Race, Islam and Power

'I have long anticipated a book that gives this kind of perspective on Indonesia: half journalistic, and half exploration through various literatures, woven together in a narrative resembling a travelogue. This has enabled Andreas to gaze into some frequently-overlooked corners, such as his dialogues with pilgrims visiting Soekarno's grave, or with the step-sister of Aceh's charismatic leader. With this approach he has the freedom to delve into some big conflicts, such as the Indonesian revolution and the tragedy of 1965, but also local sectarian conflicts that are breaking out everywhere. It's an extraordinary testimony of the interrelationship that results when power intertwines with racial and religious sentiments.'

Eka Kurniawan,
author of *Beauty is a Wound* and *Man Tiger*

'Indonesia is many lands of wonder. In this book, activist and journalist Harsono takes us through some of the most beautiful and dreadful moments of Indonesia's history in his masterful craft of eye-witness narration.'

Professor Ariel Heryanto,
Director, Monash Herb Feith Indonesian Engagement Centre

'Andreas Harsono is a human rights defender with a deep understanding of Indonesia, spending decades in his research and writing on various acts of mass violence. He's often misunderstood. Many Indonesians consider him a "traitor" or "a foreign agent." In Papua, he's often seen to be a supporter of West Papua independence but some see him to be a "government adviser." I have known him since 2008 when he was visiting my prison in Jayapura, writing and campaigning to release many Papuan political prisoners. He's actually a true Indonesian patriot who wants to see Indonesia's pimples and gangrenes to be cured. He dares to take the risk – of arrest, detention, even murder – to write what he believes and how Indonesia should act on these serious human rights abuses. This book is all about that.'

Filep Karma,
West Papua independence activist,
jailed for 11 years in Jayapura, released in 2015

'There's never been a book so thoroughly covering various sufferings and violence in the vast Indonesia archipelago. Andreas Harsono uncovered the black veil that wraps gross human rights violations as well as religious and ethnic violence in Indonesia. He moves from one group to another, from Sabang to Merauke, shocking our humanity. This book is about the importance of upholding human rights in governing Indonesia. His moral message is very clear, stop all violence, never again!'

Musdah Mulia,
Syarif Hidayatullah State Islamic University in Jakarta

Monash University Publishing
Matheson Library and Information Services Building
40 Exhibition Walk
Monash University
Clayton, Victoria 3800, Australia
www.publishing.monash.edu

Monash University Publishing brings to the world publications which advance the best traditions of humane and enlightened thought.

Monash University Publishing titles pass through a rigorous process of independent peer review.

ISBN: 9781925835090 (paperback)
ISBN: 9781925835106 (pdf)
ISBN: 9781925835113 (epub)

www.publishing.monash.edu/books/rip-9781925835090.html

Series: Investigating Power
Series Editor: Clinton Fernandes

Cover design and illustrated maps by Detego Studio: www.detegostudio.com

Text design by Les Thomas

A catalogue record for this book is available from the National Library of Australia.

Printed in Australia by Griffin Press an Accredited ISO AS/NZS 14001:2004 Environmental Management System printer.

The paper this book is printed on is certified against the Forest Stewardship Council ® Standards. Griffin Press holds FSC chain of custody certification SGS-COC-005088. FSC promotes environmentally responsible, socially beneficial and economically viable management of the world's forests.

Race, Islam and Power

Ethnic and Religious Violence in Post-Suharto Indonesia

Andreas Harsono

MONASH University Publishing

TABLE OF CONTENTS

FOREWORD

A study that encompasses the entire Indonesian archipelago is a rarity. This enormous chain of islands, straddling the equator between the Indian and Pacific Oceans, poses special difficulties for anyone attempting a careful inquiry. The time and effort needed to pull it off successfully can be daunting. Such a project calls for extensive travel, familiarity with the languages, access to Indonesia's numerous minority groups, and patience. Without these factors, a wide-ranging survey runs the risk of being superficial.

Andreas Harsono's book has been 15 years in the making. He writes about people and events in Sumatra, Kalimantan, Sulawesi, Java, the Moluccas, the Lesser Sundas, and West Papua. But this book is very different to a traveller's observations. Andreas and his contacts across the archipelago enjoy mutually trusting relationships built over many years, often in the face of intimidation from powerful entities. Andreas wears his scholarship lightly; you sense rather than see his extensive reading of the academic literature.

The result is a political travelogue in the tradition of Djamaluddin Adinegoro and George Aditjondro. The comparison is worth noting: Andreas was born just before Adinegoro's death, and cites his *Melawat ke Barat* (Travelling to the West) in the chapter on Sumatra. He studied at Satya Wacana Christian University when the great George Aditjondro taught there, and regards him as his mentor. Aditjondro, too, covered the whole of the Indonesian archipelago – one of the very few to do so. Andreas follows in this spirit and like these two luminaries is a combination of researcher, journalist and activist.

This book doesn't flinch from addressing the question of violence in Indonesia. Scholars who are sympathetic to Indonesia sometimes downplay this aspect because they don't want to give the impression that Indonesians are a violent people. But Andreas is sympathetic to the people on the wrong side of the guns – the targets of violence – who are also Indonesian and deserve the fullest ventilation of their fears, joys and hopes. His description of his visit to Indonesian-occupied East Timor is instructive: 'Are you Red-and-White'? The local military commander demands an answer, referring to the colours of the Indonesian national flag. Andreas tells him his question is irrelevant, saying that journalists should report events without having to pass loyalty tests. He is expelled from the territory forthwith. As Andreas writes in the chapter on the Lesser Sundas, 'Indonesia's longest war – the invasion and occupation of East Timor – is barely known to most Indonesians.'

Andreas Harsono is not well known to the public but he is very well known among a small network of human rights activists, dissident scholars, Indonesian journalists, and foreign correspondents. He is often the fixer behind their stories – unacknowledged, unassuming, unselfish. Now he has shown just what a superb chronicler he is in his own right. It is a privilege, as Series Editor, to bring this fine work by a writer of great integrity to print.

Professor Clinton Fernandes
University of New South Wales
January 2019

INTRODUCTION

My idea to write this book began after *The Star* newspaper in Kuala Lumpur sent me to cover the Aceh war in June 2003. I brought several books and went to Banda Aceh, travelling to guerilla war zones and interviewing dozens of Acehnese. I wrote a 15,000-word report. It got quite a response. It prompted me to look further into the questions of ethnic and religious violence in the post-President Suharto era.

The end of Suharto's authoritarian era began when the Asian economic crisis hit in July 1997. It created troubles in South Korea, Thailand, Malaysia and Indonesia. The Indonesian rupiah lost nearly 30 per cent of its value, prompting Suharto to ask the International Monetary Fund to provide a loan of up to US$40 billion. The Suharto government closed more than a dozen financially insolvent banks and promised other wide-ranging reforms. But Suharto backed off when his children and cronies protested. They suffered the heat of the economic restructuring.

Basic goods immediately vanished from the market. Indonesian students began to protest, demanding Suharto step down. The Suharto regime tried to blame economically dominant ethnic Chinese. In May 1998, anti-Chinese riots broke out in Jakarta, leading to the burning of hundreds of buildings and the killing of more than 2,500 people. The situation got worse. Student protesters occupied the parliament building, demanding Suharto step down from power.

On 21 May, 1998, President Suharto, who had been ruling Indonesia for 33 years, announced his resignation. Vice President B. J. Habibie succeeded him.

It was the beginning of a political change in multiethnic, multireligion and multilingual Indonesia. Many provinces and regencies promptly tried to find a new equilibrium, demanding more say in their political, economic and cultural domains. Some of them became involved in bloody conflict within their respective borders.

I have divided this book into seven chapters. Each chapter is about a major island in Indonesia:

- **Sumatra**: I concentrated on Aceh where guerilla fighters had fought Indonesia since 1976. Hasan Tiro, the founder of the Free Acheh Movement, criticised the Suharto regime, declaring that most of Indonesia's developments were made on Java Island. Many outer islands, such as Sumatra, had to adopt Javanese cultures if they wanted to get money from Jakarta. Hasan Tiro called it 'Java colonialism'.

- **Kalimantan**: It began with the 1997 killings of ethnic Madurese who originally came from Madura Island. In 1999, a bigger massacre took place around Sambas, seeing ethnic Malay killing around 3,500 Madurese settlers. In 2001, the racism spread to Sampit, in central Kalimantan, seeing ethnic Dayak killing around 2,500 Madurese settlers. The root of the violence was the Indonesian military campaign to remove left-leaning ethnic Chinese from the rural areas in 1967.

- **Sulawesi**: Minahasa used to rebel against Indonesia in the 1950s. It's a Christian-majority area within the Muslim-majority Indonesia. How do they avoid sectarian violence in their neighboring provinces spreading to Minahasa?

- **Java**: This is the denominator of Indonesia. It's not only Indonesia's most populated island but also the arena where the Islamists and Indonesian nationalists have battled over 'the philosophical basis' of this nation-state. Since the 1920s, the idea to formalise the Islamic sharia, implicitly discriminating against religious and gender minorities, is always challenging the idea of Indonesian nationalism. In 1998, Islamist militants revived the idea of setting up an Islamic state in Indonesia. They want to change the Constitution to oblige Muslims to follow Islamic sharia, propose bans on non-Muslim leaders in majority Muslim areas, greater implementation of sharia provisions, and the nomination of political candidates for executive office who are sympathetic to Islamist objectives. Some of the extreme Islamists even used violence to advocate their sharia agendas. Bombs were detonated in Jakarta and Bali, killing hundreds of people.

- **The Moluccas**: These islands were the scene of the bloodiest violence in post-Suharto Indonesia between 1999 and 2005. The violence took place on the islands of Ambon, Halmahera, Tidore and Ternate, involving jihadists from Java Island.

- **Lesser Sunda Archipelago**: These islands span from Timor Island in the east to Bali Island, near Java. They have witnessed violence, especially in East Timor, which became a sovereign state in May 2002.
- **West Papua**: It's about racism, human rights abuses and the manipulation of the 1969 Act of Free Choice. The American gold mine Freeport also plays a role in determining the fate of indigenous people in Papua and West Papua provinces.

I spent months reading books and analysing population statistics, trying to understand these various dynamics. But we can never fully understand complex social issues just from reading books. I decided to meet and talk with people – not only witnesses of these bloody events but also those involved in the violence. It meant that I had to travel far and wide to lands and places I had never thought of visiting.

I travelled from Indonesia's westernmost Sabang to its easternmost city Merauke in West Papua, from Miangas in the north, near the Philippines' border, to Ndana Island, near the Australian border, to learn about this communal and state-sponsored violence. This violence only dwindled after the Indonesian government organised democratic elections in 2004, 2009 and 2014. In October 2004, the Regional Representative Council, whose 128 members were elected from Indonesia's then 32 provinces, was established in Jakarta. They helped reduce regional grievances against Jakarta. There was no prosecution nor trial against those involved in the mass murders in Indonesia. The elections unfortunately also absorbed many local actors, including mass murderers, making them into leaders. Still it was a huge effort to consolidate democracy in post-Suharto Indonesia.

I initially planned to spend three years on this project. But the research and reporting stretched to 15 years. Partly this was because I also had my work for Human Rights Watch to perform, but this human rights job helped me to better understand the problems on the ground, especially in West Papua, plus the various Islamist movements in Indonesia.

Using Islam as a political tool also arose in the post-Suharto period. Perhaps this was also occasioned by Al Qaeda's terrorist attacks in New York and Washington DC on 11 September 2001 as well as President George W. Bush's order to the American military to invade Afghanistan (2001) and Iraq (2003), which created a negative reaction in Indonesia. President Barack Obama, who grew up in Jakarta in the 1960s and became the American President in 2009, helped restore the American image in Indonesia.

This book is a travelogue in conversation with those who have written on the ethnic and religious violence and territories before now. I believe that human rights protection, civil liberties, democracy, media freedom, multiculturalism and environmental protection are the answer to these problems. This book is a reminder that Indonesians still have not found the light at the end of the tunnel.

Andreas Harsono
Jakarta
December 2018

GLOSSARY

Abdurrahman Wahid (1940–2009)
: Wahid was Indonesia's fourth president in 1999–2001. He is a Muslim scholar, born in Jombang, East Java, in a prominent Muslim family. His grandfather was a founder of the Nahdlatul Ulama, the largest Muslim organisation in Indonesia. Wahid chaired the organisation in 1984–1998.

Ahmadiyah
: An Islamic religious revivalist movement, founded in Punjab, originating with the teachings of Mirza Ghulam Ahmad (1835–1908). In Arabic, Ahmadiyah means 'followers of Ahmad.' It was legally registered in Jakarta in 1953.

Al Qaeda
: A militant Islamist multinational organisation founded in 1988. Saudi millionaire Osama bin Laden helped set up this network and engineered the attack in New York and Washington DC on 11 September 2001.

Alliance of Independent Journalists
: A journalist union set up in Jakarta in 1994 during the Suharto authoritarian rule.

Bacharuddin Jusuf Habibie (born 1932)
: Habibie was Indonesia's third president. He was born in Pare-pare, South Sulawesi. He is a German-trained aeronautical engineer, becoming President Suharto's vice-president in March 1998 and replacing Suharto in May 1998. He lost his re-election in 1999.

Bhinneka Tunggal Ika, Unity in Diversity
: Indonesia's official motto. It's a quote from an Old Javanese poem by Mpu Tantular of the Majapahit empire. Sukarno used this phrase to imagine multicultural Indonesia.

Christian Evangelical Church in Halmahera
: Gereja Masehi Injili di Halmahera (GMIH).

Christian Evangelical Church in Minahasa	Gereja Masehi Injili di Minahasa (GMIM).
Christian Evangelical Church in Sangihe and Talaud	Gereja Masehi Injili di Sangihe dan Talaud (GMIST).
Christian Evangelical Church in Talaud	Gereja Masehi Injili di Talaud (Germita).
Circle of Imagine Society Timor, CIS Timor	A non-government organisation in Kupang to help displaced East Timorese after the 1999 UN-sponsored referendum.
Commission for Reception, Truth and Reconciliation in East Timor	Comissão de Acolhimento, Verdade e Reconciliação de Timor Leste (CAVR).
Communication Forum for Ahlus Sunnah Wal Jama'ah	The umbrella organisation of Sunni militias that set up Laskar Jihad in 2000 to send fighters to the Moluccas.
Communion of Churches in Indonesia	Persekutuan Gereja-gereja di Indonesia (PGI).
Darul Islam	An armed movement established in Garut, West Java, in 1949 to set up an Islamic state in Indonesia. In Arabic, Dar al-Islam means the House of Islam. It's the Arabic term commonly used to refer to an Islamic state.
East Indonesia State, Negara Indonesia Timur	This was the biggest state within the Republic of the United States of Indonesia. It was established in 1949 but dissolved in 1950.
Federal Republic of West Papua	Negara Republik Federal Papua Barat.
Forum Kerukunan Umat Beragama, FKUB	Religious Harmony Forum.

Forum Komunikasi Pemuda Melayu, FKPM	Communication Forum of Malay Youth, a militia set up in Singkawang in 1999.
Forum Mantan Tahanan dan Narapidana Politik TPN-OPM	Forum of Former Political Detainees and Prisoners.
Free Papua Movement, Organisasi Papua Merdeka (OPM)	Permenas Ferry Awom from Biak Island, a former sergeant major in the Dutch police, led a series of armed uprisings in the mountainous region of the Bird's Head Peninsula in 1965, producing this movement.
Gerakan Acheh Merdeka, GAM, Free Acheh Movement	It was set up in December 1976 as the Acheh/Sumatra National Liberation Front.
Golkar Party (Golongan Karya), Functional Group	An Indonesian political party founded in 1964 with the backing of senior army officers. It was the ruling party during President Suharto's rule between 1965–1998
Hadith	It comes from the Arab word ḥadīth that means literally 'speech' but is meant to be a recorded saying or tradition of Muhammad.
Hijab	It comes from the word al hijab, which means cover.
Himpunan Mahasiswa Islam, HMI, Islamic Students' Association	This was founded in Yogyakarta in 1947, becoming one of the largest young Muslim groups in Indonesia.
Imparsial	A Jakarta human rights NGO.
Investigating Committee for Indonesian Independence	Badan Penyelidik Usaha Persiapan Kemerdekaan Indonesia (BPUPKI).
Islamic Defenders Front	Front Pembela Islam (FPI).

Islamic Party, Jamaah Islam	It was originally named Jamaat-e-Islami, founded by Abul Ala Maududi in Pakistan. Militia leader Ja'far Umar Thalib is a Jamaah Islam leader in Indonesia.
Jihad	It comes from the Arabic word jihād, that means earnest striving in the way of God, involving personal, physical, for righteousness and against wrongdoing. It's often combined with the phrase Fī sabīl allāh, fighting in mortal combat for the sake of Allah.
Jilbab	It comes from the Arabic word al jalb, which means cleavage. It means a cloth that covers a woman's cleavage, as well as her head, neck and chest.
Joko Widodo (born 1961)	Indonesia's seventh president, in power since 2014. He was born in Solo, Central Java, from a commoner family. He was a businessman, selling wooden furniture. He is the only Indonesian president who did not come from the country's political elite or a military background.
Kerapatan Gereja Protestan Minahasa, KGPM	Minahasa Protestant Church Assemblies, a church set up in Minahasa in 1933.
Komisi untuk Orang Hilang dan Korban Tindak Kekerasan (Kontras), Commission for the Disappeared and Victims of Violence	Kontras was set up in 1998 to help find missing people in Indonesia. Kontras founder Munir Said Thalib was assassinated in 2004 inside a Garuda Indonesia flight from Jakarta to Schiphol.
Konferensi Wali Gereja Indonesia, KWI	Bishops' Conference of Indonesia.
Megawati Sukarnoputri (born 1947)	Megawati was Indonesia's fifth president (July 2001–October 2004). She is also the chairwoman of the Indonesian Democratic Party of Struggle. She's President Sukarno's eldest daughter.

Melanesian Spearhead Group	An intergovernmental organisation with four Melanesian states: Fiji, Papua New Guinea, Solomon Islands and Vanuatu plus the Kanak and Socialist National Liberation Front of New Caledonia.
Morning Star, Bintang Kejora	The name of the West Papua flag made in 1961 when the Papuan Council declared independence.
Muslim Brotherhood	Originally from Egypt (Arabic: Ikhwān al-Muslimīn).
Nahdlatul Ulama	A Sunni Islam organisation, established in 1926 in Jombang, East Java. It's the largest Muslim organisation in the world.
Pancasila	An Indonesian statement of political principle or philosophy (literally, 'five principles'), articulated at independence in 1945, consisting of five 'inseparable' principles: belief in the One and Only God (thereby legitimising several world religions and not just Islam), a just and civilised humanity, the unity of Indonesia, democracy, and social justice.
Panitia Persiapan Kemerdekaan Indonesia, PPKI	Indonesian Independence Preparation Committee.
Papuan Customary Council	Dewan Adat Papua, DAP.
Partai Persatuan Pembangunan, PPP	United Development Party.
Pasukan Gerilya Rakyat Sarawak, PGRS	Sarawak People Guerilla Forces.
Peace Brigades International	An international organisation that promotes nonviolence and human rights prevention in conflict areas.

Presidium Dewan Papua (PDP), Papua Presidium Council	It has five components: political prisoners; women's group; guerilla fighters' groups; youth organisations; and the Papua Customary Council.
Press Council	It was founded in 1968 but only became independent in 1999 with the new press law made under the B. J Habibie administration.
Protestant Church of Moluccas	Gereja Protestant Maluku, GPM.
Qanun Jinayah	An Arabic word for the Criminal Code based on Islamic sharia.
Southern Moluccas Republic, Republik Maluku Selatan, RMS	It was declared in Ambon in April 1950, seceding from the East Indonesia State.
Suharto (1921–2008)	Indonesia's second president (1966–1998). He joined a Japanese militia during the Japanese Occupation, becoming an Army officer after independence. Suharto effectively took control in Indonesia in October 1965, as he was the most senior Army general. In March 1966 Suharto received from Sukarno, via a special decree, authority to 'restore order'.
Sukarno (1901–1970)	Indonesia's first president (1945–1967). He was a Dutch-trained civil engineer but became a politician in his twenties. He formulated Pancasila, the philosophical theory of the Indonesian nation-state.
Sunnah	It comes from Arabic word sunnah/sunna. It's the body of traditional, social and legal custom and practice of Muslim communities.
Susilo Bambang Yudhoyono (born 1949)	Indonesia's sixth president (2004–2014). He comes from the military and later founded his own Democratic Party.

Ulama	Islamic cleric.
ULMWP	United Liberation Movement for West Papua.
UNESCO	United Nations Educational, Scientific and Cultural Organization.
UNHCR	United Nations Refugee Agency.
UNSC	United Nation Security Council.
WCC	World Council of Churches.
West Papua National Committee	Komisi Nasional Papua Barat, KNPB.
WPNCL	West Papua National Coalition for Liberation.

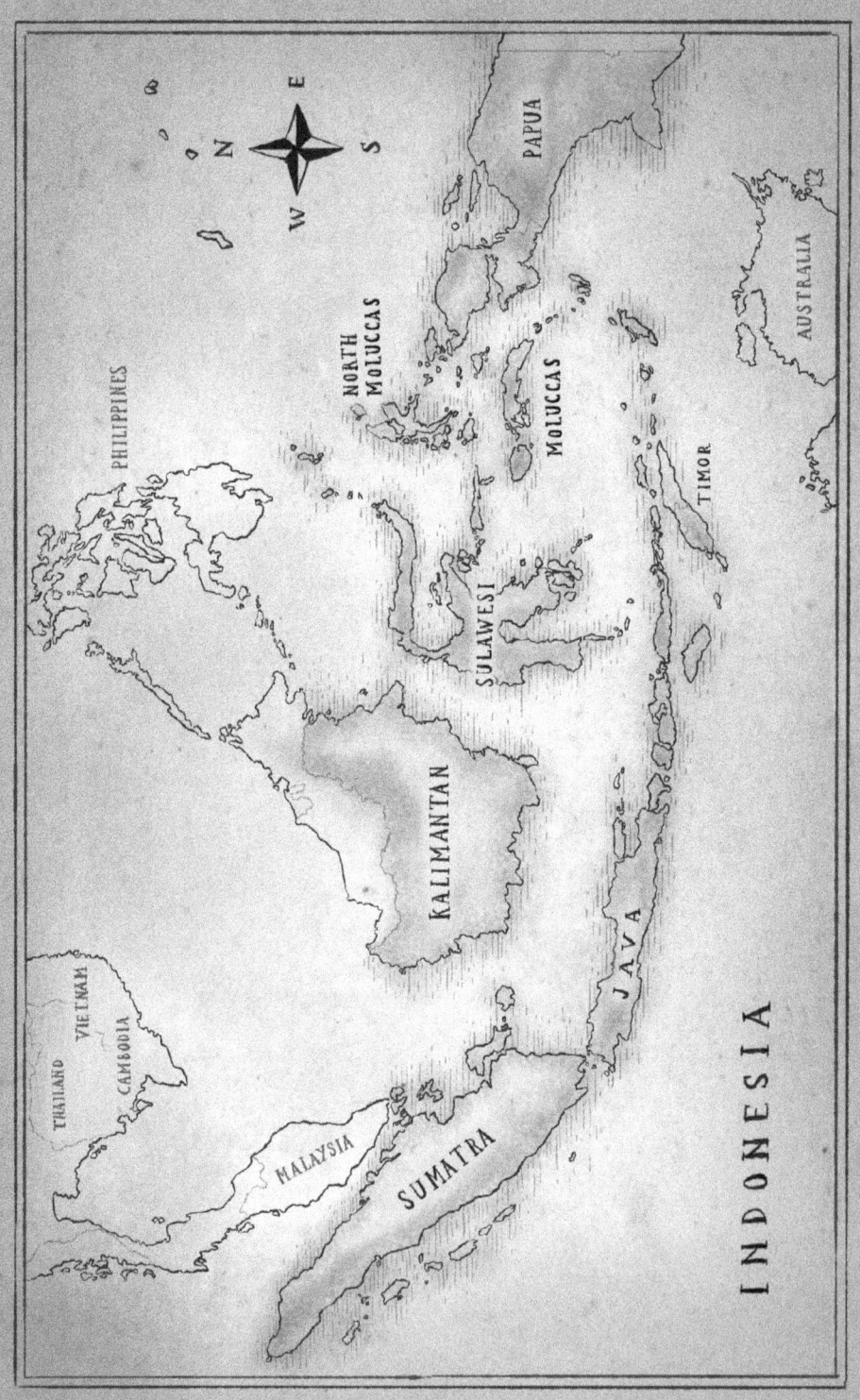

Chapter 1

SUMATRA

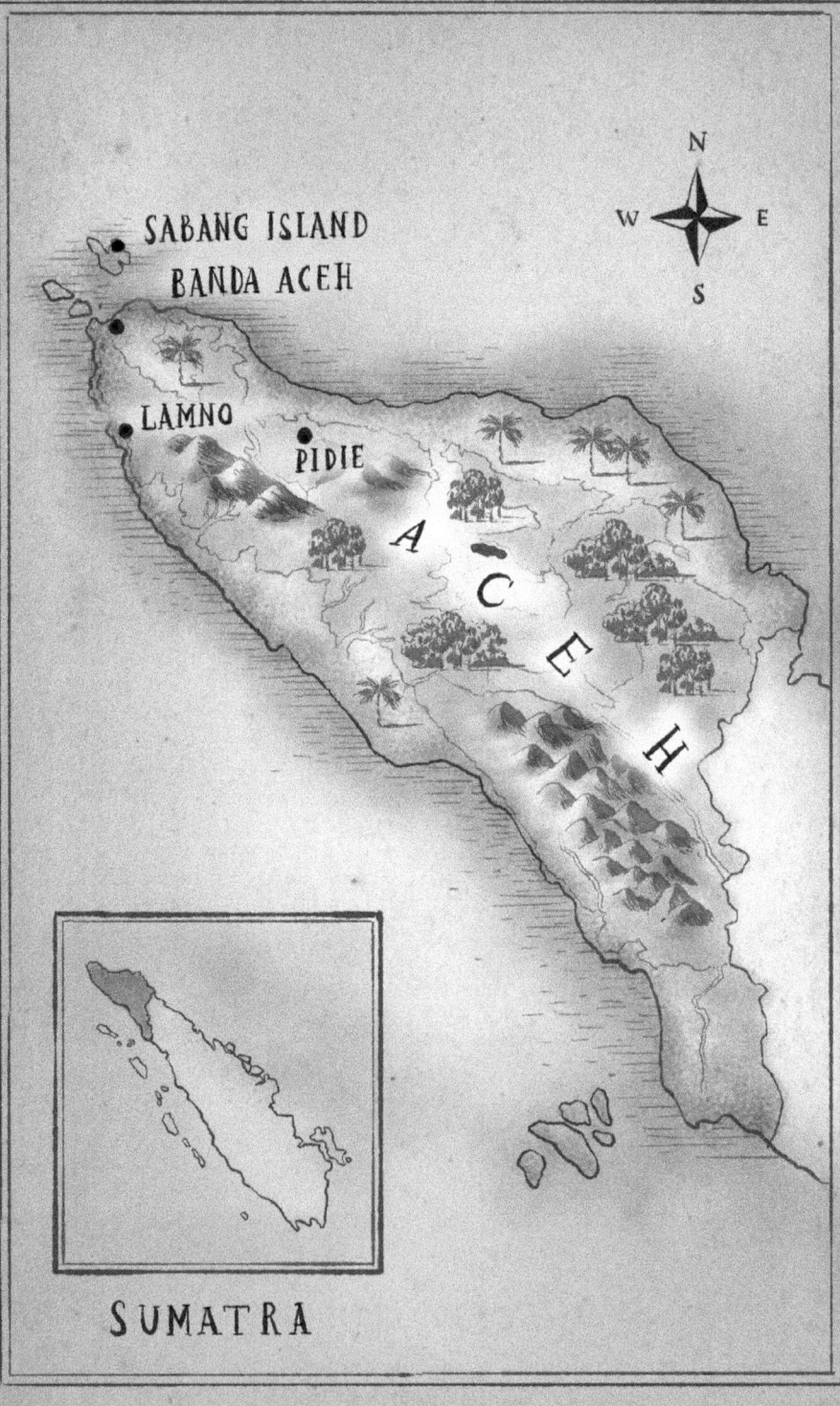

Aceh Nationalism

Sabang: Indonesia's Westernmost Symbol

In 1926, a journalist who lived in Batavia, the colonial name of Jakarta, wrote a book about his cruise to Amsterdam. In his two-series travelogue *Melawat ke Barat* (Travelling to the West), Adi Negoro described his stopovers in more than 20 cities, such as Colombo, Port Said, Marseille, Lisbon, Algiers and Southampton. It was an eye-opening book in the Netherlands Indies. Adi Negoro mixed day-to-day stories with references to books, ranging from anthropology to theology, from history to philosophy.

One stop was the seaport of Sabang on Weh Island, north of Sumatra, where the *Tambora* had stopped to load up coal. He took a car ride around Sabang and compared its harbour with the more modern British-controlled Singapore where the ship had stopped earlier. Both seaports are located on the Straits of Malacca.

Adi Negoro commented, 'If we compare only the ports, Sabang is obviously better than Singapore. But Sabang's location is not as strategic. Although the Dutch government had made Sabang into a free port, it is still not as busy as Singapore'.

Sir Stamford Raffles of the British East India Company started Singapore in 1819. The Dutch built Sabang harbour six decades later in 1887. Sabang Maatschappij expanded Sabang harbour between 1896 and 1911. Adi Negoro described it as equipped with a 2,600-ton ship repair dock with four cranes that busily loaded up coal into ships entering Sabang from Europe, China, Japan, Batavia and other places. In 1924, the company built another dock, 5,000 tons, to increase its repairing capacity.

'The livelihood of most people in Sabang depends on this seaport. There was a Chinatown near the harbour which was packed with stores and restaurants. Behind the harbour were the workers' lodgings. On the seaside were offices of shipping companies such as Rotterdamsche Lloyd and Maatschappy Nederland'. What Adi Negoro didn't write was that Sabang was a part of Aceh – the stubborn sultanate that had fought against the Dutch between 1876 and 1904. The Dutch built Sabang not only to get economic gain from the Straits of Malacca but also to help pacify the Acehnese.

In June 2003, I took a one-hour speedboat ride to reach Sabang from Banda Aceh, the capital of Aceh. It was a beautiful ride with a blue sea, seagulls and a breeze.

Outside the Sabang harbour, near a huge tree, a pedicab driver, whose motorcycle was outfitted with a locally made sidecar, approached me and offered me a ride.

'What kind of tree is it?' I asked him.

'Morai tree. This one is more than 300 years old', answered Liyan Ramli.

Its trunk was almost as big as a small wooden hut, its diameter was more than two metres. In English, its name is Manila tamarind. I decided to stay in Sabang.

Weh Island is as beautiful as Adi Negoro described. The Sabang administration preserves not only old trees but also two protected wildlife areas: Weh Island Marine Park (2,600 hectares) and Iboih Recreation Park (1,300 hectares). The Marine Park has coral gardens while Iboih park consists of beach and tropical lowland forests. Gapang beach, near Iboih, is a diving attraction. Sabang also has a little volcano, a waterfall and a cave complex inhabited by birds, bats and snakes.

During the Adi Negoro trip, the Sabang seaport was bigger and better equipped than Singapore but the difference is an extreme contrast today. In the late twentieth century Singapore was already one of the world's busiest and most modern seaports while Sabang's harbour has become much smaller. It had less equipment and almost no significance. Singapore has a population of 4 million people while Sabang has only 22,000.

Husaini, the speaker of the Sabang council, told me, 'In old photographs, we could see up to 60 ships anchored in Sabang Bay'. Now under Indonesian rule, the Sabang harbour is lucky to have a single ferry. In 1985, President Suharto's government even closed the free port on 'smuggling' grounds. Sabang citizens protested but were ignored. President Abdurrahman Wahid, who took office in 1999, reopened the free port.

Sabang plays a significant role in the psyche of Indonesians. Sabang is Indonesia's westernmost tip and the name *Sabang* itself is mentioned in a national anthem, *Dari Sabang Sampai Merauke* (From Sabang to Merauke). Its lyrics mainly describe how Indonesia *exists* in thousands of islands that span from Sabang to Merauke, a small town in West Papua, Indonesia's easternmost island. Every school student in Indonesia knows how to sing that song.

* * *

On my second day in Sabang, I rented a motorcycle from the 'Sabang-Merauke Inn' to visit a monument in the Ujong Batu area, a hill about 30 kilometres away. It's also called the Monument of the Republic Indonesia Kilometre Zero. A symbol of Indonesia's territorial integrity.

The innkeeper was not enthusiastic about my plan. He suggested his staff drive me there.

'Isn't it safe to go there alone? Are there GAM guerillas?' I asked him.

'No, no, it is the (Indonesian) soldiers that I am worried about', he answered.

GAM is the Indonesian acronym for the Gerakan Acheh Merdeka (Free Acheh Movement). It's a guerilla organisation that seeks Aceh's independence from Indonesia. The official name is the Acheh Sumatra National Liberation Front, with its base in Stockholm. These Acehnese prefer to use the spelling 'Acheh' than 'Aceh', arguing that is what their fathers and forefathers told them. The Sabang police estimated the guerillas had '20 hardcore' GAM fighters with four firearms.

I showed the innkeeper my military-issued press card. He let me rent a motorcycle.

Twenty minutes into the trip, I saw an electrical distribution station with many police officers. I also encountered a military truck with dozens of army soldiers walking beside their truck. Clad in jungle camouflage, they were fully armed and wore bulletproof vests. Their faces were painted black. They made no noise, but some looked at me curiously.

I kept riding my motorcycle and entered a village.

The road became quieter.

I saw no-one on the street. I reached Gapang beach. I saw a sign to Iboih beach and then the forest. It was filled with tall trees, ferns, red wildflowers – the anthurium. Dried leaves covered the road. Suddenly I met a crowd of monkeys. I was stunned to suddenly meet living creatures. My arm hair stood on end. The biggest male monkey looked sharply at me while sitting and showing off his big red penis. I sped up my motorcycle.

When approaching Ujong Batu, I encountered an Indonesian military checkpoint. Two Indonesian Air Force soldiers stopped me. Clad in jungle camouflage with automatic guns and sandbags, they asked my reason to be there. I told them that I was a journalist. They checked my pass.

'Are you guys not bored in this remote area?' I asked them.

'Our job is to guard this place. That's an order', said First Private Wahyu Hanes.

His colleague, First Private Sutrisno, said they're usually based in Malang, East Java, and only arrived in Sabang six months earlier. They hadn't had any firefights with the Aceh guerillas and rarely met a human being in this outpost. Sometimes visitors came to visit the monument. A German tourist visited them a few days earlier, surprisingly, by bicycle.

'When I read the newspapers about a German couple who were shot, I thought it might be him', said Sutrisno.

Luther Hendrik Albert, a German cyclist, was fatally shot by nine Indonesian soldiers while sleeping on a beach in western Aceh. It was an accident. Nervous soldiers saw two people moving in the dark. They shot Albert and wounded his wife Elizabeth Engel.

Four kilometres later I saw a billboard: You Are Entering Kilometre Zero of the Republic of Indonesia.

I was exhausted, but it was a serene environment. The deep blue sea and old trees surrounded me.

The monument park is shaped like a circle and its centre is a white three-storey monument. At the top of its dome is a zero-shaped sculpture. There is a black marble stone nearby which gives its geographical location: north latitude 5 degrees, 54 minutes, 21.99 seconds; east longitude 95 degrees, 12 minutes, 59.02 seconds. This is the symbol of the first kilometre of the Republic of Indonesia.

In this quiet place, I sat down and thought about the meaning of Indonesia.

What kind of nationalism do Indonesian opinion leaders promote?

What does this symbol mean when so many people, outside Java, are treated with contempt for what they see as injustice in their respective area? What does this symbol mean when millions of Muslims – mostly on Java and Sumatra – want to change Indonesia into an Islamic state, arguing that Islam provides justice but not Indonesian nationalism?

I also saw another island, about 20 kilometres further west, the un-inhabited Rondo Island.

Indonesia's founding President Sukarno declared Sabang to be Indonesia's westernmost town. He used the phrase 'Sabang to Merauke', borrowing that phrase from Dutch General J. B. van Heutsz who defeated the Acehnese sultanate in 1904. The slogan obviously sticks in many government propagandas. Neither Van Heutsz nor Sukarno use the name 'Rondo', which literally means 'widow'.

In Sabang, many places are named after the nationalist phrase 'Sabang-Merauke'. There is a 'Sabang-Merauke Stadium'. A billboard reads the 'Sabang-Merauke Foundation', which runs a kindergarten. It is located near the 'Sabang-Merauke Inn'. I used the 'Sabang Merauke Telephone Cafe'.

If there is an emotional tie between the citizens of Sabang and the citizens of Merauke, why is there a rebellion throughout Aceh? Why do many Acehnese seek, at least, a special autonomy? Why do Sabang citizens such as Liyan Ramli, or furniture merchant Nyik Siti Absyah or Chinese baker Su Sien Jin, feel bitter about Jakarta's decision to close the Sabang free port in 1985? Or is 'Sabang-Merauke' just a slogan that has already lost its magical power or even its real meaning?

In his classic, *Imagined Communities: Reflections on the Origin and Spread of Nationalism*, Benedict Anderson of Cornell University, himself an old hand in Indonesia, argued that a nation is an 'imagined community'. A community has members who are aware of each other's existence. But even for a lifetime, members of an imagined community don't meet or come to know a substantial number of the other members.

Indonesia is an imagined community.

Most Sabang citizens have no idea what Merauke looks like. But through a number of media – newspapers, radios, television, telephones, the internet, and the *Dari Sabang Sampai Merauke* song – these members acquire a sense of belonging to this larger group.

I asked Liyan Ramli what the 'Sabang-Merauke' meant to him. Liyan was a little bit puzzled. He scratched his head and stopped his pedicab.

After several seconds, he replied, 'Oh…that is my daily parking position. Yes, yes, right there in front of the Sabang-Merauke Inn. The next time you come to Sabang, you could find me there'.

The Free Acheh Movement

Bouncing along on one of Aceh's few good roads, you can easily spend three hours on the 160 kilometre journey from Banda Aceh to Tiro district in Pidie regency. The drive took me straight into the Aceh rebellion's heartland. It is full of the serene-looking tropical villages. The roads are filled with potholes caused by bombs. It is dotted by sandbagged Indonesian military posts.

I went there early one morning in June 2003 with Murizal Hamzah, a photographer who worked for the *Associated Press*. Murizal, himself an Acehnese, lectured me about how to enter a military operation area: (1) Always report to the closest military posts, if possible both sides, the Aceh guerillas and the Indonesian soldiers; (2) Roll down your windows; (3) Never use cars with dark windscreens.

'Don't use old Toyota Kijang van. We might be mistaken for SGI', Murizal added, referring to the Indonesian Army intelligence unit whose members often used such vans.

When I began to interview people in Sakti, a town near Tiro, he reminded me not to greet local men with the brotherly salutation of *Mas*. I should call them *Bang*.

I got the point. There is a sentiment against the Javanese – the dominant ethnic group in Indonesia – among Acehnese. Both words mean 'brother'. But the word '*mas*' is a Javanese expression and '*bang*' is an Acehnese or Sumatran one.

We went straight to the village of Tanjung Bungoeng in Malichot to visit Aisyah Muhammad, the stepsister and only remaining sibling of Hasan Muhammad Tiro, the founder of the Free Acheh Movement.

Aisyah's residence is a big traditional Acehnese house built on stilts with a large compound. I saw a satellite dish on its roof. But Aisyah was not home. Dozens of villagers, old and young, gathered outside the house and surrounded Murizal and me.

'She went out. Maybe she will stay the night away', said Muhammad Abubakar, a neighbour.

Aisyah is an elderly widow who keeps her house open for her fellow villagers. More than 20 children were playing inside her house. Some teenagers were also there. Abubakar told me that Aisyah is a Koran teacher, tutoring the youngsters about Islam and reciting Koranic verses.

When I asked him about Hasan Tiro, Abubakar said that Hasan was born in 1923 in Malichot and learned to recite the Koran in the neighbouring Tiro. Hasan is a grandson of Teuku Chik di Tiro – an Acehnese aristocrat who fought against the Dutch in 1880s. President Suharto posthumously awarded him the title 'National Hero' in 1973.

'I'm 55 years old and *Wali* is 80 years old now. I've never met him', Abubakar said, referring to Hasan Tiro whose official title is '*Walinanggroe*' or 'the guardian of the state'. Acehnese simply call him *Wali*.

I have never seen the Jakarta media reference Tiro in this way. They usually called him the GAM leader or even the more negative term: rebel leader, opportunist figure, separatist figure.

Hasan Tiro wrote in his diary, *The Price of Freedom*, that at least 10 of his forebears – six of them sultans – died in combat against the Dutch. The last sultan to fall was his uncle, Tengku Tjhik Maat di Tiro, who was 16.

The Di Tiros' saga began a century earlier, against all odds, not in Aceh, but in London, when the British and the Dutch signed the 1824 Treaty of

London. It defined a British sphere of influence over the Malay Peninsula and a Dutch sphere over Sumatra. But soon the Sumatran trade became an issue of contention. The British resented what they saw as Dutch attempts to curtail their commercial activities. One provision was the recognition of the independence of the Aceh sultanate. But Aceh controlled a large portion of the pepper trade and alarmed the Dutch by actively seeking relations with other Western countries through their representatives in Singapore, which included American consul A. G. Studer. A new Anglo-Dutch treaty, signed in 1871, gave the Dutch a free hand in Sumatra, including Aceh.

Two years later, talks between Studer and Acehnese representatives, Tengku Mohammad Arifin and Panglima Muhammad Tibang, gave the Dutch the pretext for opening hostilities. Dutch gunboats bombarded the sultanate's capital, Banda Aceh, and troops were landed. The palace was seized and the sultan was killed. The Dutch made a treaty with a new sultan, who recognised Dutch sovereignty over the area. But he was unable to control his subjects and Dutch forces became involved in a protracted guerilla war in the countryside. This war drained the Dutch colonial treasury and public opinion in the Hague became increasingly critical.

The Dutch Indies administration realised that their ignorance of Aceh had led them to commit serious errors. They didn't understand Aceh's power structure nor cultural values. C. Snouck Hurgronje, a professor of Islamic studies at the University of Leiden, was invited to advise the colonial administration. Hurgronje did his survey and published a famous book, *The Acehnese*, in 1894. A 'castle strategy', which provided fortified bases for the Dutch troops, was then introduced.

J. B. van Heutsz, who was appointed military governor of Aceh in 1899, subdued the sultanate quickly. Tuanku Muhamat Dawot, the pretender to the Aceh sultanate, submitted to the Dutch government in January 1903. As noted earlier, Van Heutsz conquered the entire region in 1904. He introduced the phrase '*vom Sabang tot Merauke*', declaring the Dutch Indies now spans from Sabang to Merauke.

Still, scores of Acehnese kept fighting a guerilla war. Hasan Tiro argued in several papers that the Aceh sultanate had never surrendered.

Hasballah Saad, an Acehnese politician who once served as a minister in the President Abdurrahman Wahid cabinet, told me that in the 1930s many skirmishes still took place in Aceh. 'I have almost never experienced peace in Aceh in all of my life', said Hasballah.

In December 1949, at the end of World War II, the Netherlands handed over its former colonies to Indonesia, a new country centred on Java. Aceh nationalists say the action was illegal: the Netherlands could not give away what it didn't own. Tiro always challenged the Dutch for handing over Aceh to 'the Dutch mercenaries' – namely the Javanese.

But Daud Beureueh, a Muslim cleric in Aceh, decided to support the new republic. He mobilised the Acehnese to donate their money and jewellery to buy Indonesia's first two airplanes. President Sukarno met Beureueh in Banda Aceh. Sukarno promised to grant a special autonomous status to Aceh. The Dutch finally agreed to hand over its power to a federal Indonesia that comprised 15 entities.

Sukarno, however, didn't fulfil his promise. In 1950, Sukarno abolished the federal states in the former Netherlands Indies, reinstating the Java-dominated unitarian state. In 1953, Beureueh took up arms against Jakarta, declaring an Islamic state, 'We regard action to set up an Islamic state as being better than living under chaotic laws, and if the Republican government understands this, it will appreciate that the only way to solve the problem is by improving the basic principles of the state and its policies'.

He continued fighting through the rest of the decade, using Islam to mobilise the resistance against the Sukarno government. Only in 1961 when Aceh was granted a special autonomy status, Beureueh dropped his fight. Beureueh died in a forced exile in Jakarta in June 1987.

Hasan Tiro missed that conflict. In 1950, he left Aceh as a young man and moved to New York. He helped buy arms for Beureueh's men. He got his PhD from Columbia University and went into business, representing major American companies overseas and negotiating deals involving oil, cattle and shipping.

In the early 1970s, Tiro left his Jewish American wife Dora and their only son Karim in New York, returning to his homeland. He visited Aceh Governor Muzakkir Walad in Banda Aceh and inquired about the possibilities for forest concessions or a contract with Exxon Mobil which operates a natural gas field in Aceh – one of the largest in the world. Hasballah, who attended the meeting, quoted Muzakkir as saying that the decision was up to Jakarta.

Since taking over power in 1965, General Suharto had centralised more power in Jakarta. He recruited American-trained economists to run the country, used his own army generals to provide security and, if necessary, to suppress even the mildest criticism. Jakarta controlled almost everything in this vast archipelago. It licensed newspapers and occasionally closed down 'recalcitrant ones'. Jokes circulated that officials in remote areas needed to get Jakarta's approval even to buy a single book.

Hasan Tiro thought that it was useless to deal with Jakarta. Fed up with the injustice, he met with his loyal supporters, hid in the jungle and began building a rebel organisation. He introduced the concept of '*bangsa Acheh vis-a-vis bangsa Indonesia*', which viewed the Javanese as Acheh's historic rival. He called the Republic of Indonesia 'a Javanese republic with a phony Greek name'. And he used the spelling 'Acheh' instead of 'Aceh'.

Hasan Tiro declared Acheh's independence in Tjokkan Hill, in the hinterland of Aceh, on 4 December 1976. 'The Dutch had counted December 4, 1911, as the day of the Dutch final "victory" over the Kingdom of Acheh Sumatra', writes Tiro in his diary. But the Acehnese never surrendered. The date 4 December became a symbol of resistance, first against the Dutch, later against the Javanese. He appointed himself guardian of state and chose Husaini Hasan, an obstetrician by training, then working in a hospital in Medan in northern Sumatra, as secretary of state.

Tiro declared that Indonesia was a fraud, an entity that cloaked Javanese colonialism.

'There never was a people, much less a nation, in our part of the world by that name. No such people existed in the Malay Archipelago of ethnology, philology, cultural anthropology, sociology or by any other scientific findings', declared Tiro. His statement was splashed on the front page of Medan-based *Waspada* daily newspaper.

That prompted a manhunt by the Indonesian Army. Tiro and his comrades-in-arms decided to head for the jungles. According to *The Price of Freedom*, which covered the two years Hasan Tiro spent in Aceh, he recounted his adventures living among the monkeys, fleeing from 'Javanese soldiers', avoiding snakes and spiders and listening to his favourite cassettes of Johann Sebastian Bach and Antonio Vivaldi.

The group carried a heavy old-fashioned press printer into the jungle. The press produced thousands of rolled-up leaflets and documents to educate his cadres. The ragtag force had only several rifles and pistols and were no match for the Indonesian Army.

'We have not been born to be anybody's slaves. We want to live as free men or not to live at all'.

In 1977, in his jungle camp, he declared Mansur Amin, an Acehnese journalist working for the Jakarta-based *Tempo* magazine, to be a spy when visiting and photographing his guerilla camp, about 40 kilometres south of Sigli. One day after Mansur's departure to Jakarta, according to Tiro, the Indonesian Army in Sigli town received a telex from Jakarta, detailing the camp's location and ordering an ambush.

The small group managed to vacate their camp about 12 hours prior to the ambush.

'We have no proof to which enemy agent made the report, but to us it could only be Mansur Amin', writes Tiro.

In January 2005, Mansur Amin told me he had never returned to Aceh after the allegation. He declined to comment further.

Husaini Hasan was wounded in an ambush in 1978 and fled in a three-night boat ride to neighbouring Malaysia. Husaini, whose weight had fallen from 65 to 48 kilograms, also discovered in a Kuala Lumpur clinic that he had malaria. He sought refugee status at the Kuala Lumpur office of the UN High Commissioner on Refugees. In 1980, he was among the first batch of Aceh migrants to settle in Sweden.

In Aceh, Tiro managed to organise a nationalist movement, created a shadow government and appointed rebel governors for much of the province. Every morning he gave lectures to his cadres. He was a smart and charismatic leader. But he was slow to get guns and his rebellion lacked international support.

When the movement was cornered, Tiro fled to Malaysia and later settled in Stockholm with Husaini and other GAM leaders. Tiro became a Swedish citizen in 1985 and accepted help from Libya for military training. By 1989, the success of the newly Libya-trained Acheh guerillas prompted President Suharto to mount a ruthless campaign.

The military strategy involved intensive surveillance, checkpoints, dawn-to-dusk curfews, house raids, and arrests on a wide scale. By 1989 and 1990, these counterinsurgency activities led to abuses that included killing of civilians at checkpoints, arbitrary arrests and detentions. According to Amnesty International, homes were raided and burned, women were taken hostage and raped, and arbitrary arrests, detention, torture, summary executions and disappearances were common into the mid-1990s. The campaign resulted in considerable social dislocation within Aceh, with thousands of Acehnese displaced from their homes and hundreds of Acehnese fleeing to nearby Malaysia.

By the time Suharto fell in 1998, human rights organisations estimated more than 10,000 Acehnese were killed. Many Acehnese hoped that Indonesia would collapse, and that Aceh would gain independence. In November 1999, President Abdurrahman Wahid, himself a former democracy activist, told a media conference in Jakarta there should be a referendum on Aceh's future. 'I support a referendum as their right. If we do it in East Timor, why not in Aceh', he said.

But Wahid wavered some months later, saying Aceh would have to wait at least three years for such a move. By July 2000, Wahid was fired by the Indonesian People's Consultative Assembly on mismanagement and corruption charges. And the referendum was shelved.

Ibrahim Alfian, an Acehnese scholar who teaches at the Gadjah Mada University in Yogyakarta, said that Aceh is a legitimate part of Indonesia. He told *Kompas* that he was involved in a heated debate with GAM leaders during an all-Aceh conference in Washington DC in 1999. He said, 'According to the statement of the Acehnese ulamas on October 15, 1945, Aceh was to merge with the Republic of Indonesia. Aceh has since become a legitimate part of Indonesia. If now some Acehnese want to be independent and to separate from Indonesia, I think they don't know history and ignore their ulamas. In Aceh, people who don't follow their ulamas are traitors'.

Ibrahim also questioned Hasan Tiro's credibility, 'How could Acehnese trust someone who claims to be the *Walinanggroe* when he himself is married to a foreign woman? Come on! If the heir of the Acehnese kingdom married a foreigner, then his successor will be a foreigner, ha?'

Formalising Islamic Sharia

Yuli Suriani is a 27-year-old student at the Syiah Kuala University. She also works as a part-time radio broadcaster in Banda Aceh. She is petite and usually wears blue jeans and a canvas jacket. Like most women in Banda Aceh, Yuli wears a *jilbab* (hijab) to cover her head, usually one that matches the colour of her dress.

'I feel imperfect without a *jilbab*. It is a symbol of women with status', she said.

Yuli decided to use the cotton scarf in 1999 to cover what she considered to be her *aurat* – an Arabic word which literally means 'scar'. The Koran has some verses around this female clothing.

According to an interpretation of the Koran, the 'scar' must be covered. That interpretation says that a man's *aurat* is an area between his belly button and his knees, meaning that a Muslim man should not wear shorts. A woman's *aurat* is from her hair to her knees. A stricter interpretation says a woman's *aurat* includes her face and voice, prompting some women to use *jalabiya* (dark robe) and *cadar* (face cover).

Karen Armstrong, the author of the book *A History of God*, writes that the Koran does not prescribe the veil for all women but only for Muhammad's wives, as a mark of their status. Muhammad encouraged women to play an active role in the affairs of the community. They expressed their views forthrightly, confident that they would be heard.

As in Christianity, Islam was later hijacked by the men who interpreted texts in a negative way for Muslim women. Once Islam had taken its place in the civilised world, Muslims adopted the customs of veiling women and secluding them in harems in Persia and Christian Byzantium, where women had long been marginalised.

Despite her own dress code, Yuli disagrees with a 2003 Aceh ordinance that requires all Aceh women to wear a hijab. She believes that faith is an individual matter, 'There are people whose appearances seem to be easy-going but who knows what is deep inside their hearts. Islam is flexible. Islam does not force people. *Jilbab* or not, it's your own business with God'.

Aceh is one of Indonesia's most Muslim-dominated areas. About 98 per cent of its 4.4 million people are officially Muslims. Its towns and villages are graced by thousands of well-kept mosques. Arab merchants introduced Islam to the region in the ninth century. The first rulers in the Acehnese region, who declared themselves Muslim, initially headed small settlements in Lamreh and Pasai. The two harbours were conveniently situated on the Indian Ocean, at the head of the Straits of Malaka, for ships coming from India and Arabia. They served Muslim merchants who married local women and built settlements.

The rulers of Lamreh and Pasai announced their Islamic credentials to men operating the Muslim sea network by taking the title sultan. They replaced their native names with Arabic ones, Sulaiman bin Abdullah bin al-Basir and Malik al-Saleh. Aceh later became the doorway through which Islam entered Sumatra and Java.

In August 2001, with the Aceh Autonomy Law passed by the Indonesian parliament in Jakarta, Aceh was granted the privilege to formalise Islamic sharia. The Aceh government set up a 27-member council of *ulamas*, whose main duty is to produce *fatwa* (Islamic decisions) and positioned itself as the fourth branch of governance in Aceh – in addition to the judiciary, the legislature and the executive.

Islamic sharia is derived from the religious precepts of Islam, partic-ularly the Koran and the Hadith. In Arabic, the term *shari'ah* refers to God's immutable divine law and is contrasted with *fiqh*, which refers to its human scholarly interpretations. It has been described as 'one of the major intellectual achievements of Islam' and its importance in Islam has been compared to that of theology in Christianity. The manner of its application in modern times has been a subject of dispute between Muslim traditionalists and reformists. Traditional theory of Islamic jurisprudence recognises four sources of sharia: the Quran, *sunnah* (authentic hadith), *qiyas* (analogical reasoning) and *ijma* (juridical consensus).

Muslim Ibrahim was the first chairman of the Ulamas' Consultative Assembly whose seats were filled by *ulamas* from Aceh's districts. Muslim Ibrahim told me that the members were initially selected from the district level. Each district nominated 10 *ulamas* who are considered 'to understand the sharia the most and fluent in Arabic'.

These nominees from all the districts in a regency were reduced down to 10 *ulamas*. These 10 regional nominees represent that regency in a provincial contest, meaning that 130 *ulamas* from the regencies plus 20 representatives from the academic circles will contest for 27 seats in the Assembly. They conducted the voting themselves.

Ibrahim was elected the first chairman. He represented the academic world. He finished his PhD in sharia from al-Azhar University in Cairo in 1984. Ibrahim teaches 'modern *fiqih* (law)' in the ar-Raniry State Islamic Institute. He was one of many Acehnese *ulamas* who applauded the 2001 law to implement sharia in Aceh, arguing that the now defunct Aceh sultanate had used sharia to run the country for centuries.

'Islam could always be appropriate in places and times', Ibrahim said, adding that the Assembly is now busy preparing local regulations on almost everything in accordance to Islam. Ibrahim said the sources for their regulations are the Koran, the words (*hadith*) and practice (*sunnah*) of Muhammad and his early companions. It also included *iqtihad* (interpretation). Caning is also a form of punishment. His office soon established the sharia police to raid small groups of gamblers or teenagers dating their loved ones. The caning is conducted in public, usually in a mosque compound after the Friday prayer. Critics say the victims are mostly women and poor people. No big-time corruptors nor Indonesian officers are ever caned.

The debate over Islamic interpretations is nothing new. In the early days of Islam, this resulted in the formation of the sharia, a code like the Jewish Torah, which was based on the Koran and the life and maxims of the Prophet. These words were collected during the eighth and ninth centuries by several editors, the most famous of whom were Muhammad ibn Ismail al-Bukhari and Muslim ibn al-Hijjah al-Qushayri. Today Ibrahim and his peers are trying to put those maxims into action.

Mohammad Dahlan al-Fairuzy al-Bagdady, the head of the Tanoh Abee Islamic boarding school in Seulimeum, about two hours from Banda Aceh, however, reminded me that today's Islam might find it difficult to be 'purified' like Islam in the old days.

His school is one of three *zauyah* (post-graduate schools) in Aceh. His few disciples usually hail him with the title 'Tengku Chik Tanoh Abee' – after his village 'Tanoh Abee' and the honorific 'tengku chik' for an elderly Islamic scholar. He is a quiet man who enjoys his daily siesta.

'Islam *kaffah* (absolute) is difficult, if not impossible, to reach. How could we claim to be *kaffah*? How many Acehnese are really faithful today? It is probably better to implement Islam individually. Just do it without claiming our Islam with symbols', said Dahlan.

'If we want to be *kaffah*, for example, we must get rid of the Chinese', said Dahlan, referring to the old Islamic communities when they rarely allowed (non-Muslim) minorities among them.

'Women and men should be strictly separated in public spaces. Is it possible to do it today?' he asked me.

Difficult or not, among the first actions that Muslim Ibrahim's Assembly immediately ruled on was the dressing code. Women were asked to use *jilbab*.

'It's in the text', Ibrahim insisted.

Upon the enactment of the 2001 law, Aceh's provincial legislature enacted a series of *qanuns* (ordinances in Arabic) governing the sharia implementation. Violations are punishable by caning and/or a fine. Many of these ordinances are discriminatory, especially against minorities (see table on page 17).

These ordinances include several features distinguishing them from the Criminal Code applied elsewhere in Indonesia. These ordinances apply not only to Aceh's predominantly Muslim population, but to about 90,000 non-Muslims residents, mostly Christians and Buddhists, as well as domestic and foreign visitors to Aceh. It soon encouraged other Muslim-dominated regencies in Indonesia to copy Aceh's sharia provisions.

A smaller faction within the Free Acheh Movement by contrast argued that the Acehnese don't need the sharia to prove that Islam is alive in Aceh. They argued that the Acehnese practiced Islam in almost everything they did. The Acehnese had already been formally practicing sharia in daily life for decades in areas such as marriage, divorce and the ban on alcohol. But they also rejected strict punishments such as the amputation of hands for theft that the sharia, in theory, can dispense.

16

Discriminatory Islamic Ordinances in Aceh

Qanun 11/2002	Promoting Islamic faith, worship and propagation (*dakwah*) which contains the Islamic attire requirement including *jilbab*; the penalty of not wearing it is 'reprimand and education' from the *Wilayatul Hisbah* (sharia police).
Qanun 12/2003	Prohibiting the consumption and sale of alcohol with maximum penalty 40 times of rattan caning.
Qanun 13/2003	Prohibiting gambling with maximum penalty 12 times of rattan caning.
Qanun 14/2003	Prohibiting 'seclusion' between unmarried men and women with maximum penalty nine times of rattan caning or a six month jail term or a fine.
Qanun 7/2013	Islamic procedure code.
Qanun 6/2014	Aceh's criminal code prohibits *liwath* (sodomy) and *musahaqah* (lesbian). It also revised the 2003 *qanuns* on Islamic attires, the ban on alcohol, gambling and casual sex. It also contains provisions that allow Islamic courts to dismiss charges against rape suspects who take *sumpah dilaknat Allah* (an Islamic oath) asserting their innocence.
Qanun 8/2014	Aceh's Principles of the Islamic Bylaw, violating the right to freedom of religion enshrined in the Indonesian constitution and international law by requiring all Muslims to practice the Sunni tradition of Islam. The ordinance imposes the Sunni school of Shafi'i as Aceh's official religion, while permitting three other major Sunni traditions – Hanafi, Maliki and Hambal – only on the condition that their followers promote 'religious harmony, Islamic brotherhood and security among Muslims'. The law excludes Aceh's sizable Shia and Sufi minorities as well as the Ahmadiyah Muslim community.

'Sharia is not what the Achehnese have been striving for, nor is it the cause of the conflict between Acheh and Jakarta. Indonesia is trying to raise this issue just for political reasons – a new, tricky move to divert the world's attention from the real issue, namely the right to self-determination of the people of Acheh', said GAM leader Husaini Hasan.

'In my opinion, if the sharia is to be implemented, those who will suffer the most are women. All interpretations and decision are made by men', said Lily Zakiah Munir, the director of the Jakarta-based Center for Pesantren and Democracy Studies, which made a survey on the sharia campaign in Aceh. Lily Munir pointed out that the 27 *ulamas* are all men. Not a single woman sits with Muslim Ibrahim.

Interestingly, in Java, large Muslim organisations such as the Nahdlatul Ulama, have openly opposed the sharia formalisation, especially the mandatory hijab, saying that the campaign is merely rhetoric. President Wahid, himself a Muslim cleric, always opposed the sharia formalisation. Nahdlatul Ulama believe that the Islamic ideals of social justice and human dignity are already being implemented in Indonesia under the state ideology of 'Pancasila'.

Indonesia was declared independent in 1945 as a rather secular state with an official ideology called 'Pancasila' – believe in one God, humanity, unity of Indonesia, democracy and social justice. Islam was not made the official state religion. Over the years, however, many Islamists in Java, Sumatra and Sulawesi campaigned to adopt Islam as the state ideology.

By August 2016, three of Indonesia's 34 provinces had adopted mandatory hijab regulations – Aceh, West Sumatra and South Kalimantan. Some other predominantly Muslim provinces, such as Yogyakarta, also adopted similar regulations but did not make them mandatory, instead 'calling on' their female Muslims to wear the hijab. The National Commission on Violence Against Women (Komnas Perempuan) has identified another 32 regencies, including those on densely populated Java, with regulations related to women's dress. In total, the best available estimate is that 8 per cent of Indonesia's population live in areas with mandatory hijab regulations and 84 per cent in predominantly Muslim areas with 'voluntary' rules.

The 2014 Ministry of Education regulation on public school uniforms gives schools the choice of national school uniform. Schools can require the hijab. That regulation prompted hundreds of thousands of schools to require the hijab, and Muslim girls must wear long sleeves to go to school, a heavy burden in a country with a tropical climate. It is not clear, however, if a school can ban the hijab, even in Christian-dominated areas such as Papua. In Yogyakarta, two Islamic universities in February 2018 attempted to ban female students from wearing the veil, with one threatening expulsion for non-compliance. But they cancelled the plan after protests from Islamist groups.

When the Islamic sharia was beginning to be formalised, between 2001 and 2003, stories were circulating in Aceh about women without 'proper attire' being stopped on the streets and asked to cover their heads by the sharia police. Some female students had also been asked to go home and change.

It seemed to me that every woman in Banda Aced was wearing the *jilbab* in public spaces, although many of them wore what college girls called 'modish' clothes. Clothing that shows their figures. I also met young women who covered their heads but showed the cleavage of their breasts.

Aceh journalists joked that even sex workers in Banda Aceh wore *jilbab*. Many students at the Syiah Kuala University used the *jilbab* at least as a formality. 'Necks are still seen. *Jilbab* are seen only as a formality', said Yuli Suriani.

I found more women without the *jilbab* in rural areas or in the free port of Sabang where women went about freely in jeans or shorts. To Muslim Ibrahim, these women are considered 'not religious enough'. But to many women like Yuli Suriani, Islam is a *presence*, not an obligation. What Aceh needs is a legal system that brings anyone to justice for crimes, including soldiers and policemen for rights abuses. That would accord with the Koranic stress on justice.

I was curious about this debate and visited Imam Syuja, the chairman of the Muhammadiyah in Aceh, to talk about the sharia, justice and mandatory hijab. I asked him the relevance of the sharia formalisation while so much violence, poverty and injustice are taking place in Aceh.

According to Imam Syuja, 'Our *ulamas* are busier talking about the sharia than justice. Our *ulamas* are busier getting close to power than nurturing their independence. It is an irony, isn't it?'

When I reminded him about his own status as a member of the 27-strong Ulamas' Consultative Assembly, Imam stopped and took a deep breath. He offered a bitter smile and didn't reply.

Indonesian Soldiers Looting Acehnese Houses

There is a popular coffee shop near the Baiturrahman Grand Mosque in Banda Aceh where many Acehnese men read newspapers, chat with friends, smoke and sip their black coffee. Chek Yuke's prices are fair. A single newspaper is usually read by more than 30 people. The shop has a view over the Kreung Aceh river, the grand mosque and the only Catholic church in town. In the morning, it provides *nasi gurih* (coconut milk-flavoured steamed rice). In the evening one can order *mie Aceh*, noodles cooked with a lot of spices.

On the morning of 12 June 2003, while having my *nasi gurih* at Chek Yuke, I noticed that the traffic outside was extremely heavy. Sedans, minivans, military trucks, jeeps, motorcycles and pedestrians were rushing to Blang Padang square, next to the mosque, where more than 5,000 civil servants were expected to attend a ceremony to pledge 'loyalty to the Republic of Indonesia'.

The civil servants were asked to line up in accordance with their respective offices. Military officers, many of whom had brought their weapons, were issuing orders and asked the civil servants to stand. They were standing before a flagpole which was erected in the centre of the square and wearing red and white armbands – the colours of the Indonesian flag.

'We worked the whole night to sew them', said an engineer with the state-owned electric company.

'Bad temper', quipped a woman who worked for the state-owned *TVRI*. She talked about the traffic jam, the crowded square, the military barking orders and the other obstacles that she had to face just to attend this ceremony. Thousands of these civil servants were cowed into following the government line. It appeared to be a case of 'join the ceremony or have difficulties with your job!'

Some days earlier, Aceh governor Abdullah Puteh had told the media that the government would 'screen' civil servants about their stance on the Aceh freedom movement. Hypothetical questions included what they would do if they had family members sympathetic towards GAM. Would they report it to the authorities or remain silent? What did they think about the unity of the Republic of Indonesia?

Puteh, himself an Acehnese, said those 'double faces' would have to deal with the 'consequences', adding that he had found out that many civil servants were sympathetic toward GAM. *Serambi*, the leading daily in

Aceh, quoted him as saying that he didn't recognise such dualities: civil servants should be loyal to those who paid their salaries.

The civil servants lined up facing the flagpole. On the other side of Blang Padang was a stage and tents which sheltered VIPs, sitting comfortably in their chairs out of the sun. Huge banners encircled the field, displaying messages such as 'GAM, people are tired of you' and 'We civil servants are loyal to the Republic of Indonesia'.

While waiting for the arrival of Governor Puteh and Major General Endang Suwarna, the Indonesian military commander in Aceh, each office coordinator circulated a file which the civil servants had to sign. Attendance was compulsory and absentees might be questioned.

The civil servants pledged their allegiance and loyalty to the Republic of Indonesia, reading a prepared oath loudly. They sang Indonesia's national anthem *Indonesia Raya* (The Great Indonesia) and recited from the Koran.

The morning's formality was the first of many flag-raising ceremonies throughout Aceh. Military officers and their civilian counterparts mobilised the ceremonies in villages and schools. Students, villagers, farmers, fishermen, civil servants and others were asked to show up, wearing red-and-white armbands. If they failed to do so, they would be putting their school or job at risk. This was the nationalism Jakarta tries to promote to win 'the hearts and minds' of the Acehnese.

Will it work? Many people doubt it.

Sidney Jones, the American political analyst who has specialised in Indonesia since the 1970s, wrote in an International Crisis Group report that such efforts were counterproductive. 'It is not possible to force loyalty to the Indonesian state by holding rallies to pledge allegiance to the Indonesian state, or by forcing people to fly the red and white flag'.

Jones wrote, 'I was in East Timor just before the 1999 referendum when militias were forcing people either to fly the flag or have their house burned. Most chose to fly the flag rather than face the loss of all their belongings, but in the process, they came to hate the flag. It had become a symbol of repression'.

Another example: Jakarta might have thought it could win the loyalty of the villagers by evacuating them from villages where operations against GAM were planned and by giving them temporary shelter in refugee camps.

But many of the tens of thousands of refugees have found that they had almost no warning of the evacuation. They were forced to leave at short notice. There was a shortage of clean drinking water and food at the sites to which where they were moved. Their livestock, electronic goods and other valuables were gone when they got home. The thieves could have been anyone, but it was the government that was blamed, particularly when Governor Puteh and General Suwarna had promised that homes would be guarded and that there would be no looting.

Two soldiers were recently tried for allegedly stealing during raids on the home of a suspected GAM member. Military prosecutor Major Maryanto Bandji accused the pair of taking 2 million rupiah (US$242) in cash and 2.6 grams of gold jewellery from the house in North Aceh.

Three other soldiers were sentenced for raping four women, with the soldiers being discharged from the military but with the heaviest sentence being just three years and six months. Another military court jailed six soldiers for between four and five months for beating up civilians at Lawang village in Bireuën during operations.

Maybe this is progress in Indonesia, where soldiers, especially high-ranking officers, often act with impunity. But it is hardly enough to win the hearts and minds of the Acehnese.

Wiryono Sastrohandoyo, Indonesia's chief negotiator, said he had found it difficult to negotiate with GAM in Tokyo in May 2003 because he had to first release the Acehnese delegates arrested by the Indonesian military. 'How could you be trusted if you arrest their negotiators?'

There is no question that Jakarta has the legal right to wage war to quell the rebellion in Aceh, as it is an internationally recognised territory of Indonesia. The question is about tactics and human rights abuses. The Indonesian military's record on incidents of human rights abuses against civilians has revealed serious shortcomings based on the 1997 Military Tribunal Law. The military justice system lacks basic safeguards necessary to ensure justice and impartiality. Indonesia is also failing to provide civilian victims of abuse at the hands of military personnel with an adequate remedy, in violation of its international legal obligations. Many of the 'GAM members' killed in this operation were, in fact, civilians. And young Indonesian soldiers, who are mostly not well trained, seem to abuse their power on a daily basis.

On 3 May 1999, these soldiers shot hundreds of protesters at a junction near the Kraft fertiliser factory in Lhokseumawe, killing at least 46 civilians. Video of the massacre circulated widely in Aceh. Chik Rini, a Banda Aceh–based journalist, reported that a military spy had gone missing in the neighbourhood three days earlier while monitoring a GAM event. This prompted dozens of his comrades from the Air Defense Artillery Guided

Missile battalion to enter the neighbourhood, questioning and beating locals. The villagers then protested on 3 May. No soldier was arrested for the massacre.

On 23 July 1999, Muslim teacher Tengku Bantaqiah and 56 of his students were shot to death near their school in Beutong Ateuh, West Aceh. The officer who allegedly ordered the shooting escaped from military police detention in November 1999.

With the screening of civil servants underway, the government will lose more support. Not only is this a decided throwback to the Suharto regime, despite all claims to the contrary, it is virtually guaranteed to be a source of bad information. Business rivals, jealous neighbours, and others could report suspicions about someone and without questions asked, that person could be isolated, fired or arrested. It also has a weird interpretation of nationalism.

In June 2003, Jakarta issued new identity cards for Aceh residents. The purpose was to differentiate GAM members from ordinary citizens. But the card design is different from the common ID cards used throughout Indonesia. The cards in Aceh have a red-and-white background. Each card is signed by a district head, a police superintendent and a military commander. Is it a symbol to say Acehnese are different from other Indonesian citizens? Officials in other parts of Indonesia have also asked their subordinates to keep a watch over all Acehnese living in their areas.

Major General Endang Suwarna infuriated media organisations by preventing foreign journalists and international observers from entering Aceh. He said that Indonesian journalists should be 'nationalists' and 'not to interview GAM', as if trying to say that the media should only cover the Indonesian side of the story. His colleague, Major General Bambang Darmono, removed *Reuters* photographer Tarmizy Harva from Aceh. Tarmizy recorded the killing of Muzakkir Abdullah, an Acehnese peasant in the village of Seumirah in Nisam on 17 June 2003. His picture won the World Press Award in Amsterdam.

What kind of nationalism do Suwarna and Darmono recognise? Is it only the either-you're-with-us-or-with-them nationalism, blind to social injustice, or the more logical understanding that citizens do live with their many complex identities?

Tsunami and the Helsinki Agreement

A huge tsunami reached Aceh's shores on 26 December 2004. The temblor began at 7.58 a.m. with a magnitude of 9.0 Richter in the Indian Ocean. Its epicentre was around 255 kilometres south-east of Banda Aceh, according to the US Geological Survey. It is the fourth largest earthquake in the world since 1900 and is the largest since the 1964 Prince William Sound, Alaska earthquake.

The subsequent tsunami, which began 15 to 30 minutes after the temblor, caused more casualties than any other disaster in recorded human history. I immediately flew from Jakarta to Aceh, witnessing rescue workers collecting corpses on Banda Aceh streets, flying with a chopper to other areas and trying to capture the tragedy.

I stopped in Lamno, a small town on the western cost of Aceh, interviewing survivors and seeing international aid workers providing food and blankets. Survivors stumbled, panicked, frightened and soaking wet, running through thick mud while trying desperately to outrun the ever-pursuing killer waves.

According to Keuchik Muhammad Ali, a survivor in Lamno, 'The first wave that reached Ujung Muloh was relatively small. As the water started rising fast from the first wave, we started running'.

Ali rushed to grab his family and get out of their house. Ali held on to his youngest daughter, who was only 10 days old. His wife, Yusmanida, who had not fully recovered from the delivery, was assisted by her mother. The couple's 13-year-old son and 11-year-old daughter ran together behind their parents. The two also held on tight to their great-grandmother as they were running. 'The waves were as tall as coconut trees', he said.

Ali lost his wife, all his children, his mother-in-law, his wife's grand-mother, gold, money, house and everything else.

'A tree trunk hit my back. I also suffered some bleeding in my left forehead. Look at this!' he said, pointing to a black scar that marks his forehead, but blaming the tsunami on 'Acehnese women who don't practice the Islamic sharia'.

Aceh suddenly became the headlines of the global media. UN Secretary General Kofi Annan, Singapore Prime Minister Lee Hsien Loong, Australian Premier John Howard, as well as celebrities like Hong Kong actor Jacky Cheung and German car racer Michael Schumacher, visited Aceh. Former US presidents George H. W. Bush and Bill Clinton paid a half-day visit, promising to bring more help to Aceh. Clinton commented, 'I've never seen anything like this in my entire life. Ever'.

US Secretary of State Colin Powell, himself a retired general, flew over Aceh and commented, 'I've been in war and I've been in a number of hurricanes, tornadoes and other relief operations but I have never seen anything like this'.

It was indeed the biggest catastrophe in Aceh's history. In Lamno, relief workers recorded that 6,375 people had been buried and 546 were declared missing out of a population of 14,634. It means 43.5 per cent of the population was killed. In total, those killer waves killed 286,000 people in 14 countries including 221,000 killed or missing in Aceh alone, according to the World Bank.

On my flight from Banda Aceh to Jakarta, the pilot decided to amuse his passengers by flying over the Krakatoa site. The pilot talked about Krakatoa's huge explosion, comparing it with the tsunami. His manoeuvre reminded me of what Simon Winchester wrote in his book *Krakatoa: The Day the World Exploded – August 27, 1883*. The catastrophic eruption on the southern tip of Sumatra had changed the world. The explosion was followed by an immense tsunami that killed nearly 40,000 people in Sumatra and Java. The effects of the waves were felt as far away as France. Bodies were washed up in Zanzibar. Most significant of all, the eruption helped to trigger in Java a wave of murderous anti-Dutch militancy among the Javanese Muslims. I am sure the tsunami will create a drastic political and economic change in Aceh, if not in Indonesia.

In Brussels, the European Union quietly asked the Indonesian government and Hasan di Tiro's Free Acheh Movement, headquartered in Stockholm, to negotiate a peace agreement. International aid organisations obviously could not deliver humanitarian assistance if both parties were still shooting at one another. Vice President Jusuf Kalla sent some of his aides to negotiate with GAM leaders. It was mediated by the Helsinki-based Crisis Management Initiative headed by former Finish president Martti Ahtisaari.

The six-month negotiation resulted in a peace agreement signed in Helsinki on 15 August 2005. GAM number two Malik Mahmud and Kalla's aide Hamid Awaludin signed the agreement. Mahmud said in his speech that Indonesia '...is not yet fully reformed from the dark days of the New Order. But this peace agreement is an important step for Indonesia away from those dark days'.

'Peace is important to Indonesia so that it can learn to live with itself, in all its diverse forms'.

'For too long, Indonesia's diversity has been allowed only so long as it conforms to a narrow nationalist interpretation'.

The agreement covers several issues like Aceh's governance (administration, political participation, economy and rule of law), human rights, amnesty and reintegration into society, security arrangements, establishment of a peace-monitoring mission and dispute settlement. Indonesia agreed to let Aceh govern all sectors of public affairs, except in the fields of foreign affairs, external defence, national security, monetary and fiscal matters, justice and freedom of religion.

There's also a clause in which Aceh is to be permitted to implement the Islamic sharia, writing its own Islamic criminal code (*qanun jinayah*)... if it does not contradict the Indonesian national law plus the two major international human rights covenants: The International Covenant on Civil and Political Rights as well as the International Covenant on Economic, Social and Cultural Rights.

In Aceh, Acehnese welcomed the peace agreement. Many GAM members went back home. Guerilla fighters took rehabilitation funds, handing over their guns. I personally helped two newspapers to rebuild their newsrooms. I also helped teach at Muslim Ibrahim's Ar-Raniry State Islamic Institute, trying to teach these young men and women to be journalists.

Acehnese also busily prepared local parties to elect their political leaders.

According to the World Bank, in eight years, Aceh became a trans-formed place. Nearly US$7 billion in contributions from the Indonesian government and international donors flowed into Aceh, fuelling a boom in reconstruction activities. The Multi Donor Fund for Aceh and Nias, managed by the World Bank, pooled funding from 15 donors and provided a mechanism for putting these funds to work. It estimated 15,000 people were killed during the three decades of guerilla war.

The post-Helsinki election was held on 11 December 2006. GAM strategist Irwandi Yusuf won the election. He secured 38.2 per cent of the votes. It was above the 25 per cent threshold, making a second round unnecessary. Irwandi Yusuf escaped from his Banda Aceh prison during the tsunami. He was serving a nine-year sentence for his political activities.

Meanwhile, Muslim Ibrahim's Ulamas' Consultative Assembly set up their sharia police, training thousands of men and women to enforce sharia provisions in Aceh. They began to increase *jilbab* monitoring, arresting more girls and women without modest attire.

In June 2007, Governor Irwandi Yusuf issued a decree on the construction of houses of worship. Yusuf made it very difficult for Christians and other minorities in Aceh to build or renovate their houses of worship. He told me that he used the majority-minority approach, 'It's something that I cannot prevent. The majority, the Muslims, do not want to have new churches in Aceh'.

A 2010 Human Rights Watch report, *Policing Morality: Abuses in the Application of Sharia in Aceh*, documented human rights abuses linked to enforcement of sharia ordinances prohibiting adultery and *khalwat* (seclusion), and imposing mandatory hijab public dress requirements on Muslims. The *khalwat* law makes association by unmarried individuals of the opposite sex a criminal offense in some circumstances. While the dress requirement is ostensibly gender-neutral, in practice it imposes far more onerous restrictions on women, with the mandatory *jilbab* and long skirts.

In April 2011, Irwandi Yusuf issued another decree to ban 14 Islamic minorities, including Ahmadiyah, Shia, Ismailiyah, Millah Abraham, as well as Druze. The Aceh parliament also produced more discriminatory ordinances.

Hasan di Tiro, the GAM founder, returned to large crowds in Banda Aceh in October 2008. He was 83 years old, having difficulties speaking due to his past strokes. He rarely appeared in public. He died in June 2010 in Banda Aceh. Vice President Jusuf Kalla restored his Indonesian citizenship the day before he died.

The tsunami reconstruction officially ended in 2012 and Aceh began to show their true colours. Aceh gradually appeared in news reports for their harsh treatment of minorities and policing morality: public caning on Fridays; harassing women without *jilbab*; criminalising homosexuality; banning Christmas and New Year celebrations; arresting women who straddle motorcycles. Scores of journalists and GAM activists, whom I knew during the war, became Islamic sharia defenders.

In June 2013, the National Commission on Violence Against Women published a report, compiling data from 16 rights organisations in Aceh. It chronicled 1,060 cases of sexual violence in 2011–12, reporting that domestic violence dominates those cases. The victims were dominantly young girls between eight and 18 years of age. The perpetrators are mostly their fathers, step-fathers, brothers, grandfathers or uncles.

Incest is the most dominant pattern, according to the 72-page report. Incest possibly increased because Acehnese villagers have loosened their safeguard against that sexual violence. They spend more time safeguarding against extra-marital affairs and seclusion.

The report authors came to Jakarta and painfully briefed several researchers. Two of them were bullied when they went back to Banda Aceh.

Still Aceh became a beacon for other Indonesian provinces to copy their sharia provisions. The Aceh sharia department provides lecturers to discuss the sharia provisions to visiting legislators and officials from other parts of Indonesia. They also like to claim that they're practicing 'moderate Islam' in Banda Aceh, tolerating women to be leaders, unlike…Saudi Arabia.

In May 2012, Sunni militants in Singkil, southern Aceh, protested 'illegal' churches and demanded that the government close them down. It produced quick results. In less than a week, the Singkil government sealed 19 churches and one native-faith house of worship. All these houses of worship were built before Irwandi Yusuf's 2006 decree; some were even established during Dutch or Japanese rule. The oldest church, a Protestant church in Kuta Kerangan, was built in 1932 during the Dutch Indies era. Some were built during the Japanese occupation in 1942–45. The newest one, the Indonesian Evangelical Mission Church, was built in 2003.

The Christians in Singkil are mostly ethnic Pakpak Batak who also live in two other neighbouring regencies: Dairi and Pakpak Bharat in North Sumatra province. They use Pakpak Batak language in their church services.

Their churches were sealed but they covertly kept using their churches via back doors.

This apparently angered the Sunni militants in Singkil.

On 13 October 2015, hundreds of Sunni militants in three cars, three pickup trucks and dozens of motorcycles, attacked one of the churches in Singkil, wielding axes and machetes. They burned down the church building. The mob moved to another church whose parishioners decided to defend themselves. Fighting ensued, a Muslim attacker got shot and killed. Police and soldiers arrived to defuse the tensions, but the mob left three churches smouldering.

About 7,000 Christians fled Singkil to neighbouring regencies in North Sumatra. They included around 1,000 children, staying in shelters out of fear that violence might escalate. In Jakarta, President Joko Widodo ordered the police and the military to immediately return those Christians and to protect them in Singkil. Those churches remained burned down.

Fifteen years after the 2001 Autonomy Law, Aceh began to apply those unforgiving treatments to about 90,000 non-Muslims residents, mostly Christians and Buddhists, as well as domestic and foreign visitors to the province. The tsunami has indeed ended the three decades of guerilla war in Aceh, but those waves obviously cannot close the area's Pandora box.

Chapter 2

KALIMANTAN

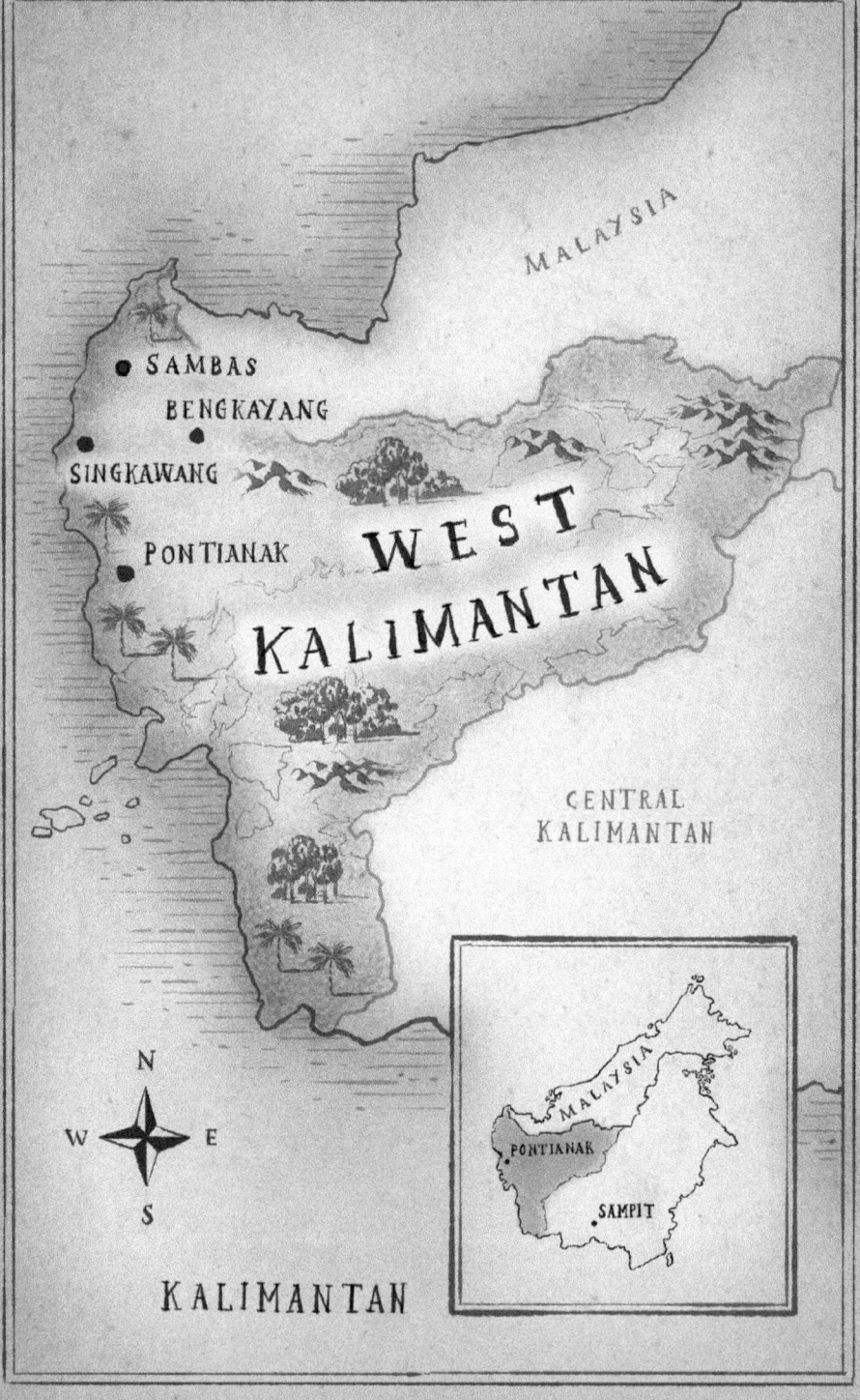

The Madurese Massacre

Sambas, the Malay Heartland

It was 2:00 in the afternoon. Someone uttered the words *'mate kabbhi'*. It means all dead Madurese.

Several other Madurese men and women came in. They sat on the wooden floor, talking about the death of their loved ones.

They talked for four hours. By six in the evening, the words *'mate kabbhi'* had been echoed. Its real meaning, I found out, is the 'ethnic cleansing' of the ethnic Madurese in Kalimantan. More than 6,500 Madurese were beheaded in the killing throughout Kalimantan, especially in Sanggau Ledo, Sambas and Sampit, between 1997 and 2001. These people at Abunawas' house are the survivors.

Abunawas himself is a cattle herder. I visited his wooden hut on Gang Dharma Putra, outside Pontianak in western Kalimantan, in December 2004. Gang Dharma Putra is a rural area with bushy lots and muddy streets. His L-shaped hut is about 30 square metres. The living room has a Sharp television, a Panasonic sound system, a video player and a Gudang Garam cigarette poster. Nothing else. Abunawas, his wife Karimah, and their 10-year-old daughter Rahayu, ate and slept on the floor.

The neighbours, who joined our conversation, introduced themselves one by one. They said they are Madurese settlers who used to live in Sambas, a fertile coastal area in western Kalimantan, crisscrossed by rivers and orange groves, about five hours by bus from Pontianak.

Next to the hut is a bamboo shelter where they kept four cows, two calves, four goats, chicken, ducks and bundles of freshly cut grass. 'The cattle are not ours. We just raise them for a living', uttered Karimah.

Mariyama, a 31-year-old homemaker, said she used to live in Senangi village in Sambas. The troubles began on Sunday, 21 March 1999, when she visited a kiosk to buy cigarettes.

'It was quiet in the kiosk. I asked the owner, "Where are all the women?"'

The kiosk owner stared back.

'The gaze was strange', Mariyama said.

'He is a Malay!'

'The mob arrived on Monday, many Malay men, coming from neighbouring villages, using spears, arrows, pistols. They attacked our village.

They burned down our houses. Our men defended our village. Many of them were killed. For four days, Monday through Thursday, I hid in the jungle. When we could not hide longer, 14 of my kin decided to cross the river in a wooden boat, trying to look for help'.

'My brother, my parents, my son, altogether 14 people in that boat'.

'Other Malay (men) also waited on the river. They shot at the boat. They rammed it. They shot Supandi, my cousin, twice in his back. They stabbed his left hip. The boat sank. They attempted to drown him. Blood was everywhere. They abandoned him'.

'Supandi, miraculously, survived. He collapsed on the riverbank and regained consciousness the following day. Some Javanese soldiers helped him. Some months later I met him in a Pontianak refugee camp. He told me that the 13 others did not make it'.

'Mate kabbhi', said Mariyama.

Sarunah also had her story. Her husband came from a neighbouring village. But 42 of their relatives were all dead, including her three brothers, a sister, several grandchildren and relatives. 'The Malays beheaded them', she said.

I visited other neighbourhoods and the story seemed to be repeated again. Chodijah, a young woman on Gang Barokah, near Gang Dharma Putra, said she was only 15 years old when the ethnic killing took place. 'I was reciting the Koran in the madrasah in Nyirih village, near Sentebang'.

'We stopped the recital when the mob attacked. I ran home. It was in the evening. They arrived with pistols, spears, some riding motorcycles. I almost collapsed. I was so scared. I told my mother to wake up. We ran into a neighbour's house. We stayed for one night. At dawn all of my siblings and my mother ran to leave our village', Chodijah said.

Sari, Chodijah's mother, added that they had run until their legs ached. 'We threw away our bags. They slowed us down'.

Jasudin, another survivor, said the most tragic killing took place in Mariyama's Senangi village. 'Babies were thrown to red ants as their mothers hid. The Malay men were waiting for their mothers. When the worrying mothers went out, they were killed'.

'There were women whose breasts were cut', said Chodijah.

I also visited the Tebang Kacang relocation area where the government resettled the Madurese. I took a four-wheel drive from Pontianak to reach this newly opened forested area. Several Madurese men built the village road. They approached me. 'The government took sides. They are not neutral', said Mat Sukri. 'Indeed, there is one or two bad Madurese but not all Madurese are bad'.

A Malay helped refugees to get some water in Segarau. In Sabaran, a Chinese man opened his warehouse and let the Madurese take rice. 'Many Chinese and Malay people are also good, but they were scared to defend the Madurese', said Mat Sukri.

According to the 2000 census in Indonesia, the Madurese numbered about 3 per cent of Kalimantan's total population of 11 million people. Around 60 per cent of them live in western Kalimantan. 'The anti-Madurese sentiment, however, makes many Madurese youths not open up about their background', said Subro, a Madurese activist in Pontianak. Subro told me the Madurese in Kalimantan are arguably more than just 300,000, saying that more than 120,000 Madurese had left their villages during the ethnic killing. 'Many are also scared to say that they are Madurese'. He disputed the census.

The Madurese still could not return to Sambas, nearly two decades after the killing.

'Why Muslims kill other Muslims? The Chinese could come from Jakarta or even Taiwan to visit the cemeteries of their ancestors in Sambas. We, the Madurese, cannot see our parents' cemeteries. We could not see our own land. Some Madurese who tried to go to Sambas were beheaded'.

'I am worse than a dog. Dogs still have masters. The Madurese have no masters', sighed Abunawas.

* * *

My next stop was the Pemangkat river port to take a *dongdong* motor boat to cross the Sambas river. It was a noisy 30-minute ride. I arrived at the Jelu Air village to reach Parit Setia with Idham Chalid, my motorcycle driver, who is also a Koran teacher.

The Malay is a dominant ethnic group in Kalimantan. They live on the coastline or along major rivers. They are Muslim people united by language and custom, formed partly by immigration from other parts of the archipelago, but more significantly by the conversion of non-Muslim Dayak, the indigenous group, to Islam.

Parit Setia is a quiet Malay hamlet. On 17 January 1999, a drunk Madurese man was caught breaking into a Malay house after midnight.

Hasan, the alleged thief, hailed from nearby Rambayan, a predominantly Madurese village, where Abunawas used to live.

Idham and I visited that Malay house.

Arman Ayub, a Malay farmer who owned the house, told me the break-in took place at about 2.00 am. 'My father caught him red-handed. My mother shouted and asked for help'.

Other villagers awoke and arrested and beat Hasan. Several hours later, the black-and-blue Hasan returned to Rambayan. His story angered the Madurese. Some of Hasan's friends and parents reported the beating to the police. The Sambas police station, however, was not a place where one could get justice.

The angry Rambayan crowd decided to take the law into their own hands. According to court records, Jabak, a Rambayan leader, told the police that they were about to attack Parit Setia. The police ignored his warning.

It also happened to be the Eid al Fitri holiday, the end of Ramadan fasting month. A Muslim usually visits his or her relatives and colleagues to ask for forgiveness.

But neither Jabak nor the Rambayan crowd took the holiday into account. Jabak organised his own men to climb into three trucks and onto a handful of motorcycles. At 3.00 pm, they headed to Parit Setia with sickles, knives, iron pipes and other weapons.

As the Madurese mob entered the Parit Setia bridge, the villagers suddenly shouted, 'The Madurese have arrived, the Madurese have arrived'.

Some Malay men shouted, '*Siap, siap, siap*'. 'Get ready, get ready, get ready'.

Arman Ayub decided to run and hide on a riverbank. But not his father, Ayub Tahir, who had caught Hasan that night. Two other villagers, Wasli Bukuan and Mahli Azis, also decided to face the Madurese group. 'My father was coming home from doing his wood work, carrying a hammer', said Arman.

Facing the three Parit Setia farmers, Jabak asked them where Hasan's attackers were. Mahli responded with his machete. Jabak and his gang attacked, hacking the three with their machetes and sickles on the village bridge. The three bled profusely and died at the spot.

'It lasted only about five minutes. The Madurese left the scene with their vehicles. We were scared. It was so fast', said Hamidi Hadran, an ironsmith and Arman's neighbour.

Arman said, 'I did not see it. I was only told that my neighbours took care of the bodies and put them in the mosque. I did not know my father also died'.

News about the raid spread rapidly throughout Sambas, Singkawang and Pontianak. Many Malays demanded the assailants be apprehended. It fuelled the Malay view of Madurese as arrogant, hot-tempered belligerents, who are keen to take the law into their own hands. Pontianak newspapers whipped up anti-Madurese sentiment by noting it was inconceivable for pious Muslims to commit such acts on Eid al Fitri. The press also revived the notion that the Madurese, as migrants, are outsiders who do not own the land. They should assimilate with and respect the Malays. The expression *'Dimana langit dipijak disana bumi dijunjung'* began to appear in daily conversations. It means something like, 'When in Rome, do as the Romans do'.

Malay support began to pour into Parit Setia. Chairil Effendi, a lecturer on Malay language at the Tanjungpura University in Pontianak, collected some money, rice and instant noodles. He told me that he had arrived in Parit Setia some days after the raid, asking the village elders 'to avoid revenge'.

Winata Kesuma, a descendant of the Sambas sultans, also arrived in Parit Setia with three close friends. According to Ronald Dachlan, one of the three friends, 'We went there not to provoke the villagers. We heard that women and children were scared. They went into hiding in the forest. We went there and used the mosque loudspeaker to invite the villagers to have a gathering', said Ronald.

According to American scholar Jamie Davidson in his thesis *Violence and Politics in West Kalimantan, Indonesia*, Winata Kesuma actually helped mobilise forces, most infamously by raising a yellow flag at his *keraton* (palace), which symbolises a call to war. Winata became hugely popular among the Sambas villagers. When I travelled in Parit Setia, Sentebang, Rambayan, Pemangkat, Jawai and other villages, it seemed to me that everyone knows him. He is affectionately known as 'Raden Wimpi' or 'Prince Wimpi'.

Hamidi Hadran, the Parit Setia ironsmith, told me that Raden Wimpi's speech 'aroused our spirit'. Tensions were brewing between Malay and Madurese youth in Pemangkat, Tebas and Jawai –the three most hard-line subdistricts in Sambas' 13 administrative groups. The Malays were mobilised swiftly. They began to arm themselves, and ironsmiths like Hamidi began receiving orders for 'samurai swords'.

'I made it from the chain saw bar. I cannot count, maybe more than 100 swords. It was so many that I had to refuse orders', he recalled.

In Singkawang, one week after the Parit Setia raid, 11 Malay leaders formed the Forum Komunikasi Pemuda Melayu or FKPM, the Communication Forum of reli. Some of these men, who are mostly in their forties, described their occupations as 'contractors' – men who usually get government contracts. After talking with them, I came away with the impression that they had backgrounds as thugs.

'These Madurese think they have a good life! They think they are great! They are overacting. They like to stab and kill. If arrested, they bribe the police. They played with the judges and the prosecutors', said Zulkarnain Bujang, the FKPM chairman.

'If we don't take a stance, we will be finished. Our girls work in the field and they were raped. So I invited some friends to meet in my house', he told me. The FKPM soon became the most important Malay group spewing ethnic hatred against the Madurese.

In Parit Setia, nearly a month after the attack, the police made only one arrest. The Malays were unsatisfied. How could the police only arrest one man when the Madurese attacked Parit Setia with three trucks and several motorcycles? Malay anger boiled up. According to his friends and wife Endang Sri Muningsih, Raden Wimpi, tried to cool down the Sambas town where his royal palace is located.

The eruption occurred on 21 February 1999 when Rudi bin Muharap, a young Madurese passenger, refused to pay his bus fare as he alighted in Pusaka village in the Tebas subdistrict. Annoyed, the fare collector, a Malay youth named Bujang Lebik, stared down Rudi.

Rudi, a civil servant, took offence. He went back home and brought his friends to look for Bujang Lebik. Rudi stabbed Bujang. Villagers brought Bujang to the Pemangkat hospital near the river port. He was bleeding from his stomach and right hand.

Zulkarnain Bujang and his FKPM comrades visited Bujang Lebik in the Pemangkat hospital. 'I suggested the nurses hide him in the delivery ward. Too many visitors arrived at the hospital'. The Malay visitors were furious.

That night, the first Malay attack took place in Semparuk village. Malay militias wearing yellow headbands burned 17 houses and killed three Madurese. The next morning, all shops in Pemangkat were closed. The mass killing had begun. Killing began to move from village to village.

It escalated again on 16 March when a Dayak worker, Martinus Amat, was mysteriously killed in Sambas. FKPM leaders insisted that Amat was killed by Madurese militia. The Dayaks joined the Malays in hunting down the Madurese. Within 24 hours of Martinus's death, over 300 Madurese houses along the Kulor–Samalantan road, the predominantly Dayak area, were razed. It became a massive ethnic campaign. The Madurese, young and old, men and women, were hunted throughout Sambas.

* * *

One of the Malay militias is Masya Hasan. The 52-year-old farmer lives in Pusaka village, Tebas district, where Bujang Lebik had stared down Rudi. Masya Hasan, nicknamed Mat Kedang, was a foot soldier, not an FKPM activist. He stormed many Madurese settlements, killing 'more than 30 Madurese settlers', especially in Senangi village where Mariyama, Abunawas' neighbour, used to live and fear for her life.

His wooden hut has two bedrooms. Mat Kedang has a beard with gray hair and is missing several teeth. He looked much older than his age. 'Come sit down. It is an honour to have a journalist visiting my place', he said, showing me his family photos and introducing me to his wife, Noursiyah binti Yahya.

He proudly talked about his two daughters, 'The youngest one killed three Madurese: a father, a son and a daughter'. Noursiyah smiled. Mat Kedang went into their bedroom and came out with a sheathed *mandau*, a typical Dayak sword.

He handed it to me.

'You can look, you can touch, but you must not open it'.

The hair on my arm quivered. I talked to other Malay men in Sambas who admitted killing Madurese. They talked about the Madurese's refusal to assimilate with the local population or their 'habit' of stealing land, chickens or coconuts. The men burned houses or in one case beheaded two Madurese victims. They, however, refused to be quoted. They obviously felt uncomfortable. I interviewed a Malay militia member in Sentebang. He showed me his long sword and his yellow Malay headband with the Arabic characters. 'After the killing, I felt very sorry. Sleeping is difficult', he said.

Mat Kedang is different. He wasn't ashamed talking about the killing. He talked about his anti-Madurese stance, saying that they are 'arrogant people'. He said he had a duty to defend the land of his Malay ancestors, 'It is a war'.

He opened the 72-centimetre-long sword. It glistened moderately. Mat Kedang held the sword as if it were a living creature.

'There is a little dent down here. Look at this! It was caused by a stubborn Madurese bastard in Senangi'.

'I hit his neck but he did not fall down. I usually took a single blow to chop off a head. But not with that bastard'.

I asked Mat Kedang how he got involved in those killings. He said it began with the Parit Setia raid and the stabbing of Bujang Lebik.

'It's a matter of solidarity. I must defend the Malay. When the Dayak fought the Madurese, the Dayak did not eliminate them. The Malay are calmer and peaceful people. But if there is a war we do it totally until the end. No more Madurese. They cannot return to Sambas'.

He smiled, 'I did the first killing against Salim. He was involved in a debate with our village head'.

'Other villagers surrounded them. I am not that patient. I shot him to death'.

'Do you know Salim?'

'Oh yes, he is a Madurese. He lived near here, down that street corner'.

He went inside his room and came out with two handmade rifles. Some black ants, which apparently nested inside, ran out of the barrel. 'I spent around 300,000 rupiahs to buy the M-16 bullets for these riffles'. He muttered about good harvest helping oil the war.

He showed me a bullet, loading it into the rifle.

'Like this!' he uttered, aiming the rifle into the living room.

I asked him about the habit of eating a victim's heart. Sometimes it is difficult to believe cannibalism still takes place in Kalimantan. I did not believe it, but some men had told me the stories.

'Why should you eat human heart?' I asked Mat Kedang.

'Our ancestors said that we must cut our enemies' heads so that they will not regroup again. Some Madurese might have supernatural power. They could do that'.

'We also must eat their hearts'.

'If you want to take the heart, you have to take them out from the back. Cut the back and grope the heart out'.

He asked to put his hands on my back, as if pretending to make a cut on my back. One hand pushed on my back and the other hand pretended to hold a *mandau* making a cut.

'It is as big as a palm, yes, the palm of our hands', Mat Kedang said.

'How did it taste?' I asked.

'It looked like a piece of tofu. Slippery. Dark red. You cut it in small sizes, maybe about 10 grams each, and everyone ate a piece', he said, using his sword to show how it cuts a bean-curd-like human heart.

'We did not eat the hearts of children and babies though'.

'Smokers' hearts tasted bitter. Most men's hearts were bitter'.

* * *

The biggest killing was in Senangi, a remote village, across Sambas river. It had remained relatively peaceful while other Madurese houses in Tebas, Jawai and Pemangkat were burned down and their owners were killed. Senangi was located outside the Malay hardline areas.

Mat Kedang recalled, 'Seven people volunteered from Pusaka to join forces in attacking Senangi. Mausere had nine men including Mawardi. Sempadung had five fighters. Mawardi was our commander'.

I remembered Mawardi bin Sude. He was a Malay militia, living in Mausere village, near Mat Kedang's Pusaka village. I once visited Mawardi's house and clearly remembered his living room decorated by letters sent by Megawati Sukarnoputri, the eldest daughter of the late president Sukarno.

Mat Kedang continued, 'We took a boat and walked to reach Senangi. We fought until dark. Difficult battles. Many stubborn bastards in Senangi'.

There were around 40 Madurese families in Senangi. The attack began on Monday, 22 March 1999. Madurese men armed themselves to defend their families. It was an unbalanced battle. Children and women ran into a nearby forest.

'Mawardi, our leader, died in the fight. He was a real leader', said Mat Kedang.

'The Madurese hacked him in the neck'.

'It was about 11.00 in the morning. I helped evacuate Mawardi. I gave my *mandau* to another colleague and decided to bring Mawardi back to Mausere. He died of bleeding on his way to Mausere'.

Later Romina, the widow of Mawardi, told me, 'We received my husband, already dead. We buried him that very day'.

Mawardi's death angered his Malay comrades. On Tuesday evening, 23 March 1999, the Madurese began to abandon their village, running to the forest or the riverbank. Mariyama, one of the Madurese victims, said she ran between Tuesday and Thursday until a group of Javanese soldiers found her. But 14 of her relatives were killed in the river. *Kompas* reported that hundreds of corpses were found in Senangi and the surrounding forest on Thursday. Madurese survivors told me it was the bloodiest killing in Sambas. Mat Kedang never knew Mariyama. I am not sure whether Mat Kedang also killed Mariyama's relatives.

'Those riots are the symbol of Malay unity. The killing should not be repeated again. The purpose is not to kill. It is their own wrongdoing, their own habit. That's all'.

Malay unity? How about Indonesian unity? How about nationalism from Sabang to Merauke? Where is the so-called Muslim brotherhood?

I left Mat Kedang's house and continued my trip throughout Sambas, seeing remains of burned buildings and 'Madurese mosques'. I saw abandoned orange groves. When reaching Sambas town, I rented a canoe on Sambas river to visit the Alwadzikoebillah palace. The view of the *keraton* from the river enchanted me. I admired its ornaments, its grand mosque and the gifts from other kingdoms such as England and China. This Malay sultanate clearly used to be rich. It employed Chinese miners to work the gold mines in Sambas in the 18th century. They also employed Dayak warriors to guard their interests.

How could these people, both Dayaks and Malays, claim to be fellow citizens when they kill the Madurese like animals? The Chinese, the third largest racial group in West Kalimantan and the descendants of the miners, also closed their eyes toward this brutality. Abunawas told me some Chinese were also involved. How could they do it? Killing their fellow citizens in the name of ethnic hatred? How could they build the nation of Indonesia when they organise such ethnic cleansing? If nationalism is not relevant, I still wonder how the Malay, who claimed to be practicing Muslims, kill their fellow co-religionists? How could they shout the name of Allah when killing the Madurese Muslim?

Chairil Effendi, a professor at the Tanjungpura University, repeated the racially prejudiced argument that the killing was the culmination of the Madurese-Malay clashes in Sambas area since the 1940s. 'There were many Madurese robbers. In smaller scales, they stole our coconuts. They stole our chickens. They harvested our paddy fields at night'.

Chairil, who grew up in Singkawang, told me that in the 1960s most of Singkawang's pedicab drivers were Chinese, Javanese or Malay. The Madurese, however, took over those jobs. 'The problem is economic', he said. 'One Madurese bought a pedicab and the other Madureses would soon follow, driving Malay, Chinese or Javanese out of business'.

The 1967 Chinese Massacre

Roban is a small suburban area in Singkawang. A grocery shop sells sarsaparilla bottled drink and fried bananas. Scores of thatched houses blared Canto Pop music. It was 2005, New Year's Day. I walked the street and talked to Lie Syak Liung, a 70-year-old ethnic Chinese.

'I once sold iced drink but not anymore. I am already old', Lie said.

I visited Roban to look at an earlier case of racial killing – the massacre of the Chinese in 1967. Roban is a Chinese resettlement camp. It is a Chinese equivalent of Tebang Kacang, where Madurese refugees were resettled after the 1999 massacre.

'I felt sorry for the Madurese. I know how they feel', he said, adding that he used to help some Madurese families.

'The police said it was dangerous to harbour the Madurese in my house'.

Lie was born in 1935 in Triak, a small village outside Bengkayang. In 1955, when Lie was 20 years old, he married Tju Nyan Tjau, then 17 years old. He also took over his father's coffee shop.

By then, the Chinese had been living in Bengkayang for three to four generations as farmers, workers, shopkeepers or traders. They were mostly descendants of Chinese miners who worked in gold mines in the 18th century.

In 1962, something that would later change Lie Syak Liung's life took place in Brunei, a small oil-rich sultanate in northern Kalimantan. Then Brunei leader A. M. Azahari won the general election, but his party was outnumbered in the National Legislative Council by delegates directly appointed by Brunei Sultan Omar Ali Saifuddin.

In December 1962, the embittered Azahari declared the creation of the Unitarian State of North Kalimantan. Sultan Omar, he said, was merely a protégé of the British colonialists.

In Jakarta, Indonesian President Sukarno enthusiastically supported Azahari's independence movement. Sukarno feared that Indonesia might be encircled by a larger and hostile Federation of Malaysia that combined the Malay Peninsula, Singapore and northern Kalimantan.

The United Kingdom rejected Azahari's declaration. London feared that Azahari might build a federation with other groups in the neighbouring Sarawak and Sabah to set up a new state in northern Kalimantan. Britain and its Western allies had an interest in Brunei's oil. They believed Azahari and his peers had some left-leaning ideology, and some Western media wrongly portrayed Azahari to have a communist link to Beijing.

In September 1963, Kuala Lumpur officially incorporated Sarawak and Sabak in northern Kalimantan into the Malaysia Federation. The Jakarta media bombarded their audience with the news, and a day later, anti-British demonstrations rocked Jakarta, culminating in the destruction of the British embassy. Sukarno launched an anti-Malaysia campaign that he called 'Confrontation', promising to 'crush Malaysia'.

According to Jamie S. Davidson and Douglas Kammen (in their paper 'Indonesia's Unknown War and the Lineages of Violence in West Kalimantan', the confrontation received enthusiastic support from the Indonesian Communist Party (Partai Komunis Indonesia, PKI). PKI asked that civilians be trained and armed to participate in the campaign. The Indonesian Army supported that proposal. It provided military training and weapons to several thousands of the 'volunteers' recruited and trained in West Kalimantan and West Java.

These volunteers had four elements: Azahari's supporters (*Pasukan Rakyat Kalimantan Utara* or Paraku, the People's Force of North Kalimantan); young ethnic Chinese supporters of the Sarawak Communist Party (its armed wing was the *Pasukan Gerilya Rakyat Sarawak* or PGRS, the Sarawak People Guerilla Forces); Indonesian 'volunteers' recruited in West Kalimantan and West Java (many were sympathetic to the PKI); and Indonesian military troops 'who had been released from their Army units'.

When the training was completed, these militias took part in dozens of cross-border raids into Sarawak. According to Canberra scholar J. A. C. Mackie in his book, *Konfrontasi*, by creating an 'external threat' these raids ironically made the incorporation of Sarawak and Sabah into Malaysia smoother than expected.

In Triak, Lie Syak Liung was busy working in his coffee shop. Tju gave birth to two sons and one daughter. While some Hakka youths joined the volunteers, Triak mostly remained unaffected.

The turning point took place in Jakarta on 30 September 1965. Three Army battalions whose commanding officers were closely linked to the PKI leadership kidnapped and murdered six Indonesian Army generals. The Army accused the PKI of masterminding the killing. The public believed the accusations, leading to massive killings of suspected communists nationwide.

General Suharto rose to power. He replaced President Sukarno's socialist policies with capitalistic approaches and ended the anti-Malaysia campaign. His government signed a peace agreement with Malaysia in August 1966. Army officers in Kalimantan were ordered to disband and to disarm the militias. The militias, however, disregarded the directive.

Meanwhile, PKI West Kalimantan chairman Said Achmad Sofyan went underground and moved into the Sambas hinterland. Sofyan is a man of Arab and Madurese heritage. He was born in Banjarmasin in southern Kalimantan but moved to Pontianak to build the PKI. He was popular among ethnic Chinese in Pontianak who affectionately called him 'Ta Ko' or 'Big Brother'. He built a coalition with PGRS and Paraku guerillas in the Sambas forest.

On 16 July 1967, Sofyan and his allies attacked an arms depot at an Indonesian Air Force base in Sambas' Sanggau Ledo, killing three officers and a civilian guard. They managed to capture 150 weapons. According to Petrus Aloysius Simuk, a Dayak schoolteacher in Bengkayang, who lived near the base, by attacking Sanggau Ledo, Sofyan and PGRS became 'an enemy of Indonesia'.

'Many PGRS leaders influenced young Chinese villagers. They wanted to set up a state within a state. Our version is that the Chinese were PGRS members', said Simuk.

The Indonesian military sent reinforcements. Simuk said many Dayak leaders helped the Army to track down the 'Chinese communist guerillas'. He said the PGRS guerillas had killed the Dayak trackmen and some village leaders.

According to Davidson and Kammen, who studied Army documents, the Army intelligence found it difficult to track down Sofyan and his PGRS allies. 'Today our enemy is a distinct ethnic group with its own community and language we don't understand, making it difficult for our intelligence to penetrate', according to an internal Army report.

Instead of penetrating these rural Chinese communities, the Army sought to uproot and physically remove them by drawing on the clichéd anti-guerilla tactic: *drain the water so the fish can't swim.*

'The water, of course, was the huge rural Chinese population', wrote Davidson and Kammen.

The military provoked Dayak leaders to attack the Chinese race and drive them from the interior to the western Kalimantan coastal areas, where they could be controlled and prevented from supplying the PGRS guerillas.

When the PGRS allegedly killed a Dayak leader, propaganda and rumours circulated that his penis had been cut off and sewn to a pole together with a note in Chinese characters, providing 'evidence' that this atrocity was committed by a 'Chinese communist gang'.

'Pak Migang (the murdered leader) and some others used to help the Kujang army unit to find the PGRS guerillas. That afternoon they were fired at by the PGRS. He was killed', said Simuk. Kujang is an Army division traditionally based in West Java.

'We put his body into a coffin and buried him in a hero cemetery in Bengkayang with a military ceremony'.

What Petrus Aloysius Simuk did not realise, or perhaps did not tell me, was that former Dayak governor Oevaang Oeray had earlier decided that it was high time to collaborate with the Army and get rid of the rural Chinese. Oeray considered the rural Chinese as 'godless communists' complicit with the PKI members and the PGRS movement. Oeray and his gang helped the Army to mobilise bands of Dayak 'warriors' to expel the 'communist Chinese' to create a Dayak-dominated economic zone in the areas emptied out. The Dayak elite also intended to ingratiate themselves with General Suharto's new regime. Oeray used to be a Sukarno protégé but now he needed to get close to Suharto. Oeray claimed that 'the initiative' to clean up the Chinese came from him.

But the Chinese community made a ritual compensation payment, despite the fact they were not responsible. It's common for the Chinese in Indonesia to do that. In October 1967, however, after another such mysterious murder, the 'red bowl' – a call of war among Dayak tribesmen – was passed and a major attack on the Chinese ensued, with no distinction made as to the political affiliations of those attacked.

On 14 October 1967, about 60 Dayaks attacked the village of Taum, killing 80 Chinese and one Dayak. The violence spread southward into the triangle of Anjungan, Mandor and Menjalin.

General Soemadi, the then Tanjungpura military commander in Pontianak, reportedly told the Dayak, '...anyone who sides with the PGRS-Paraku enemies can be beheaded like a pig or a chicken'. Soemadi also ordered his soldiers to pass out Garand rifles to Dayak families. He boasted in his book that 'the enthusiasm for taking heads (*ngayau*) flared up everywhere and the head-takers were always escorted by our soldiers'.

By November 1967, around 55,000 ethnic Chinese were displaced from the interior to coastal towns where the shortage of food and medical supplies caused more deaths. Dayak tribesmen increased the beheading of their 'Chinese enemies'.

Lie Syak Liung's difficulties began when an Indonesian soldier came to his coffee shop. 'He said it is not safe to remain living in Triak. We must leave. That afternoon we followed him, walking until dark to reach Bengkayang. Hundreds of Chinese walked together'.

'Bengkayang was a dead town. Schools became refugee shelters. We were huddled into a school building. We stayed in Bengkayang for a week'.

'I brought my wife and my children to escape the massacre. Her two young brothers and my nephew did not make it'.

They just disappeared.

'The Army brought in trucks to transfer us to Singkawang. The roads were bumpy. Many potholes. In Singkawang, we were put into a rubber warehouse. Children suffered many diseases. The dead children were uncountable'.

The Lies only stayed in the rubber warehouse for two weeks. Lie decided to take his family from the disease-infected camp and move to Tebas, where he worked as a farm labourer in an orange grove. 'I was paid 75 rupiahs per day and 20 kilograms of rice per month', Lie said.

'We raised our children in a small hut. Our eldest son was 11 years old when he quit school and began to work. The two younger children later went to school. They finished elementary school and started to work too'.

Thousands of Chinese children dropped out of school in those days.

According to the Dutch pastor who lived in the triangle area, Herman Josef van Hulten, and journalist David Jenkins of the *Far Eastern Economic Review*, about 3,000 Chinese were killed in the 1967 campaign. Anderson and Kammen called it 'Indonesia's unknown war', comparable to Indonesia's 'forgotten war' in East Timor or Indonesia's 'secret war' in Papua. Those estimates do not include Chinese villagers who died in the camps.

I asked Lie how many Chinese died in the camps.

'In the morning we saw coffinmakers selling caskets under the trees. At midday they were all sold out', answered Lie.

The Indonesian government, which was not prepared to receive the more than 60,000 refugees, couldn't help in easing the burden. The Chinese villagers were packed into warehouses, and later 'relocated' into neighbour-hoods such as Roban.

Kenny Kumala, an ethnic Chinese leader in Singkawang, recalled his German mother, nurse Alice Margot Kumala, had helped build hundreds of houses and a church building in Roban. 'I was a teenager then. I often accompanied my father and mother to help the refugees. We helped with whatever we could do. Mother asked for help from some European churches. It was difficult to count those who were dead'.

Visitors to the camps described horrifying conditions. Extreme over-crowding, pitiful food rations, scant medical supplies, leprosy, malaria, children with bloated stomachs, assaults by guards, and suicide were all common. I talked to dozens of Chinese men and women in Singkawang, Pontianak and Bengkayang, who were then children in the camps. They still felt the pain of those days. The farmers did not have land to grow food. The merchants lost their shops. There was no health care, no education, no electricity. The fortunate ones moved into big cities like Pontianak and Jakarta. Most stayed in resettlement areas.

Chin Sjin Luk, an ironsmith in Roban, told me that the Chinese were 'tormented' in Roban. The 69-year-old Chin remained single, since it was too difficult to get married and to bear another responsibility. He lived in a small hut. 'What can we do? We are accused of being communists. We could do nothing'.

On this 2005 New Year's morning, nearly 40 years after the massacres and expulsion, I could still trace the violence. Young people dropped out of school and can't find work. Young Chinese girls opted for planned marriages with Taiwanese or Hong Kong men looking for brides in poor Chinese communities such as Singkawang. These Chinese had been absorbed into the Dayak and Malay communities in Kalimantan for generations. The Indonesian military, however, uprooted them. At the same time, the Indonesian government was calling on the Chinese 'to assimilate' with the local people.

I asked Lie Syak Liung what happened to his coffee shop. He said a Dayak man took it over. 'I passed that shop a number of times over the last 30 years. But I never visit it'.

It must be painful.

Other Chinese tried other ways to survive. Khoen Sin Fah, a 56-year-old coffee-shop owner in the Bengkayang market, told me that her father had decided to marry her to a Malay man when she was 18. His name is Agus Lazim.

'My father told him, This is my daughter. It is better to see you marry her than to see her killed', Khoen told me.

'It was a very difficult time. I obeyed what my father asked me to do. Papa left Bengkayang and asked his new son-in-law to take care of our land'.

I met Agus and Khoen working together in their coffee shop in Bengkayang. Agus is the chef, Khoen the waitress.

Khoen converted to Islam and took the name Halijah – after the name of an Arab woman who was married to the Prophet Mohammad. She gave birth to six children. They recently took the hajj pilgrimage to Mecca.

When I travelled throughout the Bengkayang district, I saw Chinese merchants working in the town of Bengkayang but not outside the town. The Dayaks practically run the district themselves. No Chinese shop was seen in Bengkayang rural areas. 'Actually, they could come again. But they are scared as they have no friends', said Dayak teacher Petrus Aloysius Simuk.

The Chinese were driven out. But other outsiders threatened to derail governor Oevang Oeray's plans as Madurese immigrants began to settle in the lands mostly vacated by the Chinese. By December 1967, the Dayaks and Madurese had started to clash over the spoils of the Chinese expulsion.

In 2016, nearly 8,000 members of the Millah Abraham faith, a new religion which also used the name Gafatar, were expelled from Kalimantan, starting from Mempawah, where ethnic Chinese and Madurese were massacred. Gafatar members said that government officials and security forces had justified their role in their forced eviction as necessary to prevent a potential eruption of mass violence like the one that killed thousands of the Madurese settlers between 1999 and 2001.

Dayak Revitalisation

Stepanus Djuweng is a Dayak man with a Stalin-like moustache. He is stocky, casual and speaks with an intellectual bent. I visited Djuweng in his home in Siantan on Christmas Day 2004; he served me sweet cakes and beers.

Like most men of his stature, Djuweng wears many hats. His main job, however, is the executive secretary of the Pancur Kasih's Union of Movement for the Empowerment of the Dayak Peoples. An Australian academic simply calls him 'the Dayak main ideologue'.

In 1987, Djuweng told me, he was a young man sitting at the Pontianak airport. Some government officials, who came from Java, were sitting and talking about lost baggage.

'In Africa, we have to carry our own baggage to our plane', Djuweng remembered an official saying.

'Those Africans are similar to the Dayaks', another official responded, making an accusation that both African and Dayak people frequently steal from airport baggage.

Djuweng was shocked.

The word 'African' is a derogatory remark among many people in Indonesia. Africans are often seen as primitive and backward. Pontianak media often use words that portray Dayak as lazy natives, backward or even cannibal.

'In the market, if one would like to buy *belacan*' – stinking fish paste – 'she often says, "I want to buy some *dayak*",' Djuweng said.

His analysis went back to the 1970s when the Suharto government, with the help of the World Bank, introduced a transmigration program to ease Indonesia's 'overpopulated islands' – especially Java, Madura and

Bali – while providing cheap labour for less-populated regions such as Kalimantan and Papua.

The program provided each transmigrant family farming land plus another plot for a house. It also financially supported the transmigrants for two years. Predictably, the program created tensions with local people. Jakarta thought Indonesia was a *final product*, thinking that each citizen, especially those who are considered *pribumi*, might share their land peacefully with their *pribumi* compatriots. It was an artificial dream. Anger predictably appeared along racial and religious lines. In Kalimantan, the program created great tension with the Dayaks, who traditionally relied on slash-and-burn agriculture and foraging in their forests to survive.

Maria Goreti, Djuweng's Pancur Kasih colleague, told me, 'My parents raised pigs with a 0.5 hectare of land. Compare that with the transmigrants! They came to Kalimantan and got two hectares of land. They also got fertiliser. They also got education, roads and other facilities'.

According to Jamie Davidson, the Indonesian government granted large timber concessions as well as rubber and palm oil plantations to retired generals and business people from Jakarta since 1969, after the killing of the Chinese in 1967.

In 1969, the first four forest concessions granted in West Kalimantan totalled 370,000 hectares. Through early 1974, 16 concessions, many of which were backed by international capital, were issued for 1.31 million hectares of forest. Between 1968 and 1973, timber production increased a remarkable 25-fold.

In Jakarta, highly placed bureaucrats and soldiers gave out the forest concessions. Jakarta is also where much of the money accrued from the logging wound up. The military, however, required partners with capital, local knowledge and managerial skills. Despite the repeated charges that the PGRS insurgents were Chinese, and despite the mistreatment of the Chinese population in Kalimantan, it was only natural for the Army generals to turn to the local ethnic Chinese as business partners.

Millions of hectares of rainforest were consequently cleared in Kalimantan. Plantation workers lit fires every year to clear land, creating a haze over a vast area in Sumatra and Kalimantan as well as in neighbouring Malaysia and Singapore. It was started in the 1970s, but its global impact was only seen in the late 1990s.

The Dayak were marginalised.

'We lost our identities: our languages, our arts', said Djuweng.

He said the West Kalimantan bureaucracy was also dominated by ethnic Malay, who traditionally sought alliance with the Javanese. Malay and Javanese are mostly Muslims while the Dayak ethnic group is predominantly Christian.

'In Indonesia, there is a hidden discrimination against minorities in public services. The civil service is especially dominated by the majorities', he said, referring to the Javanese and Malay.

In 1987, some Dayak activists from Sarawak visited Pontianak, inspiring younger Dayaks such as Djuweng to begin advocating on behalf of the Dayak communities. Djuweng sought assistance from the Pancur Kasih organisation, already an influential Dayak cooperative group.

A. R. Mecer, the leader of Pancur Kasih, gave support to Djuweng's Dayak empowerment movement. The key change, Djuweng argued, would be forging solidarity to defend the Dayak land rights. He also suggested the Dayak communities map their traditional land borders.

Pancur Kasih, which means 'fountain of love', is the most influential Dayak organisation in Kalimantan. It owns a credit union, small banks, a monthly news magazine, schools, rubber tappers' union and coop stores.

Pancur Kasih began in 1982 when a group of Dayak teachers, led by A. R. Mecer, formed the Pancur Kasih Social Work Foundation. It opened the St Francis of Assisi junior high school in Siantan, across the river from Pontianak. It is a Catholic school but also a Dayak one.

West Kalimantan has 151 Dayak sub-ethnic groups with 168 languages, according to *Mozaik Dayak* book published in Pontianak. Establishing the St Francis of Assisi school was quite a bold move when the military-sponsored Suharto regime tried to create a homogenous, Java-dominated, Indonesian culture.

In 1990, Djuweng and some colleagues established the Pancur Kasih's Institute of Dayakology Research and Development. He also began to write his opinion pieces in *Kompas*, Jakarta's largest national daily, making his voice heard outside of Kalimantan.

Pontianak dailies, the *Akcaya* and later the *Equator*, rarely portrayed the Dayaks as important players. The Malay-dominated newspapers also rarely hired Dayak journalists (or Chinese or Madurese reporters either).

In 1992, Djuweng talked about empowering Dayak communities, fighting against the destruction of Kalimantan's forest and the transmigration program. These young 'indigenous activists' soon became popular internationally, working with similar 'indigenous' movements in Latin America and other parts of the world.

'Institute Dayakology quickly became very famous', Djuweng said.

They later produced Dayak-language programs with the state-sponsored *RRI* radio and a drama in the Dayak Kanayatan language. In 1994, they filed a class-action suit against President Suharto over deforestation, which was rejected by a Jakarta court.

The cooperation between Mercer, Djuweng and their other peers steadily produced similar Pancur Kasih ventures such as The Peoples' Credit Banks, the Dayak Solidarity Fund, the *Kalimantan Review* monthly magazine, as well as Djuweng's Union. It did not seek rapid, grand change, or rush to fundraise among external donors. Pancur Kasih gradually won some major funding from the Ford Foundation, the Dutch funding group Cebemo and many others.

Djuweng said the Indonesian military had 'manipulated the Dayaks' to crack down on the PGRS guerillas and to get rid of the Chinese from rural areas in 1967.

The Dayak-Madurese violence has cultural dimensions. He said the violence took place on average 'every 2.6 years' between the 1967 Chinese killings and the 1999 Madurese massacre. The Dayak fought the Madurese 14 times in 32 years. 'The first Dayak-Madurese fight happened in 1950', he said.

It means that the Dayak were involved in ethnic-motivated killing only twice in 17 years (1950 and 1967) but 14 times in 32 years during the Suharto rule (1967–99).

'It is quite natural if there are two peoples who have different habits to have so much fighting', he said.

I am not surprised to hear such statements.

Many Institute Dayakology figures, Djuweng included, like to stress the Dayak's strong *adat* (customary) system. *Adat*, for instance, forbids them to carry weapons in public spaces, in contrast to some Madurese who regularly carry knives, according to Djuweng. He said that the Madurese rely on *carok* or violent vendetta when solving their differences.

* * *

On 6 December 1996, a Madurese teenager from Sanggau Ledo, about three hours' drive from Singkawang, visited a music concert. Bakrie, the Madurese youth, approached a Dayak girl who rebuffed him. It irritated Yukundus, a Dayak youth, who told Bakrie to stop annoying her. They had a minor fistfight.

Three weeks later, on the night of 29 December, the boys met up at another concert. Bakrie had several friends with him. They attacked Yukundus and his brother with sickles. The Dayak brothers were injured and rushed to a hospital. They were treated but rumours of their death quickly spread.

In the morning, 30 December 1996, Dayak men in red headbands, appeared at the Sanggau Ledo police station, demanding the police arrest the Madurese boys. The Sanggau Ledo police called an immediate meeting of the Dayak Customary Council and two Madurese leaders to settle the dispute. The Madurese leaders apologised to the families of the Dayak victims.

According to Human Rights Watch, the police had made five arrests earlier that morning, but they were reluctant to announce it for fear the crowd would lynch Bakrie and his friends.

The apology was apparently not enough. At dusk, a Dayak mob attacked the largely Madurese transmigration areas of Lembang and Marabu, about five kilometres away, to look for Bakrie and his friends. They burned down houses and injured one Madurese.

Over the next week, the atmosphere between Bengkayang and Ledo became tense. More rural houses were burned down. In Singkawang, some Madurese youths burned the houses of some well-known Dayak figures. They stabbed and seriously wounded a retired Dayak medical worker.

On 4 January 1997, most of the destruction had stopped, not because of intervention by security forces, but because there were not many houses left to burn. West Kalimantan military authorities spread leaflets from aircrafts over the worst affected areas, stating that everything was under control and urging people not to believe rumours, carry weapons or engage in criminal actions.

The press in Pontianak reported that everything seemed to calm down. But rumours still circulated that the Madurese might strike back after the Ramadan fasting month at the end of January 1997. Rumours always play important roles in societies where there is poor quality journalism. People could not fully rely on the press. The Pontianak media, focused on military and police explanation, helplessly tried to debunk the regular propaganda about Indonesian nationalism. The propaganda basically says that the Madurese are native or *pribumi* in Indonesia – like the Dayak and the Malay. Unlike the Chinese, who were massively discriminated against in Indonesia, the Madurese were made to believe that they are 'native Indonesians' as the other *pribumis*. They were made to believe that their rights were like the Dayak – their fellow *pribumi*. They naturally wanted revenge.

The revenge took place in the wee hours of 29 January 1997 when around 30 Madurese youths raided Pancur Kasih's St Francis of Assisi high school and an adjacent boarding house in Siantan, across the Kapuas river from downtown Pontianak. Two young female Dayaks were severely injured in the attack. The word spread that they were near death.

That dawn, Madurese youths also tried to burn down the Pancur Kasih office in Siantan.

The police arrested and briefly detained nine Madurese but released them since no one could place them at the Pancur Kasih compound at the time of the raid. Four of the nine were held for 17 days before being freed, and only two Madurese men faced charges.

Attacking a Pancur Kasih institution would inevitably provoke Dayaks.

On 31 January, two days after the Pancur Kasih attack, a clash took place in Pahauman town, in which 148 Madurese were killed, including 15 members of one family. These attacks unleashed a second, and much uglier, wave of Dayak violence against Madurese. According to Richard Lloyd Parry in his book *In the Time of Madness*, headless bodies were dumped on many streets.

Lloyd Parry quoted a Dutch Capuchin priest near Bengkayang as saying, 'It was unexpected, but it was very sudden. People from all walks of life, even children, gathered outside. They were unanimous, they decided as a community to fight for their rights. Everyone wanted to go – even my friends, those boys outside, they made bamboo spears, they carried knives. They marched to Seke and Salatiga. They said that they must defend themselves. They say that the Madurese have killed Dayaks so very, very many times, but this is enough. All Madurese must leave Kalimantan'.

In Bengkayang, I talked to Petrus Aloysius Simuk, the Dayak teacher involved in both the 1967 and 1997 violence, trying to relate what Lloyd Parry had described.

'The Dayak have to lick the blood and eat the heart to make them fearless. The blood must be smeared on the forehead. It will make one fearless. It will also pump up the courage', Simuk shamanised.

Maria Goreti called it 'blood revenge…a single drop of Dayak blood means the whole Dayak community is obligated to seek revenge against the perpetrators and their peers'.

The Dayak avoided two areas. They avoided mosques, which symbolise Islam, and they avoided government offices, which symbolise Indonesia.

The Dayak, predominantly Christians, did not want to create the impression that they also attacked Madurese-owned mosques. And they did not want to create the impression that they were not happy with Indonesia. Islam and Indonesia are too big for the Dayak to make enemies of them.

In Jakarta, President Suharto did little to stop the killing. His Army chief, General Hartono, himself a Madurese, created another media brouhaha when he accused some Madurese *ulamas*, religious leaders, of stirring tension in Sanggau Ledo.

Suharto trusted West Kalimantan Governor Aspar Aswin to end the ethnic cleansing. Aspar Aswin is a prototypical New Order general-cum-governor-cum-millionaire unaccountable to West Kalimantan's populace. He was unpopular among many Dayak leaders. Aswin, himself a Javanese, was also allegedly involved in some corruption cases. At every stage of the violence, he kept saying 'everything is under control'. The newspapers in Pontianak tagged along. Aswin repeatedly blamed the Madurese for being 'exclusive' and 'violent'.

General Hartono ordered a curfew in Pontianak and Singkawang for nearly a fortnight. The violence ended in March 1997 when there were no more houses to burn. Mass graves were found in many places. Richard Lloyd Parry described a grave with six skeletons of Madurese women: 'None of the skeletons had skulls'.

The death toll ranged from 300 to 3,000. Jamie Davidson estimated 600 people were killed. In April 1997, the press reported that 3,054 homes had been destroyed, and more than 15,000 people, almost all of them Madurese, had been displaced. It was difficult to make an accurate count. Many Madurese ran away to Madura or Java islands. Others moved in with relatives in other parts of Kalimantan. Some were housed in temporary barracks.

* * *

John Bamba, another Institute Dayakology leader, wrote a paper presented in a Bonn conference in May 1998, saying that the Madurese and Dayak have many cultural differences. Bamba wrote that paper in response to a Human Rights Watch report that blamed the Dayak over the Madurese killing.

Bamba disagreed with the notion of 'Madurese ethnic cleansing' in Kalimantan, preferring to use the word 'war' between the Dayak and the

Madurese. 'The bloody conflict with the Madurese did not arise out of revenge nor ethnic cleansing. It came about as the need for the Dayak to fulfill the obligations and demands of the *adat*. Failure to do so would have resulted in great misfortune being experienced by the whole Dayak community…By killing the Madurese…the Dayak have the reason to perform the *adat*. In this case, the killing of Madurese is not for purposes of revenge, but the need to fulfill the *adat* demands. The enmity and hatred towards the Madurese is very deep and widespread. In most communities where there are Madurese, often (the) government-sponsored transmigrants, there have long been stories about the inability of the Madurese to interact with and respect not only Dayak culture, but the cultures of other ethnic groups also. The refusal of the Madurese to acknowledge Dayak *adat* has occurred continuously over a long period of time, at many different levels'.

Jamie Davidson, however, disputed Djuweng's and Bamba's arguments. Davidson is one of a few international academics who openly challenged the Institute Dayakology's explanation of the ethnic cleansing. He also disagreed with the Malay version of the Madurese 1999 ethnic cleansing.

Davidson writes in his thesis on West Kalimantan, 'In reality, we simply do not know the precise number of clashes. Despite my lengthy time in the area, I failed to specify the exact number (of Dayak-Madurese clashes) and have learned to remain suspicious of claims to veracity'.

Davidson found 17 sources that refer to Dayak-Madurese conflicts between 1967 and 1999, and examined each of them. Most were just small fights, involving individuals and petty crimes. Davidson also found inconsistencies in the two Institute Dayakology versions, a pro-Dayak book *Konflik Etnik di Sambas* and the *Kalimantan Review* news stories.

He questioned the *adat* rationale that permits a Dayak community to seek revenge against other groups when any of its members are attacked.

Institute Dayakology created the myth that the Dayak is marginalised and need to defend themselves. It noted that Kalimantan hasn't had a Dayak governor since the days of Oevang Oeray and Tjilik Riwut in the 1960s. Oevang Oeray was the governor in West Kalimantan in 1960–67 while Tjilik Riwut was in Central Kalimantan in 1957–66.

Davidson told me that the main political rivalry in Kalimantan is a tug of war between the predominantly Christian Dayaks and the Muslim Malays. Pancur Kasih's *Kalimantan Review* magazine stated that many Malay intellectuals had denied that 'their Malay sultans' used to repress Dayak people. The magazine also disputes racial prejudice in public services, saying that most government officials and civil servants in Kalimantan were not Dayak, but Malay or Javanese. 'It is about Malay-Dayak rivalry', said Davidson.

I have read several newspaper clippings in which Malay opinion leaders like Chairil Effendi worried about growing Dayak demands. They are frequently quoted in the Malay-dominated Pontianak newspapers, such as *Pontianak Post* and *Equator*, while Dayak leaders were routinely quoted in *Kalimantan Review*. Both regularly launched criticisms against one another.

The climate changed after the Dayaks had killed the Madurese in 1997 and later President Suharto, himself a Javanese, was forced to step down in Jakarta in May 1998. Dayak forces organised massive street demonstrations, demanding land rights and more Dayak representation in regental positions (*bupati*) – a stepping stone to campaign for governor offices. They organised rallies and showed their political muscles in many places throughout Kalimantan.

The first case concerned the Sanggau district *bupati* selection when Colonel Mickael Andjioe's name disappeared from the candidate list in favour of Governor Aswin's handpicked candidate, Colonel Soemitro, a Javanese. Dayaks jumped at the chance to support Andjioe. From April to June 1998, or one year after the Sanggau Ledo killing, demonstrations were held regularly at the Sanggau City Council. This constant pressure eventually led to Andjioe's appointment. He became the first Dayak regent in Sanggau since 1967.

In early February 1999, around 100 Dayaks protested outside the Pontianak Council in Mempawah. Angered that Cornelis Kimha, a Dayak, was not included among the final three candidates, the demonstrators set several cars alight. The Council preferred Agus Salim, a Malay bureaucrat. In Pontianak, dozens of Dayaks held frequent demonstrations at Governor Aswin's grand office in support of Kimha's candidacy. Jakarta eventually broke the tie, choosing Kimha.

Dayak mobilisation forced the Jakarta government to appease the Dayak. Suharto was gone but the institutions of democracy didn't exist in Pontianak. Dayak protests, which were partly backed by Pancur Kasih's *Kalimantan Review* magazine, tried to use the post-Suharto opportunities to advocate for the Dayaks.

During the 1997 killing, the Malay were not involved in hunting the Madurese. Malayness was felt only as a cultural identity. But the Dayak's awakening made the Malay nervous. Chairil Effendi and his other Malay colleagues mobilised their own Malay networks to set up Malay-based political organisations and even built a grand Malay 'cultural house' in Pontianak.

'The Malay began awaken. Sambas (killing) is a symbol of the Malay political awakening', said Jamie Davidson.

According to Davidson, the Institute Dayakology did not incite the anti-Madurese violence but it used the *adat* to justify Dayaks attacking others if an individual Dayak is hurt. On the Malay side, organisations such as Zulkarnain Bujang's FKPM, also began flexing their militia muscles.

The Madurese, a relatively small, hard-working minority, became the victim of both groups. Sanggau Ledo came first and Sambas came second. It did not stop in West Kalimantan. The Dayak awakening also spread to Sampit and Kutawaringin Timur in Central Kalimantan. In early 2001, Dayak militias beheaded between 1,000 and 3,000 Madurese settlers. KMA Usop, a Dayak leader who allegedly helped incite the violence, openly said that he copied the killing in western Kalimantan.

Djuweng chuckled when I mentioned Davidson's argument, 'Well, these foreign academics just spent some months in Kalimantan'.

After two hours in Djuweng's house, I was puzzled. Pancur Kasih is a political organisation that tries to promote Dayak culture and to empower Dayak tribesmen. Their lands are taken over by big guys from Jakarta. They are not happy with the Java-dominated Indonesia, but they also use violence in their advocacy. They played the ethnic rituals and the *adat* card. The effect was clear: It triggered racial violence against minorities like the Madurese and the Chinese.

A Little Madurese Girl

Eight years old, Novi Alfiona is the cutest little girl that I have ever met. She lives in a wooden house surrounded by bougainvillea in the Bekut swampy area in Tebas district, Sambas regency. Shyly she told me that she is a second grader.

Her proud mother Hajiah said, 'She likes to swim. Oh yes, this little girl likes to play in the water'.

Novi is a mixed Madurese-Malay girl. Her father, Thalib, a tall, cleanly shaved Madurese trader, lived in Sempadung, while Hajiah comes from a Malay family living in the neighbouring Mausere village. Thalib raised cows but does other business too.

The pair met when the young Hajiah went to school in Tebas. Hajiah was Mausere's most beautiful girl. It was only natural that the handsome Thalib felt in love with her. They were both young. Four months after dating, Thalib's parents and relatives came to Hajiah's house to meet her parents and to propose Hajiah. They got married.

Hajiah's father, Saleh, is a farmer. Her mother, Farida, is a homemaker who also works in their farm.

In December 2004, when I visited their Mausere house, they showed me around the living room and the spacious wooden veranda. It is a typical Malay middle-class family. They told me Novi won a healthy baby contest in Sambas and later in the whole West Kalimantan region. Novi became a baby model too.

'Hajiah took great care of her daughter', said Romina, Hajiah's neighbor.

Novi's victorious venture even brought mother and daughter as well as Nilasari, Mausere's midwife, to come to Jakarta at the invitation of then First Lady Sinta Nuriyah, the wife of President Abdurrahman Wahid. They have the framed photo with Sinta Nuriyah in their living room.

As is traditional among newlywed Malays, Thalib went to live with his parents-in-law. He usually slept for five days in Saleh's house in Mausere and two days in his own parents' house in Sempadung.

'He was a good young man, very decent, always talked about good things', said Farida. Thalib also befriended Mawardi, a Malay neighbor, also a militiaman, and his wife Romina. The two men liked to talk politics together. Mawardi was a loyal supporter of Suharto's adversary Megawati Sukarnoputri. Thalib was less political and more interested in raising his family.

After Novi was born, Thalib worked harder. He bought a Yamaha RX King motorcycle on credit, saying it would increase business. Having a motorcycle is also a status symbol in Sambas villages.

But their happy life changed on 21 February 1999 when Rudi bin Muharap, the Madurese passenger, refused to pay his bus fare as he alighted in Pusaka village. Rudi stabbed the Malay bus conductor and the anti-Madurese campaign started in Sambas.

Their neighbour is Mawardi, a Malay villager-cum-militia. Malay militias hunted and killed Madurese men and women, old and young. Mawardi became involved himself in leading Mausere's Malay men to hunt Madurese.

Thalib felt uneasy seeing his neighbour absorbed by anti-Madurese racism. Thalib decided to seek refuge with his Madurese relatives and friends. Hundreds of Madurese houses were burned in Tebas, Pemangkas and Jawai areas. Thalib probably thought it was safer to be with other Madurese, leaving behind Hajiah and Novi with his in-laws.

'He was gone for four days before we knew anything about him', said Hajiah. Novi was already learning to walk and beginning to speak her first sentences.

One afternoon in mid-March, Saleh was sitting on the veranda when he saw several Malay militias with motorcycles passing in front of his house. They were parading Madurese heads. A few minutes later, some motorcycles stopped near his house. A Malay youth went to the veranda, handing over an ID card to Hajiah. It was Thalib's card.

She broke down into tears.

Saleh told me, 'I actually saw Thalib's head being shown in the convoy, but I did not recognise him. I only realised that it was Thalib's head when his ID card was delivered to our house. Hajiah and Novi were lying down on a bed when the convoy passed our house. Novi was still a baby. She couldn't even talk yet. It is different to see a head, just a head. You do not recognise him, although you know him as a man, a living man'.

Saleh stopped to take a breath. He looked at the ceiling and massaged his legs.

'Hajiah received the ID card. She cried for about one hour. His head was said to be buried but we don't know where. We also don't know where his body was buried'.

Hajiah collapsed off and on for four days. Saleh was also depressed and sick for six months.

Now past histories are twisted to accommodate present circumstances. Dedi Gustian, who was away in Malaysia when his father Mawardi died, poured scorn on Thalib, 'He is a snake! When people have meetings, he eavesdropped and told his own crowd'.

'We're proud to fight the war. The Dayak did not cleanse the Madurese but we the Malay...they are finished'.

It was difficult to judge the mood in the two Mausere houses. Saleh, Farida and Farida's sister Sanimah, said many good things about their Madurese son-in-law.

Next door, when I met the late Mawardi's family, I heard anti-Madurese statements.

In another visit, I found Saleh sitting with the Mawardi family, smiling at me, offering tea and cakes.

* * *

A few weeks prior to meeting Novi Alfiona, a Madurese businessman in Pontianak, Nagian Imawan, lamented his lost cousin. He could not understand why he could not go to Sambas, now off limits to Madurese, to find his cousin. 'Every Madurese who comes to Sambas will be beheaded', he said.

Sambas is only a two-hour drive from Pontianak. Nagian is Thalib's nephew, meaning that Novi is Nagian's cousin. When Nagian was young, he lived with Thalib in Sempadung. 'My uncle asked me to take care of Novi if anything happened to him. It's been more than six years now. I don't know where Novi is'.

He sent letters to Hajiah, saying that he wanted to know about Novi Alfiona, telling her that the whole Thalib-Nagian family had agreed to hand over their land ownership in Sambas to Novi. He received no reply.

I promised Nagian that I would try to find Novi. And I finally found her in Bekut, living with her mother and her new husband, Hamidi, a Malay bus driver.

Hajiah married Hamidi two years after the killing of her first husband. She moved to live in their own house in Bekut.

When I asked her about Nagian, Hajiah said she had received Nagian's letters but it was difficult to call Nagian back. 'Our ties were kind of broken. I was worried', she said. She tried to raise Novi in the predominantly anti-Madurese Malay areas like Tebas without revealing that Novi's biological father was a Madurese. The couple had a baby girl, Novi's younger sister, last year.

It is safer to raise Novi as a Malay girl rather than a Madurese. Novi does not know that Hamidi is not her biological father. When neighbours asked whose daughter she is, she usually responds, 'I'm Hamidi's daughter'.

Hamidi told me, 'Maybe it is not necessary to explain. When she grows up and she wants to know, and she asks, then we will tell her. We will remain silent if she does not ask'.

I kept on watching Novi grow up, feeling embarrassed when I started to follow her rather unsecured Facebook page in 2016 and hearing that she had graduated from high school. Nagian helped her schooling and trained her to work in his coffee shop.

'She knows that her biological father was murdered', said Nagian.

Chapter 3

SULAWESI

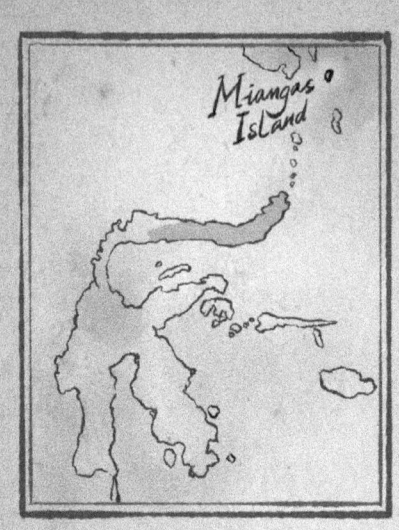

Miangas
Island

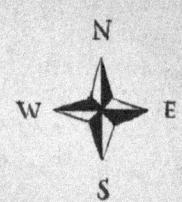

N
W ★ E
S

SULAWESI

MANADO
TOMOHON

PALU

SULAWESI

Desperately Seeking Minahasa

Miangas on the Border with the Philippines

One week prior to Indonesia's election in September 2004, I took a two-night sea trip on the *Ratu Maria* ship to the island of Miangas from Manado, the metropolis in northern Sulawesi. A government office chartered the ship to deliver election ballots to Miangas. Usually passengers must jump from island to island for about one week, or else wait for the *Daraki Nusa*, a state-subsidised ship, which heads for Miangas every 10 days from Bitung, a harbour near Manado. The trip was pleasant, with good seafood and calm seas. We also stopped in five harbours – Lirung, Melonguane, Beo, Essang and Karatung – parts of the Talaud language area. My only problem was fighting dozens of little cockroaches that inhabited my cabin.

When I reached Miangas, I was rewarded with the sight of deep blue sea, white sand, tiny boats, a white church and a hill. The island also has a small kampong, on whose gridded roads the islanders dry their fishnets or repair their wooden boats, *prao*.

Miangas has no hotel. Instead the village head, or *opo' lao*, Djonyor Namare, a dark-skinned, middle-aged fisherman, invited me to use his bedroom while he and his wife resorted to a wooden bed on their outdoor terrace. The islanders usually have these wooden beds to use when temperatures rise to between 24 to 30 degrees Celsius.

His wife, Lukring Binulang, is a big-boned cheerful woman. She served my dinner with fried tuna flavoured with the super hot *rica-rica* chilli. I loved it and sweated like hell. 'How many chillies do you use?' I asked her.

She responded by showing me a basket full of chillies. I guessed it had more than 20!

But I went to Miangas to observe how the islanders view nationalism in this Indonesian-Filipino border island. How do they reconcile their legal status, as either a Netherlands Indies- or an Indonesia-subject, with their physical and cultural proximity to Mindanao inside the Philippines? What kind of counter strategies do they use toward the bigger interests in Manado and Jakarta? How do they use the issues of nationalism to advocate their own interest? And ultimately, do they see themselves as Indonesians or something else?

Namare briefed me on some basic facts. Miangas, Indonesia's northern-most island, has a population of only 673. Almost all are Miangas natives. The outsiders include five Muslims: a Javanese couple, whose husband is a Navy official, their son and two other officials, dispatched by Jakarta to work in Miangas. The others are all Protestants. And Miangas is small, just 2.5 kilometres long and 1.6 kilometres wide. 'You could walk the whole island in two hours', said Namare.

'When I was younger, I spent like four or five hours by a *prao* to reach the Philippines', said village elder Petrus Essing.

It took a ship like *Ratu Maria* or *Daraki Nusa* between seven and eight hours to reach Karatung, the nearest island to Miangas. Their language is called the Talaud language.

The Talaud name of the island ('Miangas' or 'Meangas') means, 'exposed to piracy', referring to past attacks in Miangas from Sulu slave traders and buccaneers in Mindanao. The Spaniards, presumably the first Europeans to encounter this island, called it 'Isla de las Palmas', the island of the palm trees.

Does it really have palm trees?

Well, on my first day in Miangas, Lukas Bawala, a novice Protestant priest and a distant relative to Namare, took me on a jungle tour around Mount Batu. He brought along a *peda*, a short-curved sword, to cut tall, coarse grass. We visited the old fortress at the top of Mount Batu and saw only two palm trees left on the island. 'It was a long time ago when palm trees were gradually replaced by coconut trees. Copra is our main agri-cultural product', said Bawala.

The jungle tour reminded me that Herman Johannes Lam, a botanist at the Herbarium and Museum for Systematical Botany at Buitenzorg, then a Dutch colonial institution in Java, visited Miangas in June 1926. Dr Lam surveyed plants and animals for two days, writing that the original island flora had completely vanished.

He also wrote that 1895 was a very important year for Miangas because it marked the arrival of the then-Dutch resident of Manado, E. J. Jellesma. Jellesma visited Miangas because he had been informed that the Miangas *opo lao* had refused to accept a flag from a Spanish vessel, arguing that the island was subject to the Netherlands Indies government 'from generation to generation'. Jellesma was accompanied by a Dutch clergyman, who baptised 254 Miangas residents to be Protestants. Those visits prompted Jellesma's Manado administration to pour more help into the tiny island.

In December 1898, three years after Jellesma's visit, a treaty was signed in Paris between the United States and Spain. The treaty included the 'Isla de la Palmas', moving it into the territory of the Philippines, which was part of the Spanish colonies taken over by the Americans. The Americans didn't notice the error and the Netherlands Indies kept control in Miangas as if nothing happened. Only in 1906, an American general, Leonard Wood, visited Miangas and discovered that the Netherlands Indies also claimed sovereignty over the island.

Both the United States and the Netherlands agreed to enter into arbitration before the Court of International Justice at The Hague in 1925. The Swiss jurist, Hans Max Huber, was selected as an arbitrator. After almost three years of work, Huber finally declared in April 1928 that the island was legally a Dutch territory.

That new legal status didn't change the fact that the Miangas islanders still communicated extensively with people from their neighbouring islands of Mindanao and the Talaud Islands, or further south in the Sangihe islands. Namare's father went to school in Davao, a major city in Mindanao, but also has some brothers living in Sulawesi. Petrus Essing has two sisters who are married to Filipinos. Many Miangas islanders speak both Visayas and Tagalog, two languages that are widely used in the southern Philippines, but many also converse in Malay with the Manado dialect. 'Those who are over 60 years old speak the Filipino languages', said Namare.

Miangas' legal status changed again 21 years later, at the end of World War II, when two new states emerged from both colonies: Indonesia and the Philippines. The new republics signed four border agreements between 1956 and 1974. They opted to issue locals a 'border-crossing pass', less complicated than passports, and to set up border offices in three islands including Miangas. The Philippines, however, claimed the seas surrounding Miangas as its territory.

Jakarta tried ceaselessly to mark its sovereignty in Miangas. 'Once my boss saw the name plate *Palmas* printed in our office and asked me to immediately remove the Spanish word', said Lieutenant Hengky Vantriardo, an Indonesian army officer in Miangas. I also saw a small monument signed by Indonesian military commander General Benny Moerdani, visiting Miangas in August 1986.

More importantly, both Jakarta and Manado pour money into Miangas, subsidising rice and paying for motorboats such as the *Daraki Nusa* to extend their routes to reach Miangas. Manado sponsored scores of Miangas families to migrate to Bolaang Mongondow and Minahasa in northern Sulawesi, in the 1960s and 1970s, in a bid to reduce the Miangas population density. But the connection to the Philippines remains strong. Pop Cola or San Miguel beer come in cheaper from Davao. Many Miangas women and men choose to naturally settle in Mindanao areas.

I also met some Filipinos who were visiting the Philippines consulate to Miangas. The Philippines border-crossing officer there is Carlito Niebres. He works alone in Miangas. His 'consulate' is a two-storey wooden house. When I visited the house, Niebres was chatting with his guests in his outdoor terrace clad in shorts and a sleeveless shirt.

That morning his guests included Alfredo Papea Pagtun, a 38-year-old pastor from Sarangani, a province on Mindanao, the Philippines, who was visiting his relatives. 'My late mother is a Miangas (woman) but father is a Filipino of Belaan tribe', Pagtun said. He first visited Miangas in 1978 when he was only 11 years old. 'Then houses were very small, no roads, no electricity. Now it has improved a lot', said Pagtun.

The younger Pagtun, Adelito, cannot hide his delight in Miangas. I often saw Adelito walking along the streets or drinking cola with his three distant sisters and four cousins, 'I'm so happy here'.

According to Namare and Niebres, groups like the Pagtuns visit Miangas every week. The next morning, while swimming at a beach, I saw the Pagtuns preparing to return to Sarangani in a small wooden motorboat that takes about eight hours to reach Sarangani Island. I loved seeing their relatives give them hugs and help them board the boat, anchored some 200 metres off the beach.

Indonesia spends lots of money on Miangas. But it remains geographic- ally and culturally closer to the Philippines. Donald Rumokoy spent 25 million rupiah (around $2,300) just to charter the *Ratu Maria* to deliver the ballot papers to Miangas when it only has 450 voters. 'It is expensive, isn't it? I sometimes jokingly told my colleagues that it might be better if Indonesia sells Miangas to the Philippines'.

I felt like I was in paradise staying in Miangas, spending my time swimming, and throughout my stay, the islanders took great pride in entertaining me. They fed me grilled fish and *rica-rica* eaten with *laluga*, a sort of big aracea planted in the freshwater swamps. The lunch or dinner conversations always started with stories about their relatives, both in Indonesia or the Philippines, moved to their 'continued loyalty' toward Indonesia, and concluded with asking me to help them with some requests.

'You could write about our requests in the newspapers. The government will read your stories and give us our needs', said village secretary Jonli Awalla.

Elementary school teacher Agus Tege said his school needs a computer, a printer and new batteries for their single side band radio. Djonyor Namare said his village needs a cold storage facility, 'We could keep our fish fresh while waiting for the Filipino ships to come and buy them'. Some young mothers complained about the quality of their high school, where the teachers were regularly absent. Lukas Bawala complained about 'drunken teachers' in the elementary school. The islanders also love to pepper their conversations with reminders that Miangas is a border island, bragging about the importance of their location for the 'national unity of Indonesia'.

I tried to check on the complaints. Royke Rarumangkay, a Manado journalist who occasionally visits Miangas, told me that Miangas has relatively good infrastructure. 'We initially thought that it must be underdeveloped, but it turned out to be quite urban. The concrete road, the church and the pier, show that they are doing well. But they are isolated still. They have the transportation and communication difficulties'.

Hengky Vantriardo, the Indonesian army lieutenant, told me that he believes the Miangas people use the border issue to draw more subsidies from Manado and Jakarta. 'It is a mentality', Hengky said. 'The East Timorese (also) asked a lot, but when it comes to loyalty, they prefer to break away from Indonesia'.

Another explanation came from Joppy Luppa, the harbourmaster of Miangas, a quiet and muscled man, who also invited me to come to his house for dinner. 'If Republic of Indonesia is peaceful, we are loyal to Indonesia. But if Indonesia is not in peace, well, we're closer to the Philippines, you know. We could head for the Philippines in the morning and back in the evening, just three or four hours sailing with *prao*', said Luppa.

'What does peaceful mean?' I asked him.

'Well, you see so many riots, in the Moluccas, in Aceh, Papua and many other places. People kill one another, in the name of Islam or Christianity, in the name of ethnic or in other names'.

'But isn't Miangas an Indonesian territory?'

'It's true and I don't mean that Miangas belongs to another country. Before 1965, the Indonesian language was not widely used here. We spoke Visayas, many Miangas people also married Filipinos, but after 1972, contacts with the Philippines grew less. By 1975, there was already a *kapal perintis* (subsidised ship) to connect Miangas and Manado, and relations with the Philippines were reduced. There was also the Moro war in Mindanao. We didn't want to go there. We're scared'.

I left Luppa's house that evening, walking in the dark night, with many thoughts. The struggles of Indonesia, and to be fair, the Philippines, allowed terrorism, corruption, sectarianism, militarism and communal violence to take root in alarming ways. These troubles encourage people from small and isolated islands such as Miangas to switch sides periodically. It does not mean that they are not trustworthy, but their existence is heavily dependent on subsidies from the big brothers. Miangas is a real community, perhaps, to quote Benedict Anderson's explanation. It is also a nation, albeit a tiny one.

They switched sides when they felt that the Spaniards, who used to be the world's largest empire in the 18th century, were losing ground against the United States in the late 1890s. They thought that the Netherlands Indies was a stronger brother. But they developed closer relations with the Philippines after World War II as it provided cheaper goods, better education and a friendlier environment than the fledgling Republic of Indonesia, which was involved in several bloody conflicts in the 1950s.

During the authoritarian rule of Suharto, which produced relative stability and prosperity in Indonesia, the Miangas people showed more affection toward Jakarta. They praised General Benny Moerdani, the Indonesian military commander, when he arrived on the island. They worried again when racial and religious riots broke out in many places in Indonesia after the fall of Suharto in May 1998. In October 2016, President Joko Widodo was the first Indonesian president to step on this tiny island, officiating the opening of a small airport. The Miangas people were elated. Several months after I left Miangas, an Indonesian police officer beat Jonli Awalla to death while he was drunk. It prompted the whole of Miangas to fly a Filipino flag, switching sides again to the Philippines.

Maybe that is the fate of a small nation. They have pride but not enough political and military muscles.

European Missionaries in Minahasa

My journey continued to Manado, the major city in northern Sulawesi, where shopkeepers, housemaids and restaurant waiters were mostly Sangihes or Talauds, while the bureaucrats, the professors and the military officers were mostly Minahasans. Just listen to Jackried Maluenseng, the editor of the *Global News* daily in Manado, himself a Sangihe: 'The population of North Sulawesi (province) is 1.7 million. We're the second largest ethnic group (after the Minahasans), but not accommodated proportionally in the government'.

Alex J. Ulaen, a French-trained social scientist at the Sam Ratulangi University, himself a Talaud native, told me, 'The way this university recruits lecturers also reflects the Minahasan connections'.

Both the Minahasans and the islanders are Christians, sharing a nostalgic attachment to mission work and the sometimes awkward position of Christian, Westernised minorities in a predominantly Muslim country. But they still hold grudges against one another. Germita, the Talaud church, separated from the GMIST, the Sangihe and Talaud church. The Christian Evangelical Church in Minahasa (Gereja Masehi Injili di Minahasa, GMIM), remains the largest of the three sister churches but has its ups and downs too. Why do they prefer ethnic churches? How does ethnicity mingle with Christianity?

According to David Henley in his book *Nationalism and Regionalism in a Colonial Context: Minahasa in the Dutch East Indies*, northern Sulawesi in the early 19th century was still a tribal, largely pagan, self-sufficient and politically decentralised area. It had several languages, including the four most commonly spoken: Tontemboan, Tombulu, Tonsea and Toulour. Their cultures featured ancestor worship, shamanism and complex ritual systems connected to agriculture and fertility. All placed a strong emphasis upon divination, particularly based on behaviour of owls, known locally as *manguni*.

Willy Roroe, a German-trained theologian at the Indonesian Christian University in Tomohon, a small town about one hour south of Manado, told me, 'When I was a child, my grandfather liked to tell me to do this or to do that, in accordance to what the owl did the previous night'. They decided to travel when owls were quiet at night, meaning the following morning would be a clear day. The owl is still important in Minahasa. Manguni is the symbol of the GMIM church. Brigade Manguni, the largest Minahasa militia organisation, also uses the owl as its name and symbol. Roroe tried to teach me some owl lessons when he was walking me out of his large garden. We didn't hear any owls that night!

The Christianisation of Minahasa, the biggest nation in northern Sulawesi, began in 1831 when two young German priests, who worked for the Nederlandsch Zendeling Genootschap, the Dutch Missionary Society, arrived in upland Minahasa. One, J. F. Riedel, established himself at Tondano town, where he quickly started to make converts. His colleague, J. G. Schwarz, chose Langowan in the Tontemboan language area.

They worked hard to stamp out rivalries among the different language groups. Their main concern was tribal warfare with its headhunting and bloody rituals. Riedel once risked his life by coming between rival warriors to prevent a battle.

Other missionaries soon arrived and the number of Minahasan Christians grew. In 1847, there were fewer than 11,000 converts in a Minahasa population of 93,000. By 1880, the missionaries had baptised some 80,000 Minahasans, more than three-quarters of the population. J. G. Schwarz alone baptised more than 13,000 people.

Similar mass conversions took place among the Sangihes and the Talauds. In 1857, four carpenter missionaries came to Sangihe. In 1859, five more started work in the Talaud Islands. The leading missionary was E. T. Steller, who, with his own hands, cleared the forest and laid out a plantation which became the centre for church and society leaders.

Nicolaas Graafland, another NZG missionary, said that their aim was a united Christian community in which 'all divisions and feuds shall be dissolved into one brotherhood'. Graafland is the principal architect of the mission school system in northern Sulawesi. He used local folklore to emphasise the unity among the tribes. He reintroduced the word 'Minahasa', a term first used nearly two centuries earlier among the chiefs of several language groups in northern Sulawesi. It derived from the words *mina* and *esa*, or 'to be' and 'one'. Consequently, the word 'Minahasa' or 'to be one' was used repeatedly in the mission works.

Legend has it that To'ar and Lumimu'ut, a son and his mother, married and became the ancestors of 'Minahasa people'. Lumimu'ut is said to be the ancestral mother of all Minahasans, whom she divided into four groups: Tontemboan, Tombulu, Tonsea and Toulour. It is impossible to know how many people today actually regard themselves as direct descendants of the incestuous couple.

The missionaries used these stories to drive home the idea that Minahasa is a single community with a single past. They also set up many social institutions: mission schools, hospitals, newspapers, farming areas, clinics and orphanages. The missionaries married Eurasian women and their children married Minahasan youths. And the Minahasan laymen, teachers and preachers made possible the explosive growth of Christianity. Only 31 European missionaries were involved in the process.

The NZG schools were inseparable from the church. In fact, they usually shared the same buildings and personnel. Christian teachers taught their students who were then often partly responsible for converting their parents. Most village schoolteachers doubled up as local lay preachers.

Although many missionaries favoured, in theory, using Minahasan languages in school and church, Malay was almost inevitably the practical choice. It was easier for the Minahasans to learn than Dutch. It was also easier for the Europeans to learn Malay than the Minahasan languages. There was also the problem of linguistic diversity and rivalry within Minahasa. Malay was already the common language of commerce in Manado and the official language of administration throughout the Netherlands Indies. Therefore, the usual language of both NZG churches and schools was Malay.

Graafland nurtured the imagination of *bangsa Minahasa* (the Minahasa people or the Minahasa nation) by teaching geography. The NZG schools only taught the geography of Minahasa. Graafland supplied not only a reader listing every village in the land, but also an instructional wall map.

The NZG schoolmasters and preachers were men who had once left their home villages, albeit only for a few years, to study in one of the training colleges. There they worked alongside students from other districts, whom they came to identify as fellow-Minahasans. They were all Christians, spoke Malay and bore the imprint of their missionary education.

The mission also published a newspaper, *Tjahaja Sijang*, or Light of the Day. It first appeared in 1868 and was printed by the mission's own press in Tanawangko, on the coast southwest of Manado. Its 363 subscribers were mostly teachers, assistant missionaries and district chiefs. This small circulation conceals a much wider real audience. Copies were widely loaned out. In many villages, people also gathered to hear schoolmasters read articles aloud. *Tjahaja Sijang* gradually made the idea of Minahasa mean something, even to people whose actual circle of social contacts remained quite small.

The mission succeeded in building Christianity and the idea of *bangsa Minahasa* because one of the features of Minahasa in those days was the openness of its people toward modernity. According to Henley, the cosmopolitan atmosphere in Manado was heightened by the fact that almost half of the Minahasa Eurasians bore non-Dutch surnames, inherited from mestizo Portuguese burghers, English visitors of the British interregnum, German sailors and Belgian soldiers from the colonial army. The first six NZG missionaries, for instance, were all Germans. The Portuguese and the Spaniards also operated in northern Sulawesi and were even involved in earlier wars in the neighbouring Ternate and Tidore sultanates.

Visitors were also struck by the eagerness with which the Minahasans seemed to adopt not only Christianity but also European dress and etiquette. When the English naturalist A. R. Wallace dined at the house of a Tomohon chief in 1859, he was surprised to find his dinner served on 'good china, with finger glasses and fine napkins, and an abundance of good claret and beer'. The chief himself 'was dressed in a suit of black with patent-leather shoes, and really looked comfortable and almost gentlemanly in them'. While such goods were only affordable for the very rich, Western lifestyles represented an increasingly universal ideal. Even commoners took to wearing European dress whenever their activities and incomes permitted.

The Netherlands Indies government also helped promote Minahasa nationhood by building a dense network of roads. People could move freely throughout the country. The government schools taught Minahasan geography as a discrete subject. Schools also used a booklet by J. G. F. Riedel, a government official and a son of the pioneer missionary J. F. Riedel, on the history of Minahasa before the coming of the Dutch.

In June 1933, a group of Minahasan teachers and retired church officials, dissatisfied with the gradual decentralisation of the Dutch administrator over church matters, took matters into their own hands by inaugurating a breakaway national church called Kerapatan Gereja Protestan Minahasa (Minahasa Protestant Church Assemblies).

This pressed the Dutch pastors to hasten their own autonomy program and establish the GMIM in September 1934. Dutch administrator E. A. A. de Vreede became its first synod chairman. He argued that the name of the church should be 'the Evangelical Church *in* Minahasa' rather than the 'Minahasan Evangelical Church'. A Dutch-trained Minahasan pastor, A. Z. R. Wenas, however, advocated the name 'Minahasan church' as it was a truly Minahasan church. De Vreede won the argument because many non-Minahasans are also GMIM churchgoers, which included the Sangihes and the Talauds. Wenas succeeded de Vreede in 1942 and maintained that decision.

Arnold Parengkuan, a top GMIM cleric, who wrote his doctoral thesis on the GMIM history, told me the NZG labour in Minahasa is 'the crown' of the European mission works in Asia. The number of Christians increased 1,100 per cent in a century, from less than 10,000 when J. F. Riedel and J. G. Schwarz arrived in Minahasa in 1834 to 121,000 in 1936.

In 1947, or 13 years after the GMIM establishment, the NZG established the GMIST, combining the two names '*in* Sangihe and Talaud'. Willy Roroe told me that the GMIM and the GMIST were established separately along ethnic lines. 'It was since the very beginning, different ethnics, different churches'.

That satisfied the Sangihe pastors but apparently not the Talauds. 'The process was not clear. We were just invited to attend the conference. The GMIST was abruptly established without our involvement', Talaud cleric Firdaus Majusip told me.

In the late 1960s, many Talaud fishermen and farmers were accused of being communists as they had earlier received donations, such as hoes, from the Soviet Union via the Indonesian Communist Party. The communists were accused of trying to take over the Indonesian government in Jakarta in September 1965. This prompted the army to conduct a nationwide manhunt against the communists. The army also arrested and screened many Talaud men, discriminating against their children for three decades.

'Talaud was stamped as a communist region', said Majusip.

Their children had difficulties getting into colleges or getting government jobs. Many fled to neighbouring Mindanao, but more went to work as shopkeepers, housemaids or coconut tree climbers. The GMIST didn't provide much help, prompting the Talaud priests to work harder for a church separation.

Arnold Parengkuan championed these ethnic churches, forging agreements not to set up congregations outside their territorial area. It means the GMIM will not have a congregation in the Sangihe Islands and vice versa. 'A GMIM churchgoer could register in a GMIST church. We also have many members who are not Minahasans', said Parengkuan. This agreement was later extended to other churches throughout Indonesia.

Parengkuan said GMIM headquarters in Tomohon manages more than 800 congregations with about 700,000 members. It runs some 300 kindergartens, 370 primary schools and more than 70 secondary schools, three technical high schools, a home economics school, a teachers' college, four theology schools, a school for the deaf and dumb and two orphanages. The church also has a training centre for nurses, five hospitals and 70 clinics.

The Talaud church does not even have a single college. It is now understandable why those Talaud pastors, such as Majusip, want to be separated from the GMIST. The history has also prompted ethnic nationalism, but they simply want to handle their social works themselves!

They believe ethnic churches, with some flavour of ethnic nationalism, does it better.

Christian Minority in Muslim-Majority Indonesia

Bert Adriaan Supit's office is a two-storey wooden house on the main street of Tomohon. His working space, on the second floor, has a view toward Mount Lokon, the most beautiful volcano in northern Sulawesi. Its name originates from the phrase '*tou tua lokon*', or 'the old man'.

Supit began his career as a young medical doctor at the Bethesda Hospital, a GMIM-owned hospital in Tomohon. Supit gradually also took part in other church works, developing medical services, schools and a printing press as well as organising an Indonesian Christian conference. In 1987, at the height of President Suharto's authoritarian rule, the GMIM leadership replaced Christianity in its statute with Indonesia's state ideology Pancasila.

In his autobiography, Supit protested the decision and decided to leave the GMIM board. He argues that the synod has compromised too much. Pancasila is a matter of the state. Christianity is a principle of Christian churches. He continued his public works, however, by establishing Yayasan Suara Nurani, a non-profit foundation in Tomohon that works on rural development. It is now one of the largest non-governmental organisations in Minahasa. Supit transformed himself into an activist.

After Suharto was forced out of power in May 1998, Supit was euphoric about the emergence of democracy in Indonesia. He set up a political party and ran for governor of North Sulawesi. He lost despite a vigorous campaign with many NGOs. In February 2003, Supit set up another organisation: Persatuan Minahasa (Minahasa Union) named after an organisation established in 1927 to campaign for an independent Minahasa. Its symbol is, what else, the owl of the *manguni*. Johnny Lumintang, a retired three-star army general, chairs the new union, while Supit became its secretary general.

I visited Supit's office in September 2004 when it was certain Susilo Bambang Yudhoyono, a retired army general, had won the Indonesian presidential election against incumbent President Megawati Sukarnoputri.

We chatted about the election and Mount Lokon, but talked at length about Supit's ideas on Indonesia as a federation.

'I was born as a member of *bangsa Minahasa*. I was a Minahasan, and I was not born as an Indonesian. When I grew up I had relatives who fought for the independence of Indonesia including my cousins, Arie and Willy Lasut', Supit began.

'But I also had an uncle, Charlie Engelen, who advocated the establishment of Minahasa as a federal state in the Republic of Indonesia. I also know many Minahasans who advocated Minahasa as the Twaalfde Provincie of the Netherlands'.

Supit claimed he could fairly judge Indonesia's modern history since he knows people from both sides of the debate. He acknowledged realistic aspects of the Indonesian nationalism but also Dutch colonialism. 'Without the Dutch education, you can imagine what we are today! We will *baku bunuh* and *baku segala macam* (to kill each other and to do whatever to each other). We need to be realistic and not emotional about the Dutch'.

I asked him about Johnny Lumintang's involvement. 'Johnny is a pragmatic man. He could read the situation. Perhaps, we could collaborate as he likes to brake', Supit smiled. In other words, to slow down.

Dutch Ethical politician C. Th. van Deventer made popular the Twaalfde Provincie epithet, the Twelfth Province, in the 1910s. The Netherlands had 11 provinces. His idea was to make Minahasa into the 'twelfth province', as it was the most Europeanised area in the Netherlands Indies. Van Deventer's idea became popular among Minahasan soldiers who worked in the Royal Netherlands Indies Army. But it grew much more popular in the 1930s and 1940s among Minahasans.

One of the most fundamental problems in Indonesia, Supit believes, is the unitarian state of Indonesia. He described in his book *Melawan Arus: Wacana Federalisme Untuk Indonesia,* or 'Against the Current: A Discourse of Federalism for Indonesia', how over the past 50 years Indonesia has become 'super centralistic', culturally corrupted, repressive and discriminating against minorities.

'The provinces become beggars and not creative', he said.

'I studied the speeches of Sukarno. I don't hate Sukarno, but I am questioning what Sukarno calls Indonesia's nationalism. His nationalism is based on Majapahit. It is very imperialistic. Majapahit is worse than the Dutch'.

'The mentality of today's colonialism is copied from the Majapahit. Sukarno offered and glorified this mentality in his speeches. It is dominated by the culture and history of Java. The Javanese is over-dominant. Today our children do not know the history of Minahasa. Our children do not know anymore about *bangsa Minahasa*. It is against my identity; with the creation that God has given us. I was created a Minahasan'.

Critics said Indonesian history books are flawed, if not biased. They were designed to make school children believe that Indonesia had 'regional rebellions' against the Dutch prior to the rise of Indonesian nationalism in Java in the 1910s. Students are taught about the 'national history' from a Javanese perspective. The first 'Indonesian nationalist organisation' was listed as Boedi Oetomo, established in 1908, when in fact it was a Javanese movement. They learn to admire many 'national heroes' but the most famous is Mataram Prince Diponegoro, a Javanese aristocrat, who fought for his land rights against the Dutch from 1825 to 1830.

The Majapahit Empire was a 14th century kingdom based in eastern Java, which influenced much of Malaya, Kalimantan, Sumatra and Bali. Its greatest king was Hayam Wuruk, whose reign from 1350 to 1389 marked the empire's peak. It was a Hindu Javanese kingdom, but it didn't control the territory of today's Indonesia – contrary to what the history books say – not even the western side of Java Island.

According to the 2000 census, the Javanese make up about 41.7 per cent of Indonesia's 203.5 million population. The census showed that Indonesia had been 'Javanized', with the Javanese ranking consistently among the top three largest ethnic groups in most of Indonesia's 30 provinces.

Most Indonesian leaders, including President Suharto, Abdurrahman Wahid, Susilo Bambang Yudhoyono and Joko Widodo, are ethnic Javanese. Megawati Sukarnoputri is of mixed heritage. Her father, Sukarno, was half Javanese and half Balinese. Her mother was Malay from Bengkulu in Sumatra. But in a patriarchal Indonesia, Sukarno and Megawati are considered Javanese. President B. J. Habibie is better known as a Gorontalon from Sulawesi. His father is a Gorontalon and his mother is a Javanese. These things were different in the 1950s when the first three Indonesian prime ministers – Mohammad Hatta, Sutan Sjahrir and Amir Sjarifoeddin – were Sumatran.

The growing Javanese dominance makes Supit angry.

'We have been created equally. God has created human beings to be equal. That's basic rights. I was created as a Minahasan. Not as an Indonesian. Indonesia is a political contract. Nothing else! Because of the contract, to be united against the Dutch, it is not a religious contract, it is not a cultural contract', he said.

'We also have community rights. The ethnic rights, the religious rights, the language rights. They're all human rights. What's a state for? It is for the well being of the people!'

Supit said the Minahasa, which is culturally more receptive to Western ideas, had enjoyed a special position in the Netherlands Indies. The Dutch were gentler in Minahasa and Ambon than in other parts of the Netherlands Indies. Minahasa has also practiced democracy for longer than the Javanese have. He pointed to David Henley's book, which describes efforts among Minahasan leaders to have self-governance. This all means Minahasa has a different colonial past.

According to Henley, in May 1909 non-commissioned officers at the Magelang military base in Java founded Perserikatan Minahasa (Minahasa Association). It was the first explicitly Minahasan political organisation set up in the Netherlands Indies. It quickly attracted interest among Minahasan students and white-collar workers. By 1917, the Perserikatan Minahasa had at least 10,000 members, making it the second largest native association in the Netherlands Indies after the Sarekat Islam in Java, which had 700,000 members between 1912 and 1916. Besides unity and progress, Perserikatan Minahasa also embodied elements of another classical nationalist ideal: independence.

In 1919, that goal began materialising with the inauguration of the Minahasa Council or Minahasaraad in Manado. It had 36 elected Minahasan members who were supplemented by five appointed represent-atives of European and other foreign groups. The electorate included only adult males with an annual income minimum of 300 guilders.

Although limited in its legislative powers, chaired by a Dutch official and subject to veto by the governor general, the Minahasaraad proved more than just a talking shop. It gave Minahasans a genuine taste of the practicalities and problems of democracy. In 1924, the Dutch-trained physician-turned-journalist Samuel Ratu Langie was elected secretary of Minahasaraad. Ratu Langie did more than anybody else to generate public interest in the Minahasaraad. Its greatest achievement came in 1929, when Minahasaraad extended the vote to all male income taxpayers. This raised the number of voters from 10 per cent of the adult male population to almost 70 per cent.

'I learned a lot about Ratu Langie's ideas. I read his speeches and looked for his opinion pieces', said Supit. 'Ratu Langie advocated an independent Minahasa state in a federal Indonesia'.

In August 1927, Ratu Langie and another Minahasan intellectual, R. Tumbelaka, created a new political party, Persatuan Minahasa or Minahasa Union, to represent the civilians. That year in Java, the Dutch-trained engineer, Sukarno, set up the Partai Nasionalis Indonesia, the Indonesian Nationalist Party, which became a hugely influential party and catapulted Sukarno into one of the principal champions of the colonised people in Asia.

Ratu Langie was also selected to be a member of the 60-strong Volksraad or People's Council in Batavia, the top representative council for various *bangsa* in the Netherlands Indies. In his classic, *Nationalism and Revolution in Indonesia*, American scholar George McTurnan Kahin argues that the Voolksraad was a 'sounding board' for the colonial government. But it provided a platform for the nationalist figures in the colonies to meet each other and criticise government policy.

'The main purpose of Persatuan Minahasa is to guard the safety and well-being of *bangsa Minahasa*', Ratu Langie said. 'It cannot be called egoistical, for it is inherent in human nature. Everybody has the right and duty to look after their own selves, provided they do not damage the public interests in the process. Likewise, every *bangsa* has the right and duty to look after itself, provided it does not disadvantage other *bangsa*. For this reason, Persatuan Minahasa must give its primary attention to the local situation in *tanah Minahasa* itself. Because although *bangsa Minahasa* is now scattered throughout Indonesia, we are all tied to our birth land by spiritual bonds'.

Ratu Langie opposed the Twelfth Province ideology 'in order to avoid becoming the target of accusations in the future'. Many Minahasan intellectuals believed they should not align themselves too closely with the Dutch, especially over the nationalist movement in Java. This insecurity resulted from an awareness of the relative small size of Minahasa. According to the 1930 census, Minahasans constituted only 0.5 per cent of the 59 million people living in the Netherlands Indies. (In the 2000 census, Minahasans numbered 659,000 or around 0.33 per cent of Indonesia's 205 million people.)

Ratu Langie wasn't indifferent to the wider Indonesian struggle but he didn't want *tanah Minahasa* to be absorbed by the bigger political culture in Java. He supported a federation in which each *bangsa* in the Netherlands Indies had the right of self-governance.

In October 1928, dozens of activists, mostly students from various parts of the Netherlands Indies, gathered and pledged to set up a single state with a single language, *Bahasa Indonesia*, and a single nation, *bangsa Indonesia*. The principle was widely known in Indonesia as the Sumpah Pemuda, the Youth Pledge.

'They said because of the Sumpah Pemuda, we all have agreed to be united into a single nation, a single culture. Okay! But how many Minahasans? Only two were in the conference', said Supit.

When Japan invaded the Netherlands Indies in 1942, preparations to establish an independent Indonesia moved forward at a faster pace. Sukarno and Mohammad Hatta, released by the Japanese from Dutch exiles, agreed to cooperate with the liberators if Japan agreed to help them prepare Indonesia's independence.

In March 1945, Japan organised a committee, *Badan Penyelidik Usaha Persiapan Kemerdekaan Indonesia* (BPUPKI) or the Investigating Committee for Indonesian Independence, to prepare Indonesia's self-governance. BPUPKI had 70 members. It drafted the constitution and the principles of the state. During the first meeting in May 1945, Sukarno argued that the new republic should not be based on Islam but Pancasila. Supomo, a Javanese lawyer, spoke of 'national integration' and against individualism. Muhammad Yamin, the Sumatran poet, suggested that the new republic should include Sarawak, Sabah, Malaya, Portuguese Timor, and all the pre-war territories of the Netherlands Indies, including West Papua.

On 7 August 1945, when the United States dropped the first atomic bomb in Hiroshima, the Japanese ruler agreed to establish a smaller committee, the *Panitia Persiapan Kemerdekaan Indonesia*, to prepare a proclamation of independence. Several BPUPKI members, including Sukarno and Hatta, also joined the PPKI.

Supit examined the committees. He showed me some graphics, describing the origins of the 75 members of BPUPKI and PPKI, excluding the eight Japanese. He showed me that 63 per cent came from eastern and central Java; 13 per cent were Sundanese (western Java); Sumatra 11 per cent; Kalimantan 4 per cent; Ambon and Sulawesi four men (5 per cent). There were four Chinese, an Arab and a Eurasian in the Jakarta group.

Supit said Hatta, Ratu Langie and Johannes Latuharhary, the only Ambonese, suggested that the new Indonesia be a federation. But the other members voted them out. 'Sukarno, Supomo and Muhammad Yamin advocated a centralised unitarian state', Supit said. Latuharhary suggested the new republic hold a referendum as soon as it became independent to let the people themselves decide. The forum agreed but this decision has never been executed to this day.

On 17 August 1945, knowing that Japan no longer had the power to such make decisions, Sukarno and Hatta, with the backing of the committees, read out a brief Declaration of Independence. Word of the proclamation was spread by shortwave radio and flyers, while militias, youth groups and others rallied to defend the new independence.

A day later, the committee appointed Sukarno as President and Hatta as Vice-President, using the constitution drafted during the BPUPKI days. The BPUPKI was also remade into a temporary governing body. The group declared control by the new Indonesian government over eight provinces: Sumatra, Kalimantan, West Java, Central Java, East Java, Sulawesi, the Moluccas islands and the Lesser Sunda Islands.

As the Japanese surrendered, the Dutch intended to retake its colonies. But the Indonesians prepared to fight for their newly independent state. Riots also broke out in many places, especially against minorities, who were thought to have gotten special treatment during the Dutch period. Many Minahasans living in Java were harassed. Many Chinese and Eurasian minorities were killed. The Minahasans established a militia to protect themselves.

Arie, Supit's cousin, was a staff member of the Geological Service during the Japanese occupation period in Bandung, Java. He was immediately put in charge of the geological office after independence. When the Dutch military returned in late 1945, they sought Arie because of his mining knowledge. Arie refused to cooperate. In May 1949, the Dutch Military Police took Arie from his home and executed him.

Willy, Arie's younger brother, was a Minahasan militia, who worked with then-Lieutenant Colonel Suharto to battle the Dutch. Their battalion occupied Yogyakarta for six hours in March 1949. In 1978, Suharto appointed his old assistant, Willy, to be the governor of North Sulawesi.

Supit still dreams of a referendum to turn Indonesia into a federation. 'I think it's not too late to do it. Let's be faithful to the Republic of Indonesia in another structure. Federalism is how to manage a state. It is a matter of management. Federalism, in my opinion, is to return the pride of autonomy to the people. And the people will decide'.

In 2004, the Indonesian parliament passed the Autonomy Law which decentralises many aspects in the administration of the country. But there're six areas where local governments are not given the mandate to regulate: foreign affairs, defense, security, justice, monetary plus fiscal, and religion. On paper, religious affairs is not decentralisd. In practice, the Autonomy Law empowers new groups locally, Islamist and otherwise, as well as empowering local officials to act with less regard for what's said in the capital by officials or judges.

When I asked him my final question about the new autonomy program in the post-Suharto period, Supit replied, 'There is a saying popular among people here. "They let loose the heads but still hold the tails".'

I left Tomohon with a richer understanding of Indonesia's modern history.

Permesta Rebellion in the 1950s

During the mid-1950s, the general feeling in Sulawesi and other outer islands was that the central government in Jakarta was inefficient. Development stagnated. Money was siphoned into Java. Rivalries emerged among army officers and party leaders. Regional and ethnic grievances sparked simultaneous rebellions in Sumatra and Sulawesi.

The breakaway rebels declared the establishment of the Revolutionary Government of the Republic of Indonesia (Pemerintah Revolusioner Republik Indonesia, PRRI). The PRRI was formed in Padang, western Sumatra, on 15 February 1958, with important political leaders from Jakarta, including three former prime ministers and several high-ranking army officers among its ranks.

In March 1957, Minahasan, Bugis, Makassarese and Ambonese established the Permesta. Permesta stands for Piagam Perjuangan Semesta Alam, but its English translation varies from the 'Charter of the Universal Struggle' to the 'Charter of Inclusive Struggle'.

I wanted to learn first-hand about those rebellions from Herman Nicolas 'Ventje' Sumual, an ailing 81-year-old Minahasan businessperson, who was involved in both the PRRI and the Permesta movements. Indonesia's schoolbooks describe him as a rebel leader but many Minahasans call him a hero. He is reportedly a soldier, but others say he is simply an American agent.

I visited Sumual in his office in Jakarta in October 2004. Clad in a long sleeve batik shirt and dark pants, he invited me to sit on a sofa next to his working desk. 'Please excuse me but I need to pee during this interview. Old age and prostate problems', he smirked, pointing to a toilet inside his office. It seemed to me that he was always surrounded by a coterie of colleagues and assistants.

According to his biography, Sumual joined Indonesia's revolution in 1945 when he became a member of a militia group of Sulawesian youths, KRIS. They fought the returning Dutch soldiers as well as protected Minahasan minorities in Java. In 1948, Sumual led KRIS units incorporated into Indonesia's army with the rank of major. He rose quickly in the military. In May 1956, he was appointed to command the Eastern Indonesia military division in Makassar in southern Sulawesi.

Dissatisfaction in northern Sulawesi began when Jakarta's monopoly over the copra trade seriously weakened its economy. The Minahasans avoided the measure by doing direct trade with Singapore. In June 1956, Jakarta ordered the closure of Bitung port on 'smuggling' grounds. A storm of protests united Minahasans against Jakarta under the slogan, 'Reopen Bitung Harbor or Face Revolt'. Jakarta backed down and reopened Bitung. But it still controlled the copra trade.

In southern Sulawesi, an area dominated by the predominantly Muslim Bugis and Makassarese ethnic groups, disgruntlement began when Jakarta established a new army command in July 1956 for operations in the area. A Javanese colonel was appointed to head the new command, putting Sumual in an awkward position. The new command controlled 20 of 21 army battalions stationed in Makassar and answered directly to the Jakarta army headquarters, not to Sumual. Nine of the 20 battalions were 'on loan' from Brawijaya and Diponegoro divisions in Java. The others also included former militias incorporated into the Indonesian army.

In her book, *Permesta Half-a-Rebellion*, Barbara Harvey wrote that many of these military units were 'hardly distinguishable' from the Darul Islam (Islamic State) rebels in southern Sulawesi they were supposed to fight. 'Their commanders were relatively autonomous warlords – which made the problems of command and discipline extraordinarily difficult'.

The south Sulawesi battalions were more involved in training than fighting. Their members felt that they were looked down upon by the Javanese troops engaged in operations against the Darul Islam guerillas. Rumours circulated that the Brawijaya division would open Sulawesi to Javanese transmigration once the area was pacified.

On 2 March 1957, 51 leaders, who were predominantly Minahasan, Bugis and Makassarese, gathered in the residence of Andi Pangerang Petta Rani, a Bugis aristocrat and the governor of Sulawesi. They issued the Permesta declaration, demanding provincial autonomy and opposing the leftward trend of Jakarta's politics. The signatories made clear they still supported 'one nation, one language and one country'. Sumual was also a signatory. He also declared martial law in eastern Indonesia, including Sulawesi, the Moluccas islands, Bali and Lesser Sunda archipelago.

Jakarta responded quickly by merging the two army commands in Makassar and appointing Pangerang Petta Rani as the military governor of Sulawesi. The Javanese battalions were slowly returned to Java, departing by July 1958. It soon defused the tense situation in Makassar. Sumual lost his command job in Makassar.

Nevertheless, the inability of Jakarta to understand the deeper need to abolish the copra monopoly and recognise Minahasan identity quickly became one of the greatest sources of instability in Sulawesi. The split also became a geographic one in June 1957 when Minahasan officers, including Sumual, left Makassar for Minahasa.

The division, according to Harvey, existed from the beginning. For the Bugis and Makassarese leaders, internal security was their main concern and negotiations with Darul Islam leader Kahar Muzakkar, a former KRIS official who separated from the Indonesian army in 1950, were the main hope for a solution. For the Minahasan leaders, economic development was the prime concern. 'Permesta is a concept of development. We wanted to develop the provinces', said Sumual. The rift grew wider when the Minahasans unilaterally announced the establishment of North Sulawesi province in September 1957. Pangerang Petta Rani favoured Sulawesi to remain a single province.

They traded copra illegally with Singapore. With copra money, the new Minahasa leaders in North Sulawesi soon constructed roads, schools, bridges, churches and even a university. I talked to several Minahasans in Manado, Tomohon and Jakarta, who believed the Permesta period had been marked by popular development projects.

'I was only a teenager, but I remember the road being constructed', said pastor Arnold Parengkuan.

'It was the first time I saw a diesel stone roller. Everybody knows the Manado-Tomohon road was widened by Permesta', said F. H. Ruata, now an aide to Sumual, but was a 16-year-old boy living in Ratahan, southern Minahasa.

Meanwhile, on Indonesia's westernmost island, Sumatra, tension against Jakarta turned into armed conflict. In January 1958, Colonel Ahmad Husein, western Sumatra's military commander, organised a regional meeting in Sungai Dareh, a small town about 110 kilometres east of Padang, in which several dissident colonels and politicians, the former prime ministers, as well as Sumual agreed to join forces. They wanted a new central government, one in which Mohammad Hatta – seen as a champion of non-Javanese minorities and a federalist Indonesia – would play a role. They also wanted regional autonomy and a ban on communism in Indonesia.

After the three-day conference, Husein, Sumual and Soemitro Djojohadikusumo, a former finance minister who ran away to Padang to avoid arrest in Jakarta, went to Singapore to meet Foster Collins, the Central Intelligence Agency (CIA) station chief. He asked for Collins' assistance to ship Permesta weapons from Italy to Manado. Collins promised to help.

Husein's colleague, Colonel Maludin Simbolon, began building relations with the CIA from his home base of Medan in northern Sumatra. Playing on his anti-communist stance, Simbolon asked the CIA to help with cash, weapons and training.

The US government was interested in supporting an anti-communist movement in Indonesia. US State Secretary John Foster Dulles had for some years worried about the growing strength of the Indonesian Communist Party, fearing that President Sukarno was building a closer alliance with communist countries. In an October 1953 briefing, Dulles said, '...as between a territorially united Indonesia which is leaning and progressing towards communism and a break up of that country into racial and geographic units, I would prefer the latter as furnishing a fulcrum which the United States could work later to eliminate communism in one place or another, and then in the end, if they so wish, arrive back again at a united Indonesia'.

Sumual was in Manila to talk with Filipino intelligence officials when his Sumatran colleagues issued a five-day ultimatum on 10 February 1958, threatening to set up a separate Indonesian government if Jakarta didn't meet their demands. The deadline expired and Jakarta did nothing. The dissidents had passed the point of no return. They immediately declared formation of the PRRI. Sjafruddin Prawiranegara, a former caretaker Indonesian president and central banker, was named prime minister. Simbolon took the foreign minister portfolio, while Djojohadikusumo was placed in charge of education.

Four Permesta leaders from Sulawesi were also put in the PRRI cabinet: Sumual (army chief), Saleh Lahade (information minister), Mochtar Lintang (religious affairs minister) and Joop Warouw (deputy prime minister). Both Lahade and Lintang are Bugis figures. The Sumatran leaders announced the line-up without consulting the four. During the next 24 hours, Sumual stalled in Manila and sent an aide to arrange for a return flight to Minahasa. 'I was trying to buy time. We're not prepared', said Sumual.

He cabled the ranking Permesta officer, Lieutenant Colonel Daniel Somba, to postpone any decision until Sumual's return. Sumual thought they needed to consolidate their network with their colleagues in southern Sulawesi, western Java and Jakarta.

On 17 February 1958, when Sumual turned on the radio, he was in for another shock. Over the airwaves of Radio Manado came Somba's voice, announcing that the northern Sulawesi dissidents supported Sumatra.

Permesta had now become the eastern wing of the PRRI. It was another fait accompli that Sumual had to face.

Incredibly, Sumual continued to stall in Manila. On the morning of 22 February, two B-25 bombers appeared from behind the mountainous area southeast of Manado, strafing and rocketing Manado's radio station and transmitter. The Indonesian Air Force also began a bombing spree in Padang. The war had begun.

When Sumual arrived in Manado, he asked Somba whether he had received his cable.

'Yes, I received it'.

'Why did you make that decision?'

'People said that I am a coward! They said I was bribed (with a promotion). I needed to show that I was not!' Sumual recalled that conversation.

Indonesian army chief Abdul Haris Nasution had just then promoted Somba to colonel. Nasution was the officer who led the attacks against the dissident officers. Nasution obviously tried to prevent Somba from joining Sumual, prompting the quick tempered Somba to declare war.

'When you go to Minahasa, a lot of people talk about Permesta as a rebellion. Permesta as a fighting unit of the PRRI, well, it is okay, but not a separatist organisation. Permesta is a development movement in the region', Sumual said.

Kenneth Conboy and James Morrison wrote in their book, *Feet to the Fire: CIA Covert Operations in Indonesia 1957–1958*, that the CIA quickly supplied weapons and advisors to the Sumatran troops. But Nasution, himself from Sumatra, moved faster. Like Sumual, Nasution knew very well that speed was the key to their success. The CIA operation was supposedly a secret, but rumours in Jakarta were widely circulated that the Americans were helping the rebels. The CIA assistance would make the dissidents stronger if Jakarta didn't move fast. Nasution parachuted commandos into Pekanbaru in eastern Sumatra without much resistance. The Marines landed in Padang in mid-April 1958. By early May 1958, Nasution took over Padang, sending the troops of Simbolon and Husein into the forests to conduct a guerilla war.

Many Permesta signatories also retracted their commitment to participation, including Mohammad Jusuf, a Bugis aristocrat and a top army officer in Sulawesi, who led the army to arrest Kahar Muzakkar. Jusuf immediately reported his loyalty to Nasution in Jakarta, prompting Nasution to appoint Jusuf to be the Sulawesi military commander.

Sumual recalled, 'Jusuf likes to say that he is still Permesta but the difference between him and me is that he is a peace Permesta and I am a war Permesta'.

Jusuf's loyalty led President Suharto to appoint him in the 1970s as the commander of the Indonesian Armed Forces.

But Sumatra was an entirely different matter.

In Sumatra, ethnic and religious diversity had proved the rebels' weakness. Most of the Simbolon troops were Batak Christians, Husein's troops were largely Muslim like the Javanese soldiers that dominated Indonesia's army. By contrast the Minahasans were psychologically ready to fight Jakarta. In northern Sulawesi, most of its residents were staunchly opposed to the excesses of Jakarta. GMIM chairman A. Z. R. Wenas condemned the rising influence of the communists in Java, saying in his sermons that the Minahasans should refrain from 'atheism'. More than 2,000 retired Netherlands Indies soldiers turned up at the Permesta headquarters one day after Daniel Somba made a call for help.

In Washington DC, President Dwight Eisenhower suggested that the CIA help build a covert air force for the PRRI in northern Sulawesi. Eisenhower recalled the CIA's positive experience in organising an operation in Guatemala to overthrow the left-leaning Jacobo Arbenz government in 1954. Soon CIA operatives looked for aircrafts and bombs to aid the Permesta air operations.

It hired two Filipino pilots, four Poles and several Americans to run Permesta's Revolutionary Air Force from the Mapanget airfield in Manado. Two Indonesian Air Force officers, Major Petit Muharto and Captain Hadi Supandi, who were Javanese, sided with the Permesta. Muharto led the small air force. Though both officers were Javanese, like Djojohadikusumo, the PRRI welcomed them as their presence added a desired ethnic dimension to the anti-Jakarta struggle.

The small air force radically changed the equation. Sumual even drafted a plan to take over the 'unconstitutional government' in Jakarta in four stages. Stage One was to involve an amphibious landing to seize Morotai island as a secure air base near Sulawesi. Stage Two called for grabbing Palu in central Sulawesi. From there, Permesta air and ground forces would leapfrog to the southern coast of Kalimantan. In the final stage, Sumual told me, 'My plan was to bomb oil stations in Jakarta, Bandung and Surabaya. Our colleagues in Java would help us. We expected the ground transport in Java to collapse and we would land in Cilincing to take over Jakarta'.

Stage one and two were successful. But on 18 May 1958, Captain Ignatius Dewanto, piloting his Mustang fighter above Ambon Island in the Moluccas, shot down CIA pilot Allen Pope in a dogfight. Pope and his gunner, Jan Harry Rantung, who had been flying a B-26, were arrested on Hatala Island, near Ambon.

The Pope fiasco created turmoil in Washington DC. CIA Director Allen Dulles reported the shooting to his brother, State Secretary John Foster Dulles, in a telephone conversation in the middle of a CIA meeting. CIA officer James Glerum, who attended the meeting, said few other words were spoken. Returning the handset to its cradle, Allen Dulles looked straight to Glerum: 'We're *pulling the plug*'.

The instruction was to pull out of Mapanget. In three days, the CIA operatives took their planes and returned to Clark Base in the Philippines. Sumual and his colleagues were devastated. 'We could have conducted a guerilla war for decades just like what Ho Chi Minh did. But we thought, 'What for?' Both Nasution and Ahmad Yani (army chief) were anti-communist like us. The fighting would make the people suffer', said Sumual.

Internal conflicts began to take place among the Permesta guerillas. Nasution's troops occupied major towns in northern Sulawesi, while Jakarta offered amnesty for the surrendering PRRI troops. Somba and Kawilarang surrendered first, followed by Husein in Padang and Simbolon and his Batak colleagues. Sumual finally surrendered in October 1961. The last Permesta leader to surrender was Lieutenant Colonel Jonkhy Robertus Kumontoy, who had holed up in the rugged interior of Halmahera island. Between 20,000 and 30,000 people, mostly civilian Minahasans, died during the war.

Some intellectuals in Manado told me the effect of both the Sumatran and Sulawesi upheaval was to strengthen exactly the trends the dissidents had hoped to weaken. Central authority was enhanced at the expense of local autonomy, radical nationalism in Java gained strength over pragmatic moderation, the power of the communists and Sukarno increased while that of Mohammad Hatta waned. When General Suharto overthrew Sukarno in 1965, Sumual and the others were released from their prisons, but Suharto became even more authoritarian than Sukarno.

Muslim Minorities in Manado

Lalampa is a rice cake made of glutinous rice. The steamed rice is moulded around a piece of fish, wrapped with banana leaves and barbecued over charcoal. It is finger-sized, rather oily, but also a little bit sweet. It is popular throughout Sulawesi with tea or coffee. My favourite *lalampa* vendor is in Manado's Jalan Roda, a crowded alley, where more than a dozen food stalls cater to office workers, middlemen, students and activists.

What I like about Jalan Roda (Wheel Street) is that I could easily choose a table and mingle with others, joining their chats and listening to political gossip and the wildest conspiracy theories. It's located next to the 45 Market – the largest market in Manado – dominated by Muslim traders, mostly from Gorontalo, south of Minahasa.

Yuni Husain, a bank clerk in Manado, whom I met on a Monday evening, said that she likes to drop in to Jalan Roda after-office hours, 'Everybody is equal here and the ambience is comfortable'.

'The prices are fair; the crowd practically knows one another. People also call it the street-level parliament', said Muin Sumaila, a high-school teacher.

Sumaila's joke has a ring of truth in it. A Jalan Roda visit is mandatory for politicians, government officials, artists and public intellectuals to test their ideas. Sumaila told me that new appointees, such as Manado police chiefs, also visit Jalan Roda. The talk is mostly about self-governance and public welfare.

'When the Ternate and Ambon violence exploded, nothing happened in Manado. You know why? Many government officials came to Jalan Roda to have informal discussions', said Arudji Radjab, a Manado-born politician, who works for the Muslim-based United Development Party.

Radjab said that Sulawesi is an ungodly island, awash in weapons and conflicts, where crime, corruption and politics are often intertwined. These facts make conversations in Jalan Roda very lively. Visitors talked about the violence in the neighbouring islands of Ternate and Ambon as well as in Poso in central Sulawesi, where racial and religious tension produced deadly fighting. They also talked about the creeping influence of money politics in Jakarta.

Religious violence in Poso had taken place since December 1998. In three years of episodic fighting between Christians and Muslims, death toll estimates ranged from 1,000 to 2,500, with thousands more injured. Scores of churches and mosques had been torched. Nearly 100,000 had fled their burning homes. Islam supremacist groups set up bases in Poso, spreading hatred and intolerance as well as organising sporadic attacks. In December 2016, when I visited Palu, central Sulawesi, the police had just shot dead an Islamist terrorist in Poso.

When violence in the neighbouring Poso and Moluccas islands climaxed in 2000, Aif Darea, a journalist-cum-activist made a breakthrough in Jalan Roda. Darea was then working for 'Radio Al Khairat' FM 102 MHz, the largest Muslim-based radio station in Manado. He decided to launch a weekly political talk show in Jalan Roda. Every Monday from 7.00 am until 10.30 am, he broadcast live from a small table in the Warung Pak Hari stall.

'I also added a loudspeaker so that the program could be heard outside the food stall. People were very proud to talk on radio', Darea said, adding that he usually invited one or two commentators and four other sources take part.

Warung Pak Hari is a hole-in-the-wall eatery on Jalan Roda. It provides delicious *lalampa*. It is always crowded in the morning and evening. Next to Warung Pak Hari is a billiard place. Some other food stalls also provide space for their customers to play cards. A brothel with a small entrance is nearby.

'I have known Warung Pak Hari since I was a kid, selling newspapers or scavenging for plastic bags. I sometimes slept in this food stall and called the couple that own it Papa and Mama', Aif Darea said.

Interestingly, most of the customers in Jalan Roda are Muslim. Sumaila is a Muslim from Tidore Island. Yuni Husain's father is Acehnese. Arudji Radjab is a mixed blood. His ancestors include Palembang, Ternate and Bantik. Most customers come from Gorontalo, a predominantly Muslim region south of Minahasa, or Bolaang Mongondow, a Muslim enclave inside southern Minahasa.

Many customers told me that this religious affinity goes back to the 1930s, when cattle traders from Gorontalo parked their bullock-carts in the neighbourhood while selling their cattle in a nearby market.

The Jalan Roda visitors also share a general feeling that they are a Muslim minority inside a Christian enclave, although Minahasa itself is located inside a huge Muslim country. Many of the Jalan Roda visitors are also critical of the social structure in Minahasa. Most Minahasans control the bureaucracy, the academic circles and the military. The Chinese control businesses. The Gorontalons are middlemen or street vendors. The Sangihes are shop keepers, coconut climbers or restaurant waiters.

Adil Polontalo, an activist with the National Mandate Party, told me that discrimination is widespread in student life, especially at the Sam Ratulangi University, the largest college in northern Sulawesi. The Minahasan students get most scholarships. The Muslim students are mostly sidelined.

'Discrimination does exist. Virtually no Minahasans fight against this discrimination. It is a structural problem, but we don't want to fight it. If some Muslims are given positions, it is merely for balance. Just to be proportional. If we move against it, there might be Muslim groups from outside Manado coming here. It will sharpen the dispute', said Radjab.

'The Gorontalons also want to climb the social ladder. There is a feeling of being marginalised...the hegemony of the Minahasans', said Suardi Hamzah, a Gorontalon activist in Manado.

Friko S. Poli, an editor of the *Komentar* daily whose founding editors were mostly Minahasans, denied such allegations, saying that one might see it as a discrimination but such a view 'underestimates those professions (street traders)'.

Poli believed that the Manado government must enforce the law, including sometimes eradicating street vendors from sidewalks, but strictly on a legal basis. The street vendors, he stressed, were not removed because of their racial or religious backgrounds. They were removed because they took over pedestrian areas.

Ironically, the Minahasans themselves frequently feel that they are a tiny minority, whose total population is less than 1 per cent of the whole population in Indonesia. In 1999 when Christian-Muslim violence broke out in the Moluccas islands, killing nearly 25,000 people, many Minahasans established militia groups. Their leaders didn't have confidence that Jakarta could contain the violence from engulfing Minahasa.

The largest group is Brigade Manguni, whose members in black uniforms are frequently seen on the streets of Manado. They stress their Indonesian nationalism and Minahasan identity: red-and-white flag and *manguni* or owl in their insignia. But they shied away from anything which symbolises Christianity.

'It was too stupid to use Christianity in such a dangerous time', said Denni Pinontoan, a Minahasan theologian in Tomohon. Pinontoan mentioned the now defunct *Telegraf* daily which covered the communal violence with a Christian bias, 'It was quite provocative, but pragmatism finally wins'. Pinontoan stressed that Brigade Manguni also has Muslim members, showing that pragmatic Minahasans want to keep the social fabric in North Sulawesi.

Suardi Hamzah helped his fellow Gorontalons forward their demands to the Jakarta government, indicating their desire to break away from North Sulawesi and become a separate province. They succeeded in December 2000 when the Indonesian parliament passed a law to split North Sulawesi into two provinces: North Sulawesi with Manado as capital and Muslim-dominated Gorontalo in the south with Gorontalo as capital.

But activists such as Hamzah became frustrated, probably also wiser, when the new Gorontalo parliament elected a notorious businessman and an old Golkar Party hand to become its first governor. 'I'm not returning to Gorontalo as long as Fadel Muhammad is still governor', said Hamzah, referring to the businessman. Golkar is the political party established by Suharto in the late 1960s.

Reiner Ointoe, a lecturer at Manado's Sam Ratulangi University and himself a regular Jalan Roda visitor, believes that the street is a public forum in which outrage and criticism could be channelled. This forum, he said, does help to maintain civil liberties in Manado.

When I left Manado, I thought maybe this kind of forum, with its delicious *lalampa* and sweet coffee, could help prevent communal violence in post-Suharto era. I am not sure how this small enterprise could save the much bigger project in Indonesia.

Chapter 4

JAVA

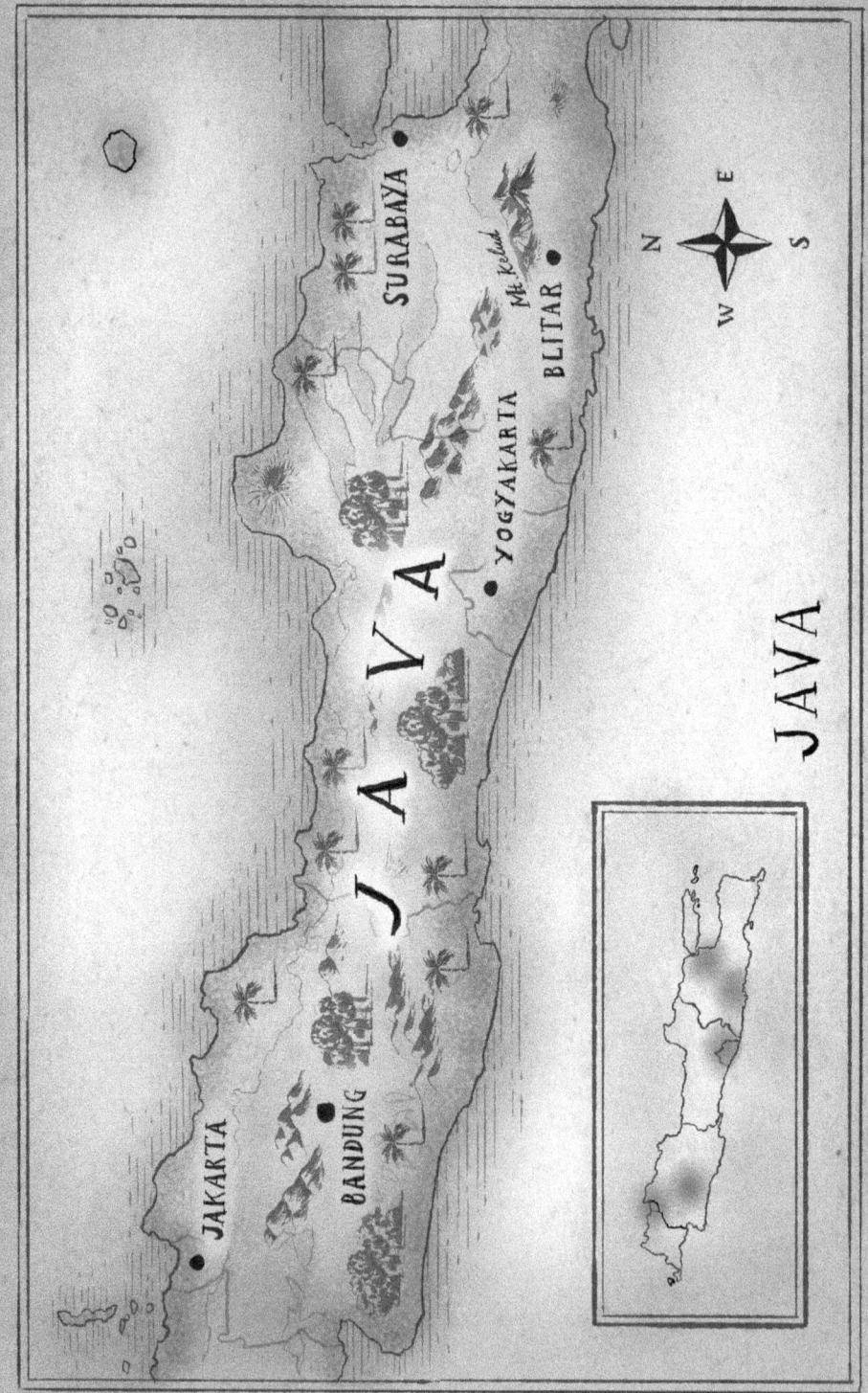

Indonesian Nationalism versus Islamic State

Myth about Indonesia from a Hindu Temple

In 1817, Thomas Stamford Raffles published *The History of Java*, revealing many temple ruins scattered on Java. One was a Hindu temple that Raffles discovered at Panataran village, about 12 kilometres north of Blitar, on the slopes of Mount Kelud.

This temple turned out to be the most important archaeological remains from the Majapahit kingdom. It has a tall stone called the Palah monument, written in Old Javanese, which says that this temple was built by the king Crnga of Kediri in 1197.

Crnga ruled his kingdom between 1190 and 1200. The temple was meant to worship 'the Mountain God'. Various inscriptions reveal dates from 1197 to 1454, recording continuous construction for more than 250 years.

I visited the Panataran temple one morning in May 2006. The temple stands majestically with the background of Mount Kelud. I saw a group of primary school students with their teachers. The entrance has two statues of the *dwaraphalas* (fearsome giants). Their pedestals were dated 1320.[1]

It was quiet. The complex has three buildings. The first temple is the smallest. Palaeographers later called it the Dated Temple with a giant statue of Lord Ganeca inside. An engraved dragon surrounds the second temple. It is called the Dragon Temple. The third is the largest and called the Main Temple.

Only the first temple is fully reconstructed. The second and third temples have only their foundations. The engraving on the foundations is impressive. One section depicts the story of Hanuman, the monkey king, who helped Rama and Shinta in the Indian epic Ramayana, burning their enemy's kingdom. The temples are obviously a Hindu house of worship.

Some visitors invited me to sit with them under some trees.

'I think this is the Maja trees', said Nur Ismiati, a Javanese trader from Sampit in Kalimantan, referring to the name *Majapahit* kingdom.

'People said that it's bitter. It is sweet when ripe'.

---

1   All dates at the Panataran temple used the Hindu Saka era. It was introduced by Indian Prince Aji Saka where year 1 Saka corresponds to 78 CE (Common Era) in the Western calendar. Javanese and Madurese civilisations still widely use the Saka lunar calendar.

The word '*pahit*' means 'bitter' in Javanese.

Nur Ismiati and her family came to Blitar to learn about Majapahit's history. In 1976, they moved to Kalimantan in a government-sponsored transmigration program. They apparently prospered in Sampit, opening a butcher shop and regularly returning to Java, seeing relatives and taking care of their businesses.

Her husband, Choirul Anam, said that the temple is important to Javanese migrants like him, 'Since Majapahit, all kingdoms in the Nusantara area, ranging from the Malay peninsula to Papua, were defeated and ruled by Majapahit'. He lectured me on the greatness of the Majapahit.

Nusantara is a *name* found in a Majapahit manuscript, widely believed to be the old name of Indonesia, at least, among Indonesian citizens.

This dates to 1894, when Dutch troops defeated the Balinese dynasty, also a Hindu power, that ruled Lombok. The Dutch found in the royal library many manuscripts, including a copy of the *Deśawarṇana* (Writing about Territories). It was written in Old Javanese and only translated into Dutch in 1902 as *Nagarakrtagama* (State with Sacred Religion). The translation project was widely reported in the Netherlands. The author of this epic is a Javanese chronicler named Prapanca.

The manuscript refers to a territory that it called 'Nusantara'. It was written in 1365 or around 175 years after the Panataran temple was built. The manuscript is a perfect complement of Thomas Raffles' book, published almost a century earlier. It reported that Majapahit rulers regularly visited a temple on the slopes of Mount Kelud to worship the Mountain God. Majapahit was very likely established by descendants of king Crnga.

This epic poem chronicles situations in the Majapahit kingdom under the rule of king Hayam Wuruk, who reigned from 1350 to 1389, receiving gifts from smaller kingdoms in 'Nusantara'.

Most of the text tells of Hayam Wuruk's journey to Blambangan and Singosari in Eastern Java. The death of his prime minister Gajah Mada was also written about. Another part of the text is about Majapahit's territory and their tribute. Interpretations of this part remain controversial. It says that Majapahit has ruled '...*muwah tikhan i wandan, ambwan athawa maloko wwanin*'. It translates, '... *as it was in ambwan or maloko wwanin*'.

Ambwan is probably Ambon in the Moluccas islands. Wwanin means the Onin Peninsula, an area near Fakfak in Papua, and Maloko is a place on Halmahera island. The name 'Maloko' probably inspired the Portuguese to call the archipelago *Maluco*, and later to be the Moluccas.

Choirul Anam, the Javanese butcher, said that the Majapahit power had continued until today. Throughout Indonesia, he believes, the Javanese play the greatest role in administrative matters.

'We could find Javanese *lurah* (village head) in many areas throughout Nusantara. Please tell me if you could find a Dayak *lurah* in Java?' Anam quoted Sampit regent Kusnan Daryono, himself a Javanese, as saying that Sampit had developed because of the Javanese transmigrants.

'I came here to see how Gajah Mada had built Majapahit into such an influence'.

I'm not surprised to see how people like Choirul Anam relate to Majapahit as a reflection of his own situation.

Anam's bother-in-law, Daud Mesriadi, told me, 'From the textbook in my elementary school, I learned that the Majapahit kingdom expanded its power from here to the Malay peninsula under the premiership of Gajah Mada'.

According to *Nagarakrtagama*, Gajah Mada was born a commoner. He rose to power on his intelligence, courage and loyalty to king Jayanagara of Majapahit. Jayanagara sexually abused the wife of his personal physician who later killed him. He had no offspring. He was succeeded by his step-mother Dyah Gayatri. Soon Dyah Gayatri retired to become a nun. Her daughter Tribhuvana Wijayatungga Dewi ruled as regent (1328–50).

Gajah Mada gradually became the most powerful figure in Majapahit. In 1331, a rebellion took place in Sadeng in eastern Java. Gajah Mada sent a military expedition and won the battle. When Gajah Mada was appointed as prime minister, he took a solemn oath before the council of ministers that he would not enjoy *palapa* – privileges of vacation or the revenue from his estate – before he conquered the 'whole archipelago' for Majapahit. In 1976, President Suharto named Indonesia's first satellite after Gajah Mada's oath: Palapa. Now Indonesia has almost a dozen Palapa satellites to electronically unite Indonesia.

The manuscript only described Gajah Mada's activities in Java and Bali. It didn't say whether he also led similar expeditions to other islands. It was under his patronage that Prapanca began writing *Nagarakrtagama*. It's a court chronicle and this genre is renowned for exaggerating the greatness of rulers. Gajah Mada died in 1364.

According to Slamet Muljana, a Javanese historian, the death of Gajah Mada and the emergence of Islamic influence in the northern coast of Java Island signalled the beginning of the end of the Hindu golden era.

In the 1920s, knowledge of Prapanca's claim that Majapahit had an influence over Nusantara became widely known among the new middle class in the Netherlands Indies. Javanese had the Dutch conception of Majapahit, a mighty empire, to replace their own version of Majapahit as a kingdom defeated.

Radical nationalists such as Muhammad Yamin found in the Dutch interpretation evidence for an archipelago-wide political and cultural entity existing for centuries prior to Western colonial rule. In 1948, Yamin published *Gaja Mada* play, taking their subjects from the Majapahit history. Yamin had the audacity to take Majapahit as an inspiration in his campaign for Indonesia's independence and a justification for imagining the new country as the successor state to Majapahit. Yamin wanted to create a single past for his Indonesia.

The term of *Indonesia* is compounded by 'Indie' or 'Indo' (Latin word for India or Hindus) and 'nesos' (Greek word for island). It was coined by James Richardson Logan, a jurist-cum-journalist who was born in Scotland, working in Singapore and buried in Penang. Logan introduced the terminology in his 1850 writing 'The Ethnology of the Indian Archipelago' in which he said: 'The name Indian Archipelago is too long to admit of being used in an adjective or in an ethnographical form. Mr (George Samuel Windsor) Earl suggests the ethnographical term *Indunesian*, but rejects it in favour of *Malayunesian*. I prefer the purely geographical term *Indonesia*, which is merely a shorter synonym of Indian Islands or the Indian Archipelago'. Logan didn't include Papua but incorporated the Philippines.

Dutch author Eduard Douwes Dekker introduced the terminology *Insulinde* in his famous 1859 book *Max Havelaar or the Coffee Auctions of the Dutch Trading Company*. Insulinde is compounded by 'inseln' (islands) and 'indie' (india). Other writers introduced other terminologies like 'Malay Archipelago' or 'Le Grand Archipel Malais' or 'Nusantara Malayu Raya'. The first political party in Java, which consciously tried to move out of racial boundaries, was named *Indische Partij* in 1913 and later renamed Insulinde Party after Dekker's *Max Havelaar*.

Ethnologist Adolf Bastian of Berlin University, however, popularised the name 'Indonesia' through his 1884 book *Indonesien oder die Inseln des Malayichen Archipels*. Adolf Bastian is known as a founder of ethnography. His book was widely read among European scholars, including Dutch bureaucrats, whose colonial rule gradually controlled the Dutch Indies archipelago, conquering one kingdom after another.

According to Merle C. Ricklefs' standard *A History of Modern Indonesia*, the Dutch didn't create Indonesia. They defined its territorial extent. By establishing that territorial extent, the colonial power also determined who was to be Indonesian and who was not. In the 19th century, European ethnologists often regarded Filipinos, and even Malagasies, as Indonesians. But the perception of Indonesia as a nation or a territory only began to materialise after the Dutch empire established control over the territory in the 1910s.

The conversation in the Hindu temple reminded me of a lecture by nationalism guru Benedict Anderson of Cornell University, in Jakarta in November 1998. It was a high profile event. *Tempo* magazine, which was banned by the Suharto regime in 1994 and began republication that November, invited Anderson to speak, himself having been banned from entering Indonesia since 1972.

Anderson began his speech by talking about Javanese Prince Diponegoro being made Indonesia's number one hero in the 1950s. He said that nationalism is widely misunderstood to be something very old and inherited from 'absolutely splendid ancestors'. Many misunderstand nationalism as arising 'naturally' in the blood and flesh of each Indonesian citizen. In fact, nationalism is a new entity; in countries such as the United States and France it is little more than two centuries old, and in Indonesia, which declared independence in 1945, it is in its infancy.

Another misunderstanding is that 'nation' and 'state' are, if not exactly identical, at least connected like a happy husband and wife. In fact, the reality is often just the opposite. Anderson debunked the idea that only Westerners could colonise 'native people', reminding the audience that 90 per cent of the government officials of the Netherlands Indies were 'natives'. In the 1950s, when Indonesia began to govern itself, these native colonial officials became the ruling elite.

During the Dutch colonial period, repression took place but was not as extreme as what Anderson observed during Suharto's regime, such as torture with electrical cords connected to activists' genitals. And such violence was especially common in areas like Aceh, Papua and East Timor.

'I see too many Indonesians still inclined to think of Indonesia as an "inheritance", not as a challenge nor as a common project. Where one has inheritance, one has inheritors, and too often there are bitter quarrels among them as to who has "rights" to the inheritance: sometimes to the point of great violence', Anderson said.

'The situation is today very serious and can only be remedied by a radical change in the mindset of the political leaders in Indonesia'.

These Javanese visitors in the Hindu Majapahit temple only consumed what they were taught. Majapahit power was exaggerated, but turned into a myth of inheritance. Too many Indonesian elite have manipulated that logic and, worse than that, also fanned racism and sectarianism.

Sukarno's Tomb

Blitar is a small town of little shops that formed itself along the government road. Its most important landmark was the tomb of Sukarno.

The 1.5-hectare tomb complex is divided into two compounds. The first compound is the museum, a library and a park. The collections included a huge Sukarno painting, his memorabilia and hundreds of his photos with world leaders: Chou Enlai, Gamal Abdul Nasser, Ho Chi Minh, Jawaharlal Nehru, John F. Kennedy, Josep Broz Tito, Mao Zhedong.

Hadi Purnomo, a museum guide, told me that it employs 40 workers, 'In accordance to the tradition of the Javanese, the roof of this two-storey building should not be higher than the grave. When building the museum, we dug this place'.

The second compound is the tomb area with wall panels. The entrance is outfitted with a pair of stone gates. They call it the Majapahit Gate... what's else? Several vendors sell flowers and incense. A line of shops sell Sukarno T-shirts, Sukarno mugs, Sukarno posters and other Sukarno-related souvenirs. The tomb has a Javanese tall roof with crafted wood ceiling. The tomb is connected to a mosque. The epitaph is made of black marble. Visitors must take off their shoes to approach the cemetery.

Sukarno was the son of a Javanese schoolteacher and a Balinese mother from Buleleng. Soekeni Sosrodihardjo originates from Blitar. His only son, Sukarno, was born on 6 June 1901 in Surabaya when Sosrodihardjo was assigned to teach there.

Sukarno was admitted into a Dutch-run school as a child. When his father sent him to Surabaya in 1916 to attend a secondary school, he stayed at the house of Tjokroaminoto, a leader of the Islam Union. Tjokroaminoto was Sukarno's first political mentor. Sukarno was fluent in several languages, especially Dutch and his native Javanese. He also speaks and writes Malay.

Suwanto, a keeper of the tomb, told me that around 600 visitors come to the tomb every day. 'Mostly they come from Java, but we also have visitors from abroad including Japan, the Netherlands and England. Local tourists come from Lampung, Borneo, Ende, Kupang, as well as Aceh'.

Bahasa Indonesia to Unite Indonesia

In the late 19th century, the Dutch-led administration in the Indonesian archipelago became denser, companies expanded, and authorities in Batavia began to think about expanding education for the 'islanders' to engage them in bureaucracy and business life. The need to enforce a standard language became more urgently felt.

In 1872, the basis of this policy was laid down in the so-called Regulations of primary education for islanders in which it was stated that: 'Malay will be taught following the rules and spelling of the pure Malay as commonly used on the Malay Peninsula and the Riau'. It was called High Malay in opposition with Low Malay or Sino Malay – written mostly in ethnic Chinese-owned publications. It took a long time until this High Malay effectively gained the authority of a standard, not only because the competition with Low Malay was vehement and confusing, but also because other local languages had to be neutralised as possible alternatives: Dutch, Javanese and Sundanese.

Indonesia has more than 1,000 ethnic languages, ranging from the Javanese, spoken mostly on the island of Java, to much smaller languages like the Tomean on Tomea Island or hundreds of languages in Papua and Kalimantan. Malay was shared by a wide variety of people in this archipelago, in many variations and forms. It could be resorted to in the exchange of information, in trade, in conveying religion, anxiety and political ideas. In Minahasa, they call it Bahasa Manado. In Kupang, people call it Bahasa Kupang. In Papua, people call it Bahasa Papua. Sukarno grew up during this period when a name and a standard language had been adopted by the Dutch government.

According to Claudine Salmon of the French National Centre for Scientific Research, in her monograph *Literature in Malay by the Chinese of Indonesia*, Malay was already a marketplace language in the 18th century. It was written mostly in Arabic or Javanese characters. Dutch printers and missionaries, however, pioneered the use of printing presses to initially publish their own Dutch-language publications, prompting the later romanisation of the Malay too.

Several newspapers in romanised Malay appeared in Java in the mid-19th century: *Soerat Kabar Melajoe* (1860), *Soerat Chabar Betawie* (1858),

Selompret Melajoe (1860) and *Bintang Soerabaja* (1860). The usage of the romanised Malay spread to other parts of the Netherlands Indies including Minahasa where the Nederlandsch Zendeling Genootschap mission published the *Tjahaja Sijang* newspaper in 1868.

In her research, Salmon found 806 Sino-Malay authors and translators as well as 3,005 Sino-Malay book titles, spreading from 1870s until the 1960s. This is considerable when compared to the list of *Modern Indonesian Literature* (1979) published by Dutch scholar Andries Teeuw, with 284 islander authors and 770 works. Salmon challenged the generally accepted ideas that 'modern' Indonesian literature had nothing to do with Sino-Malay literature.

When Sukarno was a teenager in Surabaya, he was obviously reading this Sino-Malay literature. He also observed a debate between D. V. J. Westerveld, a Dutch teacher with socialistic leanings in Semarang, and Tjipto Mangoenkoesoemo, a Javanese doctor with a great interest in the emancipation of the Javanese commoners.

Westerveld argued that an educational policy that focuses on Dutch language is fundamentally wrong – teaching Dutch to islanders means that they lose contact with their own languages and cultures. The educated ones will no longer be able to show their people 'the way to emancipation and, ultimately, to independence'. Education in their own indigenous languages is the key for emancipation.

Tjipto Mangoenkoesoemo took a radically opposite stance: the Javanese tongue no longer meets the requirements of the present day, unable and unwilling as it is to express modern ideas and convey scientific knowledge, and this holds for all languages in the Dutch Indies. Mangoenkoesoemo advocated the Dutch language.

His Indische Party colleague, Suardhy Surya Ningrat, a Javanese educator, made a speech about language at a Congress for Colonial Education in The Hague in 1916. It was inspired by a clear idea that Malay should be stimulated as the language of administration and education. Other native languages should be taken to be less important.

In the ongoing discussions about language, some themes were to emerge again and again: Malay should be developed as the language of administration and education, Malay needed a standard, and the knowledge of Dutch among islanders should remain restricted. The Dutch colonial administration followed a compromise: local languages, much Malay, little Dutch.

In the 1910s, Malay slogans, phrases and rallies were launched by the Indische Party, Muslim associations, trade unions and the Communist Party. Everyone knew that the future 'national language' was to be Malay, the language that for several decades had been the most used language in government offices and in colonial educational efforts since the 1872 regulation.

The racial and religious diversity also enriched the romanised Malay media. Benedict Anderson argued that the first generations of journalists in the Dutch Indies were '*jagoan*' (champions): F. Wiggers, F. D. J. Pangemanann, G. Francis, H. Kommer, J. H. Pangemanann, Kwee Kek Beng, Marah Sutan, Mas Marco Dikromo, Soewardi Soerjaningrat, ter Haar, Tio Ie Soei, Tirto Adhi Soerjo. They mixed Malay with Dutch vocabulary, Javanese words, Hokkian expressions etc. Malay became a communicative language, a popular lingua franca. This rich and diverse journalism naturally helped create a public discourse about an imagined community that people were going to call 'Indonesia'.

In 1921, Sukarno moved from Surabaya to Bandung. He studied at the Technische Hogeschool, majoring in civil engineering. He soon learned to speak Sundanese – the language of the natives in western Java.

In 1922, Mohammad Hatta, a Sumatran student in Rotterdam, suggested his organisation change its name from Indische Vereeniging (Indies Association) to Indonesische Vereeniging (Indonesian Association). It is the first organisation to use the name that James Richardson Logan introduced in 1850.

Hatta was born in Bukittinggi on 12 August 1902 into a prominent and strongly Islamic family. His father died when Hatta was a baby and he was raised by the family of his mother. Little Hatta studied in a Dutch school and recited the Koran after school. When he was 17 years old, Hatta went to Batavia to attend a Dutch high school and finished with distinction in 1921. He departed for what was to be a decade's residence in the Netherlands. He continued his learning in the Rotterdam School of Commerce, studying several fields of economics and completed all requirements for his doctorate except for the thesis, which he never finished because of his immersion in political life.

In 1927 Sukarno and his comrades set up the Indonesian Nationalist Party, which adopted 'Bahasa Indonesia' as its official language. Both Sukarno and Hatta adopted a militant policy of noncooperation with the Dutch government. They campaigned rigorously for Indonesian nationalism.

In October and November 1928, the Malay newspapers in Batavia covered the Second Meeting of Indonesian Youth convened on 27–28 October by several youth organisations – Jong Sumatra, Jong Java, Jong Islamieten Bond, Jong Ambon, Jong Batak. Local periodicals covered the speeches and discussions in report-like narratives, each with a different emphasis and with different heroes, all of them rather low-key and cautious.

Most Malay newspapers mentioned some 1,000 participants on the first day; some suggested that that number dwindled on the second day. Many conversations and discussions in the Congress, the newspapers told their readers, were in Dutch. That should not come as a surprise: the youth that came together in Batavia to discuss past, present and future were Dutch educated.

Dutch scholar H. M. J. Maier of Leiden University wrote that the greatest novelty took place on the second day when the composer Wage Rudolf Supratman played a melody on his violin; only after loud applause and exhortations he recited the text, 'Indonesia, my homeland...', and under more roaring applause he proposed to make it the 'national anthem of Indonesia', even though many leaders thought it too Western and not native enough. He entitled his song, 'Indonesia Raya' – a song that now, decades later, must be sung by Indonesian school children every week in their school compound.

The most important speech was arguably delivered by Muhammad Yamin of Jong Sumatra, entitled 'Unification and Nationalism of Indonesia'.

Yamin said, 'A nation is a soul, a spiritual principle. Two things, which in truth are but one, constitute this soul or spiritual principle. One lies in the past, one in the present. One is the possession in common of a rich legacy of memories; the other is present-day consent. The desire to live together, the will to perpetuate the value of the heritage that one has received in an undivided form'. He talked about Majapahit as the single past of the future Indonesia.

H. M. J. Maier wrote that the meeting could be called a local inter-pretation of Ernest Renan's famous 1882 lecture *Qu'est-ce qu'une nation?* A Malay translation of Renan's speech was circulating among students in Batavia. Yamin also regularly gave out the material for many discussions and polemics. Renan is the only writer Yamin explicitly refers to in his speech, in a quotation that reads like a creative transposition of Renan's words, 'Our love is growing. Of course, our love for the house that we ourselves built is even greater, the house, that is, that we will leave to our descendants as a sacred heritage'.

106

Finally, almost all newspapers make prominent mention of the resolution, unanimously accepted without discussion, in which those present acknowledged the idea of Indonesian unity. The text of the resolution was published in several newspapers:

> We sons and daughters of Indonesia declare to be of one place of birth, the Indonesian land.

> We sons and daughters of Indonesia declare to be of one nation, the Indonesian nation.

> We sons and daughters of Indonesia revere the language of unity, the Indonesian language.

It is a short text, only three sentences. It didn't elaborate the land and sea borders. It didn't talk about religion. It didn't talk about the Islamic sharia. It didn't talk about governmental structure. Perhaps, the speakers understood it was very difficult, if not impossible, to talk about those issues in such a meeting.

But it's important to note that the Javanese speakers had agreed not to make Javanese into Indonesia's national language. What would Indonesia's literature look like if Javanese writers like novelist Pramoedya Ananta Toer, or poet W. S. Rendra and Wiji Thukul, or columnist Goenawan Mohamad wrote in Javanese?

Tjipto Mangoenkoesoemo's idea of using Dutch as the administrative and educational language was gently rebuffed. Dutch schools are famous for their multilingual classes (Dutch, English, French, even German). Perhaps young Indonesian students today would have had a much better command of English if his proposal was accepted.

In Blitar, Wajiman, a cleaning serviceman from nearby Sleman, visited the Sukarno tomb with his wife Sutinem. They had been married for nine years but still had no baby.

'We come here as it is a holy, sacred place. If we ask sincerely, God will grant our wishes', Wajiman told me.

The Sukarno tomb, unsurprisingly, has attracted not only visitors who wanted to learn about the past but also many who wish for wealth, fame, a spouse and power.

Islamic Sharia in the Jakarta Charter

In 1942, Japan invaded Pearl Harbor and occupied Southeast Asia. In Jakarta, it has been recently acknowledged that Sukarno and Mohammad Hatta agreed to cooperate with Japan's war effort. They were given access to speak on the radios. They helped the Japanese to promote paramilitary organisations. It was the first time ever in Java that a ruling government trained thousands of young men to be involved in politics militarily. They later became famous as *pemuda* – young people, mostly men but also many women – who were courageous and eager to sacrifice themselves for independence. The Japanese banned the Dutch language, prompting a wider use of Bahasa Indonesia. Japan also closed Dutch-inherited newspapers, publishing only a few tightly controlled Malay-language ones.

Japan partitioned the Indies for the first time since its unification under Dutch rule. The new political centre was now Saigon, the headquarters of the Southern Area Forces under Field Marshal Terauchi Hisaichi. Sumatra now fell with the Malayan Peninsula under the 25th Army based in Singapore. Java was under the 16th Army based in Jakarta, while Eastern Indonesia was ruled by the Makassar-based Second South Sea Squadron of the Navy. The Japanese had a war to conduct and ruled the region militarily. Southeast Asia was made to provide resource-poor Japan with the raw materials it needed to wage war.

On 7 September 1944 Japanese Prime Minister Koiso Kuniaki announced in Tokyo that Japan was 'prepared to acknowledge the Indies' independence in the future'. The announcement was greeted with fanfare in the Japanese-controlled media in Indonesia. Sukarno spoke over the radio about his stirred emotions, urging the people to fight for life or death besides 'Dai Nippon'.

In Makassar, the announcement led to a tentative proposal to set up an equivalent to the Sukarno-led Djawa Hokokai, to be called Kominkai, and chaired by Minahasan politician Sam Ratu Langie. Shibata Yaichiro, the new Navy commander in Makassar, abandoned the conservative de-politicisation policy of his predecessors towards the more mobilisational approach like what the Japanese Army had organised in Java.

In March 1945, the Japanese Army set up a committee, the Investigating Committee for Indonesian Independence (*Badan Penyelidik Usaha Persiapan Kemerdekaan Indonesia*, BPUPKI), to prepare Indonesia's self-governance. It had 70 members including eight Japanese officials. It was to discuss the Indonesian constitution, the national language, and related issues. Indonesian textbooks usually say it had only 62 members, omitting the presence of the eight Japanese members, as if trying to create the impression that Indonesia's independence was a totally local initiative.

In its first meeting, committee chairman Radjiman Wediodiningrat put a question to its members: 'What was the philosophical basis to be used for a free Indonesia?'

A long debate soon emerged: Islam or secularism?

Muslim politicians Bagoes Hadikoesoemo of Muhammadiyah and Wahid Hasjim of Nahdlatul Ulama advocated an Islamic state. Strongly opposed to them were bureaucrats Hoesein Djajadiningrat and Wongsonegoro, as well as the Ambonese Christian politician Johannes Latuharhary. In between were many well-known figures, including Sukarno, Agoes Salim and Soepomo.

Sukarno proposed five values as ideal 'principles of the state', calling it Pancasila and including a vaguely religious value of Theism.

They made a compromise through an informal subcommittee of nine. It didn't make Islam the state religion but could be interpreted to mean the state had a special responsibility to uphold the so-called Islamic sharia. Just after the phrase on Monotheism, the draft now contained seven words (in Indonesian): *'With the obligation for adherents of Islam to practise Islamic sharia'*.

The work of the subcommittee was known as a 'gentleman's agreement' but later acquired the label Jakarta Charter. Heated debate in subsequent plenary sessions, again on Islam versus secularism, ended in exhausted acquiescence. Wahid Hasjim's further suggestion that the President should constitutionally be a Muslim was even accepted.

What kind of state structure would be adopted?

Jurist Soepomo, a prominent member of the BPUPKI, proposed a unitarian state. His idea basically laid out a centralised state, whose capital was Jakarta. Soepomo's inspiration was Adolf Hitler's Germany. Soepomo believed the protection of individual rights might disrupt the state management.

Another question was about Indonesia's territories. What would be the boundaries of independent Indonesia?

Muhammad Yamin, the voluble politician from Sumatra, theorised about three Indonesias: Indonesia Part I was the Srividjaja kingdom in Sumatra in the seventh century. Majapahit was Indonesia Part II.

'Today we're talking about Indonesia Part III', he claimed, describing in length the territories of these ancient kingdoms. He suggested that the new republic or Indonesia Part III should include southern Thailand, Sarawak and Sabah in northern Borneo, the Malay Peninsula, Portuguese Timor, and all the pre-war territories of the Indies, which included West Papua.

Sukarno backed Yamin's proposal, saying that Indonesia should include southern Thailand and the Malay Peninsula. Sukarno claimed Indonesia would not be a strong nation if it was to control only one side of the Malacca Strait: Sumatra. Indonesia should also include the northern side of the Malacca Strait: the Malay Peninsula and Singapore.

Others suggested that Indonesia should be only the pre-war Indies. Another camp thought Papua should probably be included, even though the Melanesian was racially very different, with invitations extended to northern Borneo and Timor.

Mohammad Hatta said, 'I'm worried to learn the arguments on Papua. If the logic is to be continued, we will eventually want the Solomon Islands too and later half of the Pacific Ocean. We have to be careful with the German theory, *Kultur und Boden*, that Mr Muhammad Yamin used. It's very dangerous as it's the base of German imperialism'.

Finally, the 70 members voted. Yamin's idea won the majority with 39 votes. The realistic camp, including Hatta, received the least with 19 votes.

The victorious Allies, which soon controlled Southeast Asia, would disagree with such a proposal. London and Washington thought that the former British colony in the Malay Peninsula and northern Borneo should wait a little bit longer to have independence. London was obviously much stronger than The Hague.

On 7 August 1945, the Japanese regional headquarters in Saigon announced a smaller committee, the Indonesian Independence Preparation Committee (*Panitia Persiapan Kemerdekaan Indonesia*, PPKI). The smaller committee had 21 members. In formal terms, the PPKI contained respectively twelve, four and five representatives of the territories under the 16th Army, the 25th Army and the Navy's Second South Sea Squadron:

- Java had 12 representatives including Sukarno and Radjiman Wediodiningrat as well as ethnic Chinese leader Yap Tjwan Bing;
- Sumatra had four representatives including Mohammad Hatta;
- The Navy representatives in Eastern Indonesia had five representatives including Kalimantan politician A. A. Hamidhan, two Sulawesi representatives Andi Pangerang Petta Rani and Sam Ratu Langie, the Lesser Sunda with only I. G. Ketoet Poedja of Bali, and the Moluccas' Johannes Latuharhary.

The Japanese Navy accordingly sent its representatives to Jakarta to be involved in the independence preparation. The Navy imagined a federal structure in which Eastern Indonesia would be governed by a coalition of the traditional aristocracy and a modern intellectual elite. It was different from the structure discussed in Java and Sumatra.

On their way to Jakarta, these representatives stopped in Surabaya on 9 August for a one-week consultation with the Navy officers. Intense Allied bombing raids sent their meeting into a shelter from time to time.

The Navy delegation obviously came too late in Jakarta. The BPUPKI, drawn only from Java, had already made fundamental decisions which were to be simply presented for ratification to the smaller but more widely representative PPKI.

BPUPKI members had debated and agreed with a draft constitution. BPUPKI had agreed with the state structure: it was to be a unitary republic. BPUPKI had agreed to give Islam a prominent place with the Jakarta Charter. BPUPKI had elected a president and vice-president.

Johannes Latuharhary, who lived in Jakarta, was the only member of the five-strong Eastern Indonesia delegation to have attended the BPUPKI sessions. He had protested unsuccessfully against the enthusiastic unitarism of most participants, and even more so, against the inclusion of the Islamic sharia.

The Navy-based Eastern Indonesia group had no difficulty agreeing that Indonesian citizens should have equal rights. Islam should not have a special status. Their argument was that the Jakarta Charter would 'threaten national unity' by marginalising adherents of other religions especially the Christians and Hindus in Eastern Indonesia. Behind that argument probably lay a familiar aristocratic mistrust of claims of religious homogeneity over which they had no control.

The group was aware of the strong unitarist feelings in nationalist circles in Java. They agreed not to challenge that directly, but rather to lobby for a high degree of autonomy for the regions: Kalimantan, Sulawesi, the Moluccas and the Lesser Sunda archipelago. They also agreed that in this time of war it was best for Eastern Indonesia to remain under its own Japanese Navy administration, which would then deal with the Jakarta-based Japanese Army government.

In a bid to prepare the independence declaration, the Japanese had hurriedly flown Sukarno, Mohammad Hatta and Radjiman Wediodiningrat to Saigon.

On 11 August 1945, Terauchi Hisaichi, the Japanese top commander of Southeast Asia, met his Indonesian guests in his villa in Dalat, near Saigon. Terauchi promised an immediate transfer of independence. Sukarno and Hatta were also inducted as chairman and deputy of the PPKI. They were told to coordinate closely with the Japanese Liaison Guidance Committee for the Preparation of Independence. Sukarno believed that the date for Indonesia's independence was 24 August. Hatta said he was 'thrilled' to know that Indonesia would soon gain independence.

On their way back to Jakarta, they stopped in Taiping in Perak in the Malay Peninsula, meeting two Malay politicians, Burhanuddin Helmi and Ibrahim Yaacob. The agenda was the unification of Malaya and Indonesia to form the 'Greater Indonesia' – a plan that never materialises.

Arriving in Jakarta on 14 August 1945, Sukarno, Hatta and Radjiman faced a new reality: news of the Japanese surrender began to emerge. Also, that day, the Navy delegation arrived in Jakarta and was met by Ratu Langie's former boss Rear Admiral Tadashi Maeda, who appeared enthusiastic about the prospect of Indonesia's independence.

At around 4 o'clock in the afternoon, Sutan Sjahrir, a Sumatran intellectual, met his long-time friend Mohammad Hatta, telling Hatta in his house that the Japanese had surrendered to the Allies.

Sjahrir listened to uncensored radio broadcasts from San Francisco. Japan had reportedly accepted the Allies' ultimatum for unconditional surrender following the nuclear bombing of Hiroshima and Nagasaki.

Hatta was 'very surprised' to hear the news.

Sjahrir urged Hatta to declare independence unilaterally, saying that they must grab power in the ongoing political vacuum.

Hatta responded that he couldn't do it without Sukarno. Hatta and Sjahrir immediately went out to see and to persuade Sukarno.

Sukarno declined, saying it was better to wait for an official explanation and to avoid a bloodbath. Anyway, the Japanese Army was still in total control of Jakarta.

Sjahrir became furious, calling Sukarno 'a transvestite'.

This crisis was the situation faced by the Eastern Indonesia delegates. An effective partitioning of the archipelago during the Japanese occupation had merely deepened pre-war divisions between the Outer Islands and Java.

Java had an undercurrent of populism largely absent in the more stable Outer Islands. The Outer Islanders were not immediately made welcome in the whirl of events around Sukarno and Hatta, and sought out one another for advice.

On 15 August news spread that the war was over. Radios were still censored. Sukarno and Hatta spent the whole day finding a Japanese official who could confirm the Japanese surrender. Admiral Maeda finally confirmed the radio report but told them to wait for an official explanation.

Sutan Sjahrir became reckless. He had prepared an independence text widely distributed among his underground network.

Early in the morning of 16 August, Sukarno and Hatta were abducted by unknown elements. Delegates were told the PPKI's work was imperilled. Some speculated they were arrested by the Japanese military police or even murdered. It turned out that Indonesian youth activists had kidnapped the duet, pressuring them to declare independence in a farm house in Rengasdengklok, a village on the outskirt of Jakarta. Sukarno declined the offer. They were released later in the afternoon after Admiral Maeda had sent a delegation to pick them up. Sukarno believed Sjahrir was behind the kidnapping.

In Jakarta, Sam Ratu Langie was the effective leader of the Eastern Indonesia delegates. According to Gerry van Klinken, in his book on Christians in Indonesia, Ratu Langie contacted Dr Mohammad Amir, a PPKI member from Sumatra, and the Indo-European P. F. Dahler, both former *Penindjauan* weekly colleagues with whom Ratu Langie worked in the 1930s. Dahler was involved in the BPUPKI. Dr Amir was an ally in the federal idea, while Dahler represented Ratu Langie's connection with the slightly elitist mestizo nationalism of Indische Party's founder Douwes Dekker.

Ratu Langie tried horse-trading behind the scenes by means of proxies. His daughter, Emillie Agustine Ratu Langie, brought him in contact with a group of medical student activists in Jakarta. At a dinner hosted by BPUPKI member Alexander A. Maramis, also a Minahasan, Ratu Langie took Maramis to task for agreeing to the Jakarta Charter which included the Islamic-sharia phrase.

Ratu Langie thought it was to create serious consequences: 'Alex, this is a serious matter, you can't just ignore it'.

According to Oscar Eduard Engelen, a Minahasan medical student who attended the dinner, 'We, the students, never skipped those opportunities to have a feast'. That night more than a dozen Sulawesi students, both Bugis and Minahasan, joined the dinner. Ratu Langie promised the students he would do what he could.

Meanwhile most PPKI members were kept uninformed about what to do while Admiral Tadashi Maeda, several Japanese Army officers, Sukarno and Hatta worked out a compromise. The 16th Army banned Hotel Des Indes, where the delegates stayed, from hosting any meetings. But Maeda persuaded an Army general to let the PPKI members have a 'coffee drinking gathering' that night in his official residence. The Japanese general agreed if the Army *officially* didn't know about the plan to declare independence.

Finally, at night on 16 August, all 21 PPKI members gathered in Tadashi Maeda's residence. They agreed to declare independence in the morning. Sukarno proposed that all 21 members sign the declaration, but others disagreed. They didn't want to create the impression that the independence declaration was a Japanese-sponsored declaration, with or without the PPKI name. They assigned Sukarno and Hatta to sign the declaration 'in the name of the nation of Indonesia'. The meeting ended at 5.00 am on 17 August.

Five hours later, in the morning of 17 August 1945, Sukarno and Hatta read out a brief statement, proclaiming Indonesia's independence outside Sukarno's house – a few blocks from Maeda's residence. The statement didn't confront the Allied Forces, which expected a Dutch Indies status quo, but also didn't go for a legal transfer of authority from the Japanese. They told the small audience that the PPKI will deliberate other matters the following day. The activists soon used telephone and telegraph systems to spread the news (radios and newspapers were still under the Army control). They managed to send the news to Bandung and Yogyakarta. The students moved along the Jakarta streets, putting up banners and scrawling graffiti in English on the walls. The Malay word 'Merdeka' or 'Freedom' was soon widely used in urban areas throughout Java.

'We fight for freedom, sovereignty and independence'.
'Go to hell, imperialism! Merdeka!'
'We are free, Indonesia is free'.
'Indonesia never again the life blood of any nation'.

Reinstating Pancasila

At beautiful Hotel des Indes, the horsetrading began some hours later. O. E. Engelen, who was involved in the dinner discussion at Alexander Maramis' house, and his Acehnese colleague, Teuku Tadjoeoedin, visited Hotel des Indes to meet the Outer Islands delegation. They first talked to I. G. Ketoet Poedja of Bali about the religious aspects of the draft constitution. Other delegates were in the corridor.

Andi Pangerang of Sulawesi, himself an aristocrat in the Bone sultanate, said the new state should be separated from Islam.

Ratu Langie joined them and said, 'Eastern Indonesia will make its move'.

Later that day Ratu Langie and some delegates – Johannes Latuharhary, I. G. Ketoet Poedja and Andi Pangerang, plus two politicians from Kalimantan – visited Engelen's dormitory and asked the students to approach Mohammad Hatta and tell him that if this draft constitution was not changed, Eastern Indonesia would not join in Indonesia. They talked about the modern concept of a nation-state, separating state affairs from any religion.

These students came from their dormitory on Prapatan Street in Jakarta. It is one of three influential Dutch-speaking dormitories. These medical students was headed by Eri Soedewo, a Javanese student. Its political section was headed by Teuku Tadjoeoedin whose buddies included Piet Mamahit, a Minahasan, and Moeljo Hastrodipoero, a Javanese. The students also had a Chinese Jakartan, named Tan Tjeng Bok, to help organise their security. O. E. Engelen himself oversaw propaganda.

The group eventually asked three students – Piet Mamahit, Moeljo Hastrodipoero and Tan Tjeng Bok – to meet Mohammad Hatta. They possibly requested Nishijima Shigetada, an assistant to Admiral Maeda, to make an appointment with Hatta, saying they had a message from Ratu Langie.

In the evening of 17 August, Hatta met them and took the message seriously enough to convey it to Sukarno. The three students managed to persuade Hatta that the Islamic sharia provision would relegate minorities to be second-class citizens.

Separately, Sukarno had already been told by Mohammad Hasan of Aceh that Ratu Langie had said Eastern Indonesia would not be happy to join Indonesia unless the draft constitution was changed.

The following morning on 18 August, Hatta, himself not in favour of a sacralised state based on Islam, met with four Muslim politicians to discuss the issue: Mohammad Hasan, Bagoes Hadikoesoemo, Wahid Hasjim and Kasman Singodimedjo.

Hatta was a devout Muslim who believed firmly that Islam could help Indonesia to greater social justice. But his belief in Europe's secularism was also deeply rooted. This reputation helped Hatta to persuade the Muslim politicians.

Mohammad Hasan stressed the importance of national unity. It was imperative not to drive important Christian minorities – Batak, Minahasan and Ambonese – into the arms of the returning Dutch by provisions that, at least one of which, appeared to relegate Christians to second-class citizenship.

The Muslims agreed to excise the Islamic sharia section.

Sukarno announced the excision of the Islamic provisions in the plenary session and was met with applause.

Wahid Hasjim asked that a ministry of religious affairs be established, replacing the sharia provision. He said that it would be 'a bridge' connecting the state and Islam.

Johannes Latuharhary rejected the idea, but Sukarno and Hatta accepted the proposal.

Sukarno also presented the plenary session with what he called a 'lightning constitution', a 'revolutionary constitution', asking the PPKI to ratify it in only one day's deliberations. Mohammad Amir and Ratu Langie were the first to jump into the debate. Realising the terms 'federalism' and 'commonwealth' had already been ruled out, both argued for 'the greatest possible deconcentration' of powers to the Outer Islands. But most Javanese members, including Sukarno, chose centralised governance, fearing that a federalist state might work in favour of the Dutch's divide-and-rule tactics. They said the unitarian status fits for the revolution. Ratu Langie did not get what he wanted.

Hatta's excision of the provisions for Islamic law for Muslims, and for a Muslim president, was certainly irregular. Hatta died 35 years later in 1980 without revealing the identities of the 'Navy officials who represented Eastern Indonesia'. Hatta probably hid Sam Ratu Langie's name, assuming it might create unnecessary reaction among Islamists in Java and Sumatra. Ratu Langie died much earlier, in 1949, also without writing about his group's involvement in excising the Islamic sharia component.

* * *

The Indonesia revolution began when it became clear that the Dutch Kingdom intended to retake its colonies. Dutch troops returned to Java and other islands along with the British-led Allied Forces. They quickly took over power from the Japanese military. *Pemuda* organisations in Java prepared themselves to defend their newly declared independence. They also sent delegates to the Outer Islands, trying to campaign for Indonesia's independence. In Java and Sumatra, fighting broke out in many places but also violence and looting against minorities, who were considered to get special treatment during the Dutch period. Many Minahasan and Ambonese living in Java were harassed. Many Chinese and Eurasian properties were looted.

In November 1945, Sutan Sjahrir published a pamphlet entitled *Perdjuangan Kita* (Our Struggle). It was basically a bitter inventory of the darkest features of the Japanese occupation: forced labour, compulsory rice deliveries, lawlessness, corruption and brutality. It particularly focused on what Sjahrir felt to be the two most permanently dangerous consequences of the war years. First, the rise of a considerable group of nationalists whom he regarded as having sold out to the Japanese. Second, what he saw as the corruption of Indonesian youth by the militarist and fascist attitudes inculcated through various Japanese-sponsored organisations. This corruption had resulted in atrocities and terrorism against Dutchmen, Eurasians and Indonesian minorities such as Christian Ambonese and Minahasan.

It laid out the problems facing 'our struggle' in creating a 'democratic revolution'.

Sjahrir wrote, 'Our revolution must be led by revolutionary, democratic groups and not by nationalist groups, which have let themselves be used as servants of the Fascists, whether the Dutch-colonial Fascists, or Japanese military Fascists. Those who have sold themselves and their honor to Japanese fascism must be thrown out of the leadership of our revolution – that is those who have ever worked for the Japanese propaganda organisations, the secret police, in general, everyone who has worked for the Japanese fifth column. All these persons must be considered as traitors to our struggle and be distinguished from the common laborers, who have had to work for the enemy to support themselves. These collaborators must be considered as our own fascists, as the running dogs and tools of the Japanese Fascism'.

Sjahrir's thoughts were widely praised. Sjahrir was seen to be a reliable Europe-educated intellectual and an anti-fascist activist. The Allies considered Sjahrir to be the right person to negotiate with. He also decided to join Sukarno and Hatta, becoming Indonesia's first prime minister and starting negotiations with the Dutch under the mediation of the Allies. In January 1946, fearing possible assassination by Dutch troops, Hatta and Sukarno moved to Yogyakarta, leaving Sjahrir to head negotiations with the Dutch in Jakarta.

It was a revolutionary period. Sjahrir understood very well that the Dutch controlled all islands in Indonesia but not all parts, especially not Yogyakarta, in Java.

Others didn't see it that way. Tan Malaka, a Sumatran activist and a former Communist International representative to Southeast Asia, and more importantly, a living legend in Java, unexpectedly appeared in public and offered a resistance solution. He published his pamphlet, *Moeslihat* (Strategy), which basically asked for '100% Merdeka' through a revolutionary resistance like what Ho Chi Minh did in Vietnam against the returning French power.

Tan Malaka argued that the real aim of the struggle is freedom. He insisted that 'provided all the conditions of resistance are understood and carried out, 70 million human beings cannot be colonized once again'. The Dutch also could not conceivably muster more than 200,000 troops, while the resistance could mobilise many times that figure. Geographical conditions were clearly in favour of Indonesia. Her natural fertility and tropical climate meant that the resistance could easily obtain food and the little clothing it required. He stressed that the victorious winnings of World War II was divided between the Anglo-Saxons and the Soviet Union. The resistance should use these divisions.

Both Sjahrir and Tan Malaka had their respective supporters. Sjahrir asked how a ragtag of militias could win over a military power that had just won World War II. He also understood that the Dutch were not at all discredited in the Outer Islands. Many areas were suspicious of a Java-centric Indonesia.

Benedict Anderson wrote in *Java in a Time of Revolution* that from a larger perspective, Jakarta and Yogyakarta came to symbolise the opposition between diplomacy and resistance. 'If one lived in occupied, cosmopolitan Jakarta, it was hard not to become convinced of the imperative need for diplomacy. But if one lived in unoccupied, traditional Yogyakarta, where scarcely a white face was to be seen, how could one not believe, watching and experiencing the city's turbulent vitality, that resistance was possible and necessary?'

The division was soon mixed up in the lawlessness that evolved in Java. Sukarno ordered dozens of opposition leaders arrested, including Tan Malaka in March 1946. He remained imprisoned until September 1948. Upon his release, he fled Yogyakarta for rural East Java, where he hoped he would be protected by anti-Republican guerilla forces. He was captured by Republican forces and executed in February 1949.

In November 1949, the negotiation with the Dutch over the structure of Indonesia was finally agreed. It was a federation consisting of seven states (including Republic of Indonesia in Yogyakarta) and nine territories. It was organised under Bijeenkomst Federaale Overleg, or the Federal Consultative Assembly, headed by Sultan Hamid of West Kalimantan and I Gde Anak Agoeng Gde Agoeng of East Indonesia State. The Queen of the Netherlands would be the symbolic Head of State while Sukarno and Hatta would continue as President and Vice-President of the new federation called the Republic of the United States of Indonesia.

On 27 December 1949, the Dutch transferred its legal sovereignty to the new republic. Mohammad Hatta received the handover from Queen Juliana and Prime Minister Willem Drees in The Hague. In Jakarta, Javanese Sultan Hamengku Buwono IX did a similar ceremony with Dutch representative A. V. J. Lovink. Benedict Anderson concluded that the Indonesian revolution never became more than a 'national revolution'.

It ended when Sukarno moved into the palace where Dutch governors-general had ruled for generations.

The 1965–66 Massacres of the Communists

The bloodiest violence in Indonesia's history began on 30 September 1965, when a force of three battalions moved to kidnap several Army generals in Jakarta. They also took over several key points in Jakarta, including the telecommunication building, Jakarta's main radio station and areas around the presidential palace.

It began at 7:15 in the morning of 1 October 1965 when Jakarta radio broadcast an announcement, reporting 'a military move with the Army in Jakarta'. A body styling itself the September 30th Movement, led by Lieutenant Colonel Untung, had arrested the so-called 'Council of Generals' and seized important installations in Jakarta and Yogyakarta.

The September 30th Movement claimed to place President Sukarno and other leaders under its protection. It said that these actions were taken to prevent a planned coup by the Council of Generals, sponsored by the CIA and scheduled to take place prior to 5 October. Finally, it denounced 'power-mad generals and officers who have neglected the lot of their men, and lived...in luxury, led a gay life, insulted our women and wasted the government funds'.

These soldiers did not arrest but killed six generals, including Army chief General Ahmad Yani, and brought their bodies to Halim military airport in Jakarta.

At 9.00 am, President Sukarno arrived at Halim airport, but he did not issue a clear statement of support for the movement. Two other prominent figures were already there: Air Force Commander Marshall Omar Dhani, who gave the coup leaders permission to operate out of Halim, and D. N. Aidit, the PKI chairman, who had allegedly planned the movement along with those officers.

D. N. Aidit was the top decision maker of this movement. According to Taomo Zhou, a Chinese scholar who researched using declassified documents at the Chinese Foreign Ministry, Aidit met China's Chairman Mao Zedong in Beijing in August 1965. Aidit was reportedly told by his Chinese comrades that the Indonesian Army might take over power from ailing President Sukarno. He told Mao that he had developed plans to prevent the Army takeover when Sukarno was to die. It was not clear whether Mao and the other Chinese leaders agreed with Aidit's plans.

That morning, Major General Suharto, then the commander of the Army Strategic Reserve, backed by Defence Minister General A. H. Nasution, was able to quickly mobilise the necessary units to take control of Jakarta. Nasution was shocked to learn that his small daughter and his adjutant were gunned down in his failed kidnap attempt.

President Sukarno issued an order to appoint Major General Pranoto Reksosamudro, perhaps the most Sukarno-minded of the top officers, to be the acting Army chief. Suharto ignored the appointment. He sent word to the military airport that he was in command and intended to assault them unless the September 30th Movement abandoned it. At Halim airbase, attempts were apparently made to persuade Sukarno to accompany the rebels to Central Java, to make a stand there against the Army. Sukarno rejected the proposal and at about 10.00 pm departed by car for his palace in Bogor. D. N. Aidit flew to Central Java at about midnight in an Air Force plane shared with Omar Dhani.

The Army immediately blamed the Indonesian Communist Party, saying that PKI chairman D. N. Aidit and other PKI top leaders had swayed Lieutenant Colonel Untung and other officers to kidnap the generals to take power from ailing President Sukarno. The Army accused Aidit of using the PKI Special Bureau to infiltrate those military units. It was headed by two men known as 'Pono' and 'Sjam' or Kamaruzzaman.

In his trial, Kamaruzzaman admitted that D. N. Aidit was responsible for the entire direction of the coup, even down to writing the decree concerning the establishment of the Revolution Council and its composition that were broadcast over Jakarta radio.

In his defence speech to the court that sentenced him to death in 1967, PKI secretary general Sudisman admitted that D. N. Aidit and some other leaders were involved in the coup attempt. They feared that the Army was intending to move against the PKI. He acknowledged that it was 'adventurous' and accepted full blame for it.

But a lot of questions remained unanswered. The Suharto regime issued propaganda to blame the whole communist party, ethnic Chinese, the leftists and many other actors while conducting a witch-hunt for more than three decades. Aidit expected President Sukarno to protect the communists but Sukarno did not do that.

New facts only began to emerge after the fall of President Suharto in May 1998.

Colonel Abdul Latief, one of the coup leaders, revealed several critical facts upon his release from prison. The evening before the coup Latief went to an Army hospital where Suharto was with his small ill son, Tommy, to alert him to the intended move against Nasution and the six generals. Suharto took no action. 'I think it is clear Pak Harto used the opportunity of the arrest of the generals to blame the PKI and reach power'.

In his essay *Petrus Dadi Ratu*, Benedict Anderson questioned, 'Why were the two generals who commanded directly all the troops in Jakarta (Suharto and Umar Wirahadikusumah) not 'taken care of' by the September 30th Movement, if its members really intended a coup to overthrow the government, as the military prosecutor charged? The reason is that the two men were regarded as friends'.

It was also revealed that months before 30 September 1965, Ali Moertopo, then Suharto's intelligence chief, was pursuing a foreign policy kept secret from both President Sukarno and General Ahmad Yani. Ali exploited the contacts of former rebels in Sumatra and Sulawesi to make clandestine connections with the leadership of Malaysia and Singapore, then enemy countries, as well as with the United States. Benny Moerdani, another Suharto advisor, worked to further this connection from Bangkok, where he was disguised as an employee of Garuda Indonesia's airline office. It was at the height of the Vietnam War when the three countries – the United States, Malaysia and Singapore – obviously preferred to work with these officers than the leftist Sukarno government.

In 2017, declassified US State Department documents – a cache of almost 30,000 pages of declassified embassy paperwork spanning from 1965 to 1968 – show that American officials approvingly reported that Army units and Muslim groups were working together to arrest or to hack and club to death at least 1,500 suspected PKI sympathisers per day, sometimes parading their heads on sticks. This enthusiasm for the bloodbath reflected the US and the Indonesian Army's strategic and political interests.

Jess Melvin has written that the Army was using the anti-Malaysia structure to immediately launch the 1965–66 massacre. The Army had trained civilian militia, ranging from gangsters to members of Muslim organisations, under that separate structure. When Suharto gave the order, their response was swift and catastrophic.

Hundreds of thousands of members of PKI-affiliated groups, who had nothing to do with the September 1965 movement, spent years in prison, without clear charges against them, and without any due process of law. They suffered excruciating torture on a routine basis. To say nothing of uncountable losses of property to theft and looting, casual, everyday rapes, and social ostracism for years, not only for former prisoners themselves, but for their wives and widows, children, and kinfolk in the widest sense. There were stories about wives who slept with soldiers who guarded their husbands. Dozens of intellectuals and activists were exiled to Buru island in the Moluccas archipelago. Journalists were not spared. Adam Schwarz, in *A Nation in Waiting*, writes: 'In 1965–1966, about a quarter of Indonesia's 160 or so newspapers were shut down because of alleged communist links and hundreds of journalists were arrested'.

When General Suharto officially took over power from Sukarno in 1968, Suharto began to enhance what Sukarno had started, but in a more vicious way. He changed the school curriculum, blaming the communists for the September movement but not adding a single line about the mass murders. In 1971, Suharto introduced a new spelling for Bahasa Indonesia, bringing in a lot of euphemism. Many new words were instituted with twisted means. For example, the word '*diamankan*' literally means 'to be secured' but in fact, it mostly meant someone 'to be detained' – mostly also to be tortured, and in many cases, also be killed.

Joshua Oppenheimer portrayed these massacres in his two award-winning films – *The Act of Killing* (2012) and *The Look of Silence* (2014). The films discussed not only extrajudicial killings but also forced labour, disappearances, gang rape, arbitrary detention, discrimination, repression of expression, sexual abuses, media censorship and, obviously, military dictatorship in Indonesia. Oppenheimer made them as powerful reminders of the culture of impunity and the lack of rule of law continuing to weigh on Indonesia. Impunity expresses itself in a systematic failure to hold accountable members of the security forces and Islamist militants who commit abuses against religious and gender minorities across Indonesia.

In the 1970s, when the Suharto regime became stabilised and won the support of the Western governments, he prioritised economic development, building infrastructure and introducing new approaches to mass agriculture.

Suharto imposed severe legislative restrictions on freedom of speech, assembly and association. The Anti-Subversion Law is one of the most repressive measures used by his government to imprison critics. The regime closed dozens of newspapers and imprisoned many journalists, creating an atmosphere of fear and consequently self-censorship.

'In 1946, when Sutan Sjahrir was writing his pamphlet, it was as if Sjahrir was predicting the arrival of the New Order, a fascist regime whose leaders are Japanese-trained militias, exactly someone like Suharto', said Rahman Tolleng of the Forum for Democracy, a dissident group during the Suharto rule.

Suharto systematically took control of as much as he could into his own hands. He pressured all political parties to merge into two, ensuring his own party, Golkar, would always win the pseudo general election that he organised every five years; it was always won by him – six consecutive times!

His cronies were granted monopolies. He carefully balanced his generals, pitting one officer against another. He set up foundations to collect levies for his own purposes. Later when his six children became adults, he recruited them to run super-rich foundations and to have their own businesses.

He also targeted the Chinese minority. Laws passed at the time made it illegal to teach Chinese languages in schools. The military-backed government also closed all ethnic Chinese organisations. Mandarin and other Chinese languages were banned. Chinese-language publications couldn't be printed or imported into Indonesia. The military regime also prohibited celebrating Chinese festivals in public spaces. It changed the terms 'Tiongkok' (China) and 'Tionghoa' (Chinese) to the derogatory term *Cina* (for both China and Chinese). Suharto also 'restructured' Chinese temples, changing them into Buddhist temples. The Chinese couldn't have their native religions: Confucianism, Taoism. They couldn't have their Chinese names. They were not allowed to join civil and military service. Ironically, many Chinese businessmen, closely related to the regime, became extremely rich. It was a divide-and-rule strategy, using the politically weak Chinese to work on the economic side of his regime.

A Village Near Jakarta

Among people who live in overcrowded and polluted Jakarta, Puncak may be the most popular weekend destination. It's a mountainous area only about a three-hour drive from the city. It has fresh air and it's green.

I also like to visit Puncak, bringing my family. Puncak has a little known villa located in Sirnagalih village. It has a grass lawn, a swimming pool, a tennis court and nine two-storey bungalows. It's called the Tempo House – a villa that belongs to the Jakarta-based Tempo media group.

It's a historic villa for the struggle of press freedom in Indonesia.

In June 1994 President Suharto banned three news weeklies: *Detik, Editor* and *Tempo*. Thousands of journalists, human rights lawyers, artists and students protested the ban, demanding the Suharto government reissue their publishing licences. Suharto's men accused the three weeklies of repeatedly breaching the press law. Sadly, the government-sanctioned Indonesian Journalists Association stated that it 'understood the banning'.

Street protests soon turned bloody. Indonesian soldiers dispersed the protests in Jakarta using rattan sticks and arresting many protesters.

I was among those angry reporters, helping to organise the street protests but knowing that it was not enough. Those young journalists decided that it was high time to be confrontational in fighting for press freedom in Indonesia. We knew very well that it was illegal to establish a journalist union. The Suharto regime only sanctioned a single organisation for each profession: farmers, teachers, workers, doctors, engineers and journalists too.

Another handicap. The government practically monitored all public spaces in Jakarta. We needed a safe place to discuss this plan. Goenawan Mohamad, then the editor of *Tempo*, let us use the Sirnagalih villa.

More than 100 journalists eventually went to the villa, having a one-night deliberation. On 7 August 1994, 57 journalists and writers declared the establishment of the Alliance of Independent Journalists in a statement called the Sirnagalih Declaration.

The Declaration stated that the signatories will fight for press freedom and the welfare of journalists. In Sundanese, the name of that village was coined from the words 'sirna' (fade away) and 'galih' (body). These journalists, mostly in their thirties, pledged to leave their bodily needs and to fight for press freedom.

The Alliance soon established branches in more than a dozen cities nationwide. It published a monthly magazine with stories that mainstream media would not publish. These journalists obviously disregarded the licensing regulation. In a few months, some members and a printer were arrested and sentenced to prison terms. This prompted the group to work underground, moving our office into some secret locations. We began to use pseudo names and codes.

Goenawan Mohamad thought that another group was needed, asking some journalists, including me, to set up the Institute for the Studies on Free Flow of Information. It was to organise media research, to have public discussions on democracy, to publish books and to support the alliance. 'The second organisation should be legal so that we could raise money, but we should use the money to support press freedom', he said.

Meanwhile, this opposition against Suharto was itself challenged. An opposition party, a much weakened nationalist group that Sukarno established in 1927, elected his eldest daughter, Megawati Sukarnoputri, to be their chairperson. Megawati consolidated the Indonesian Democratic Party, expecting to get more votes in the 1997 election.

But Suharto considered her move to be a threat and ordered the military to crack down on them. In a textbook Suharto move, the military appointed a puppet politician to challenge Megawati's leadership, organising a 1996 bogus congress in Medan, North Sumatra, unseating her and installing that politician to be the party boss. Megawati's camp, however, resisted, controlling more party branches and their headquarters in Jakarta. It was a difficult situation.

In June 1996, the Indonesian Armed Forces invited around 40 newspaper and television executives to have lunch. Military spokesman Brigadier General Amir Syarifudin asked the editors 'not to exaggerate' their coverage on Megawati. He asked the editors not to use the words 'to unseat' and 'to topple' in their reporting, suggesting the editors use the name 'Megawati Kiemas' – the surname of her husband – rather than 'Megawati Sukarnoputri' after her father. He also asked the editors 'to defend the dignity of the government', denying earlier media reports that the military was behind the Medan congress.

It was a sign that the military was going to use force to finish her faction. On 27 July 1996, the military deployed hundreds of thugs and soldiers to take over the party head office in Jakarta. Dozens of people died in the melee. Megawati moved the party businesses to her own spacious house in southern Jakarta.

Goenawan Mohamad, who admired the philosopher Albert Camus, who joined the French resistance during World War II and published an underground newspaper, suggested his peers set up an underground media operation. It should operate like a news service, having a network and paying their reporters.

A question emerged. What should we prioritise? Democracy or press freedom? We unfortunately did not have the luxury to focus on both challenges. But we knew that censorship, intimidation, harassment and media bans were nothing new in Indonesia. These measures dated back to at least 1745 when the Dutch ruler closed the *Bataviasche Nouvelles*, the first newspaper in Java. Hundreds, if not thousands, of newspapers have been closed by the Dutch, the Japanese, the Sukarno and the Suharto regimes. In Indonesia, self-censorship has become a ritual. We chose press freedom, using our network to publish not only uncensored stories but also to try to be as accurate as possible.

These underground journalists knew that their first duty was to respect the truth, to defend the principles of freedom in honest collection and publication of news, and to honour the right of fair comment and criticism.

The publications on national news, East Timor, Aceh, Papua and so on had different names and consistently provided daily news reports, initially using fax machines, photocopiers and later the internet. We later learned that those stories were printed and faxed widely. Once a lecturer at Duta Wacana Christian University in Yogyakarta was arrested. He was accused of distributing electronic mail messages relating to the July 1996 riots.

A George Washington University media historian, Janet Steele, wrote about this underground media in her book *Wars Within: The Story of Tempo, an Independent Magazine in Soeharto's Indonesia*, calling this network 'a ghost operation'. A reviewer elaborated: 'It's like a ghost. Mysterious. Even among fellow activists, many did not know where it was'.

But it was growing rapidly. I remember one evening I signed payments to 110 people. I did not realise that it was employing that many staff: full-time and part-time. The network ended up managing six wire services: politics, economy, analysis, East Timor, West Papua and Aceh – the three provinces that wanted to secede from Indonesia. Our favourite was the seventh one: political jokes. The main victim was indeed Suharto.

In July 1997, the Asian economic crisis hit Thailand, South Korea and Indonesia. The rupiah lost its value by 10 per cent...20 per cent...30 per cent and up to 60 per cent by February 1998. Suharto was under a lot of pressure. His son-in-law Prabowo Subianto, himself the commander of the Special Forces, published a leaflet in January 1998, blaming the crisis on a conspiracy of ethnic Chinese, Jewish bankers and the White House. His soldiers began kidnapping activists. Some were probably killed. We thought that Suharto's power would come to an end in only a matter of weeks.

In May 1998, Suharto stepped down from power. Freedom was in the air. One day after his resignation, the still-outlawed Alliance of Independent Journalists circulated a list of demands that they considered essential to press freedom. Suharto's successor, B. J. Habibie, apparently listened to these demands and promised to revoke regulations that strangled press freedom.

Habibie's Minister of Information Lieutenant General Muhammad Yunus Yosfiah annulled the 1984 regulation on the mandatory journalist association. Yosfiah also reviewed the repressive press law, asking the United Nations Educational, Scientific and Cultural Organization (UNESCO) in Paris to advise his ministry in reviewing the press law. UNESCO even sent some experts to help write the new press law. I was involved in the meetings to draft the new law, working closely with some legislators, who understood that it was a priority in the post-Suharto era. In September 1999, the new press law was passed by the parliament. President Habibie signed it.

I knew that Indonesia was in a difficult period. Mass violence took place from Aceh to Kalimantan to the Moluccas to East Timor to Papua. On Java, Islamist groups began to organise themselves, peacefully or violently. In 2018, Janet Steele wrote, 'If I have learned one thing from following press developments in Indonesia and Malaysia for the past 20 years, it is this: all reforms follow from press freedom, and journalists themselves must take the lead in demanding it. If anything secured the transition to democracy in Indonesia, it was the 1999 Press Law, which was drafted and passed largely because of how journalists kept up the pressure on the new government'.

In November 2014, I had a conversation with Pak Dadang, the manager of the Tempo villa in Sirnagalih, who had known me since the 1994 declaration. He reminded me that after the journalists had left the villa, he had some military officers visiting the villa and asking him to go to their command.

'They accused me of helping to organise treason', Pak Dadang said. Some officers beat him, making him lose two teeth and causing bleeding to his face. Pak Dadang replied he was only working at the villa, taking orders from Goenawan Mohamad and Goenawan brought the many journalists. He was detained a few nights, but the officers released him.

'I never regret doing my work. I'm proud to be a witness of those days when this villa was made into the trigger of the reform movement'.

Java has Too Many People

Pramoedya Ananta Toer is arguably Indonesia's most renowned author. He was jailed for 14 years without trial from 1965. On Buru, where he was required to do forced labour, he wrote on waste paper. Upon his release in 1979, he published his Buru Quartet, a collection of four novels, published between 1980 and 1988, about Indonesia's nationalism. The royalties from their English translation meant he was able to save money.

He lived in a six-storey white house with blue pillars and a swimming pool in Bojong Gede, outside Jakarta. In April 2006, I took a train to visit him.

Pramoedya welcomed me. When I asked him about the big house, he reminded me that the Indonesian Army had seized his house in 1965. The Army burned his library. A soldier hit his head with a rifle butt, making him lose the hearing of his left ear.

'For me, to resist is just to keep writing. I proved that I could overcome my enemies by my writing'.

We sat in his spacious living room with many posters of his novels.

I told him that I had travelled into the jungles of Aceh and Papua, using boats in the swamps of Kalimantan. I went to see the sectarian violence in the Moluccas. I learned that the Indonesian dream in post-Suharto Indonesia is quite violent when opinion leaders use ethnicities, religions and nationalisms to mobilise people and to find new equilibrium in Indonesia.

More than 6,500 Madurese were slaughtered in Kalimantan. Poverty and corruption are still huge problems in many places in Indonesia. Corruption is another huge problem. Islamists are getting stronger, hoping to revive the Jakarta Charter, introducing hundreds of discriminatory regulations against religious and gender minorities. Many political interests also use the 1965 blasphemy law to get more power. Post-Suharto Indonesia seems to be a messy state.

Pramoedya listened carefully.

He suddenly shouted, 'The only one that unites Indonesia is Bahasa Indonesia. That is the source. The Papuans also speak Bahasa Indonesia, not Papuan languages. Java had 40 million people, but their elite was easily bribed. Just hundreds of men in ships, passing by, these Javanese regents surrendered. They took bribes. Java became a colony without a war but through bribes. Even a small European country with only hundreds of men could colonise Java'.

Pramoedya smoked his clove cigarettes, thinking and sipping his black coffee.

'If Indonesia is to break up, wars will happen continuously. Java has too many people. Java, for more than 100 years, sends murderers to Aceh, Bali and other islands, since the Dutch period. Once there were some friends coming from Aceh here. I apologised to the fact like this. I apologised. But I refuse the idea of breaking up Indonesia. It will create wars continuously'.

Pramoedya reminded me of Mohammad Hatta's 1960 speech in New York in which Hatta stressed that two-thirds of Indonesia's population lived in Java. But Java had only 7 per cent of Indonesia's land mass. The biggest concentration of poor people is also located on Java. The Javanese could not survive without the other islands. The Javanese should be able to go to the other islands to survive.

Pramoedya repeated, 'Java is the source of murderers. Indonesia is the product of young people. Its peak was the Youth Pledge in 1928. It was the beginning of this country. The history of Indonesia is the history of young people. It is not understood by Indonesian leaders after Sukarno. Javaism is to be loyal and obedient toward your bosses. It does not have rule of law, justice and truth. It is a victim of fascism. If Indonesia is to break up, wars will take place everywhere. Java has too many people and they are mostly poor'.

He saw that the mind-set among the ruling elite in Java hadn't changed. They saw Indonesia more as a territorial matter than a nation-building process.

Pramoedya, already 81 years old and suffering from lung disease and a kidney problem, smoked his cigarette. When he came back in the living room after excusing himself to go to the toilet, he shouted: 'My ideology is Multatuli's creation, "Human's responsibility is to be human". It means, humanity is the most important issue'. It was a reference to Multatuli's 1859 book *Max Havelaar* – Pramoedya calls it 'the book that kills colonialism'. Multatuli is the pen name of Dutch author Eduard Douwes Dekker.

It had already been two hours and I stopped the interview. He needed to take a nap.

Pramoedya walked me to his carefully manicured garden outside his house. 'This house is even bigger than the old one', he giggled.

He promised me he would continue the interview with me next week. But next week never came. Pramoedya succumbed to his long illness and died on 30 April 2006.

A Christian Governor in Jakarta

In March 2011, a few weeks after more than 1,500 Muslim villagers attacked and killed Ahmadiyah members in a small village in western Java, Basuki Tjahaja Purnama, a member of the Indonesian parliament, agreed to meet me and discuss rising religious violence in Indonesia.

Purnama, who goes by the Hakka Chinese nickname Ahok, asked me many questions. We talked about Indonesia's 2008 anti-Ahmadiyah regulation, which discriminates against this Muslim minority and, incorrectly, accused them of having another Islamic prophet after the Prophet Mohammad. The discriminatory regulation was often used to close their mosques, kick them out of their villages and deny them government services such as marriage registration.

I told Ahok that the discrimination began with President Sukarno. In January 1965, Sukarno issued the blasphemy law, declaring that Indonesia is only to protect six religions: Islam, Protestantism, Catholicism, Hinduism, Buddhism and Confucianism. The law threatened to sentence anyone who blasphemes against any of those six religions with a maximum penalty of five years imprisonment. The anti-Ahmadiyah regulation was also based on the 1965 blasphemy law.

Sukarno never used that law himself. Suharto, ruling from 1965 to 1998, used the blasphemy law only eight times. Suharto's successors – B. J. Habibie, Abdurrahman Wahid and Megawati Sukarnoputri – never used it. Wahid even tried to revoke the law, arguing that it is unconstitutional. But Susilo Bambang Yudhoyono, who became president in 2004, aggressively enforced the blasphemy law. Yudhoyono not only issued the anti-Ahmadiyah decree in 2008 but also strengthened the blasphemy law office nationwide. More than 100 individuals were prosecuted for blasphemy when Yudhoyono was in power.

In 2006, President Yudhoyono also set up in Indonesia's 34 provinces and some 500 regencies the so-called Religious Harmony Forum (Forum Kerukunan Umat Beragama, FKUB) comprised of advisory bodies to governors, mayors and regents. His regulation stipulates that the composition of FKUBs should 'mirror the composition of religions' in each area. Consequently, the dominant religion in any given area – whether it be Islam in Java and Sumatra or Christianity in Eastern Indonesia or Hinduism in Bali – has the most members in a 17-strong FKUB (in a regency or mayoralty) or a 21-member provincial FKUB. The decree also restricts the construction of houses of worship to the 'real needs' and 'composition of the population' in the area.

The result of the decree has been a legally sanctioned block on construction of new houses of worship for religious minorities, mostly in areas where Muslims are in the majority, but also in some areas with Christian or Hindu majority. In some cases, in conservative Muslim areas, the decree has even blocked Christian congregations from renovating existing church buildings. Militant Islamists effectively hijacked the decree and imposed vigilante-style enforcement of alleged violations.

The Communion of Churches in Indonesia, the national grouping of Protestant churches, criticised the 2006 decree as more repressive than President Suharto's 1969 regulation, which decentralised the permit application of building houses of worship to local governments. Yudhoyono essentially swapped the constitutional principle of 'religious freedom' in Indonesia's 1945 constitution with 'religious harmony', which introduces majorities and minorities in legal consideration.

Ahok, himself a Protestant, is familiar with the 2006 discriminatory regulation. Ahok thought that the police should protect Ahmadiyah members and charge the perpetrators. It was sickening to see the video of those Ahmadiyah men being chased, clubbed and beaten. He said it's difficult to curb rising religious intolerance in Indonesia as it already had many discriminatory regulations. But he repeated a popular mantra: Indonesians are mostly moderate Muslims.

I said goodbye, and that I hoped he would use his legislative power – dealing mostly with the Ministry of Home Affairs – to slow down the implementation of many of those discriminations. He promised to see what he could do although he stressed that it was not going to be easy: 'Ahmadiyah is a very sensitive issue in the parliament'.

Two years later, in October 2012, Ahok surprised me when he won the Jakarta election as the deputy governor along with his ally, a former furniture trader, Joko 'Jokowi' Widodo, who was running to become the Jakarta governor.

Jakarta is a metropolis of 18 million people. It is Indonesia's richest city. I wished them well although I was nervous with Ahok's sharp tongue. It was not politically helpful that he's ethnic Chinese and a Christian. He's also a transparent politician, putting his income and tax report on his blog.

Still Jokowi and Ahok were the dream team: Jokowi with vision, Ahok crunching the numbers. They soon handled Jakarta's notorious traffic jam and annual flooding, building Jakarta's first underground train and cleaning up rivers. They cut red tape, computerising government tenders and tendering government jobs.

They became popular, prompting Jokowi to run for president. It was a difficult campaign. Demagogues used anti-Chinese, anti-Christian sentiments to attack Jokowi. In July 2014, Jokowi defeated his opponent, Prabowo Subianto, a son-in-law of Suharto. It automatically meant Ahok replaced Jokowi as the Jakarta governor. Ahok took another transparency step: live streaming his official meetings.

Indonesia's transition from the Suharto military-backed dictatorship to democracy has created space for more freedom of expression for all Indonesians, including Islamists. There are many examples of the Indonesian state that Mohammad Hatta and Samuel Ratu Langie tried to mould gradually changing into a state that enforced Islamic sharia.

Some Islamists called Hatta a 'Muslim traitor' and mocked him for meeting 'Japanese genies' in August 1945. Islamists advocated sharia-inspired regulations in Indonesia's Muslim-dominated provinces, aspiring to set up a global Islamic caliphate.

The National Commission on Violence Against Women (Komnas Perempuan) repeatedly aired their concern against these discriminatory regulations, updating their database every year since 2007 and calling on the central government, particularly the Ministry of Home Affairs, to revoke those ordinances. Komnas Perempuan listed not only gender discriminations but also religious ones including against Muslim minorities such as Ahmadiyah and Shia. In August 2017, Komnas Perempuan listed 421 discriminatory regulations against religious minorities, women and LGBT communities.

In her 2013 book, *Negotiating Women's Veiling: Politics and Sexuality in Contemporary Indonesia*, Dewi Candraningrum estimated '...almost 80 per cent of veiled women do so in the name of religion, compelled by parents and schools, as well as formal law'. She used samples on Java (60 per cent) and Sumatra (40 per cent) islands, arguing that school regulations were the most effective method of making the putton on of the hijab mandatory. Candraningrum herself is a lecturer at the Surakarta Muhammadiyah University in Surakarta, Central Java.

Some Islamist groups even go the extra mile by using terrorism. Abubakar Baasyir, a Muslim cleric associated with the Jemaah Islamiyah, a satellite organisation of Al Qaeda in Southeast Asia, said that Indonesia will always be problematic as it never radically solves its problem: the morality of the nation sanctioned by the Jakarta Charter.

'It's like we bathe in a river, but our body is always dirty. It turns out there're rhinos at the upper courses of the river. They're muddy and they always shit. If you want to bathe, of course, you have to get rid of the rhinos first'.

Jemaah Islamiyah was involved in several suicide bombings in Jakarta and Bali between 2001 and 2005, killing hundreds of civilians. A 2006 survey by the Indonesian Survey Institute showed that 11 per cent of the respondents believe suicide attacks are 'sometimes justifiable'. The survey also showed a higher rate of support in all Indonesia's provinces for such groups as the Islamic Defender Front, often perceived as violent organisations, than for the cerebral Liberal Islam Network.

Governor Ahok's situation changed when he announced he would seek re-election in 2016. The Islamic Defender Front campaigned against him, declaring repeatedly that Muslims should not have a non-Muslim leader. On 27 September 2016, when meeting with fishermen in the Jakarta Bay, Governor Ahok told them it's understandable that they would not vote for him because they are being 'threatened and deceived' by some groups using a Koranic verse about leaders among Muslims. His office, like usual, uploaded his speech on YouTube.

The Islamic Defender Front reported Ahok to police, accusing him of committing blasphemy against Islam. On 2 December 2016, several Muslim organisations, including Hizbut Tahrir and the Islamic Defender Front, organised a huge protest in Jakarta, estimated to number at least 500,000 Muslim protesters, demanding the police charge Ahok.

The police finally charged Ahok. He campaigned while also having his weekly blasphemy trial.

Ahok lost the election to his rival Anies Baswedan despite his approval rating being at 70 per cent. He got only 47 per cent of the votes.

On 9 May 2017, Ahok was sentenced to two years in prison for blasphemy. The verdict endorsed an Islamist narrative of blasphemy. One of the five judges, reciting the Koran's Al-Maidah 51 verse in Arabic, stressed that Muslims should not elect non-Muslim leaders. The court also adopted the Islamist's position that non-Muslims should not comment on Koranic interpretations.

The verdict paints a frightening future for moderate Muslims and non-Muslims who believe in Indonesia's pluralist society. Non-Muslims will think twice before making comments in public or on social media about diversity and pluralism. Ahok might be sharp-tongued but he's fair and transparent. Ahok's mouth might not have been a problem if he wasn't an ethic Chinese and Christian.

It was unfortunate that Sukarno wrote the blasphemy law, and that Abdurrahman Wahid was unable to have it revoked. I always remembered Benedict Anderson's lecture, especially his warning that Indonesia, especially the elite opinion makers, should always work and rework on its nationalism. Indonesia is not final. Indonesian nationalism is still in its infancy. Discrimination is not going to help nurture Indonesian nationalism.

Chapter 5

THE MOLUCCAS

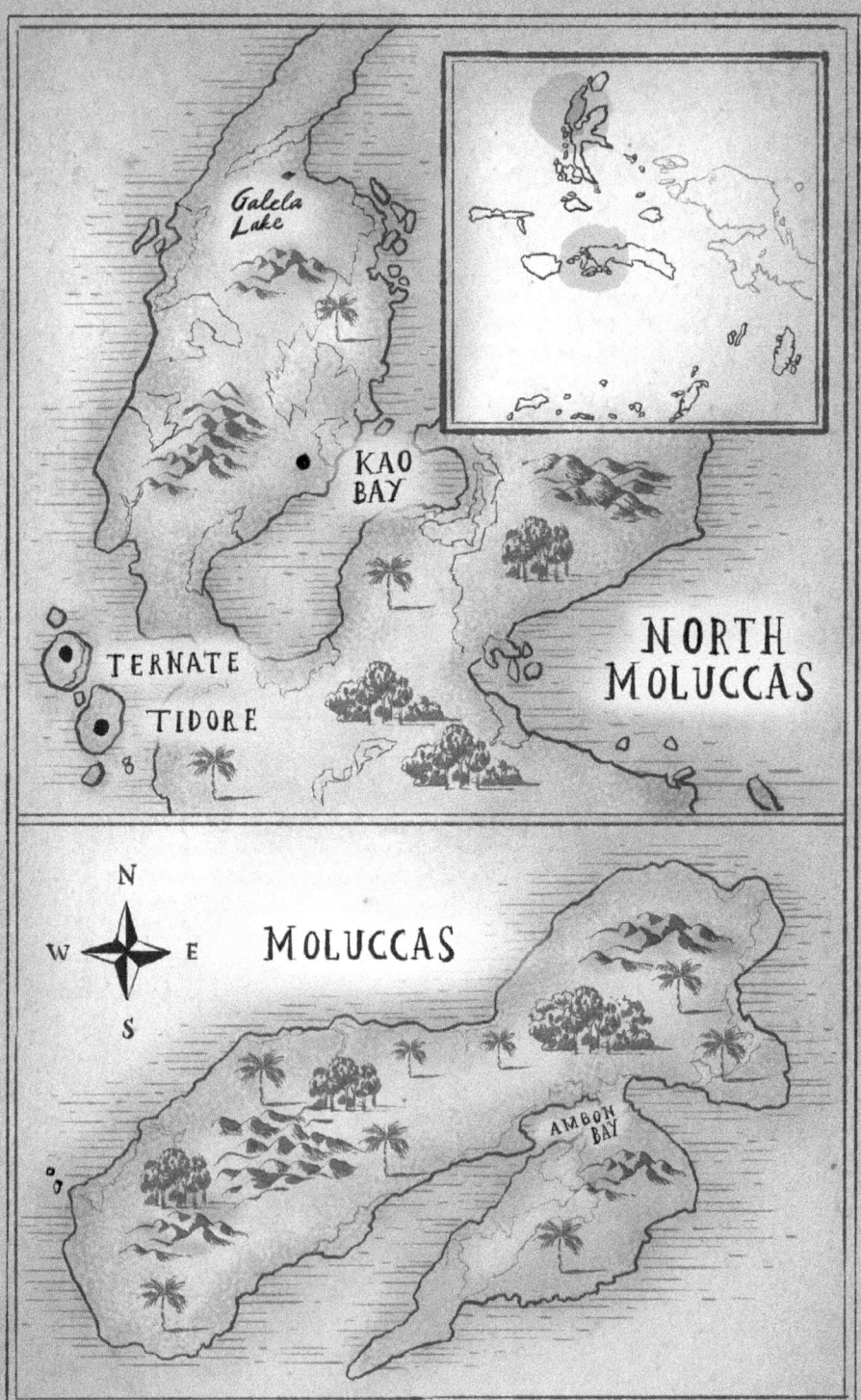

Sectarian Violence

Ambon Island: Muslims versus Christians

If you visit the Moluccas islands, you won't see sacred tombs nor watch ancient ceremonies. But you will learn how Muslims and Christians fought against one another, using machetes, fire burners, slingshots, spears, Molotov cocktails and automatic rifles. Nearly 10,000 people were killed in the fighting and close to 700,000 were made refugees – this equalled one-third of the population of 2.1 million. The fighting also drew in Muslim militants and Afghan war veterans. Groups such as al Qaeda-linked Jemaah Islamiyah and the Java-based Laskar Jihad swarmed into these islands, fuelling sectarian battles.

The fighting has also created a divided society. Even businesses are split. 'BCA opened a new office in a Muslim neighbourhood', said Insany Syahbarwaty, an Ambon journalist, referring to a large private bank. Ambon, the main southern Moluccas island, now has Christian and Muslim newspapers. Civil servants are divided. Police, soldiers, prosecutors, judges and many others are split: *kitorang* and *mereka*. Us and them.

The Moluccas, or the Maluku Islands, were famous for their nutmeg, cloves and other spices that grew only here until the 1800s. In Middle Ages' Europe, these spices were extremely expensive. Arab, Chinese and Malay traders initially carried the spices overland to the Mediterranean. After the Turks captured Constantinople in 1453, effectively shutting down the overland spice trade, European navigators began searching for a sea route to the Moluccas. One of them was stranded in a place that we later called America!

The spice trade left behind pockets of Christianity and Islam. On Ambon Island, for instance, if you drive from the Laka airport to downtown Ambon, you will see dozens of segregated areas – Muslim village, Christian neighbourhood. The border of each neighbourhood has a checkpoint, with militias on guard. You can easily spot the difference. If a neighbourhood has some churches and remains of mosques, it is obviously a Christian village. If a neighbourhood has burned churches, it must be a Muslim area.

In November 2005, I met two women, Wa Malia and her elderly mother, Wa Djalia, who recalled their nightmares since the violence broke out in January 1999. They are Butonese, a predominantly Muslim ethnic group.

Many Butonese moved from Buton island, off Sulawesi's southeast coast, to work in Ambon as street vendors, farmers or sailors. Wa Malia was born in Ambon in 1975. She currently clerks at Ambon's Education Office. Her father, La Bessy, is a sailor, who moved from Buton to Ambon in the late 1960s.

On 19 January 1999, the day the violence started, Wa Malia was shopping in downtown Ambon when she suddenly saw people running frantically. Some shouted about a violent fight in the crowded Mardika area. Shop owners immediately closed their doors. Motorists sped up to avoid emerging roadblocks. Wa Malia also hurried back to her house.

'I heard that people were already slaughtered. Houses were burned and shops were looted', she said.

Earlier that afternoon, a Christian Ambonese bus driver, Yakub Leuhery, stopped at an intersection near Mardika market. Nursalim, a.k.a. Usman, a Muslim Bugis youth, asked Leuhery for money. It was a common petty coercion. Leuhery turned Nursalim down, saying he hadn't made enough money yet that day. It was an Eid al Fitri holiday, the holiest day for the Muslims. Business was rather quiet. Leuhery decided to continue his bus route. Sometime later he returned to the intersection. Nursalim asked for money again. They quarrelled. Nursalim took out a blade. Leuhery grabbed a machete. Then Nursalim ran away and shouted for help.

Fighting soon broke out between the young men of Batumerah, a predominantly Christian neighbourhood, and Mardika, a Muslim area. Such fights are quite common in Ambon. They used machetes, sticks and stones. The police and the military were thinly stretched. Their commanding officers were mostly newcomers, knowing almost nothing about the social and political culture in Ambon. They didn't move quickly enough to stop the fighting.

In Jakarta, the ruling elite, including President B. J. Habibie and his advisors, were baffled about the chaotic post-Suharto situation that was breaking up much of Indonesia. A group of Madurese villagers earlier that day attacked the Parit Setia hamlet in a Malay-dominated area in Kalimantan. That Eid al Fitri attack triggered a massive campaign against the Madurese in Kalimantan. In Aceh, freedom fighters held gatherings openly, displaying their troops and arms. Papuan leaders went to Jakarta, telling President Habibie that they wanted to be independent from Indonesia. That month, Habibie also granted the East Timorese the freedom to vote for their own future.

In Ambon, Wa Malia saw young men with red headbands and spears appearing near Mardika. They looked for what they called the *BBM* – the

Bugis, the Butonese and the Makassar people. The Bugis and the Makassar also originate from Sulawesi. They are Muslims and mostly involved in trading. They're better organised and economically stronger than the Butonese. Wa Malia tried her best to avoid the Christian Ambonese checkpoints.

The following morning, the *Suara Maluku*, the only daily newspaper in Ambon, did not publish. It was technically difficult to travel and to work in a burning Ambon.

'Our delivery boys are mostly Butonese', said editor Rudi Fofid.

Christian militants and Muslim fighters established checkpoints throughout the island. The Ambonese use 'red headbands' while the Muslims wear 'white headbands'. People relied on private communication like telephones or small gatherings to get their information. Rumours swirled through the islands. It was difficult to verify information. BBM ethnic circles believed that the Ambonese were about to burn mosques. The Ambonese circulated rumours that the Muslims were acting as if they were 'the owners' of the Moluccas and were going to attack churches.

Southern Moluccas islands, including Ambon, were predominantly Christian during the Netherlands Indies period. The Dutch favoured Christians, recruiting many Ambonese into their civil service and military. The northern Moluccas, on the other hand, were home to four traditionally Muslim sultanates.

When Indonesia became a sovereign state at the end of World War II, the Moluccas islands became a single province. Johannes Latuharhary, a Christian Ambonese, joined the Japan-made committees in Java to work with Sukarno and Mohammad Hatta to prepare Indonesia's independence. Latuharhary became the first governor of the Moluccas. Since the 1970s, migrations from Sulawesi and Java have changed the balance of the population. The World Bank sponsored this transmigration program, moving people from densely populated Java to islands such as Ambon, Kalimantan, Sumatra and Papua. By 1997, the comparison between Christians and Muslims in Ambon's 311,000 total population was respectively about 57 per cent and 42 per cent, according to the government statistics.

In the 1990s, in an apparent bid to favour the Muslims in Indonesia, President Suharto appointed Saleh Latuconsina, a Muslim Ambonese, as governor. Latuconsina was a member of a 'Muslim intellectual' association, whose influence was on the rise throughout Indonesia. In an archipelago where nepotism rules, a Muslim activist governor meant many other government jobs for fellow Muslims. The Christians themselves tightened their control of the Ambon mayoralty and state-owned Pattimura University.

Being a civil servant is a prestige in Ambon. The change of balance created a feeling of being besieged among the Christian Ambonese.

When Suharto stepped down from power in May 1998, his absence created political vacuums throughout Indonesia. Rival groups, based on ethnicities or religions, tried to secure their respective interests. And violence often erupted.

In late November 1998, Muslim militants killed some Ambonese thugs in Jakarta, prompting the Jakarta administration to send home dozens of other Ambonese thugs. James Nacthwey, an American war photographer, took pictures of the Jakarta killing, showing an Ambonese man running away from more than a dozen Jakarta youths armed with machetes and clubs. Another picture showed a young man pressing his machete on the throat of the Ambonese. Those Muslim militants later set up the Islamic Defenders Front in Jakarta. The Ambonese thugs' arrival back in Ambon helped create more tension.

In December, Governor Latuconsina also convened a meeting in Ambon, meant as precautionary, but sadly it instead sent more jitters into an already nervous city. The meeting impressed upon Ambon's Muslim and Christian communities the need to be on alert for trouble and to guard against rumours. Both sides went home and set up command posts with a network of mosques and churches connected by both cellular and regular phones. The meeting foreshadowed the fighting before it started.

Suara Maluku commenced publishing again 11 days later with a headline, 'Ambon is Under Control'. It reported that daily activities in Ambon had 'returned to normal'. But Ambon was not going back to normal at all. Its editors avoided using the words 'Muslim' or 'Christian', using instead 'certain group' against 'another group'. They avoided the words 'mosques' or 'churches'. Like most journalists in Indonesia, they believe by not highlighting religion, they help deter further violence. They also developed a theory that the violence was instigated by 'certain parties' or unidentified 'political elite' or 'puppeteers' or the ever popular 'provocateur' associated with the Suharto regime.

In her paper, 'Fire Without Smoke and other phantoms of Ambon's violence', Patricia Spyer of Leiden University writes: 'Whatever its aim, this lack of specificity to the agents of violence may in fact produce a sense of phantom danger, which lurks both nowhere in particular and therefore potentially everywhere in general, provoking fear and, perhaps even, new violence'. Who were the so-called provocateurs? The newspapers and the electronic media almost never mentioned their names until the later stages

140

of the violence. But gossip and informal conversations revealed the names of some retired Army officers. The first was Ambon-born Brigadier General Rustam Kastor, formerly the chief of staff of the Army command in Jayapura, Papua, who had also been stationed at the military headquarters in Jakarta. Kastor was associated with militant Muslims in Ambon. Kastor also published three angry books about the injustices committed by Ambonese Protestant Christians. Kastor often talked about international Jewish and Christian conspiracies, of groups planning to Christianise Indonesia. Kastor had contact with disgruntled Army officers under Major General Kivlan Zen in Jakarta, evidently somewhat of a dirty tricks specialist.

Rudi Fofid of *Suara Maluku* remembered Kastor attending a fast-breaking gathering at his newspaper a few days prior to the violence, during which Kastor talked about the need to be vigilant. 'If a conflict is to break out in Ambon, it is going to be very difficult as Ambon has no majority. It is a 50-50 composition', Fofid quoted Kastor as saying.

Militant Protestants also had a champion in Lieutenant General Leo Lopulisa. These generals are among 'the provocateurs' that the media mentioned but never explicitly identified. Kastor regularly wrote op-ed pieces for *Suara Maluku*. Its editors also befriended these strongmen.

Tension soon spread to other islands like Kei in the southeast and Tidore in the northern Moluccas. *Suara Maluku* stopped publishing regularly. Their journalists still went to work in the *Suara Maluku* office in Halong Atas, a Christian area. But it became more and more difficult, and expensive, for its Muslim editors and reporters to penetrate the many checkpoints to reach the newsroom. The state-owned *RRI* and *TVRI,* whose offices were located in Christian areas, set up second offices in Muslim areas.

Novi Pinontoan, an editor at *Suara Maluku*, said that Christian militants even threatened to burn his office. 'We told them that it is true the newspaper owners are Muslims but take a look at us. We're Christians'.

Suara Maluku is a subsidiary of the Jawa Pos Group, a giant media company established during the Suharto period, which controls more than 140 newspapers throughout Indonesia. The Moluccas operation is controlled by its division in Makassar in Sulawesi. The Jawa Pos Group assigned Widjojo 'Tony' Hartono, a Javanese executive, to be its general manager. Christian militants saw it as either a Bugis or a Javanese newspaper.

Meanwhile, Wa Malia hid herself at home. She finally took a walk around Ambon a month after the Eid al Fitri violence. Burned buildings and dead bodies were scattered in the downtown area. Ambon barely had enough fire engines to deal with all the fires. 'I could take my salary, walking through different areas, ours and theirs', she said (meaning that she could go to ATM machines or the post office to retrieve money). Her mother, Wa Djalia, was relieved to know that the violence had quieted down.

What they didn't know was that a bigger conflict was brewing between Muslim and Christian journalists at the *Suara Maluku* that eventually helped enlarge the violence and trigger the involvement of thousands of militias from Java. Some Muslim executives, including Widjojo Hartono and business director Machfud Waliulu, asked the Jawa Pos Group management in Surabaya to open a new newspaper for the Muslims. Hartono had been discussing the idea since 1998. Wailulu's argument was that Muslim journalists could not go to work. 'A lot of my neighbours asked me why *Suara Maluku* always blamed the Muslims?' Waliulu said.

Suara Maluku had 10 Muslim employees out of more than 30 workers. Muslim reporters sent stories by fax or asked someone to deliver diskettes to their office in the Halong Atas area. Only Christian editors worked in Halong Atas. Muslim reporters began to quietly complain that their stories, especially about Christian militias attacking Muslim enclaves, were not printed. But stories on Muslims attacking Christian areas were always sent to press, creating an image that Muslims were the aggressors.

'When I wrote ceremonial reports, such as officials visiting an area or activities in the Governor's office, the reports were published. But it did not happen if a Muslim neighbourhood was under attack', said Ongki Anakoda, a Muslim reporter.

On 1 March 1999, dramatic fighting took place in Ambon when some Muslims died inside a mosque. It was reported that the Christians had attacked the Ahuru mosque in a dawn raid. Several street rallies took place in Java, demanding President B. J. Habibie take firm measures against the Ambonese. For those in other parts of Indonesia, it was emotional to read stories of fellow Muslims being shot at and killed while at their dawn prayer.

Suara Maluku did not publish stories about the killing, raising more suspicions from its Muslim reporters. Novi Pinontoan, a Minahasan Christian, denied the allegation, 'The phrase *subuh berdarah* (bloody dawn) was inaccurate because the fighting had taken place at around 7.00 am. There was indeed fighting and some of the Muslim victims were evacuated into the mosque. Some died inside the mosque. They were not shot inside the mosque when having their dawn prayer'.

Pinontoan decided not to publish the story, seeing its inaccuracies, but also did not try to find an accurate one. The Muslim journalists couldn't accept his argument.

In April, Machfud Waliulu brought some soldiers to guard him when he visited the *Suara Maluku* office and took cash from its safe. He apparently already had approval to start a Muslim-managed newspaper. And he needed the money. Pinontoan said the Christian journalists kept running the daily using only circulation money. There was no normal business during the fighting and no advertisements anyway.

In May, the Jawa Pos Group management held a meeting in Makassar. Waliulu brought up his proposal, calling his new newspaper, *Ambon Ekspres*. Darmosius Sosobeko, a Christian editor, disagreed with the division. 'In Ambon, everything was divided along the religious line. We have Muslim buses, we also have Christian buses. We have Muslim boats but also Christian boats. Should we add to this with a Christian and a Muslim media?'

But he was a minority voice.

'Muslim journalists have not worked for four months. Where should we employ them? They need a place to write', said Ahmad Ibrahim, a Muslim editor, who was appointed to edit the new daily.

In the Makassar meeting, they finally agreed to divide their Moluccas operation into two religion-based newspapers.

In July, *Ambon Ekspres* began publishing, copying what *Suara Maluku* did. *Ambon Ekspres* only reported stories from the Muslim side. The two newspapers began to be involved in the ethnic and religious wars themselves. Their reporters rarely went to a news scene. They didn't have the money to do that. They just made phone calls only to their co-religionists.

The violence grew bigger, spreading to other islands in southern Moluccas such as Banda, Saparua and Buru. Ambon was almost flattened to the ground. The historical Silo Church and An Nur Mosque also burned. Some elders told me that Ambon's destruction was similar to what they had witnessed during World War II and the South Moluccas Republic guerilla war in the 1950s.

In his book on the Ambon media, *Media dan Konflik Ambon*, Eriyanto wrote that *Ambon Ekspres* tended to bury news reports when Christian areas were attacked. 'They headlined reports if Muslim villages were attacked by Christian militias', said Eriyanto. The same happened with *Suara Maluku*, who portrayed Christians as victims and Muslims as aggressors. The division created two warring newspapers that helped fuel hatred in the Moluccas, escalating the killing and worsening ethnic relations. The journalists put their religion above their professionalism.

Dahlan Iskan, the CEO of the Jawa Pos Group, who was frequently criticised for agreeing to such a division, said that, if possible, he would 'to bomb' his printing house in Ambon. Iskan claimed his hands were tied. He could not stop his employees in Ambon from dividing the newspapers.

Eriyanto wrote that the division was based on pragmatic business approaches rather than an eagerness to provide Ambon residents with the quality journalism they needed to understand the violence better. The Jawa Pos Group controlled supplies of paper, ink and other needs in Ambon. If Dahlan Iskan wanted to, he could have easily stopped the supplies. 'He didn't need to bomb the printing press', Eriyanto told me.

People like Wa Djalia gradually felt the increased hostilities. Fifteen months after the first Fitri fighting, her family was forced to move out of their house.

'One day later they burned our home', she said.

Some Christian neighbours tried to help but were threatened by fellow Christians. The family moved to two different places prior to settling down in a burned shopping area where I met them in their makeshift house.

'We thought it was over when we moved out. It is worse', said Wa Djalia.

Seven years later, they still live in fear.

'Now things are getting calmer. Living during the wars was miserable, extremely miserable', Wa Djalia told me.

The Southern Moluccas Republic

It was raining when Yany Kubangun and I used a Honda motorcycle to visit the Waiheru prison on a narrow gravel road about 45 minutes from downtown Ambon. Kubangun, a reporter of the *Ambon Ekspres* daily, helped me secure a court permit to interview Semuel Waileruny, a leader of the Moluccas Sovereignty Forum that advocates for the Moluccas' separation from Indonesia.

Waileruny is a lawyer. He initially worked in an Ambon social service office but later headed the legal team of the Moluccas Protestant Church, the largest reformed church in southern Moluccas. His team represented churchgoers involved in the sectarian violence. While handling the legal cases, Waileruny began to realise that the violence was political in nature.

Fileo Pistos Noija, his team member, earlier had told me that the team only understood that Waileruny was involved with 'the forbidden organisation' when Indonesian police arrested him in April 2002. Waileruny was detained for more than one year. He was found guilty of 'subversive activities' by a Jakarta court and served four years in prison.

While in the prison, Waileruny was interrogated continuously until he was freed in March 2006. He stayed in Jakarta for another month. When he finally flew back to his homeland, he was arrested on his arrival at the Ambon airport, again on 'subversive charges'.

'He is the man who moved from one prison to another, from Ambon to Jakarta, from police detention to military interrogation. He's stubborn despite our objection', said Noija.

The drizzle stopped when we reached the front gate of the white-walled prison. We knocked on the iron gate. Prison guards checked my permit and brought me into an open meeting space with cement benches. It was quiet.

A dark stocky man in a grey T-shirt and training pants entered the area. He approached me, 'You're looking for Semmy? I'm Semmy'.

We shook hands. I began my introduction and used the word *'bangsa Indonesia'* in describing my interview. Waileruny interrupted, 'What do you mean by *bangsa* Indonesia? There is no *bangsa* Indonesia. A *bangsa* is a commitment of a people in a particular land. Do we have that commitment in Indonesia? Do we have such an Indonesian people? I am a member of *bangsa Alifuru*, descendants of the Melanesian peoples. We have such a commitment. This is our land. These are our people. This is our *bangsa*. But *bangsa Indonesia* is a bizarre and vicious manipulation'.

His speech stunned me. He reminded me of Hasan di Tiro's arguments in Aceh. Waileruny delved into history to spread his views about the Moluccas liberation movement. Waileruny told me that the Moluccas have suffered from the 'Javanisation' of their islands, politically, culturally and economically.

In 1920, the first Indonesian Ambonese organisation was established in Semarang, in Java. The Ambon Union was set up to help Ambon citizens in Java, but especially in their native Ambon. It demanded the Dutch Indies be more open to self-governance. The Dutch administration set up the legislative Ambon Raad in 1921, covering Ambon and Saparua islands.

I asked Waileruny about the involvement of many Ambonese politicians in setting up Indonesia. In 1923, Ambon Union leader A. J. Patty returned to Ambon from Java, persuading Ambonese leaders to establish a similar union. Patty considered that most educated Ambonese live elsewhere, especially in Java, depriving their native island of leadership. He was not popular with other Ambonese leaders. Two years later, the Dutch arrested and exiled him to Bengkulu in Sumatra. In 1928, a young Dutch-trained lawyer, J. Latuharhary, took the leadership of the Ambon Union and moved its head office from Semarang to Surabaya in eastern Java. Latuharhary chose to cooperate with the Dutch administration. When the Japanese took over power in 1942, Latuharhary joined the Japanese effort to prepare for the establishment of Indonesia in Java.

According to Waileruny, Latuharhary and Patty didn't necessarily represent the Ambonese in the Moluccas. 'They worked in Java, very far from Ambon', he told me. The Java-based activists didn't even get the blessing of the traditional South Moluccas Council, whose leaders tended to be more Molucca nationalists than Latuharhary. During the Japanese occupation, the Ambonese in the Moluccas, generally seen as close to the Dutch, suffered a lot.

The Moluccas, the Lesser Sunda Islands including Bali, and Sulawesi agreed to establish East Indonesia State (*Negara Indonesia Timur*) on 23 December 1949. Four days later, the Dutch handed over its authority to the Republic of the United States of Indonesia.

'Indonesia' – the federalist Indonesia – became a new state and won international acceptance. East Indonesia State became the second strongest state in the federation after Republic Indonesia in Yogyakarta.

But Hatta's rival Sukarno soon accused Dutch Governor General Hubertus van Mook of creating a federalist Indonesia to allow a continued Dutch presence. Sukarno wanted to establish a unitarian state as Professor Soepomo had wanted – the Javanese lawyer who promoted the German-inspired political thought behind the 1945 Constitution.

In Ambon, many leaders viewed Sukarno's intentions nervously. They saw no future in a Republic dominated by what they perceived as a Muslim majority. They expected that the unitarian state would be dominated by Javanese under Sukarno. Moreover, this poor backwater was dependent on the wages civil servants and colonial soldiers had regularly remitted to their families and villages from the Netherlands Indies administration. Rumours were widespread that Javanese soldiers would islamise the Ambonese, Minahasan and Timorese.

Moluccas nationalists led by Dr Christiaan R. S. Soumokil, then the attorney general of East Indonesia State, held a 'national conference' in the predominantly Muslim Tuhelu village on Ambon Island. Soumokil also asked Jabir Sjah, then the sultan of Ternate in northern Moluccas, to secede from Indonesia and to establish an independent state. Jabir Sjah refused that idea, stressing his own idea of a federal Indonesia. But Muslim and

Christian Ambonese agreed to separate the southern Moluccas from East Indonesia State, proclaiming the independence of the Republic of Southern Moluccas (RMS) on 25 April 1950.

Johannes Leimena, an Ambonese advisor to Sukarno, took the initiative to negotiate with the RMS figures. East Indonesia State in Makassar sent Jabir Sjah, who was its home affairs minister, to visit Soumokil. The RMS refused to let them land in Ambon. Ethnic Moluccas politicians in Java met in a two-day conference in June, recommending the Jakarta government grant autonomy to the Moluccas and asking the Dutch to disarm their former Ambonese soldiers. The federalist state lasted only a few months. In August 1950, Sukarno dispersed the federalist Indonesia, believing that it was a Dutch-made product to disintegrate the new republic. He declared the RMS a dangerous anti-nationalist movement. He labelled the movement as 'foreign colonialist' and 'the labour of Dutch reactionary elements'. Sukarno sent his soldiers to Ambon. They fought briefly and the RMS lost in November. About 4,000 Ambonese soldiers, those who used to work for the Dutch, were evacuated to the Netherlands with their families.

Dr Soumokil, who had become the RMS president in 1954, went into hiding in the jungle on Seram Island, the largest island in southern Moluccas, and organised a guerilla resistance. The Indonesian Army captured him on 2 December 1962, and tried him in a military tribunal in Jakarta. He was sentenced to death and executed on 12 April 1966.

Waileruny told me, 'I was born in a family who hated the RMS. My father received an honour from Sukarno because of his participation in cracking down the RMS fighters. My father was a farmer. He even once met SBY when he was still a minister'. SBY is the nickname of President Susilo Bambang Yudhoyono.

The RMS set up an exile government in the Netherlands. The first president in exile was Johan Manusama. He listed the RMS to the Unrepresented Nations and Peoples Organization whose members include indigenous peoples, occupied nations, minorities and independent states or territories. They join together to protect their human and cultural rights, to preserve their environments and to find non-violent solutions to their repressions.

'I was still a kid when the RMS movement was repeatedly used (by the Indonesian military) to suppress the people in Moluccas', said Waileruny.

Ricky Rumoruson, a *Suara Maluku* journalist, told me the sad story of his maternal grandfather, Demianus Nussy, a retired Dutch Indie soldier involved in the RMS movement. 'My grandfather never told me he was an

RMS. Every April, he was summoned to the local Army command and intimidated so he wouldn't fly the RMS flag. He grew so tired of being beaten every 25 April. When he got older, his sister, who lived in the Netherlands, sent him money to vacation in her house every year for about three months just to avoid the month of April'.

During the Moluccas wars, Waileruny concluded that the RMS issue was used as a 'justification' to provoke hostilities against the Molucca people. He objected to what some Muslims liked to say, that RMS stands for *Republik Maluku Serani* (Southern Christian Republic). He said many Moluccan Muslims also supported the Moluccas republic. The meeting to declare independence took place in Tuhelu, a Muslim village, on Ambon Island. The RMS is a nationalist movement.

He pointed out that the Ambonese are vulnerable in a predominantly Javanese Indonesia. Hundreds of churches in Java were burned down by Indonesian Muslims. He said Indonesian regulations discriminate against Christians when they want to build churches. Sukarno also banned the usage of family names, a practice mostly used by many ethnic groups, including the Ambonese, but not the Javanese. Christians do not believe they receive adequate protection in Indonesia. He fears Javanese trans-migration into Ambon will leave them a powerless minority in their own land.

Waileruny joined with physician Alex Manuputty, a conspiracy theorist, to establish the Moluccas Sovereignty Forum, whose main political activities were to commemorate the 25 April celebration. Hundreds of people raised the RMS flag, on that day, prompting the Indonesian police and Muslim militants to take harsh action.

'The RMS is a legal state recognised by the United Nations', Waileruny insisted.

Gerry van Klinken of KITLV Leiden analysed the Moluccas wars using Ted Gurr's study of communal conflict in Africa. In his paper, 'The Maluku Wars: Bringing Society Back In', van Klinken argued that Moluccas leaders had manipulated ethnicity, not to break away from Indonesia, but to grab a bigger share of state power for themselves. Ted Gurr was a political scientist of the University of Maryland. Gurr labelled this kind of conflict the 'communal contenders' conflict. The Molucca leaders didn't necessarily want to secede from Indonesia.

Ahmad Ibrahim, the chief editor of *Ambon Ekspres* disagreed with this argument, saying that the RMS does exist and wants to be independent.

'It's serious enough', Ibrahim argued.

Other scholars saw the Indonesian government's failure to prevent the outbreak of violence in the Moluccas as evidence the Indonesian military fomented violence to deflect attention from investigations into human rights abuses, to bolster their role in a changing Indonesia, or to protect their business interests. In several cases, according to both Muslims and Christians, it appeared that local commanders were not willing to place their troops in harm's way and took no action at all. The armed forces were in a catch-22: if they did nothing they were criticised for their failures; if they acted they often were accused of human rights violations. The military's desire to profit from the conflict also hampered their efforts to stop the violence.

Manuputty escaped a prison term and moved to California. Waileruny decided to face the prison and lived with his struggle. Waileruny spoke to Yani Kubangun in their mother tongue. Waileruny protested some news report in Kubangun's *Ambon Ekspres*. They also talked about their fate, being fellow Moluccas.

I left the Waiheru prison that evening with Yany Kubangun, driving by motorcycle back to Ambon and back to the Indonesia reality. Waileruny is politically much too weak and too localised to be able to pose a serious challenge to Indonesia.

I know that no state supports the Moluccas separation from Indonesia. It's also not even on the agenda of the Netherlands let alone the United Nations. Waileruny apparently does not understand the international mechanism, the extreme difficulties, in creating a nation-state. But the feeling of injustice, sadly, has increased among the Christian Ambonese.

Ternate: White versus Yellow Militias

My next destination was Ternate, the most important commercial centre in northern Moluccas. I took a flight from Ambon to Ternate and stayed for one week. The wars in northern Moluccas were started differently from those in southern Moluccas. The fighting began as an ethnic dispute, but later transformed into a religious one. The ending was also different from in Ambon, which unfortunately has never stopped.

The twin islands, Ternate and Tidore, and Halmahera, Moti, Mare, Bacan as well as Makian to the south, were once the world's only source of cloves. They were controlled by four ancient sultanates: Ternate, Tidore, Bacan and Jailolo on Halmahera. The Portuguese were the first Europeans to reach the islands, establishing themselves on Ternate and Tidore in 1521. The Spanish arrived 50 years later. Intrigues between the two Iberian powers lasted until the turn of the century when Ternate sided with the Portuguese while Tidore supported any European powers against Ternate.

When the Dutch arrived in the early 17th century, they allied themselves with the Sultan of Ternate and forced out the Portuguese and Spanish. The Dutch East India Company (VOC) negotiated a monopoly on the clove trade. In 1607, the Dutch built Fort Oranje in Ternate when they set about enforcing a monopoly on the cloves.

Ternate is beautiful, with majestic views on every side. In 1858, British naturalist Alfred Wallace made the little island his post during his explorations of the archipelago. Charmed by the forest-clad slopes of Mount Gamalama, the coral-filled seas and the remains of earthquake-crumbled fortresses, Wallace returned again and again to Ternate. The beauty of Ternate, and its twin island Tidore, is unchanged since Wallace's day.

Today this archipelago still has three sultanates: Ternate, Tidore and Bacan. Jailolo is already closed. I talked to M. Adnan Amal, a retired Ternatean judge, who wrote a history book on North Moluccas. Amal believes that the source of the current conflict was initially economy and politics but later spread to religion and racial division.

'Religion eventually dominated the conflict'.

Economic squabbling began in 1998, when PT Nusa Halmahera Mineral, a goldmine company owned by Australia's Newcrest, began operation in Malifut, a land traditionally owned by the Kao people. It triggered competition between the people of Makian and the Kao ethnic group. Many Makian people from Malifut, migrants known as hard workers, were doing well as labourers at the mine. The Makian got nearly 90 per cent of the jobs. This made the Kao envious. They are the original tribe who have inhabited the area for thousands of years but find employment hard to come by.

The conflict dated back to the passage of Government Regulation No. 42/1999 that created a new Malifut subdistrict for the Makian in the southern half of the district. The Makian people had been moved to Halmahera in 1975, after the Indonesian Institute of Vulcanology predicted that the volcano on their home island was going to explode. The government moved everyone on Makian (many against their will) to supposedly empty land in the southern half of the Kao subdistrict. Eventually 16 Makian villages, complete with their original names, sprang up around the village of Malifut.

Syahrini Sad, a sister to Sultan of Ternate Mudaffar Sjah, the son of Jabir Sjah, the royal family who traditionally rules the Kao area, told me that the Makian were placed temporarily in the Kao land with her brother's agreement, 'Of course, they could stay there. But if the mountain didn't explode, they should return to Makian island', she said. Jabir Sjah was East Indonesia State's home affairs minister who tried to negotiate with Soumokil in Ambon in 1950.

I stayed in Ternate for one week, including a quick trip to Tidore.

I decided to take a speedboat to reach Sidangoli, a small port on Halmahera, the largest island in the Moluccas archipelago. From Sidangoli, I rented a car to visit the Kao-Malifut region along the wide and deep Kao Bay. During World War II, the Japanese maintained a naval base in this bay. I stopped in Tahane, the most strategic Makian village, and stayed at a house of village head Munawar Ahmad.

Muhlis Idrus, a Tahane villager, recalled his 1975 eviction. 'We were forced to move from our island', said Idrus.

They initially stayed in a warehouse in Malifut. The government gave them rice, sugar and tea but no money. They eventually built their own houses, creating 16 villages named after their original homes on Makian. Their Kao neighbours helped them survive, giving them food, as well as existing banana, cassava and coconut gardens. Slowly the Makian rebuilt their lives.

Yuningsih Saibaka, a Kao teacher in Sosol village, next to Tahane, said that the Makian, as well as the Javanese transmigrants also living in the Kao district, are hard working people. 'The Kao people are just ignorant', said Saibaka.

In 1975 the mountain didn't erupt. But the Makian didn't return to Makian island. They assumed that the land they occupied was government land. More Makian people bought land in the Malifut from Kao farmers. The Indonesian government still considered Malifut legally a part of the Kao subdistrict. Makian villagers told me they travelled to Makian every time they have to deal with administrative matters.

When President Suharto stepped down from power in May 1998, Makian students and leaders saw an opportunity to make Malifut an independent district. They lobbied government officials and parliamentarian members in Ternate, Ambon and Jakarta. The Makian disproportionately dominate bureaucracy and university positions in North Moluccas. Bahar Andili was the regent of Central Halmahera and a senior civil servant. Syamsir Andili, the brother of Bahar, was the mayor of Ternate. The Makian lobby also included Abdullah Assegraf and Thaib Armaiyn, respectively deputy regent and regional secretary of North Moluccas. Rivai Umar and Yusuf Abdurrahman were current and former rectors of Khairun University in Ternate. Abdurrahman was also the chairman of the Indonesian Council of Ulamas in North Moluccas. They gradually convinced Jakarta's Ministry of Home Affairs to draft a government regulation on establishing the Malifut district. President B. J. Habibie signed the regulation in May 1999 and called the subdistrict 'Makian Mainland in Malifut'.

The decision in Jakarta to create the North Moluccas province triggered a fierce debate in the new capital. The new province would consist of the island of Halmahera and surrounding islands such as Ternate, Tidore, Obi and the Sula archipelago to the southwest. Mudaffar Sjah, the Ternate sultan who headed the Golkar Party in Ternate, suggested Ternate be capital. His Makian opponents attacked this plan, saying that the new capital should be Soasiu on Tidore. They finally agreed to set up the capital in Sofifi, a small village on Halmahera.

Tensions in North Moluccas increased in May 1999 when a document entitled 'Protestant Church of Moluccas Invasion Map for Ternate' began circulating in Ternate. The map purported to show the Christian invasion plans for North Moluccas. Local security forces soon discovered that the document was actually a map from a church report detailing the location of GPM congregations in North Moluccas rather than points of attack.

Regional political differences were evident in the debate over the questions of who would become the first governor of North Moluccas. One local contender was Mudaffar Sjah himself. His rival was Bahar Andili, the Makian regent of Central Halmahera. Decentralisation exacerbated pre-existing fault lines in North Moluccas society rather than creating new ones.

Academic Chris Wilson has written that the Kao objected strongly when they first heard of the release of the Government Regulation No. 42, setting up a Makian-controlled subdistrict. The Kao argued that Makian people, who had moved to other areas in Halmahera, such as Central Halmahera district and Ibu in northern Halmahera, had not established new Makian subdistricts. When Javanese transmigrants settled in Kao land, they assimilated with the Kao administrative structure. They especially objected to the name 'Makian Mainland' as it strongly implied land ownership. They told Makian leaders and government officials to change the name to 'South Kao subdistrict'. The regulation also included five Kao villages, such as Sosol and Wangeotak, into the 'Mainland Makian in Malifut' subdistrict. The Kao strongly objected to being separated from their fellow Kaos.

Violence finally broke out on the evening of 18 August 1999.

Some men and women, both Makian and Kao, told me that the trigger was rumours between some people in Sosol and Tahane, whose border is only a 3-metre-wide village road that I crossed every day during my stay in Tahane. Muhlis Idrus, a Tahane villager, heard someone shouting, *'Islam cukimai, keluar ketong baku bunuh'*. It literally means 'Islam, motherfucker, go out and we fight'.

'Perhaps, if they shouted 'Makian *cukimai*', we wouldn't go out. But they blasphemed against Islam. People spontaneously began fighting', said Muhlis Idrus.

'They were prepared. They already had Molotov cocktails and spears'.

Soon they threw stones one at another. Husin Syawal, a Tahane farmer, told me at about 10.00 pm there was a call from the Tahane mosque's loudspeaker, *'Allahu akbar, Allahu akbar'*.

'I immediately prepared my weapons', said Husin Syawal.

The attack left two Sosol villagers dead: Eliezer Moumou and Eras Dodowal.

According to Yuningsih Saibaka, Moumou was hacked in the face by a sword at around 10.00 pm in front of his house. Dodowal was cut on his back, and bled to death. The fight went on till dawn when village head Munawar Ahmad ordered an ambush of Sosol. Their objective was to get rid of the Kao in the Makian-dominated area.

On the other side of the battle, Erwin Makahiking of Sosol recalled, 'We tried to defend our village for one night. We left the village the following day. Everything was burned including our churches'. Makahiking lived a stone's throw away from Muhlis Idrus' house.

At 10.00 in the morning, a tow ship from PT Nusa Halmahera Mineral helped evacuate the Sosol villagers. Soldiers guarded the evacuation process.

'My house was burned at 10.00 am I ran to the rectory of the Pentecostal church. Some Bugis Muslims also took refuge there. But at 1.00 pm the rectory was also burned. We ran again until around 3.00 pm, when soldiers picked us up by a truck. They brought us to Kao', said Yuningsih Saibaka. Villagers of Wangeotak, another Kao village 100 to 200 metres away from Sosol, also ran away. The Makian farmers burned down the two villages.

Muhlis Idrus said, 'If we wanted to, we could eliminate everyone in Sosol. Sosol is surrounded by Makian villages as you can see'.

Sosol and Wangeotak villagers took refuge in the main Kao subdistrict, about 10 kilometres north of Malifut. Their removal upset fellow Kaos. Some government officials and Sultan Mudaffar Syah travelled to Kao and met with Kao leaders, agreeing with the Kaos that the Makian had violated traditions and that the four sub-ethnic Kaos should not be separated. Mudaffar Syah stressed that the problem should be resolved through traditional forms of resolution, not through violence.

Kao leaders formed a group called The Team of Nine to represent them to the government in Ternate and try to negotiate an end to the conflict. The team included five Protestants, three Muslims and one Catholic.

Kao people are predominantly Protestants, with a significant number of Muslims. They have a smaller number of Catholics. All share the same Kao language. Unlike most religiously mixed ethnic groups in Indonesia, traditionally Kao villages have just one cemetery for everyone. They believe they are neighbours in life and should also be neighbours in death. The team demanded the cancellation of the Government Regulation No. 42 and the rebuilding of Sosol and Wangeotak. The team returned to Kao in late August and waited for more than a month.

Regrettably, the Ternate government did not respond. It was too busy with the inauguration of the new North Moluccas province. More importantly, many members of the parliament, especially Makian politicians, believed that the Ministry of Home Affairs in Jakarta had already authorised the regulation. They wanted the Kaos to accept it.

Scattered skirmishes erupted, including some between Muslim Kao and Muslim Makian. Rosdiana Din, a Makian teenager from Bobowa village, told me that rumours spread about an incoming attack. 'I only slept with my bra and underwear. My mother told me to quickly find clothes but we didn't have the time. I just used a blanket to run away from our house. We took refuge at the Bobowa mosque'. Nothing happened that night and Rosdiana returned to her house.

But two weeks later, on 25 October 1999, Bernard Bitjara, a Kao leader, led approximately 15,000 Kaos in a massive attack on Malifut. They used traditional weapons – bows, spears and machetes – and wore 'red headbands' that symbolised bravery in Halmahera (the colour is thus similar to those used by Christians in Ambon). They also made a powerful Molotov cocktail with sulphur extracted from bombs found on several Japanese World War II battleships sunk in the Kao Bay.

Bitjara, better known as Benny Doro after the name of his village, told me his men had earlier found the bombs on the shores. The Kao troops attacked and burned down all 16 Makian villages. The speed with which the Makian were driven from Malifut meant that only three people were killed.

Bitjara ordered his troops to protect the Makian mosques. He wanted to show that the Kao Muslim community was supportive in the attack and to demonstrate that this conflict was not 'about religion'. Some Kao leaders told me that their goal was to drive the Makian from the area, not to kill large numbers of them. But the scale of destruction was massive. Every house was either bombed or burned. The entire Malifut infrastructure was destroyed, including the government buildings, although several schools and all mosques were left untouched. Benny Bitjara took a military officer to each mosque in order to confirm that they were not destroyed.

Husin Syawal, the Tahane villager, told me the Makian men tried to defend their territory, 'We used arrows and (homemade) bazookas. They used arrows and homemade bombs, long bows, made of bamboos'. The Kao troops attacked from north, south and the sea. 'The Kao Muslims attacked from the south', Syawal said, adding that the main problem in the dispute was territory, not religion.

Kao leaders calculated the Islam factor into their strategy. Muslims are an obvious majority in North Moluccas, making up anywhere from 60 to 85 per cent of the population, depending on who is doing the calculation. The Kao leaders, both Muslims and Christians, told me they realised they couldn't play the religious card.

'We finally flew the white flag. We negotiated. They wanted us to vacate the Kao land', said Husin Syawal.

'It happened at around 4.00 pm. At 1.00 am we boarded a truck to go to Sidangoli and to take refuge in Ternate', said Rosdiana Din. Around 17,000 Makian from Malifut eventually took refuge in Ternate and Tidore.

Poniyem, a meatball seller and a Javanese migrant in Tobelo told me, 'These Kao people, both Muslims and Christians, are fully united. They didn't break apart. They maintained their tribal solidarity'. Her husband, Suyanto, said the Javanese transmigrants, predominantly Muslim farmers, were not disturbed at all during the violence. About 500 Javanese families stayed in two villages in the Kao district. 'But the Javanese became nervous', said Poniyem.

Chris Wilson wrote that the violence was caused primarily by ethnic solidarity and competition; the importance of traditional land to the Kao; and Makian frustration at the refusal of the Kao to recognise what they saw as their rights. Kao Muslims and Christians maintained ethnic solidarity. Kao Muslims were involved in retaliatory attacks against Muslim Makian. Kao relations with other Muslim communities in the Kao Bay area, including the Javanese transmigrants, remained civil until the end of the fighting. No other Muslim or Christian ethnic groups assisted the Makian or Kao until members of the Makian elite subsequently reframed the conflict in terms of religion.

A contentious letter began circulating around Ternate and Tidore that shifted attention to the religious aspects of the conflict. It was addressed to the 'Head of the Halmahera Synod in Tobelo' from the Synod of Moluccas. This letter contained plans for the removal of the Makian from Halmahera and the establishment of Christian control over the island and its wealth. Muslim readers saw the letter as evidence of the church's role in the violence in Malifut. It also drew a link between the events in Kao-Malifut and the violence in Ambon. The letter was signed by 'Semi Titaley'. This connection led many Muslims in Tidore and Ternate to believe the letter was genuine. In fact, there were many signs that the letter wasn't authentic. It carried no official church letterhead. Samuel P. Titaley also usually used 'S. P. Titaley' plus his academic title 'S.Th.' when signing a church document. The Protestants churches implicated in the letter, GPM and GMIH, denied its authenticity and quickly released statements that decried it as a blatant attempt at provocation.

The Evangelical Church of Halmahera (GMIH), the immediate successor of the Dutch mission church, has long held a near monopoly over Protestant Christianity in North Moluccas. It remains the dominant church in most of North Moluccas except for Tidore, Obi and Bacan, which are under the Protestant Church of Moluccas (GPM).

Muhammad Amin Faaroek, an elder in Tidore, also received the letter but saw the signature to be a fake. 'It didn't look like Sammy Titaley's signature', Faaroek told me.

On 3 November, officials in Soasiu, Tidore island, used a loud speaker to invite Muslims, Christians and other peoples to meet at the Indonesiana subdistrict office. They also invited Reverend Arie G. Risakotta, the GPM head in Tidore, to talk about the letter. GPM runs the largest church in Soasiu, called 'Maranatha', located right across the Indonesiana village office.

Indonesiana is a Soasiu subdistrict created after President Sukarno launched his campaign to take over Papua by force in the 1950s. Sukarno made Zainal Abidin, the sultan of Tidore, the governor of Papua. Zainal Abidin organised the Papua campaign from Soasiu. Many people from other Indonesian islands came to Tidore to work on the campaign by becoming 'volunteers' to penetrate the Dutch-controlled New Guinea. Thus, a multicultural community temporarily established themselves in Soasiu.

Zainal Abidin changed the name of an area where most outsiders work, from 'Goto' to 'Indonesiana'. The temporary settlers, including Christians, also built a church. Some Soasiu residents told me both Muslims and Christians worked together to build the Maranatha church.

That night, several Christian leaders who went to the Indonesiana meeting quickly left, they said, due to the anger among the largely Muslim crowd. Risakotta refused to attend until police chief Captain Muhar picked him up and took him to the meeting. Risakotta attended the meeting and tried to explain the counterfeit letter. Before he could finish explaining, the angry crowd threw chairs at him. Village head Ali Muhammad suddenly turned off the lights. The crowd brought Risakotta out and killed him. A riot ensued as the crowd left the meeting, and proceeded to burn Christian homes and churches. Local security forces were unable or unwilling to stop the rioters. Eventually the Indonesian Navy evacuated the small Christian community to Bitung seaport in Minahasa.

Faaroek told me those who killed Reverend Risakotta were not Tidorean. In the morning, after the burning, Faaroek took a walk in the Indonesiana area and met many people whom he didn't recognise. Faaroek is a native Tidorean. He knows almost everyone on the island. He heard a new term circulating among the newcomers, 'Only Two Hours'. It meant that the mob took 'only two hours' to kill eight Christians, Risakotta and to kick away 800 Christians from Tidore. Faaroek suspected Makian refugees were among the attackers. 'They cut the throat of Risakotta', said Faaroek. He added he knew the Risakottas and hid Risakotta's wife that night when the crowd burned down the Maranatha church. Jan Nanere, who wrote a book on the violence entitled *Halmahera Berdarah*, blamed Indonesian officials, including Ali Muhammad and Muhar, for inflaming the public meeting.

As Tidore burned, the situation in Ternate, with a larger Christian population, remained tense but peaceful. The arrival of the Makian refugees from Malifut on 22 October 1999 led many Christians to stay in their homes. The local government did its best to reassure the Christian community that they had nothing to fear. It sent cars with loudspeakers through various neighbourhoods telling everyone to remain calm. Despite these assurances, violence broke out on 6 November. Hundreds of armed Muslims appeared in the streets wearing white headbands (similar to those worn by the Muslims in Ambon), ready to attack Christian homes. By this point, the police and army had been rendered powerless due to their inability or unwillingness to take control of the situation. They only guarded their own installations.

That prompted Sultan Mudaffar Syah to deploy approximately 4,000 of his *pasukan adat*, or customary guard. These troops were primarily ethnic Ternate Muslims from the northern part of the city or from the countryside, where many supporters of the Sultan live. Kao villagers traditionally send their men to serve with this customary guard. When the violence began, these customary guards did their best to protect Christians from rioters. They are called the 'yellow troops' due to the colour of their traditional uniforms. Mudaffar Syah said, 'These forces become the de facto guarantors of order in Ternate after the Indonesian security apparatus had collapsed'. These efforts earned the customary guards a pro-Christian reputation among opponents of the Sultan.

Some Makian and Tidore figures felt suspicious of the 'Ternate elite'. The Newcrest goldmine lies on land traditionally controlled by the Ternate sultanate. Suspicion grew when Mudaffar Syah 'very quickly' brought his customary palace guards into the action to stop the rioters in Ternate.

'This made the Makian feel the Ternate elite were against them', writes Ternate-born Smith Alhadar of the Indonesian Institute for Democracy Education in Jakarta.

Both the Makian and the Tidore people dislike the Ternate elite. They soon chose businessman Jaffar Syah, a descendant of Zainal Arifin, who died in 1961 without an heir, to revive the Tidore sultanate. More generally, Tidore people dislike the recent campaign by Mudaffar Syah, Syahrini Sad and their colleagues to return to 'traditional values' in which the Sultan plays the decisive role in administrative matters. Like their father, Mudaffar and his sister, Syahrini, believed that Indonesia would be a better country if based on federalism.

'The current autonomy program sometimes goes forward, sometimes backward. If one element is seen to disadvantage the central government, then they move backward. But if the element is seen to benefit the central government, then they move forward. The central government never genuinely consider the interests of the regions', Syahrini told me.

Tidore people began to worry that their traditional enemies on Ternate were preparing to revive the cultural dominance they had enjoyed in the past in order to justify a resurgence of their political power. Between the 13th and the 17th centuries, Ternate was indeed 'the first among equals' out of the four sultanates. The Tidoreans have no pleasant memories of that past.

'His (Mudaffar Syah) popularity decreased as he was seen to take sides with the Christians. He should be more neutral between the Muslims and the Christians. No sultans have ever been scorned like him', said Adnan Amal.

The riots in Tidore and Ternate marked the point where the conflict's narrative definitely shifted from being about ethnic divisions and economic spoils to being dominated by religion. One evening after dinner, when I crossed the village road that borders Tahane and Sosol, I realised that the road is physically only 3 metres wide, but politically it is a deep and wide valley full of prejudice and ignorance.

Halmahera: Ethnic Kao Fights Ethnic Makian

I decided to test the atmosphere in Tobelo, the busiest seaport in Halmahera and a predominantly Christian area. Jeanne van Diejen, a Belgian woman, lived here between 1921 and 1941 and describes Tobelo intimately in her biography *Ibu Maluku*. Van Diejen described Tobelo as being surrounded by several villages. Three plantations also surrounded Tobelo, and beyond those lay virgin forest. She had two riding horses and several coolies, living in bamboo houses and *gaba–gaba*. They worked in her coconut plantation, also planting corn and sweet potatoes and running a pig farm. She worked with Sultan Mudaffar Syah's father to treat sick people during World War II.

On 27 December 1999, two violent clashes occurred in Ternate and Tobelo. That day, Sultan Mudaffar Syah's troops burned down Kampung Pisang neighbourhood in Ternate, in retaliation for the Muslims burning down an old Catholic school used as headquarters by the Sultan's troops. The yellow and white troops clashed in street fighting for weeks. The Sultan's troops suffered a defeat and Mudaffar Syah left Ternate for Jakarta in January 2000.

In Tobelo, December began with troubling rumours. Febyola Lilipory, a reporter for SPB 103.6 FM radio in Tobelo, told me that people talked quietly about the so-called 'Semi Titaley' letter. Her radio didn't report on the fake letter but called on its audience to be on alert when receiving such a document. Tobelo was a nervous town. If an ordinary fight took place in the market, people assumed religious violence had broken out.

The violence began when some drunken youths kept celebrating their Christmas parties on 27 December. A shouting match broke out between Christian and Muslim drunkards. They ended up fighting one another.

Christian women and children soon gathered in churches. The Muslims gathered in two Muslim enclaves: Gorua in Tobelo and Gamhoku in southern

Tobelo. Christians who lived inside Muslim areas were hacked to death. Muslims, trapped in Christian-controlled areas, were also hacked to death.

The Catholic church, which owned Lilipory's radio station, closed its operation, moving its equipment to Manado in Minahasa. It wouldn't reopen for another two years.

'It was a very dangerous situation. We didn't go to each other's area', said Lilipory. Once she left the church to pick up some clothes at her house. It was a rather quiet day. She saw Muslim heads being paraded in pedicabs, motorcycles and cars. She witnessed a Muslim being burned alive. 'I dared not look. I just saw the fire'.

Victor Magany, a Tobelo electrician who had a radio communication licence, became involved in the fighting. 'Someone who holds the radio is similar to someone who holds a sword', Magany said. Every village has a walkie-talkie. Communication was power. 'I happened to know the radio communication code of conduct', Magany told me. The warring sides sometimes used radios to communicate, especially to help the wounded or trapped women and children.

Unlike Ambon, which had a rather developed media, the media in Ternate and Tobelo were much less developed. They had only a limited number of weekly papers in circulation when the conflict began. Radios reached bigger audiences in the islands. Their journalists were primarily based in Ternate. Ternate journalists mostly travelled with Muslim forces in Halmahera. They had little access to, and in some cases little interest in, information from other parties in the conflict.

Ani Sawal, a Muslim woman who ran the Maro Ona eatery, told me, 'The Christians cut the Muslims like cutting fishes. But the Muslims also cut the Christians like fishes. Who's to blame?'

Sawal and her husband, Tellong Haji Lombe, a tailor, decided to leave Tobelo for Manado in a Navy ship. From Manado, they returned to her husband's hometown in southern Sulawesi. He was traumatised and hospitalised for two months.

'He couldn't close his eyes. He used 34.5 bottles of intravenous fluid. He was extremely depressed and died'.

The Tobelo violence also provoked the reds and the whites to fight in Galela, north of Tobelo. The Christians in Dokulamo, aided by re-inforcements from the nearby Christian villages of Duma and Soatabaru, defeated the Muslims in Dokulamo and took over the village. Red forces eventually controlled Galela and Tobelo. The Muslims ran to the Muslim-controlled village of Soa-sio in Galela.

Around 1,000 people died in the violence in Tobelo and Galela. Most were Muslims. Images of the Muslim massacres in Popilo village circulated throughout Indonesia in magazines and VCDs, while Muslim newspapers in Java headlined the massacres. The horrifying images of a bulldozer pushing corpses into a mass grave created a sense of outrage, helping spread the violence to other parts of Halmahera and other islands in northern Moluccas.

The Indonesian military was unable, or unwilling, to overcome the fighting. The military forced the Javanese to move out of their two villages, sending them back to Java. Suyanto of Toliwang village said only 40 of 500 Javanese families remained in the Kao area. 'We had no electricity. We had no school. Our children didn't go to school for two years'. Suyanto and his wife stressed that the soldiers didn't understand the nature of the conflict.

* * *

The massacres prompted Rustam Kastor, the Ambonese Muslim general, to speak at press conferences organised by two Islamist organisations in Jakarta. Kastor raised the idea of sending Muslim militias from Java to the Moluccas. He claimed 'the Dutch-supported Christians' were planning to establish an independent state and to wipe out the Muslims. In his opinion, which he later shared in a book, the GPM church supported the RMS movement. He also blamed the Ambon chapter of the Christian-nationalist Indonesian Democratic Party for Struggle, which was led by Sukarno's daughter, Megawati Sukarnoputri. His statement led to a declaration of jihad (holy war). *Suara Maluku* fiercely questioned Kastor's views, reporting that the church had opposed the RMS revolution since the 1950s.

Amien Rais, the chairman of Indonesia's People Consultative Assembly and the founder of the National Mandate Party, earlier addressed a rally in Jakarta's National Monument Park. Rais said the government of President Abdurrahman Wahid had failed to restore peace and security. Muslims had a duty to defend their Muslim sisters and brothers in the Moluccas. Amien Rais was Wahid's political opponent and would eventually play an important role in unseating Wahid in July 2001.

Their calls bore fruit. On 6 April 2000, more than 5,000 Muslims, some armed with swords and daggers and dressed in white robes, gathered at a Jakarta stadium to mark the Eid al Fitri holiday by calling for the jihad in the Moluccas.

Ayip Syarifuddin of the Communication Forum for Ahlus Sunnah Wal Jama'ah, a Wahabi organisation, said that if the government stopped his forces from entering the Moluccas, they would wage war on the densely populated island of Java instead.

'It's up to them to choose', Syarifuddin said.

Ja'far Umar Thalib, the head of the Communication Forum, said that the Wahid government had failed to protect the Muslims in the Moluccas. Now the Muslims themselves should be ready to fight 'the enemies of Islam'. He said his group had established Laskar Jihad, a militia of 10,000 young men to fight a holy war in the Moluccas.

About 1,000 protesters boarded buses and took their protest to the Merdeka Palace, where they were halted by a police blockade. Six protest leaders could meet President Wahid. Ja'far Umar Thalib, Ayip Syarifuddin, Rustam Kastor, jihad commander in Ambon Ali Fauzi as well as jihad commanders in Tidore, Abu Bakar Wahid al-Banjari and Tasrif Tuasikal, entered Wahid's office.

Thalib immediately barked at Wahid. He criticised Wahid policy on the Moluccas and his proposal to revoke a 1966 ban on Marxism-Leninism. Wahid angrily rebuffed them. They only met for about five minutes, a palace spokesman said.

'He threw us out', one of the Muslim leaders told journalists. Wahid threatened 'stern action' against anyone conducting a jihad and ordered a naval blockade to stop the militias.

Thalib told journalists he would lobby military officers and politicians to help his cause in the Moluccas. He also opened a military training camp in Bogor, near Jakarta, and used his school in Yogyakarta for Islamic courses. He employed jihad fighters who used to fight in Afghanistan, Moro and Kashmir, to train the Laskar Jihad new recruits, denying allegations that Indonesian officers were involved in his military training camp.

Ja'far Umar Thalib was born in Malang in eastern Java in 1960, the son of a Yemeni trader-cum-preacher. In 1986, while studying at a Saudi-supported college in Jakarta, the young Thalib won a scholarship to study at the Maududi Institute in Lahore, Pakistan.

The institute is named after Sayyid Abul Ala Maududi, a Muslim thinker who founded the Jamaat-e-Islami (Islamic Party) in Pakistan. Maududi condemned the degraded nature of contemporary Muslim communities. He claimed Muslim governments that do not implement Islamic law were apostate and commanded true believers to wage jihad against them. He once wrote that an ideal Islamic state bears 'a kind of resemblance' to the fascist and communist states. Maududi died in Buffalo, New York.

In Lahore, Thalib read much about the Muslim Brotherhood in Egypt and its leader Sayyid Qutb. Sayyid Qutb got his master's degree at the Colorado State College of Education in Greeley, Colorado. Returning to Egypt in 1950, Qutb joined the Muslim Brotherhood and wrote several books, including his 30-volume commentary of the Koran *Fi zilal al-Qur'an* (*In the Shade of the Koran*) and his manifesto of political Islam *Ma'alim fi-l-Tariq* (*Milestones*). Qutb's thoughts are radically anti-secular, based on his interpretations of the Koran, Islamic history, the social and political problems in Egypt and his American experience. He argued that 'physical power' and jihad had to be used to overthrow governments, and attack societies, 'institutions and traditions' of the Muslim world. He was executed by hanging in 1966 by the Gamal Abdel Nasser's government. But he remains an inspiration to radical Islamists such as Thalib.

Thalib didn't finish school. But his interest in activism grew stronger. In 1987, he joined the Mujahedeen forces fighting the Soviet Union in Afghanistan under the direction of the World Islamic League, established by Saudi Arabia in 1965. While working in Afghanistan, Ja'far Umar Thalib claimed to meet Saudi-born millionaire Osama bin Laden.

In 1989, Umar Thalib returned to Java and oversaw the building of a network of Koranic boarding schools. He bought land in Yogyakarta in 1993 and established the As-Sunnah boarding school. In 1998, his Communication Forum for Ahlus Sunnah Wal Jama'ah was established. That group advocates for the establishment of sharia as Indonesia's supreme governing force.

By May 2000 about 3,000 Muslim fighters, who had finished their military training and indoctrination courses, had arrived in Ambon. Ja'far Umar Thalib had obviously secured a green light from certain officials in Jakarta. They included none other than Vice President Hamzah Haz. The press reported that Indonesian soldiers quietly provided them with automatic weapons such as AK-47 and SS-14, and welcomed their arrival in Ambon. President Wahid's order to blockade state-owned ships that brought Laskar Jihad fighters to Ambon was ignored.

Clashes between Christian and Muslim communities soon escalated. In Ambon, many Christian police officers helped their fellow Christians. The war also drew other Islamist groups such as Laskar Jundullah, Laskar Mujahidin, the Jemaah Islamiyah and al Qaeda. Several men, later associated with the Bali bombings or the bombing of 36 Indonesian churches on Christmas Eve 2000, turned out to be alumni of the Moluccas fighting. They became global jihadists like Omar al Faruq (killed in Iraq in 2006), Taufik bin Abdul Halim (a Malaysian sentenced to life in Jakarta for a 2001 mall bombing), Azahari Husin (a Malaysian killed by Indonesian police in Batu in 2005), Encep Nurjaman (his nom de guerre is 'Hambali', caught in Ayutthaya, Thailand, in 2003, detained in Guantanamo Bay) and Abdul Azis (better known as Imam Samudra, who received the death penalty for the 2002 Bali bombing and was executed in 2008).

Husin Syawal, the Tahane villager, told me that he first heard of the call for jihad troops while living in refuge on Makian island. His seven-month old daughter and his young son died while they were moving from Malifut to Makian. He wanted to take back his land and seek revenge against the Kaos. He went to Tidore to register at Abu Bakar Wahid al-Banjari's place.

The main goals of the white troops were to avenge the killings in Tobelo and return Makians to their homes in Malifut. To achieve these goals, they had to retake the subdistricts of Kao and Tobelo. Their strategy was to attack Kao from the south via Jailolo and to attack Tobelo from the north and northeast via Galela and Morotai respectively. The plan required additional white troops to make the short crossing from Ternate to Jailolo and sweep north, destroying the red troops in Kao.

Husin Syawal told me 48 men from Tahane joined the jihad forces. Al Banjari, however, named his troops 'Pasukan Jihad' or 'Jihad Troops', differentiating them from Ja'far Umar Thalib's Laskar Jihad. The Tahane group was initially sent to fight near Jailolo, on the east side of Halmahera.

He stayed in Akelamo, near Jailolo, for 20 days prior to crossing the jungle to reach Malifut. It was a difficult crossing. His group of 18 men walked for two nights inside the jungle under heavy tropical rain. They fought a battle near Malifut that lasted only about 30 minutes. 'Four men from Tahane died in the jihad', he said. Benny Bitjara's troops defended the area. Al Banjari, who arrived with another white group, tried to negotiate with the red troops. The red and white troops could not defeat one another, since many Kao Muslims also defended the southern border. The white troops retreated back to Tidore, prompting the red troops to retreat from Malifut to the Kao mainland, creating a barrier for Tobelo.

Ja'far Umar Thalib began appearing in Ambon, making speeches on a Laskar Jihad–owned radio station. He repeatedly talked about 'the enemies of Islam' or 'the conspiracy of international Zionist-Crusaders', imploring Muslims 'to prepare our bombs and ready our guns'. Laskar Jihad also used the internet to spread their cause, creating a ripple effect as their reports were reproduced or quoted by Islamist media. But when Osama bin Laden's al Qaeda network attacked the World Trade Center and the Pentagon in September 2001, Thalib openly scorned bin Laden. Thalib said bin Laden's understanding of Islam was misguided.

The increased violence in the Moluccas prompted several international human rights groups and church organisations to call on the Indonesian government to remove the jihad forces from the Moluccas. The Indonesian Communion of Churches asked for UN-supervised peacekeeping forces, doubting the neutrality of the Indonesian military. 'There are indications that this movement will continue with the goal to eradicate the presence of Christians and the Church in Moluccas, which is the oldest Church in Asia', it said in a 8 July 2000 statement. Other human rights groups asked the Indonesian government to allow an independent international team to enter the Moluccas and evaluate the need for humanitarian assistance and protection for the hundreds of thousands of refugees. They also wanted to examine chances for reconciliation between the warring sides.

But the Indonesian government refused to allow international aid agencies to offer humanitarian assistance. International journalists based in Jakarta were also blocked from visiting Ternate and Ambon.

Such requests, however, prompted government prosecutors to accuse Ja'far Umar Thalib of sowing hatred against Christians. He was detained for several months. In October 2002, just days after Jemaah Islamiyah fighters triggered suicide bombings in Bali, killing 202 civilians, Laskar Jihad unexpectedly announced it was disbanding, saying, 'There were deviations in implementing the methodology and morality of the jihad'.

Another reason was that a Yemeni sheik, Muqbil bin Hadi al Wadi'I, on whom Laskar Jihad depended for directions, criticised Laskar Jihad as 'too political' and die going beyond simply defending Muslims. A Jakarta court acquitted Umar Thalib in January 2003. By then the focus of the international community had shifted to al Qaeda attacks and the subsequent American invasions of Afghanistan and Iraq.

I stayed for one week in Tobelo, swimming in the ocean and talking with people. Tobelo, as you would expect, is a quiet little place like Jeanne van Diejen has described. Perhaps, if I had not become aware of what happened after, I would have assumed that it remained just an ordinary small town.

Desecrating a Christian Cemetery in Galela Lake

It was perhaps 5:30 in the evening when I reached Duma village on Galela Lake. The birds were still chirping. Big trees surrounded the lake. I could even hear a fisherman throwing his net into the water…splash…splash… splash. A giant mango tree stands majestically beside the lake. I enjoyed the serene sunset.

I visited Duma with Hernata Lasamahu, whose father, husband and son died in the violence. She brought me to see their mass grave next to the only church in Duma.

While sitting in the graveyard, she told me her story. Hernata was born in 1972 in Duma. Her father was a schoolteacher, her mother a homemaker. She had one sister and two brothers. In the late 1980s, when she was still in her high school in Tobelo, she noticed a young teacher that arrived in her village and taught at a Duma school.

The young teacher, Josephus Lasamahu, came from Seram Island and had finished his teacher training in Ambon. 'I was watching TV in a neighbour's house when I first met him', said Hernata.

'I was interested in him, since he already had a job. Unlike other boys, who *like to ask for this and that*, he never asked *this or that*', Hernata giggled, noting that Josephus was a gentleman.

'I also thought that I always wanted to marry a teacher. He would love me like my father loves my mother'.

They began dating. Soon Josephus came to meet her parents and proposed to her.

In 1990, when Hernata was 18 years old, they got married in Duma. Their first daughter was born in 1992. The second child, a baby boy, was born in 1993. 'His papa named him Roberto Zico. His papa's favourite team is obviously Brazil'. The second son was born in 1997. It was a simple and happy marriage, as Hernata recalled Josephus as a loving father.

Things were turned upside down by the violence in Ambon, and later Malifut, Tidore, Ternate and finally Tobelo. Duma became tense. Duma has a beautiful GMIH church called 'Nita' or 'Bright' in Galelarese. Duma is also the first Christian village on Halmahera.

Hernata's father and husband took turns guarding their small village. 'They didn't go attacking others. They just guarded our village using machetes', said Hernata. But others contradict that view. Christopher R. Duncan writes that Duma men had 'played a major role' in the violence that occurred from 27 December 1999.

Christianity arrived in the northern Moluccas with the Portuguese and Spanish traders in the 1500s. The Ternate sultanate allowed Iberian priests to work in Halmahera. But Christianity did not grow significantly until 1866 when the Utrecht Mission Union sent Hendrik van Dijken to Galela. The Galelarese invited van Dijken to their village. They suggested that he settle in Morodoku, an uninhabited area on the Galela Lake, deeply feared by people in that region. The area was the land of the Moros, or the living-dead ancestral spirits.

Van Dijken accepted the challenge. A debilitating eye disease struck him, and his home was destroyed by a storm. Gradually several villagers, including the Muslims, became Christians. The name of the village was changed from Moroduku ('land of the giants') to Duma. Related to the local phrase 'Duma wi doohawa', it means, 'But he [van Dijken] was not harmed'. A new church was dedicated in July 1874. Van Dijken planted a mango tree by the lake that I spotted in my trip. He and his Minahasan wife, Maria Soentpiet, also trained several people as pastors and Bible teachers. Van Dijken did not rush the conversion process. He was meticulous in his attention to the pietistic tradition, insisting that those interested in Christianity be thoroughly prepared for their decisions. Van Dijken died in June 1900 but the church continued to prosper.

When the Japanese built a Navy base in the Kao Bay area, Christian leaders in Halmahera were suspected of being Dutch spies. Many Tobelo, Kao and Galela leaders were imprisoned in Ternate. Church buildings were used as arsenals. Many Christians fled into the jungle to worship in secret with Allied bombs exploding around them. The church survived without any Dutch pastor. In 1949, the Christians established the GMIH independent from the Dutch missionaries. Christianity began growing in Halmahera when the fledging Indonesian nation made it compulsory for each citizen to declare a religion.

When the white troops didn't accomplish their mission in the Malifut area, they had no option but to seize control of Galela in a bid to take over Tobelo and Kao. The jihad fighters made a camp in Igobula, across the lake from Duma. They used loud speakers to warn the Duma villagers to move out.

'They wore white, all white', said Hernata.

The white troops also offered the Christians in Duma safe passage out of the village. The Christians did not take those opportunities. They decided to stay and fight. Hundreds of villagers took refuge inside the church.

On 19 June 2000, just two days after the centenary of Van Dijken's death, a force of more than 4,000 jihad fighters attacked Duma.

The attack began at 9:00 in the morning when a bomb was set off in the backyard of the church. 'We panicked. We heard automatic gun shots', said Hernata. 'Children and women gathered inside the church. We shouted for help. The soldiers, manning their positions near the village, didn't move', she recalled. 'The church was soon burned. We left the church through broken windows'.

Hernata held her youngest son, Niksen. Hernata's mother grabbed her eldest granddaughter. They crawled outside the burning church. Josephus held their eldest son, Roberto Zico. Bullets showered the church. Some reports mentioned that Indonesian soldiers, clad in their jungle camouflage pants and white shirts, were also seen firing into the church. The family tried to jump over the church wall.

Hernata suddenly saw the six-year-old Roberto Zico stand up and walked slowly into the gunfire. Zico was immediately shot in his right eye and fell. 'His back skull was detached from his head', said Hernata. Josephus froze knowing Zico was dead. 'Nata, Ongen! Ongen!' Josephus shouted to Hernata, using Zico's nickname.

'I have seen it', Hernata replied. But Hernata couldn't reach her husband. She jumped over the wall with her mother and the two children.

Suddenly a Galelarese Muslim with a long sword approached Hernata. 'I was scared', Hernata recalled. The Muslim fighter said, 'Don't be scared. Come with me'. They passed rows after rows of jihad fighters. He held Hernata when other jihad fighters said, 'Just kill her. Just kill her'.

'The man replied, "Go and find men at the church",' Hernata recalled. The family reached a military post at about 3.00 pm. The Muslim man left her there and joined the fight again.

Other Muslim troops apparently went to the Duma village cemetery and dug up Hendrik and Maria van Dijken's graves. Their bones were reportedly taken out and burnt.

Hernata brought me to see the empty holes in the cemetery. The cemetery itself, which had been beautifully built and restored in recent years, was destroyed. Every cross on every tomb was desecrated.

In the afternoon, the battle finally ended. The tiny village was destroyed. Hernata, her mother, her sister and other women found a small cart to look for their loved ones. Graffiti was found on the charred church: 'This place is only suitable for dogs'.

'I found my husband with a wound in his head. Perhaps, a bullet hit him. His body was undamaged. I still remember him wearing a blue jacket and blue pants. He died next to our son', said Hernata.

She also found the bodies of her father, Alfons Leledana; her father's brother, Yosep Leledana; her mother's nephew, Max Sumtaki and her sister's husband, Abner Ewinones. 'In a single day, my mother, my sister and I became widows', she cried.

The villagers buried the dead that night.

According to the GMIH Crisis Center, 207 people died in Duma that day, including 88 men, 79 women and 40 children, while 292 homes were destroyed. The villagers brought 519 wounded people to Tobelo. Hernata considered the Muslim fighter as her saviour since many other women and children were indiscriminately killed. Almost 2,000 survivors sought refuge in Tobelo.

The port in Tobelo was a scene of panic, filling with people, mostly women, desperate to escape. They fought their way up the gangplanks, carrying their luggage and children onto badly maintained and overloaded ferries. Two weeks later, when the *Cahaya Bahari* ship entered the Tobelo port, about 300 refugees boarded the ship to leave for Manado. They brought 30 people, who had been injured during the Duma attack, to be transferred to hospitals in Manado. The *Cahaya Bahari* left Tobelo with 198 passengers and crew as well as 290 refugees. It was only licensed to carry 250 passengers.

It sank on 29 June 2000.

A passing ship found just 10 survivors, who had spent three days and four nights clinging to debris. They suffered from severe sunburn and dehydration. The six men and four women explained that the wooden vessel had capsized after it was engulfed by huge waves during a storm near Karakelong island in the Talaud archipelago.

'There were too many passengers, but it was forced to set sail anyway', said survivor Reny Sopacua, adding that some passengers fought with knives to get hold of one of the few life jackets on board, as the overloaded ferry started to go down.

Indonesia's National Search and Rescue Agency chief reported that rescuers also picked up the body of another passenger believed to be part of the survivors group but who had died. The remaining 477 passengers and crew were considered missing. In Rome, Pope John Paul II conveyed his grief, 'I express deep pain for the victims…and I invoke with all my might peace and security in those islands tormented by violence'.

The loss of the *Cahaya Bahari* only begins to highlight the desperate situation facing the people of the Moluccas – both Christian and Muslim.

During the war, most of their plantations were destroyed. 'Ninety per cent of our crops, like clove and nutmeg trees, were cut down', said Makian farmer Muhlis Idrus, referring to Malifut's main product. Husin Syawal told me he first came to Malifut as a poor man. Now he was poorer.

'Nobody wins, nobody loses. The winners become ashes, the losers become dust', said Kao teacher Yuningsih Saibaka. The Kao people let the Makian refugees return to Malifut. The Muslims were also returning to Tobelo while the Christians went back to their places in Ternate, Galela and elsewhere.

Jacob Matheis Soselisa, a Tobelo politician, views the problem in Halmahera and other Moluccas islands as related to the fact that Eastern Indonesia suffered 'structural marginalisation' in the fields of education and health care and was neglected 'in the hands of the central government'. Soselisa stressed that the state did not exist during the violence. The Indonesian police, the military and the government practically stopped functioning. 'They sometimes moved victims, especially women and children, out of the conflict areas but their main concern was to guard their own assets'.

Chapter 6

LESSER SUNDA ARCHIPELAGO

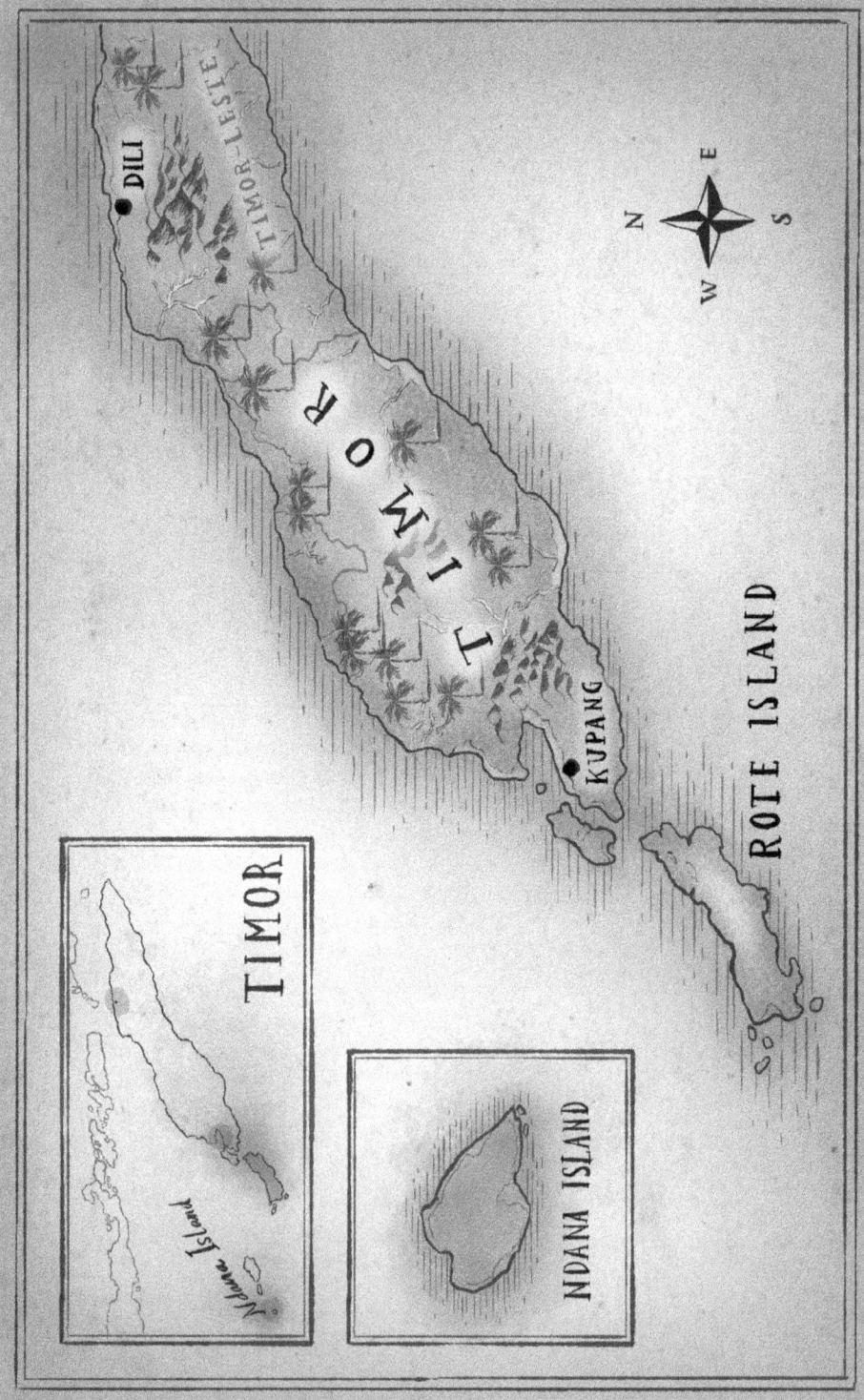

East Timor's Independence

Ndana Island: Indonesia's Southernmost Tip

Indonesia's southernmost island is Ndana, a tiny islet with white sand beaches, a little forest, thousands of deer and a lot of sea cucumbers. It belongs to the Messakh family, the descendants of Thie rajahs on the neighbouring Rote Island.

In March 2005, I began my Ndana trip from Kupang, the commercial centre in western Timor. It took a one-hour ferry ride from Kupang's Tenau seaport to Rote Island. It brought me straight to Baa, a small town in central Rote.

In Baa, I met Jerzy Messakh, a descendant of the Thie rajahs. He is a handsome man with a Stalin-like moustache in his forties. We talked a lot about his family tree. He offered to bring me to visit Ndana with his van. We drove to reach the southernmost fishing village in Rote prior to taking a boat to Ndana.

The common Rote landscape is dry steppe where cattle wander freely to find available grass. In some areas the greenness gives an image of fertility. In some places, I saw generous water springs. It is very beautiful. Perhaps, this is the kind of impression that created the *Mooy Indie*, or Beautiful Indie, artistic movement from the Dutch Indies period, freezing the beauty of the archipelago into paintings.

The Messakh is one of 18 royal families in Rote. In 1908, all of these families agreed to hand over Ndana Island to the Thie kingdom after a marriage dispute. Jerzy showed me a document with dozens of signatures acknowledging that handover. The Messakh still keeps its royal house, a three-storey wooden structure in Oebafok village, about 14 kilometres south of Baa. It has a thatched roof with chickens, goats and pigs, roaming around in the compound. Some men chewed betel nuts. They call it *Umaina* or the Mother House.

According to Ruth Messakh, Jerzy's wife, who joined the trip, women are traditionally not allowed to visit Ndana Island, 'If we visit the island, most likely our marriages will have problems'.

Ruth decided to wait for us at the house, when Jerzy, his driver and me continued our trip to Oeseli, a fishing village in southern Rote, closest to Ndana.

According to the Messakh family tree, the Thie kingdom began in 1570 when their ancestor, Lunggi Helo, became quite rich and established his power in the Oebavok village. European powers were already in the region by this stage. The Portuguese seized Malacca, on the west coast of the Malay peninsula, in 1511, and competed with the Dutch for control over the eastern wing of the archipelago. The Dutch seized Kupang in 1652 and built Fort Concordia. Portugal and the Netherlands later divided Timor island into Dutch West Timor and Portuguese East Timor. The two powers demarcated a border in 1859, confirming it at the Permanent Court of Arbitration in The Hague in 1914. Lunggi Helo's descendant, Voeh Mbura Messakh, converted to Christianity, built a Western-oriented school in Rote and introduced Christianity there too. This would be the cornerstone of Western education in Rote. It also made most Rotenese families convert to Christianity.

After the Dutch handed over sovereignty to Indonesia in 1949, the Indonesian government took nearly 15 years to establish its rule there. Jakobus Arnoldus Messakh, then the rajah of the Thie kingdom, was inaugurated to be the *camat* or the district head of Rote. The long delay shows that Rote was practically ignored by the power struggle in Java.

The Indonesian government does not recognise feudal kingdoms or indirect rulers like the Dutch. Jakobus Messakh, who had 40 wives, automatically became the last rajah of the Thie kingdom.

'He is my paternal grandfather', said Jerzy. Jerzy's father is the eldest son of this last rajah.

When reaching Oeseli village, we took a small *prao* with two fishermen to reach Ndana. Its engine didn't run very well...blek...blek...blek. Inside the *prao*, Jerzy told me about the surfing competition that the Rote Tourism Office regularly organises on Nemferala Beach, near Oeseli.

'The waves here are some of the best for surfers in the world', he said.

It took us only 70 minutes to reach Ndana. We stepped onto a stunning white beach. Ndana also has sizeable ebony woods. I spotted green-and-purple coloured doves. Swallows make their nests near the woods. Danau Darah, or Blood Lake, is located right in the middle of the island. The bottom of the lake is red. Ndana is an uninhabited island.

'Many people came here to settle. I asked them to move away', said Jerzy. 'Last year Tomy Winata and Ryamizard Ryacudu came here with a chopper'.

Winata is a well-connected Indonesian tycoon with alleged links to the underworld in many places throughout Indonesia. He heads the Artha Graha business group. Ryacudu was then the commander of the Army Strategic Reserve Command. He led his troops to 'crush' Aceh guerilla fighters.

'They wanted to take a look!' said Jerzy.

According to Jerzy, in 1992 or 1993, the Indonesian government asked permission from the family to establish a flag pole, the Red-and-White, on Ndana Island. 'We let them do it'.

While walking along the Ndana beach, I met a group of two families. Some women and children were also there, working on the beach and picking up some things. Stefanus Benggu, the group leader, told Jerzy that his group was only occasionally visiting the island to catch fish and to collect seagrass.

Benggu told me separately that this island is claimed by the Messakh family. 'If it can be a human habitat, many people would be willing to live here. We found many water springs'.

I also found remnants of a bonfire, probably used to boil water and to cook some meals.

Jerzy said the family usually appoint some fishermen to guard this island. 'I once fired a guard who allowed men to hunt deer'. The deer population has decreased lately due to illegal hunting by Indonesian soldiers.

In 1993, Indonesia's Ministry of Forestry declared Ndana Island a protected area. It means that no one could build settlements or hunt inside the island. Ironically, the government never assigned a ranger to enforce the declaration. Only the Messakh family tries to keep undisciplined Indonesian soldiers from hunting deer and to ask settlers, like Benggu, not to live on Ndana. Jerzy has become the guardian of this tiny island.

A problem might arise, if a businessman like Tomy Winata, one day finds something economically interesting in Ndana. It was said that Winata was looking for a place to build a casino with hotels, a seaport and other facilities. If it is to happen, I wonder whether the family might be able to keep guarding the island.

Local newspapers reported that the Indonesian Air Force base in Kupang patrols the surrounding islands twice a week. A radar stationed in Buraen village, near Kupang, also guards these islands from 'foreign intrusion', presumably coming either from East Timor or Australia.

Ndana reminded me of Miangas. Miangas is legally also an Indonesian territory but its people over the last 200 years switched sides in times of troubles: the Spaniards, the Dutch, the Philippines and Indonesia. The Thie kingdom also sought endorsement from the Dutch power in Batavia. Unfortunately, both Batavia and Jakarta have no genuine interest in raising the public welfare in places such as Miangas or Rote. Small islands, perhaps, always have these political natures. In Ndana, I realised Indonesia is obviously too big, too diverse and too complicated to be understood by the Jakarta elite. They have neither the imagination nor the intellectual prowess to professionally manage this vast archipelago.

We returned to Oeseli with the *prao* again. It was much faster as we were travelling with the current. When seeing two turtles floating on the surface, one of the two fishermen suddenly jumped into the sea. 'They're mating. They're mating! They could mate for three weeks connected. It's an easy catch', said Rie Tayang, the fisherman. He threw the turtle into the *prao*.

'We usually sell a turtle for $3 in the Oeseli fish market!'

The turtle was struggling with her sudden seizure. I had no heart to look at her.

* * *

I stayed some more days in Rote and realised that Ndana is not seen as the southernmost island among the islanders. In their view, their southernmost border is Pasir Island, or Sand Island. Legally, Pasir Island is an Australian territory. It is named Ashmore Reef after British Captain Samuel Ashmore, the commander of the *Hibernia*, who landed on the reef in June 1811. The nearby Hibernia Reef, which is also an Australian territory, was named after his ship. It has some islands, sometimes submerged under the tide, sometimes connected one to another, located about one night's sailing from Oeseli.

Sarah Lerry Mboeik, a Rotenese human rights campaigner, told me that Captain Ashmore claimed to find the island in 1811. But there is evidence that Rotenese sailors had worked on the island since the 17th century.

'The Dutch Indies government unfortunately didn't include the island into its map. Pasir Island simply became an Australian one just because one British sailor, Captain Ashmore, was accidently stranded there', said Mboeik.

'Sailors from Rote Island had travelled to Ashmore Reef for more than 200 years. We could even see cemeteries of those fishermen. Now the Australians claim to own the island'.

Interestingly, many Afghanistan and Iraqi citizens, who wanted to seek a better living in Australia, used Pasir Island as their transit point. They enter Indonesia legally through Jakarta and later fly to Kupang.

Once they had landed on Ashmore, asylum seekers could claim to have entered Australian territory and request to be processed as refugees. The use of the remote island for this purpose created great notoriety in 2001, when the issue of refugee arrivals became a major political issue in Australia. In 2002, the Australian government designated Ashmore Reef a 'port' so it could be excised from Australia's migration zone. The government then intercepted asylum seekers' boats and sailed them through the Reef so that they could be detained indefinitely as having arrived 'offshore'. Hasan Saidah, another Oelaba fisherman, told me about his experience when he was arrested by the Australian Navy. Hasan usually sails to catch sharks near Pasir Island waters. He was sailing in a traditional sail ship without navigational equipment, manned by seven people, including himself. They were taking a rest when an Australian patrol boat approached them. An officer showed them a map, saying that they had entered 25 miles into Australian waters.

'We have no electronic equipment to know our exact location', Hasan told me.

'It was about 7 o'clock in the morning. We had just finished our breakfast and were about to unfurl our sails'.

They had a small dispute, but nobody spoke English. The Australian officials speak neither Rotenese nor Malay. The officers asked them to move to the Australian ship. The officials bombed the *Matok*. They were under arrest.

It took two days to bring them to Well Creek, a small town in Western Australia, where they were put into a house to await trial. 'It was not a prison. It was only a house to accommodate foreign fishermen caught in their waters. We could roam freely around the area'. A translator and a lawyer were assigned to help them. Hasan said two days after his arrest, the Indonesian Consulate in Perth were informed about their case. Some of them also talked to an Indonesian diplomat over the phone. 'He did nothing. He just said, "When you sail, you have to be careful. Don't embarrass our country"', said Hasan.

One week later they were brought to trial in Broome. They were found guilty of unintentionally entering Australian waters. They were given a probation period of two years. If they were caught doing it again, the sentence would be a three-year jail term in Australia or an eight-month imprisonment in Bali.

They were freed but warned not to repeat such an offence. They were flown to Perth where they were given immigration letters, Perth–Bali plane tickets with Garuda Indonesia and $40 Australian dollars each. 'I still have the tickets stubs', Hasan said.

'It was the first time ever I flew with a Garuda plane and I think I will never have a chance to fly again'.

'I got arrested and flew back in a plane!' Anwar laughed.

In Bali, they used the money to purchase a ship ticket to return to Kupang and later Rote Island. 'My mother thought that after sailing, I went directly to Papela (in northern Rote) to sell the shark fins. She was surprised when I told her I went to Australia. She didn't believe it until I showed her my plane ticket'.

'It's been two years and I never fished sharks again'.

That evening in Baa, I concluded that territorial borders might please the needs of the ruling elites in countries such as Indonesia and Australia, or perhaps a global organisation like the United Nations. But borders could hardly accommodate ordinary people like Hasan Saidah, who live in marginal places like Oelaba.

Borders in post-colonial countries like Indonesia were made during the British, Portuguese, Dutch or Spanish colonial periods. The Malay people in the Malay Peninsula and Sumatra might share similar Malay cultures but they belong to two different countries: Malaysia and Indonesia. Ironically, the people of Flores, Timor and Rote, whose cultures are starkly different from the Malay, must share a single country, a single identity, with Sumatra. The difference is made absurd with the imposition of a single identity called 'Indonesia' sanctioned by the ruling elite in Java.

The Occupation of East Timor

I went to Kupang after staying for almost one week in Baa. It was March 2005. I visited an East Timorese refugee camp, meeting some human rights workers and dining in a Chinese seafood restaurant. It served tasty smoked beef called *daging sei*. Soon I realised that the much bigger story of Timor Island is not in the western side of the island, but in its eastern part. I decided to go to Dili in the newly independent *Democratic Republic of East Timor*.

East Timor is roughly half of Timor island, the largest island in the Lesser Sunda archipelago. Two dominant language families – the Malay-Polynesian, or Austronesian, and the Papuan, or non-Austronesian – break into more than 30 district linguistic groups in East Timor. However, Tetun has become a sort of *lingua franca*.

I took the *Timor Tour & Travel* bus from Kupang to border town Motaain, sitting next to a young woman who told me that her father is Lopez da Cruz, an Indonesian diplomat and a former East Timor politician, who chose to live in Jakarta. She said she works in Dili. In Motaain, interestingly, passengers must unload their baggage, cross the border, pay visa tax and put their bags into another *Timor Tour & Travel* bus – 'It's too expensive to pay the $30 visa', said the new driver – that will take us to Dili.

The bus passed Liquica, a little village with a lovely beach with a breathtaking view of the Ombai Strait. Liquica is one of the districts that suffered greatly during the Indonesian military campaign. The Liquica Church massacre took place in April 1999 when the Indonesian military and East Timor militia killed some 200 East Timorese.

When reaching Dili in the evening, I checked in at Hotel Turismo on the Dili Bay. Dili has an Iberian feel in the architecture of its seafront and many other buildings. This Portuguese-built hotel always reminded me of my first Dili visit back in November 1995 when as a cub reporter I had to cover the commemoration of the Santa Cruz massacre. Dili was very gloomy then. It was already deserted at 7.00 in the evening.

Today after taking a shower, I went out for a walk and looked for a street vendor for dinner. Teenagers roamed freely in the downtown area. People wined and dined along the beach or just sat with their friends. I dined in a small cafe with a group of teenagers who had just finished their soccer practice. 'Our favourite team is obviously Portugal', said one of them.

On 12 November 1991, Indonesian soldiers opened fire and killed 271 East Timorese protesters at the Santa Cruz cemetery in Dili during a procession to mourn the fatal shooting of a youth activist two weeks before. A New Zealand student was also killed but a British cameraman was able to record the shootings and broadcast the killings worldwide. This created an international outcry against Indonesia, sparked the international solidarity movement for East Timor and was the catalyst for the action to stem the flow of US and European weapons and other military assistance for Indonesia's military. Ali Alatas, then Indonesian foreign minister, called the massacre a 'turning point', which set in motion the events leading to East Timor's independence.

In November 1995, scores of international activists such as Irish senator David Norris, Maori leader Naida Pou, Aboriginal poet Lionel Fogarty, Indonesian Muslim leader Abdurrahman Wahid, Namibian legislator Daniel Botha and New Zealand's first female Anglican minister Reverend Ann Batten planned to commemorate the massacre. The commemoration was organised by a coalition of international NGOs. In Tetun it was called 'Ahi Naklakan' or 'Light the Candle'.

Nine activists had already boarded an Indonesian plane from Surabaya to Dili when Indonesian officials asked them to leave the plane in their transit on Bali. Others reached Dili from Kupang airport. I met them at Hotel Turismo. One of them, medical doctor Andrew McNaughtan of Sydney, asked me whether I would like to join them for dinner.

I brought a friend, Irawan Saptono, an Indonesian journalist editing the Dili-based *Suara Timor Timur* daily, to join our dinner. We dined at the Bidau Massau restaurant. The owner was East Timor's most famous chef Olandina Caeiro. The Porto meals were excellent. Irawan told us we were being monitored closely. The plainclothes officers sat inside the restaurant. Others waited in cars outside the restaurant. Olandina Caeiro quietly met some of us inside a backroom near the toilet, praising our courage and telling us to be careful.

The following morning, the plainclothes officers came to the hotel, inviting the activists to come to the dining room. The officers said that 'foreigners' should leave Dili that day. Five of the activists, however, managed to persuade the officers to let them climb Fatucama Hill to see the 'Christ the King' statue, a Dili landmark. They allowed us, but we were to report wherever we went to our respective 'minders'. Hotel Turismo staff, mostly elderly men, were obviously terrified.

McNaughtan invited me to join them in going to the hill. They lit candles at the foot of the statue. McNaughtan made a short speech. Lionel Fogarty sang an Aboriginal song and repeatedly said, 'This city has no love', pointing to Dili below the hill.

They also read a statement from U2 rock singer Bono:

> *There is no silence deep enough.*
> *No blackout dark enough.*
> *No corruption thick enough.*
> *No business deal big enough.*
> *No politician bent enough.*
> *No heart hollow enough.*
> *No grave wide enough to bury your story and keep it from us.*

Back in Dili, Indonesian soldiers clad in jungle camouflage guarded checkpoints in a number of areas such as Comoro, Becora, Matadouro and areas surrounding the campus of East Timor University. The Santa Cruz cemetery was totally off limits. Irawan courageously headlined the arrival of the activists to commemorate the massacre in his newspaper. I faxed my story from Irawan's newsroom.

One day later, the officers came to my hotel room and asked me to meet their boss, Lieutenant Colonel George Toisuta, on the hotel verandah. Toisuta directly asked me about my patriotism. 'Are you Red-and-White?' asked Toisuta. I replied that I am just an ordinary journalist, covering the event and doing my reporting. He asked again, 'Are you Red-and-White?' I told him that his question is irrelevant, saying that East Timor is internationally still a disputed area. Journalists should be able to be independent from their biases when covering issues like this. He ordered my expulsion to his men, right in front of me, at the verandah. There is no point arguing with a closed-minded officer like Toisuta. The officers also asked another journalist, Hugh O'Shaughnessy of the *London Observer*, to leave Dili that day.

O'Shaughnessy was expelled after having had an argument with an immigration official, Yohanes Triswoyo, who politely asked his 'kind understanding to leave East Timor' but refused to use the word 'expulsion'.

O'Shaughnessy told me, 'It illustrates very clearly how afraid the Indonesians are of people observing what is going on in this territory. It will confirm the worst fears of the outside world as we approach the fourth anniversary of the Santa Cruz killings'.

I remembered those 1995 scenes while watching these East Timorese teenagers now chatting and laughing about European football. Dili had changed tremendously. East Timor is now a sovereign state, a member of the United Nations.

Olandina Caeiro is not only running her restaurant but was a commissioner of the Commission for Reception, Truth and Reconciliation in East Timor. Hotel Turismo is now an elegant and historical hotel in Dili. Indonesia, however, has not changed much. George Toisuta became a four-star general after commanding some of Indonesia's military commands in Aceh, Papua, Jakarta and Bandung. I am afraid the narrower your view on Indonesian nationalism, the easier it is to build your career and possibly to enrich yourself.

Commission for Reception, Truth and Reconciliation

I spent my lunchtimes mostly at a canteen in Dili's Farol neighbourhood. It's a food vendor inside an NGO compound. Many NGOs and foreign embassies have their offices in Farol. It is easy to meet activists there. They were mostly toddlers when Indonesia invaded their country. They grew up in Indonesian schools, speaking Bahasa Indonesia and learning Indonesia's official history. What they learned at school was totally different from what they saw in their real life. I heard this over and over throughout Indonesia.

One afternoon, a man in his forties picked me up and drove me, in his new car, to a new coffee shop in downtown Dili. His name was Jacinto Alves, a former clandestine leader and one of the architects of the Commission for Reception, Truth and Reconciliation in East Timor, or CAVR in its Portuguese acronym. CAVR is arguably one of the most important organisations in East Timor's history. CAVR is trying to find the truth in East Timor's past. CAVR's website quoted Alves as saying, 'We must have the courage to direct and offer, in a just way, our spirit of reconciliation to all Timorese people, for the sake of East Timor's future'.

Indonesia failed to create such a commission despite the enormous needs to answer for its bloody past. The Abdurrahman Wahid administration tried to establish such a commission to deal with Indonesia's bloody past – the massacres in 1948 and 1965 in Java, the killings in the 1950s like the ones in Minahasa, the Moluccas and going on to Aceh, Papua and Borneo in the 1960s to the 1990s – but Wahid's plan was later, sadly, shelved by Indonesia's Constitution Court.

When the Santa Cruz massacre took place, Jacinto Alves, then a clandestine leader in Dili, recalled, 'Two of us were already arrested. We decided that the seven of us had to move forward and to take the responsibility'. He was initially detained at the Dili police station. Indonesian prosecutors asked Indonesian judges to sentence him to eight years imprisonment for treason.

In his defence statement, Alves claimed that he was not guilty. He described East Timor and Indonesia as two parallel lines. They will never meet. 'I feel myself as an East Timorese, not an Indonesian', he recalled. African people never think of themselves as Portuguese. History forms our identity. It is dynamic and irreversible. Timor Island was divided by the Portuguese and the Dutch. It separated East Timor from Indonesia. It is irreversible'.

His speech apparently didn't please the judges. They condemned him to 10 years imprisonment, spending his prison terms mostly in Semarang, Java. The Indonesian government released him on 30 December 1998, a few months after the fall of Suharto. He returned to Dili and established an association of ex-political prisoners to help activists like him, and their families, adjust to normal life.

In January 1999, against a backdrop of international pressure as well as violence throughout Indonesia, Suharto's successor President B. J. Habibie unexpectedly announced that the East Timorese would be allowed a referendum to decide whether they wished to accept or to reject autonomy within Indonesia.

In his 2006 autobiography, *Decisive Moments: Indonesia's Long Road Towards Democracy*, Habibie wrote that he was feeling alone, then. He faced so much turmoil those days in Java, Aceh, Papua, Borneo, the Moluccas and other places. He felt he should make a sound decision. A small error, he believed, might provoke the Indonesian military to use force in repressing separatist movements in Indonesia.

Habibie argued that the Indonesian military likes to portray, and to think of themselves, as the guardian of Indonesia's territorial integrity. But Habibie believed the use of force would only disintegrate Indonesia, like Yugoslavia, where the Serbian-dominated military were attacking Yugoslavia's minorities. International opinion would not tolerate violence on a mass scale. Habibie decided to bet on Indonesia's only internationally disputed card: East Timor.

Even if the referendum were to be lost, his bet was that Indonesia would keep the other cards: Aceh and Papua.

He chose to reveal his 1999 decision in an interview with BBC correspondent Jonathan Head. I still remembered that night when Jonathan joined us, some foreign correspondents, playing electronic games and drinking at Jakarta's Hard Rock Cafe. He caught his breath and told us about his exclusive interview with Habibie.

A formal agreement between Indonesia, Portugal and the UN was reached on 5 May 1999 which charged the United Nations Mission in East Timor with organising a referendum. Indonesia was to provide the security for the ballot. Voter registration began on 16 July 1999. But independent observers reported political violence by the Indonesian military and militia groups, allegedly designed to intimidate voters.

The referendum was held on 30 August 1999. Five days later, the UN announced in New York and Dili that 78.5 per cent had voted against East Timor remaining as part of Indonesia. It meant East Timor voted for independence. Three days later, Indonesia released Xanana Gusmão, East Timor independence leader, from his Jakarta house arrest.

When Xanana arrived in Dili, the Indonesian military were forcibly evacuating more than 260,000 villagers, or around 30 per cent of East Timor's population, to western Timor. Their plan was to later use these

East Timorese to be evidence that many of them were not happy with the referendum. In their departure, the Indonesian military organised widespread looting, burning and killing. They destroyed 70 per cent of East Timor's infrastructure, built mostly during the Suharto years, and killed an estimated 1,500 independence supporters.

The East Timorese militias also fled across the border into western Timor. They alleged that the UN mission was biased in organising the referendum. They attacked the UN office in border town Atambua and killed three UN workers. They also attempted sporadic armed raids along the border. Australian and New Zealand troops, soon deployed in East Timor, managed to fend the militia off. Pressure from the United States and international opinion forced Indonesia to withdraw their tacit support toward the militias.

When Dili was burning, Jacinto Alves brought his family to hide in Dare, a small town about 80 kilometres south of Dili. He only returned to Dili when the Australian troops had secured East Timor. 'I found only the ruins of my house. I checked my kitchen, where I stored many documents, and found only ashes. I couldn't stand it. It was about 75 centimetres thick, all my imprisonment documents. I cried quietly, knowing that my personal documents were burned to ashes'.

After a visit to Lisbon by Xanana Gusmão, Portugal agreed to recognise East Timor's independence scheduled on 20 May 2002. A massive international program, led by the UN, manned by civilian advisers, 5,000 peacekeepers and 1,300 police officers, led to substantial reconstruction in both urban and rural areas. Thousands of refugees returned to their respective East Timor villages. This successful UN effort was headed by Special Representative of the Secretary-General, Sérgio Vieira de Mello, who also helped Jacinto Alves and his colleagues to establish CAVR.

On 19 May 2002, Dili welcomed representatives of more than 90 countries to attend the independence event. They included UN Secretary-General Kofi Annan, Indonesian President Megawati Sukarnoputri, Portuguese President Jorge Sampaio, Australian Prime Minister John Howard, New Zealand Prime Minister Helen Clark and former US President Bill Clinton.

After Kofi Annan's speech, as midnight struck, the UN flag was lowered while singer Barbara Hendricks sang a song dedicated to freedom. Six former guerilla fighters carried the East Timorese flag to the stage and presented it to members of the new East Timor Defence Force. The ETDF raised the flag after Parliament President Francisco Guterres declared East

Timor's birth as an independent nation. Guterres then proceeded to swear in Xanana Gusmão as East Timor's new President.

'Today we are a people standing on equal footing with all other people in the world. On the celebration of independence, we wish to take upon ourselves this commitment before you: to work solely and exclusively for our people', Gusmão said in his speech.

Xanana told President Megawati, 'We warmly welcome your presence here among us, not only in your capacity as the head of state of the brotherly and neighboring country...but also as a symbol of the democratic journey of the brotherly people of Indonesia'. Wearing a traditional Timorese scarf, President Xanana paid tribute to the 'bravery' of B. J. Habibie.

Upon independence, East Timor declared the day Indonesian soldiers massacred the Santa Cruz marchers (12 November 1991) as National Youth Day, and 28 November as Declaration of Independence Day. On 28 November 1975, the Revolutionary Front for an Independent East Timor, known by its Portuguese acronym Fretilin, declared independence. Indonesia launched a full-scale invasion nine days later. The invasion day 7 December 1975 was to be known as National Heroes' Day. The East Timorese government also named Dili airport after Fretilin president Nicolau Lobato who made the 1975 declaration.

Jacinto Alves's CAVR sped up its work, having six national and 28 regional commissioners. CAVR established representatives and organised hearings in 13 districts and 65 subdistricts throughout East Timor. They documented and taped victims' testimonies.

I had earlier visited Jacinto Alves's office in Balide, a sleepy Dili neighbour-hood, meeting some CAVR translators and advisors, including Nugraha Katjasungkana, an Indonesian human rights activist, and Pat Walsh, a Melbourne researcher who used to edit *Inside Indonesia* magazine. That office was formerly a Portuguese-built prison known as Comarca. During the Indonesia occupation period, it was used by the Indonesian military as an interrogation and detention centre. Thousands of East Timorese men and women, and some children, were jailed here between 1975 and 1999.

Like most visitors, they showed me a cell called 'the submarine'.

Indonesians apparently bricked up the cell's doorway so that the cell could be filled with water, thereby providing an effective place of punish-ment. Prisoners had to stand for long periods or drown.

There were frequent disappearances and executions without trial in Comarca; inmates spent months without bedding or clothes in grossly over-crowded, dark cells in which human excrement frequently fouled the floor;

there were horrific beatings, torture with electricity and water; and, not surprisingly, appalling food. Death due to illness, violence and starvation was common.

For many people, the first hours spent in the prison were a foretaste of what was to come. Jacinto Alves, when arrested in 1992, was taken to a rock in the quadrangle that had the words, 'Welcome to Comarca'.

'We had to say "Welcome to Comarca" repeatedly for hours in the heat of the sun – from early in the morning until we fainted. Then we were splashed with water to get up. "Welcome to Comarca, welcome to Comarca", until we fainted again', Alves said.

'Then they beat us until we were swollen, puffy and bloody, and we couldn't stand it anymore. Then we lay down over there and slept exhausted in the mud'.

He was later moved to the Kedung Pane prison in Semarang, Java, and received relatively better treatment. When staying inside the Kedung Pane prison, he read a statement from Amien Rais, then the chairman of the Muhammadiyah, one of the largest Muslim organisations in Indonesia, who criticised the East Timorese for allegedly discriminating against Muslims.

He told me he sent a letter to Rais. 'Amien Rais made a statement as if the East Timorese, predominantly Catholics, do not respect the Muslims. Amien is obviously wrong. We want to state that there is no sectarianism in the East Timor struggle. The East Timor people hate men without principles. We respect people like Mari Alkatiri, although their religions are different from ours, but they are consistent with their principles. We respect people like them more than our co-religionists without principles. The evidence is that Mari Alkatiri, a Muslim, became our prime minister and the leader of a big political party (Fretilin). Leaders without principles are men who have no integrity. Indeed, they will be rejected'.

'Now after independence', Alves told me, 'the East Timorese welcome Indonesian citizens with sympathy, including those who used to be spies and informers of the intelligence. They remain here. There are quite a lot, mostly involved in business'.

It was late in the evening when we finished our interview. Jacinto Alves drove me back in his car, from the coffee shop to Hotel Turismo.

* * *

A few months later, I read in the newspapers that CAVR had launched its report, entitled 'Chega!' or 'Enough!' in Portuguese. They handed over the 2,500-page report to President Xanana Gusmão in October 2006. It listed a range of human rights abuses:

- Unlawful killings and enforced disappearances;
- Forced displacement and famine;
- Detention, torture and ill-treatment;
- Violations of the laws of war;
- Political trials;
- Sexual violence;
- Violations of the rights of the child;
- Economic and social rights.

CAVR received the assistance of Benetech, a California-based nonprofit organisation devoted to using technology in the service of humanity. It worked with CAVR to build a database of three independent sources: narrative statements, a retrospective mortality survey, and a census of public graveyards.

The first source consisted of approximately 8,000 narrative testimonies in which patterns of abuses such as arbitrary detentions, torture, rape and massive property destruction were reported to the CAVR. In turn, the CAVR developed a Human Rights Violations Database.

The second source was a survey of 1,396 households that were randomly selected from East Timor's approximately 180,000 households. Each sampled household gave information about their residence pattern and household members and relatives who died during the occupation. While these mortality surveys are standard procedure in governmental statistics, no truth commission had previously conducted one.

The third source was the graveyard census database, developed by visiting all public cemeteries in East Timor and recording the name, date of birth and date of death for every grave for which the information was available. The researchers established that there were approximately 319,000 graves in the sample, of which about half had complete name and date information. Once again, this was a first for a truth commission anywhere.

There had been numerous reports of mass killings and famine during the 24 years of Indonesian rule, but various apologists for the occupation had questioned high-end estimates of death tolls. *Chega* provided a scientifically credible estimate of a minimum of 102,800 deaths. It did not provide a maximum estimate but suggested that it may have been as high as 183,000. Sarah Staveteig, a demographer at the University of California, Berkeley, who worked with Benetech, reviewed these figures and Benetech's methodology. She applied standard demographic methods of indirect estimation and found that 'a reasonable upper bound on excess deaths during the period [was] 204,000'. Staveteig considered it 'likely that 204,000 is a conservative upper-bound estimate on excess mortality'. This makes the death toll in East Timor the highest relative to total population since the Holocaust during World War II in which Nazi Germany, aided by its collaborators, systematically murdered some six million European Jews.

Chega relied on Indonesian military records and intelligence from international sources. It documents a litany of massacres, summary executions of civilians, rapes, looting and the torture of 8,500 East Timorese. I almost vomited when reading the report. No wonder that Benny Moerdani, who played a huge role in East Timor, tries to keep a distance from the area in his biography.

Xanana went to New York to present the report to UN Secretary-General Kofi Annan. The report created a hysterical reaction in Java. A scheduled meeting between Xanana and President Susilo Bambang Yudhoyono was cancelled. Xanana publicly opposed CAVR's findings, arguing that cordial relations with Indonesia was more important than a potentially impotent quest for justice. Three months later, Xanana and President Yudhoyono agreed to ignore *Chega*'s conclusions. They decided not to discuss the findings, which recommended that Indonesia and Australia, among other countries, pay reparations to the fledgling nation.

Yudhoyono said the two nations had instead decided to focus on their Commission on Truth and Friendship, a new body that has frequently been criticised as merely cosmetic. Indonesia refused an international tribunal and promised to punish their military officers in Jakarta. But this was an empty promise. Not a single Indonesian officer has ever been punished. The Indonesian Army, the direct descendant of Japan's fascist military, still holds to its tradition of impunity. Accordingly, when the Commission on Truth and Friendship released its report in 2008, it stated its unswerving commitment to 'the conclusive truth', then said that the 'nature of the process by which East Timor was integrated into Indonesia has been the subject of controversy. The two parties to the conflict have opposing interpretations of this process which it is difficult to reconcile'. This means that Indonesia is yet to make an official admission that there was even an Indonesian invasion of East Timor. It hasn't changed its position, expressed in 1975 by Information Minister Mashuri, who said that 'Indonesian volunteers' had helped 'the combined forces' of 'our brothers in Portuguese Timor', and that the Indonesian military went there only after the formal integration on 17 July 1976. Consequently, Indonesia's longest war – the invasion and occupation of East Timor – is barely known to most Indonesians.

East Timorese Militias in Kupang

On a quiet Sunday, I rented a car and visited Tuapukan, an East Timor refugee camp, about 30 minutes drive from Kupang. I wanted to meet some militias. The camp is about 18 hectares, accommodating about 20,000 refugees. They live in semi-permanent huts built around an open area. Children played on the dusty roads. Women sat near their huts, gossiping and looking for hair lice.

In 1999, the Indonesian military built this camp in the heart of the Tuapukan village after driving away more than 260,000 East Timorese from East Timor. 'It was usual to see three families building their huts in our front yard and two families in the backyard', said Yakob Dethan, a village leader. His wife, Selvince, showed me their well, used by more than two dozen families. 'Sometimes we have to close the well, for about two hours, as the water is already too muddy', said Selvince.

I saw several huts located inside the Dethans' compound. Meri Djami, a student volunteer at the Tuapukan camp, who accompanied me on my walk around the camp, said that many villagers are frustrated. Their income from producing palm sugar had dropped from 10 boxes to four boxes in a season. Tuapukan used to be a cool and breezy area. 'Now it is very hot', Djami said.

Cultural differences also create a problem as most refugees originate from East Timor's eastern area, including Baucau and Los Palos. They are predominantly Catholics. The Kupang residents are predominantly Protestants and mostly speak Tetun. The refugees speak little Tetun. 'They don't necessarily understand each other. Most refugees are also illiterate', said Winston Rondo, who coordinates students like Meri Djami, in an organisation named Circle of Imagine Society Timor, based in Kupang.

The refugees, mostly militia families, have their own stories. Alfonso Soares, one of the East Timorese refugees, told me that his group had left their home village of Karaobalao in Viqueque, four days after the UN announcement of the East Timor referendum result.

Soares said, 'Indonesians are better than the Portuguese. Children could go to school. The Portuguese only sent mestizos to their schools'.

Soares now lives with his wife and four children, 'Two children were born here'.

Olandina da Silva Ximenes, another Tuapukan refugee, told me that her husband, Manuel da Silva, used to work for the Indonesian military. He was an Indonesian sergeant. He was killed in a Falintil ambush in August 1997. 'He was about to go home when he was killed. My husband died for the Red-and-White', Olandina said. She currently lives alone in a one-room hut. Her two youngest teenage daughters live in a Catholic nunnery in Kupang. Her eldest daughters live in Dili.

'When my second eldest daughter died, I was denied a visa to enter East Timor border in Motaain. It really hurt me', she said. 'My children can't communicate with their eldest sister in Dili. Perhaps, in the future, they won't recognise each other'.

There is no question that Olandina is an East Timorese, but she refuses to live in her Viqueque village. She also has no Indonesian passport.

According to Winston Rondo, refugees started to enter Western Timor in October 1999, with this reaching a climax in November. Rondo said eventually there were more than 260,000 refugees and 20,000 soldiers moving into western Timor. The soldiers included members of 12 Indonesian military territorial commands and two reserve commands (Battalion 744 and 745) in East Timor. Kupang's football stadium then hosted more than 10,000 refugees.

Rondo and his colleagues helped the refugees. He recalled, 'We asked for donations, clothes, food and everything through the churches and campuses'. International organisations such as UNHCR, European Commission of Humanitarian Office, Uniting Church of Australia, World Council of Churches, Catholic Relief Service and CD Bethesda (a Christian hospital in Yogyakarta) sent thousands of aid workers to help the refugees in 175 camps scattered throughout western Timor, including Tuapukan.

The militias thought they were 'war heroes', defending the sovereignty of Indonesia. The camps were organised like military barracks with flag raising ceremonies, territorial mapping, watchtowers, etc. According to Rondo, 'They sing *Indonesia Raya* and hold a flag raising ceremony every morning. They like to loudly talk about their heroic battles, victory after victory. Once a volunteer was beaten for walking over the shadow of the Red-and-White. He was accused of not being nationalist enough. We, who were born as Indonesians, were confused ourselves. What kind of nationalism is this?'

Slowly the East Timorese realised that others, including the western Timorese, did not think the militias nor the military were heroes. Worse than that, the Indonesian media, based mostly in Jakarta, ignored these militias. They slowly became frustrated when the Indonesian government also ignored them. It depressed the militias.

Alfonso Soares is one of these 'depressed war heroes'. He told me his parents died in the forest in 1977 when taking refuge from the Indonesian invasion. 'I don't know whether Fretilin or Indonesian soldiers shot them. I was still very young', said Soares. In 1980, he joined an Indonesian Army unit, as a child soldier, bringing their things and cleaning up their barracks.

In 1991, when a teenager, Soares began to operate weapons himself. It started with an SICS rifle equipped with a bayonet. 'I could operate any rifle, FNC rifle, SS-1 that were used by Battalions 743 and 744. We could shoot down a chopper with an FNC. But my favourite was the AR15 lightweight rifle. It was light and really tough if we took it into muddy places. I could use Minimi. Just bring me everything. Basically, whatever weapons the Indonesian military used, I could operate it, guns, rifles and pistols'. He sat down in front of his hut with his wife and some neighbours. 'I saw on TV that GAM guerillas used AK47 in Aceh'.

In July 1994, Soares was involved in a battle with Falintil guerillas in Los Palos. It was about 4 o'clock in the morning. Three Bugis-Indonesian soldiers of Battalion 431 were killed. Soares was seriously wounded and was treated for three months in the Gatot Subroto Army hospital in Jakarta.

Indonesia treated him well. He toured Jakarta and returned to Viqueque as a battle-ready tracker. But President Suharto stepped down from power in 1998 and many things changed.

'Habibie is illogical. We protected him from the Fretilin. Why should he hand over East Timor? Why should he give that option?'

In the August 1999 referendum, Soares did not vote. 'I was too scared although Indonesian soldiers asked me to vote'. Earlier that year, he claimed that five pro-independence activists cornered him in a transmigration village in Viqueque and beat him black-and-blue. I cannot independently verify this account from the CAVR website.

Soares, with his wife and two children, left Viqueque on 8 November 1999 in an Indonesian military convoy and later a Navy ship. His group arrived in Tenau seaport and later in Tuapukan.

'TNI said houses, clothes, rice were all readied. "Don't be scared"', he quoted the Indonesian military as saying. When arriving in Tuapukan, it was difficult to find food. His family lost three of their bags in the chaotic Tenau seaport. 'Arriving here, everything that they promised did not exist at all'.

Tuapukan was still a forest. He tried to build a hut and took some *gewang* leaves. 'When cutting the leaves, they (the local people) became angry and threw stones. It was really horrible. We finally paid some money for the leaves. How could you expect us to live without a roof over our heads? It was important to sustain the heat. We slept under the *gewang* leaves, just on the ground without anything'.

Gewang or nibung palm is a tall (up to 25 metres) densely clumping palm, with up to 50 trunks, all of which are covered with long black spines, with drooping leaves. The hard and water-resistant spines are usually used in places like Timor and Flores to build roofs and hut walls.

Yakob Dethan, the Tuapukan village leader, separately told me that some Indonesian military officers had initially visited his village, saying that they needed a place for the East Timor refugees. A state-owned factory let the military use its abandoned land. The villagers hesitated. A Kupang officer argued the refugees would stay for 'around three months'.

'Those who are strong enough will return and fight with our troops in East Timor. They will take over and return to East Timor', Dethan quoted the officer as saying. 'I asked him, "Is it true?" And they replied the young and the strong ones will return to East Timor with them'.

The next morning, the Indonesian military brought in wood planks and zinc roofing. When the refugees arrived, Dethan felt pity, '...especially seeing the children. They came here like ocean waters, wave after wave'. Dethan organised the building of huts, allocating spaces and giving them some plots of land to grow cassavas.

Assistance only arrived three months later. The UNHCR gave the refugees some cooking utensils, a plastic bucket, some blankets, a kerosene stove, a kerosene lamp and mosquito net. 'The Indonesian government closed their eyes', said Alfonso Soares. He became very disappointed toward his military bosses.

'We live and die under the Red-and-White. What fate do we have now? We are the ones who defended the Red-and-White in East Timor. What does the Indonesian state do to defend us? You know the other meaning of the Red-and-White?' he asked me. 'Red means I will be back. If I am back only with the white (flag) one, I don't want it. Red means bravery.

Let me die here without the red one returning to East Timor', he answered himself.

'If the Red-and-White is already in East Timor, I will also return. If the Red-and-White doesn't return, even if I must eat leaves here, I am ready to die here'.

I asked him whether he could eat the Red-and-White. He was furious, shouting and yelling at me, 'I know you're a journalist. You're lucky! If you're a soldier, I'd shoot you down. I will shoot you down!'

Mery Djami's face turned pale. She reminded me to be careful. The militias still have their weapons.

Winston Rondo said that the East Timor militias, including Soares, had regularly conducted a sweep against 'pro-independence' East Timorese in the 175 camps. They paraded in military trucks, moving from one place to another, holding their rifles and machetes. They liked to use Red-and-White headbands or Red-and-White clothes. They rallied almost every day in the streets of Kupang. They brought their homemade weapons with their long hair, entering shops and leaving without paying.

'They shot people's pigs and said, "Um, this belongs to Indonesia, right? Let's eat it together"'.

I wonder how Muhammad Yamin, the myth maker, would react when seeing his mystification of the Red-and-White turned to banditry?

According to Rondo and his CIS Timor colleagues, the refugees brought many electronics, such as laptops, and motorcycles. Each camp had some stores selling things at extremely low prices. 'We could buy a Honda Tiger (motorcycle) for only two million rupiahs', said Rondo. This is only one-sixth of the market price. People assumed that these things were looted from East Timor.

'Xanana once visited Kupang and met us all at the Kupang stadium. He said, 'We're all hurt. Here is hurt but there, in East Timor, is also hurt', said Olandina.

Olandina da Silva said, 'I don't like Ramos-Horta. He is a mestizo. He was not fighting in East Timor. I consider Matan Ruak (Falintil commander) to be the murderer of my husband. It still hurts me when talking about my late husband'.

Between 2000 and 2002, the international organisations helped return around 150,000 refugees back to East Timor. Statistically, there were 268,407 East Timorese grouped in 48,000 families arriving in western Timor after the 1999 referendum. By June 2001, 105,450 people had chosen to retain their Indonesian nationality. On 31 December 2002, the status of western Timor as a refugee area was terminated. But there were still nearly 100,000 East Timorese living in western Timor.

East Nusa Tenggara Governor Piet Tallo said his province can accommodate only about 6,000 families, or one-eighth of the refugees. The cash-strapped government stopped the supply of food assistance to the refugees, offering them the choice of either staying in other places within Indonesia or returning home to East Timor. Many of them ran out of food. Some began to eat cassava. Others eat rice or porridge, but only twice a day.

Villagers, like the Dethans, demanded the government to return their lands. 'We dare not to ask them out. They used to burn our houses. Their number is seven times bigger than ours', said Yakob Dethan, meaning they dare not ask for their expulsion. The East Nusa Tenggara government is helpless. The Kupang government offered three options: (1) repatriation back to East Timor; (2) resettlement in the East Nusa Tenggara province; (3) empowerment with training and education.

Hello, where are the military officers?

'They are gone, and their successors obviously claimed no responsibility', said Dethan. Rondo and his CIS Timor colleagues used video recorders to tape interviews between East Timor and western Timor, showing East Timorese village leaders calling on their countrymen to return. It helped reduce the number of refugees.

More than 17,000 refugees chose the resettlement program. They were moved to live on the islands of Alor, Flores, Sumba and Lembata. The majority chose to live in western Timor as it is easier and closer to visit their families and relatives. By July 2007, eastern Timor still had 5,000 families or around 25,000 refugees, living in 70 camps.

In Jakarta, Major General Zacky Anwar Makarim wrote a magazine column blaming 'foreigners' for writing the CAVR report. Makarim was the most senior military officer in East Timor in 1999, yet he had no real job description known to the public. He was allegedly in charge of a black operation to undermine the UN free ballot. Makarim also blamed President Gerald Ford, State Secretary Henry Kissinger and Prime Minister Gough Whitlam for encouraging the Indonesian government to take over East Timor in 1975. On 24 February 2003, Makarim was charged in absentia with crimes against humanity before the Dili special panel. In his column, Makarim skipped the manipulation of the Balibo declaration. He also skipped the Indonesian military covert operations in East Timor. The perpetrators refuse to admit their crimes. They also refuse to apologise.

Chapter 7

WEST PAPUA[2]

---

2   The name of this territory, Indonesia's western part of New Guinea Island, is *very confusing*. During the Dutch Indies period, it was named West New Guinea. In 1961, the Dutch-sponsored and ethnic Papuan-dominated West New Guinea Council decided to name their land 'West Papua'. Indonesian President Sukarno, who ordered the invasion in 1961, gave it another name: *Irian Barat*. When General Suharto came to power in 1965, he changed the name to *Irian Jaya*. In 1999, President Abdurrahman Wahid let Papuans use their own name: *West Papua*. Later President Megawati Sukarnoputri divided the territory into two provinces: *Papua* (capital Jayapura) and *West Papua* (capital Manokwari). I am using these provincial names – Papua and West Papua provinces – when referring to administrative terms but have used 'West Papua' as a whole.

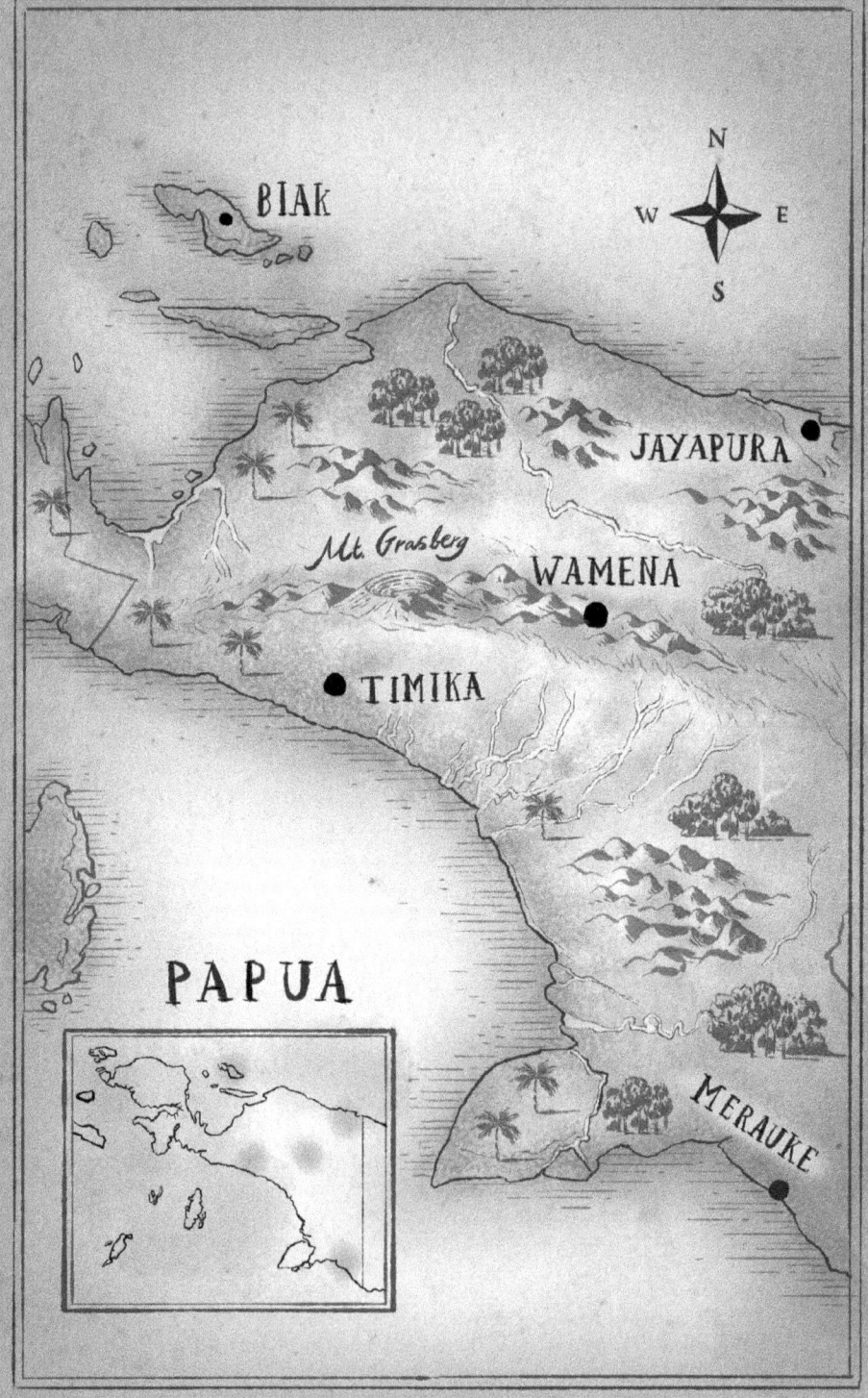

Racism versus Separatism

Merauke: Indonesia's Easternmost Mark

In June 2006, I arrived in Merauke, Indonesia's easternmost symbol in Papua province, about 35 months after starting my journey from Sabang island in Aceh. Merauke is a low land, close to the Indonesian border with Papua New Guinea, whose border crossing is located in Sota, a town about 80 kilometres east of Merauke. It means that geographically and legally Sota is Indonesia's easternmost border – not Merauke. It reminds me of Rondo Island, a small unpopulated islet north of Sabang island, the geographical westernmost border of Indonesia.

It should be from Rondo Island to Sota. But President Sukarno used the slogan 'from Sabang to Merauke' when launching a campaign to seize then Papua Guinea in 1961. Ironically it was created by J. B. van Heutsz, the Dutch Indies governor general, who defeated the Acehnese in 1904, killing 2,900 people, including 1,100 women and children. Van Heutsz, who used the slogan '*vom* Sabang *tot* Merauke' to describe the Dutch Indies territory, perhaps did not know Rondo and Sota, or knew Rondo and Sota but decided on the bigger Sabang island and Merauke town.

Journalist Agapitus Batbual accompanied me in Merauke, showing me Merauke's straight and wide streets patterned in a grid system. Batbual showed me a dark side of Merauke: a prostitution alley behind the Merauke hospital.

It was so dark that I could not even see my own hands.

I slowly adjusted my eyes to the darkness and saw rows of wooden huts. Each hut had three or five small rooms. I could see some straight-haired women inside. Outside a food stall, some men were smoking and talking in low voices, almost whispering.

Merauke is the first place where HIV/AIDS virus was found in West Papua. In 2005, an estimated 90,000 to 130,000 Indonesians were found HIV positive and 30 per cent of them were in West Papua. Unluckily, West Papua contains only one per cent of Indonesia's population. West Papuan nationalists likened the spread of the disease to Indonesia's harsh military occupation. It is also a reason to suggest the Papuan race is facing 'slow motion genocide'.

Batbual introduced me to Anita Ayu Sulandari, a 25-year-old sex worker, who worked in the alley but sometimes also on the main streets of Merauke.

Ayu is a Javanese Muslim. She grew up in Surabaya in eastern Java, but decided to run away from home to Makassar in southern Sulawesi after a dispute with her mother. She became a sex worker in Makassar and later moved to Merauke. In Merauke, she initially worked in a karaoke bar called Nikita. She worked there for three years until she decided to 'freelance' in the hinterlands of Kaname Island.

'I was considered old', she said. 'In Kaname, I did business, looking for the *gaharu* in the villages'.

The *gaharu* tree produces a hard, black resin that ethnic Asmat peoples burn to connect with their ancestors and cast spells. Outsiders value *gaharu*, or agarwood, as the source of expensive incense for the Asian and Middle Eastern market.

Ayu traded sex for *gaharu*, selling the *gaharu* to middlemen in Kaname. It's a widespread practice in West Papua, including in the remote mining and logging areas where workers could easily find sex workers. 'If the *gaharu* is of low quality, 1 kilogram buys a short time. If the quality is excellent, it could be one full night'.

Her clients were mostly Papuan men who found *gaharu* in the forests. But in October 2002, Ayu fell seriously ill and returned to Merauke. Doctors told her that she had contracted HIV. Devastated, she decided to stay in a Catholic-run HIV treatment house called Santo Antonius Foundation. It's managed by the Congregation of the Seven Sorrows.

In 2005, Ayu decided to leave the Santo Antonius facility and worked again on the street. 'I can't stand to live there. The (pocket) money was not enough. It's also depressing to see my housemates die one by one'.

I asked her if her consumers used condoms. 'They refuse to use condoms. They said it is not natural'. She said she sometimes only serves five clients in a single night. But her maximum was up to 30 men in a single day when money was high.

She recommended I meet her Merauke pimp: an Indonesian Army soldier.

* * *

Chief Sergeant Ukas lives in a white two-storey house next to his store on the outskirts of Merauke.

'I'm a retiree now', he smiled.

I told him that I had interviewed Anita Ayu Sulandari and that she is dying. He was sorry to hear that Ayu got HIV. They have not seen each other for some time. 'What can I do? She left Nikita a long time ago'.

His karaoke business began in 1996 when he was made the treasurer of the Merauke Military Command. 'We usually bring in girls from Java or Makassar. We contract them for three or four months. The girls sometimes went out with the guests. What can we do? We cannot say no, can we? But we also regularly checked their health'.

Ukas is one of thousands of Indonesian military officers who profit from shadowy side jobs in West Papua: prostitution, alcohol distribution, illegal logging, illegal mining, illegal trade of protected birds. They know it is illegal but the practice is so pervasive, it's almost taken for granted.

'Our salaries are not enough. We have to find extra income', Ukas argued.

Many Papuans say they are dying as a nation, among other things, due to the spread of HIV and poor health services in West Papua. They often compare the population of West Papua and PNG in 1962 when Indonesia started to rule West Papua.

In 1962 West Papua had a population of 800,000 people, mostly (718,000) dark-skinned Melanesian people. In 1962 PNG had a population of 2 million and this was 5.3 million by 2000. In 2000 West Papua had 1.5 million Melanesians, meaning the West Papuan population grew 2.8 per cent annually in 38 years. The Melanesian population in PNG grew roughly 4.3 per cent in the same period.

Yulianus Bole Gebze, an ethnic Malind chief and a former Merauke legislator, told me that HIV is not the only problem. They also have a problem with the huge migration into the area. 'Migration is natural in human civilisation. The Dutch Indies administration also brought workers from Java in the 1920s to Merauke'.

'We need migrants but not like the present number', said Gebze. 'It is now impossible for Papuans to develop. Job opportunities are almost all occupied by non-Papuans. Papuans are not Indonesian. Papuan culture and lifestyle are Melanesian'.

Transmigration is the Indonesian government process to move poor people from overcrowded Java and Bali to less populated islands such as Sumatra, Kalimantan, Sulawesi and Papua. In the 1970s, when President Suharto launched the program, Indonesia got help from the World Bank, as it believed transmigration had a significant impact on employment, migrant welfare and regional development in Indonesia. It was actually a program initiated under the Dutch Indies government in 1905. The Indonesian government believes that transmigration is also important to unify various racial groups in Indonesia.

Merauke is a very important transmigration destination area. It is a symbol of Indonesian nationalism. The Indonesian program began in 1983 when thousands of Javanese settlers were shipped into Merauke seaport mostly from Banyuwangi and Jember in eastern Java. Now it has more than a dozen transmigration villages with Sanskrit Javanese names: *Sumber Mulya, Sumber Harapan, Jaya Makmur, Rawa Sari, Marga Mulya, Sumber Rejeki, Harapan Makmur*. Javanese is widely spoken in Merauke.

When driving through these villages, I saw an entire settlement built on a grid system that, from the air, looked like a giant square. Four straight roads ran into the square, meeting at its centre: the Benny Moerdani statue – the Indonesian Special Forces captain involved in a covert operation to infiltrate Merauke in 1962. In the 1970s and 1980s, Moerdani became a very powerful assistant to then President Suharto, planning the East Timor invasion in 1975 and the streamlining of the Armed Forces in the 1980s.

It has military checkpoints in strategic locations in the area. Each village has administrative buildings, a police station, a post office, shops and some gas stations. Each settlement has a school and several mosques. The population are mostly Javanese Muslims with a small percentage of Papuans. I spoke Javanese when doing my business there, from buying meatballs to talking to officers.

In downtown Merauke, Perwita Sari of Statistics Indonesia told me that *'pendatang'* (migrants) are more dominant than *'penduduk asli'* (natives). Her office does not do an ethnic census due to 'limited budget'.

I visited Merauke again in March 2009 and June 2010, doing more interviews for Human Rights Watch, visiting the transmigration villages and interviewing Malind people in the swamp areas around Merauke.

Jim Elmslie in his book *Irian Jaya Under the Gun: Indonesian Economic Development versus West Papuan Nationalism*, wrote that there is actually little suitable land available for transmigration settlements in West Papua. Land ownership in West Papua is different from Java. He believes that the real motivation is to populate West Papua, an economically important Indonesian territory, with people mainly from Javanese descent for *security reasons*. The transmigration settlements are mostly located along the

Papua-PNG border, from Merauke in the south to Arso in the north with a border point at Wutung.

Spontaneous or unsponsored migration is the movement of individuals or families into Papua. They get no government sponsorship. Many Papuans like to refer to the "white ships" which dock in Jayapura or Nabire seaports, bringing in many of these migrants to their land. (The ships, from a state-owned company formally a part of the Dutch East Indies company, are always painted white.) This form of migration is bringing a larger influx of people than the official transmigration program, according to Elmslie. Local wages are relatively high in Papua and it is seen as a land of opportunity. Papua also has more rapid economic growth than most other provinces in Indonesia, due to mining and logging activities.

In 2010, the Indonesian government started a mega project, inviting big companies to open up palm oil plantations and industrialised agriculture in Merauke. It is expected to cover a million hectare area, or a quarter of Merauke. It provided more jobs to Indonesian migrants, inviting more workers from outside West Papua and sidelining more native Papuans.

In 2011, Jim Elmslie published another analysis of the racial breakdown in Papua and Papua Barat provinces, using the result of the 2010 Indonesian census. He showed that the ethnic Papuan population had increased from 887,000 in 1971 to 1,505,405 in 2000 with an average annual growth rate of 1.84 per cent. The non-Papuan population, mainly Indonesian migrants, increased from 36,000 in 1971 to 708,425 in 2000 with an average annual growth rate of 10.82 per cent.

He used those rates to calculate the number of non-Papuan people based on the 2010 census, finding the number of 1,882,517 or 52.10 per cent of the total population in the two provinces. By 2010, he estimated the indigenous Papuan population to be 1,730,336 or 47.89 per cent of the total population.

This shows the growing domination of the population by non-Papuan migrants where the indigenous Papuans are in the minority from being an overwhelming majority (96.09 per cent) in 1971, less than four decades ago.

Elmslie used historical growth rates to predict the racial breakdown for 2020, showing the increasing marginalisation of the Papuans. He assumed that the Papuan 2010 population of 1,760,557 continues to increase at an annual rate of 1.84 per cent. There will be 2,112,681 Papuans in 2020. If the non-Papuan population continues to increase at its historical rate of 10.82 per cent there will be 5,174,782 non-Papuans in 2020. This would give a total population of 7,287,463 of which Papuans would make up 28.99 per cent and non-Papuans 71.01 per cent.

Non-Papuan migrants are drawn to West Papua by the economic opportunities generated by the massive natural resource extraction industries led by gold and copper mining, oil and gas, logging and agriculture. Plans to convert millions of hectares of rainforest into oil palm and other plantation crops such as the ones in Merauke may even increase this rate.

Yulianus Bole Gebze might not have read Elmslie's analysis. He died at 65 in 2008 due to his liver problem. Anita Ayu Sulandari, that nice young woman, died three years after our interview. She was only 28 years old. I also had more and more Papuan friends – a very bright young columnist, a popular TV presenter, a musician and a leading human rights defender – dying because of HIV. West Papua was not only losing its population but some of its sharpest minds.

The Free Papua Movement

In May 2005 I rented a car, driving north for two hours from Jayapura, the capital of Papua province, to Wutung, the border town between West Papua and Papua New Guinea in the north. I wanted to see the security concern in the resettlement of thousands and thousands of Javanese migrants along the West Papua-PNG land border, approximately 760 kilometres, from Merauke in the south to Wutung in the north.

Angela Flassy, a Jayapura-based journalist, accompanied me. She had just read an anthropological study on ethnic languages in West Papua, briefing me about 265 languages in the western half of Papua Island.

When we were about to enter Wutung, we were stopped at an Indonesian military post with machine guns and sandbags. The sign declared that it was a post of the 432nd Infantry Battalion from Maros, South Sulawesi. A soldier stopped us and introduced me to his commander First Lieutenant Irvan Tarigan.

Tarigan is 27 years old. He has 14 soldiers at the post.

Private Husni Ali said, 'It's very quiet'.

They eat mostly instant noodles, eggs and salted fish. Their daily allowance is IDR15,500 (around US$1.25) per soldier. It's relatively low for the standard of living in West Papua. 'Our meals are basically simple and practical', said Tarigan.

Their battalion has about 450 soldiers distributed into three companies. 'It's a territorial duty. We're just guarding the Wutung area'.

I asked Tarigan about Mathias Wenda, a West Papuan guerilla leader, who used to be active in Wutung. 'Mathias Wenda is old now. He's not active, staying mostly in PNG'.

Wenda was a West Papua independence activist since he was a teenager in his Pyramid village, Central Highlands. He moved to Wutung in 1980, becoming a guerilla fighter under Jacob Prai, the head of the Defender of the Truth (Pembela Kebenaran, Pemka) within the armed wing of the Free Papua Movement.

In April 2001, when jailed in PNG, Wenda wrote a public letter, 'I am now imprisoned in my own land, Papua, by my own tribesman, Papuan and staying here in my own prison. Because of fighting against exploitation of my land and my people, against destruction of my ecology and ecosystem'.

Despite the affinity between people on the two sides of New Guinea Island, a border was drawn down the middle by European colonialists in 1895 and 1910 that officially separated them. The British and Germans claimed the eastern half and the Dutch claimed the west. The Netherlands claimed West New Guinea in 1828 mainly because of its proximity to the Dutch Indies.

In November 1949, when The Hague was negotiating to cede sovereignty to Indonesia, they agreed to talk about the status of Papua, then West New Guinea, in further talks to take place within a year. Mohammad Hatta, the Indonesian chief negotiator, agreed, as he himself thought it was more practical to deal with the other territories.

But Sukarno annulled the federal arrangement in August 1950, concentrating power in the central government in Jakarta and sparking rebellions in the Outer Islands including the Moluccas as well as Sumatra and Sulawesi. This prompted The Hague to retaliate, setting up three advisory councils in Papua in May 1951 to advise the Dutch government and to prepare the Papuans for autonomy.

Both sides tried to negotiate about West Papua but continuously failed. In December 1957, the Indonesian government ordered around 50,000 Dutch nationals living in Indonesia to leave the country. In August 1960, the Dutch Embassy to Jakarta was closed and the diplomatic Dutch-Indonesian ties were severed. Indonesia brought the West Papuan dispute to the United Nations, stressing that West New Papua was a part of the Dutch Indies territory and it should be a part of Indonesia.

I brought a book written by John Saltford, *The United Nations and the Indonesian Takeover of West Papua, 1962–1969: The Anatomy of Betrayal*, during my trips to Merauke and Wutung, trying to learn about the process in the United Nations.

According to Saltford, in September 1961 Dutch Foreign Minister Joseph Luns presented a proposal to the UN General Assembly in which the Dutch would withdraw from West New Guinea and terminate its sovereignty, to be replaced by a UN administration and the establishment of 'a member state study commission'. The UN would supervise the administration and organise a plebiscite to decide the territory's final status.

Walt Rostow, a National Security Affairs advisor, disagreed with Luns' proposal. Rostow wrote a memo to President Kennedy asserting that Indonesian control of the territory was the only permanent solution, to avoid Jakarta being 'driven into the arms' of the Soviet Union. Rostow was known to be a supporter of the US involvement in the Vietnam War. He also advised the US government to be frank with The Hague, telling the Dutch that self-determination for 'stone-age' Papuans was rather meaningless.

But the UN General Assembly decided to have a vote on Luns' proposal and the American government supported that idea. Still the proposal received half of the votes. It was quite a lot but not enough to pass that proposal. The Dutch suddenly had no other alternative on West New Guinea.

On 1 December 1961 the Dutch-sponsored West New Guinea Council voted to rename the territory 'West Papua' with a national anthem and a national flag, *Bintang Kejora* or the Morning Star, which flies alongside the Dutch tricolour. It also passed a resolution supporting Dutch Foreign Minister Joseph Luns' plan to establish a UN administration in West Papua in a bid to supervise and organise a plebiscite to decide West Papua's final status. The West New Guinea Council also called on all nations to respect the rights of the Papuans to self-determination.

This infuriated Jakarta. President Sukarno immediately called it a Dutch 'puppet state'. On 19 December 1961, Sukarno made a major speech at a rally in Yogyakarta in which he called for a mass mobilisation to 'liberate' West Irian. Sukarno rejected the name West Papua. It was a declaration of war against the Dutch in West Papua.

Benny Moerdani and his men were parachuted to Papua. This increased the American pressures on the Netherlands although these infiltrators did not match the strength of the Dutch and the Papuan forces on the ground. An important consideration for the Dutch was that it could not win a war so very far away from Europe. Neither Australia, Britain nor the United States would give any commitment to provide military support. The Dutch were not prepared to fight alone.

In February 1962, US Attorney General Robert Kennedy, a brother of US President John F. Kennedy, travelled to Jakarta and The Hague to broker talks between Indonesia and the Netherlands. The talk took place in Middleburgh, Virginia, in March 1962, officially under the United Nations but sponsored by the US, which chose Ellsworth Bunker, an American diplomat, as mediator. The result was the New York Agreement, signed on 15 August 1962. It said that in six weeks, a UN administrator was to manage Papua, and in nine months, control was to pass to Jakarta. It was a great victory for Indonesia. The Hague accepted the agreement, at least, to avoid having a war with Indonesia.

There was one actor missing from all of these negotiations: Papuans themselves.

They tried to speak up but got arrested. Some of them tried to go to New York via Port Moresby but got delayed. It was the beginning of the independence movement in West Papua. They felt they were not heard.

The United Nations Secretary General U Thant appointed a Bolivian diplomat, Fernando Ortiz Sanz, to be the UN representative in West Papua. Ortiz Sanz had worked as a lawyer, journalist, legislator, academic, award-winning novelist and poet. He also served as Bolivia's under secretary for foreign affairs and the Bolivian representative in the United Nations.

Soon Ortiz Sanz faced the refusal of the Indonesian government to have a one-person-one-vote procedure in West Papua. The Indonesian government wanted to use an electoral system in which the territory was to be divided into eight regencies. Each of these would have a number of electors. Indonesia calls this electoral system *musyawarah* or consensus.

On 20 April 1969, the selection process for the Act of Free Choice electors began without any UN involvement and in early July 1969, these electors were reportedly isolated from the rest of the Papuan population. Indonesian military briefed them on Indonesian nationalism and the Dutch divide-and-rule strategy.

The voting began in Merauke on 14 July in which the Merauke assembly voted unanimously to integrate with Indonesia. This continued in Wamena on 17 July and again the Wamena assembly voted unanimously to integrate with Indonesia. The voting subsequently took place in Nabire (19 July), Fakfak (23 July), Sorong (26 July), Manokwari (29 July), Biak (31 July) and finally in Jayapura on 2 August. *In total 1,026 representatives voted unanimously to integrate with Indonesia.*

On 19 November 1969, the United Nations General Assembly in New York voted by 58 to 31 with 24 abstentions to reject a move by the Republic of Dahomey for an adjournment of the so-called Act of Free Choice. It then voted 60 to 15 with 39 abstentions to reject a Ghanaian amendment to the resolution on the Act of Free Choice for a further voting in Papua by the end of 1975.

In the end, the UN General Assembly voted 84 to none with 30 abstentions to pass the unamended resolution of the Act of Free Choice. Papua became legally an Indonesian territory.

Dutch historian Pieter Drooglever, who wrote an 854-page historical monograph on the process, concluded, 'In the opinion of the Western observers and the Papuans who have spoken out about this, the Act of Free Choice ended up as a sham'.

In the 1960s, colonialism was indeed a dirty word.

Indonesia won the United Nations vote by exploiting the word 'Dutch colonialism'. Many UN members, who opposed colonialism, interestingly, also objected to any Dutch moves toward granting independence to West New Guinea. Some African countries remained sympathetic to the Papuan cause but the crucial point to remember about the 'anti-colonial' states during the debate was their strong adherence to the doctrine of *uni possidetis juris*. This basically argues that territorial boundaries of post-colonial states should match those of the colonial territories that they replaced. The logic behind this was that it minimised territorial disputes among post-colonial states, thereby avoiding unnecessary conflict.

In his book, John Saltford quoted poverty and human rights scholar Michael Freeman of Essex University who asserts that *uni possidetis juris* is a flawed argument, 'Most states were multinational or polyethnic, and many subordinate ethno-nationalist groups perceived the doctrine of *uti possidetis juris* to be an ideology that justified the domination of weak peoples by groups that had managed to seize state power. Consequently, secessionist wars and anti-secessionist repression became pervasive features of the post-colonial world order. The UN states system could not live in peace with the nationalism that it had itself encouraged. It would only recognise states while it denied to many peoples the right to their own states'.

Indonesia managed to convince most of the anti-colonial movement that West Papua had been an inherent part of the Dutch Indies. Under *uti possidetis juris*, it belonged to Indonesia. If the Dutch granted independence, it would be an act of separatism against Indonesia.

In December 1999, John Saltford interviewed Fernando Ortiz Sanz in his retirement in Sucre, Bolivia, and asked him how he felt about the Act of Free Choice in 1969. Ortiz Sanz replied that the result was 'wise and sensible...But this does not make me rule out that, in the future, the population of West Irian should again have the opportunity to decide their own fate. I told them: be patient. The moment will come, do not fear. Go to school, learn everything there is to know about the principles of democracy and the road will be open to you'.

In Wutung, First Lieutenant Irvan Tarigan let my car pass his military post, going to the border. Twenty minutes later, I passed the border crossing without anyone stopping me. It was quiet. No border guards. No police. A man was sleeping right on top of the large immigration counter. A 20-metre zone is a no-man's-land between Indonesia and PNG.

On the PNG side, there was an immigration office where Angela Flassy had to show her Jayapura ID card. It also had a drug store selling medicine and PNG souvenirs. The shop assistant told me that the most popular souvenirs were PNG caps and PNG T-shirts. 'Anything with a PNG flag is popular', he said.

I also met a small truck of PNG citizens returning from Jayapura. They bought mostly instant noodles, cigarettes, clothes, blue jeans and other food. 'Cheaper in Jayapura', one said.

Flassy's mother is Javanese. She went to school in Java, graduating from college in Solo and later worked in Jayapura. She got to know her father's family in Jayapura. Her husband was a Papuan civil servant. It's tough to live in two opposites. 'In Papua, I am often accused of being a Javanese. But in Java, people called me Papuan. If only Indonesia got Papua in a proper way', she sighed.

A Big Man in Sentani

If you fly to Jayapura, you will land at the Sentani airport and see a single cemetery outside. It's the only cemetery on a plot of land right in front of the airport. It's the burial ground of Theys Hiyo Eluay, arguably the most influential West Papuan leader and a Sentani native, assassinated on 10 November 2001.

I often passed this cemetery, sometimes stopping by, putting some flowers and trying to remember this big, and complicated, man.

I knew Theys Eluay since he began to emerge as a West Papuan leader in post-Suharto Indonesia, mostly staying at the five-star Hotel Indonesia in Jakarta and often inviting journalists to cover his media conferences. He was tall and heavyset, with a white-tinged afro and frizzy beard. He had a straightforward way of talking, often peppering his speeches with jokes.

Theys Eluay was born in Sentani in 1937. In the 1960s he worked as a Dutch West Guinea meteorological assistant. He later replaced his father as the chief of his Sentani tribe. Eluay supported West Papua's integration into Indonesia. In 1969, Eluay was appointed an elector in the UN-sponsored Act of Free Choice which voted 100 per cent for Indonesia. In 1971, Eluay became a legislator in Jayapura with the Indonesian Christian Party, moving to Golkar – the political party that Suharto used to win bogus elections during his 33-year authoritarian rule – in 1977 and keeping his legislative position for a decade.

In July 1998, two months after Suharto's fall, the Indonesian parliament sent a fact-finding delegation to Jayapura to investigate widespread protests in West Papua. A Golkar politician led the delegation.

They hosted a talk with local leaders of Golkar and some other Papuan intellectuals in an upscale hotel in downtown Jayapura. The Papuans presented the Jakarta politicians with a litany of human rights abuses in Papua, including the Biak massacre on 5 July 1998. The Golkar man responded with a monologue about West Papua's integration into Indonesia. The audience got bored.

'Suddenly someone stood up', said theologian Benny Giay, who recalled the event to American anthropologist Eben Kirksey, 'It was Theys Eluay'. Eluay's big physique immediately commanded the attention of all eyes in the room.

Giay recalled, 'Theys shook with anger. As he picked up a chair to hurl at the parliamentarians, we restrained him'. Eluay shouted, 'We didn't come here to listen to your canned history, but to initiate a dialogue. The problem with the political status of West Papua is not just a national problem but an international problem'.

This outburst caught the Indonesian parliamentarians off guard. Theys Eluay, one of the 1,026 electors who had voted West Papua's integration into Indonesia in 1969 and been a Golkar politician for two decades, was rejecting Indonesia's historical claims to West Papua. Theys Eluay also had close ties to the Indonesian military. He allegedly helped the Indonesian military to identify West Papuan freedom fighters in Sentani in the 1980s, men who then disappeared. Theys Eluay also allegedly executed Julianus Joku, a young man openly critical of the Indonesian military, in Sentani.

Days later, Theys Eluay returned all the material artefacts associated with his career as a member of the Golkar party – awards, certificates, gifts bearing the banyan tree logo – to the local Golkar headquarters in Jayapura. He also asked a pastor to perform a full immersion baptism on him in Lake Sentani. In his Biblical interpretation, he talked about a born-again conversion: 'Before I was Saul and now I am Paul'.

In *Freedom in Entangled Worlds: West Papua and the Architecture of Global Power*, Eben Kirksey used rhizomes to describe political resistance in West Papua, also from people such as Theys Eluay. Rhizomes, in a botanical sense, are stems that spread laterally in the topsoil and send down roots. Rhizomes are different from roots. They ceaselessly establish connections among organisations of power, social struggles and other heterogeneous forms. These forms are extremely difficult to disrupt or to kill. When plans with rhizomes are mowed down, they grow back. When chopped up and left for dead, they resprout.

Kirksey argued that during Suharto's authoritarian rule, the West Papuan freedom movement had already been moving quietly underground in the form of rhizomes, evading detection and fuelling dreams of breakouts into the light of day.

Initially the Free Papua Movement (Organisasi Papua Merdeka, OPM) had an identified leader: Permenas Ferry Awom, from Biak island, a former sergeant major in the Dutch colonial police, who led a series of armed uprisings in the mountainous region of the Bird's Head Peninsula in 1965. After Awom surrendered in 1970, and his reported murder, the OPM became a rhizome. A multiplicity of competing leaders, representing various linguistic and cultural groups, including Seth Rumkorem's Victoria faction and Jacob Prai's Pemka, in the border area, became linked together under the umbrella of the OPM – an *organised anti-organisation*.

These rhizomes, according to Eben Kirksey, were crawling and attaching themselves around the Indonesian state, symbolised for Kirksey by the banyan tree.

Suharto's Golkar Party also uses a banyan tree as its symbol. Golkar's logo is a green banyan tree surrounded with yellow rice and cotton ornaments. Rice is to symbolise food. Cotton is to symbolise clothing. Golkar virtually eliminated all forms of political opposition. His military-backed regime only tolerated two other, deeply tamed political parties: the Islamic United Development Party, symbolised by the Kaaba in Mecca, and the nationalist Indonesian Democratic Party which helped catapult Megawati Sukarnoputri to prominence in 1996, two years prior to Suharto stepping down from power.

Theys Eluay is a part of those rhizomes. But he also kept his dark side. On 11 August 1998, less than two weeks after his confrontation with the Golkar leaders, Theys Eluay had a secret meeting with former president Suharto at his residence in Jakarta. Suharto and his allies were trying to distract the Indonesian public from a nationwide campaign to bring Suharto to trial over his corruption, by fanning the flames of freedom in West Papua. It was Suharto and his cronies who paid Eluay in his struggle for freedom in West Papua.

Benny Giay, who wrote a book about Eluay, encouraged Kirksey, then a first-year graduate student, to investigate Eluay's connection to Suharto and the Indonesian military. Eluay embarked on an independence campaign, helping set up the Papua Presidium Council with many other Papuan leaders.

On 6 October 1998, Theys Eluay and four of his close associates were arrested for treason. But the arrest turned him into a martyr and increased his popularity in Papua. New organisations and new figures emerged, catapulting the freedom movement to a new height. The five men were soon released but the momentum had already built.

President B. J. Habibie, who succeeded Suharto, agreed to have a dialogue. His state secretary agreed to have seven West Papuans, led by Cenderawasih University lecturer Willy Mandowen, to coordinate the dialogue. On 26 February 1999, a delegation of 100 Papuan leaders were invited to meet President Habibie in the presidential palace in Jakarta. *Kompas* correspondent in Jayapura, Octovianus Mote, who used to work in Jakarta, helped organise for the delegates to go to Jakarta.

It was a diverse delegation, coming from different parties, ethnic groups, gender groups and civil society organisations. But it excluded Theys Eluay. 'Independence was the strongest aspiration I heard from the Papuans in all my experience of working eight years as a journalist. Wherever you go in Papua, all over, in the streets or the highlights, civil servants to intellectuals to villagers, everybody has the same voice', Mote is quoted saying in a 2007 book, *The Testimony Project Papua*, by Charles Farhadian.

Mote was nervous that many of the delegates, especially those with government ties, would refuse to endorse their joint statement. Surprisingly, all 100 delegates signed the declaration, presented to Habibie. It confirmed his belief that most Papuans wanted to separate from Indonesia.

Tom Beanal, an elder statesman from the Amungme tribe in Timika, was selected to read the declaration: 'We the people of West Papua have the intention to leave the Unitary Republic of Indonesia for freedom and for full sovereignty among the other nations on the surface of the earth'. It was a frank statement – aspiration for freedom not aired behind the backs of the Indonesian officials.

Habibie cancelled his prepared statement and talked with the delegates 'heart to heart'. He thanked them for making diplomatic efforts, 'Your method of presenting your aspirations has been very congenial, in contrast to other regions'.

Habibie called their effort 'honest and pure'. He also used the name 'West Papua' – not Suharto's Irian Jaya. But he did not explicitly reject or accept their demand. He just wanted them to go home in peace and to contemplate.

The delegates went back to West Papua but Mote felt that the Indonesian military suspected him. 'The military put me in a situation where I was acting like a politician, which was sad because I'm not a politician. I was just a journalist, they thought I was one of the masterminds of the Papuan movement for independence. They knew the aspiration for Papuan independence was already there before I was born in 1962'.

In April 1999, his friend Obed Badi, an academic at a Catholic college, died inside a police station apparently after being attacked somewhere else. Mote believed it was intended for it to be him. 'His face is similar to my face. He may have been killed by mistake...there was no independent investigation about the killing', Mote said.

A few months later, Mote went to San Francisco and Washington DC on a two-week State Department program along with two other Indonesian academics. But Jakarta newspapers accused him of running away. 'I decided to stay in the US. The State Department understood my situation. They changed my visa. Eventually I got a visiting fellow position at Cornell University', he said.

It was the beginning of his move to the United States, being a fellow at Cornell University and befriending Benedict Anderson and other professors at Cornell. He later moved to Yale University, doing research on genocide while delivering pizzas to pay his bills.

On 29 May 2000, Eluay opened the one-week West Papuan Congress in which nearly 3,000 delegates from all over West Papua talked about human rights abuses, environmental destruction, the marginalisation of indigenous Papuans as well as the aspiration to be an independent nation. This was held in a stadium in downtown Jayapura. The Morning Star flag was flown all over West Papua. In Jakarta, President Abdurrahman Wahid ordered his troops to tolerate the Papuans. Wahid even donated some money to finance the event – one-third of the total budget, according to Agus Alua who chaired the congress.

On 2 June 2000, about 15,000 ethnic Dani men and women, the biggest ethnic group in West Papua, joined the congress in the stadium, clad in their colourful paraphernalia – bows, arrows, blackened spears and lots of birds' feathers. Ethnic Mee, the second-largest racial group, also sent thousands of men and women, also in their traditional dress. They danced and sang for two days till the closing ceremony on 4 June.

The atmosphere was nothing but *merdeka*. Independence.

Theys Eluay joked, 'When my time has come, I would sure go to heaven. But if I see Indonesians there, even a single Indonesian, I would run and leave heaven. If the angels of God asked me why I run away, I will say, "Well…I see Indonesians there, I am afraid they will again colonise Papuans"'.

In Jakarta, various politicians reacted with disdain. On 27 June 2000, President Wahid received four West Papuan Catholic church leaders, including two bishops, asking them about the congress. They gave him a long list of human rights abuses and the marginalisation that Papuans had suffered since the 1960s. In their report, they talked about *memoria passionis* – the collective memory in West Papua of their decades of suffering and humiliation. They told Wahid that Papuans felt that they were not treated as equals inside Indonesia.

On 4 July 2000, seven West Papuan leaders, including Theys Eluay, Tom Beanal, Thaha Alhamid and Willy Mandowen, met President Wahid in Jakarta, briefing him about the congress' recommendations. They told him about their eagerness to separate from Indonesia. They also thanked Wahid for giving money to support the event.

Wahid said that he appreciated their peaceful gathering, saying that West Papua was relatively peaceful despite the huge turnout at the congress. He said other areas in post-Suharto Indonesia, such as Aceh and the Moluccas, were facing great violence. He said that he had told his military and police commanders that the Papuans had simply expressed their political aspiration. It was a matter of freedom of expression. He would set up a team, including his Papuan advisors, to discuss the recommendations.

The seven Papuan leaders were also talking about Wahid's presidency, knowing very well that Wahid might lose his job. Theys Eluay said West Papuans respected and loved him. They were going to wait for Wahid's policy on West Papua.

But Wahid did not stay in power long enough. In July 2001, the People's Consultative Assembly unanimously voted to impeach President Wahid and to replace him with Vice-president Megawati Sukarnoputri. In Jayapura, rumours began to circulate that the Indonesian government, the deep state which controlled the banyan bureaucracy, was going to eliminate some Papua Presidium Council leaders including Theys Eluay, Tom Beanal and Agus Alua.

Theys Eluay was target number one.

On 10 November 2001, Theys Eluay attended the Heroes Day's reception at the Special Forces' base in Hamadi, Jayapura. When it was over, Lieutenant Colonel Sri Hartomo, the commander, walked Eluay to his Toyota Kijang van. A journalist, who happened to cover the reception, walked with Eluay, asking Eluay if Eluay could give him a ride. But Eluay did not respond. Two Special Forces officers entered the car, sitting on the back seat, probably to provide security until Sentani.

According to witnesses in Benny Giay's book, Theys Eluay's car was stopped in a place known as Skyline, the highest point in Jayapura. Four men entered his car, kicking away Eluay's driver, Aristoteles Masoka. But the driver managed to hang onto the car for around 50 metres, screaming while it was driven away with Eluay inside. It created a minor traffic jam in the area.

The driver asked for help and a passing Suzuki Carry van stopped. Masoka reportedly asked the Suzuki driver, who was driving with some passengers, to bring him to the Special Forces base in Hamadi, about 8 kilometres away.

Wearing socks but shoeless, Masoka said he wanted to protest to Lieutenant Colonel Sri Hartomo. He told them six Special Forces officers had kidnapped his boss, Theys Eluay.

'The commander was a decent man, but his men were rude', recalled the Suzuki driver, quoting Masoka. Masoka reached Hamadi and entered the Special Forces compound. The Suzuki car continued to Jayapura. Masoka made a short phone call at around 10.00 pm, telling Eluay's home that 'Father Theys' was abducted by 'amber' – a local word for non-Papuans. As the driver was speaking, the phone was cut off, according to Eluay's family. It was the last time Masoka was known to be alive. The driver is still missing.

On the morning of 11 November 2001, Theys Eluay's body was found inside his Toyota van in Koya, about 60 kilometres east of Jayapura, near the border with Papua New Guinea. His death was due to strangulation, according to the forensic examination.

That evening, two shops, two banks, a pharmacy, and a hotel in Sentani were burned down. Police fired into the air to stop the angry mob. Lieutenant Colonel Sri Hartomo denied involvement in the assassination. But international outrage prompted the Indonesian military police to investigate. In 2003, a court in Surabaya found seven Special Forces soldiers, including Lieutenant Colonel Hartomo, guilty of mistreatment and battery leading to Eluay's death, but crucially not of murder. Sentences served by the seven ranged from two to three-and-a-half years.

But President Megawati's Army chief of staff, General Ryamizard Ryacudu, hailed the convicted men as 'Indonesian heroes' for the killing of a 'rebel'. No further investigations have been undertaken into who ordered the killing and no senior officer has been held accountable. Hartomo and those six officers appealed and got a lighter sentence. I spent five years trying to get hold of their verdicts but failed. Hartomo became a two-star general, becoming the head of the military intelligence agency in 2016.

Munir Said Thalib, Indonesia's human rights defender, spent some time investigating the assassination. He revealed a Ministry of Home Affairs memo on West Papua in which some leaders, including Eluay, were to be targeted in a 'clandestine operation'. Munir was poisoned to death on 7 September 2004 during a Jakarta-Amsterdam flight.

This shows the deep state, the banyan tree, in its darkest hour. Banyans are polymorphic: some have a single trunk, while other trees grow into a whole grove of interconnected secondary trunks. In tropical regions, banyans assume dominant positions in gardens, crowding out other plants and overgrowing human architecture.

Beneath banyan trees, other plant life is shaded out and has difficulty growing. The towering canopy of banyans also stunt civil society organisations in Indonesia. Suharto used the Indonesian military and civil bureaucracy to suppress any dissent. These did not fade away when Suharto stepped down from power.

Theys Eluay had become a key node in a polycentric, entangled network of the West Papuan resistance. When he was killed, the banyan tree expected that the independence movement in West Papua might die down, if not become paralysed. Perhaps it was justifiable to think that but it turns out this was wrong, as new leaders slowly began to step forward.

In December 2008, I passed Theys Eluay's cemetery in Sentani and saw a group of young men placing flowers. Buchtar Tabuni, a 29-year-old activist, used the graveyard to fly tiny Morning Star flags. I did not realise that it was the birth of another mass organisation in West Papua called the West Papua National Committee (Komite Nasional Papua Barat, KNPB).

Rhizomes, when chopped up and left for dead, resprout.

A Political Prisoner in Abepura

On Christmas Day 2008, I visited the Abepura prison in Jayapura, joining their Christmas celebration. A priest was giving a sermon. It was a small chapel with around 50 prisoners and some choir members. A Papuan man with a Karl Marx-like beard, in a light brown shirt, sat behind me. He put a Morning Star flag on his chest.

'Filep Karma', he shook my hand.

In May 2005, the Abepura district court found him guilty of treason for organising a pro-independence rally on 1 December 2004, and sentenced him to 15 years of imprisonment.

He was born in 1959 into an elite Papuan family on Biak island. His father, Andreas Karma, was a Dutch-educated bureaucrat who retained his position under Indonesian rule, and was appointed deputy regent of Jayapura in 1968. He became the regent of Wamena, Central Highlands, from 1970 until 1978. In 1979, he moved to Serui, becoming the regent there for a decade until his retirement. Filep's cousin, Constant Karma, is a former Papua deputy governor and was later the head of Papua's AIDS Eradication Commission.

Karma told me he had overheard his father and uncle talk quietly about the mistreatment of native Papuans under Indonesian rule. He learned how his father, then the regent in Wamena, locally the highest government official in the area, had to face a Special Forces officer, using a gun to ask for money inside his father's office.

'I am pretty sure that Papuan governors also face similar threats'.

In 1977, when Karma was 18 years old, the Indonesian army conducted a military operation in Central Highlands, killing and starving to death thousands of native Papuans. This took place after some OPM guerillas had attacked a group of Indonesian soldiers during a football match on 20 April 1977 in Kobakma village. They killed one officer and wounded two others, prompting the local military to ask for assistance from their headquarters. Two army battalions from Central Java and South Sulawesi were deployed to the area. Three OV-10 Bronco planes were also deployed, conducting aerial bombings in the mountainous area. Asia Human Rights Commission has the names of 4,146 victims killed in 15 districts between April and July 1977. It reported various atrocities including rape, torture and mass executions.

The events emboldened young Karma to help his fellow Papuans, thinking to get involved in the Papuans' struggle using political means rather than violence. In 1979, he studied political science at the March 11 University in Solo, Central Java. He graduated in 1987 and began to work as a civil servant in Jayapura. He married his college sweetheart, Ratu Karel Lina, a Javanese-Malay woman, and they had two daughters.

In 1997, he received a scholarship to take an 11-month course at the Asian Institute of Management in Manila. When he returned to Indonesia in May 1998, he travelled in Java and learned about widespread student protests against President Suharto. On 1 July 1998, a few hours after the Morning Star was flown in Jayapura, Tanjung Karma, a member of the prominent Karma family, talked to two prayer groups on Biak island. They decided to mobilise their members to raise the flag, also in Biak. Tanjung suggested his cousin, Filep Karma, to speak at the event. Filep had just returned from his studies in Manila. He was considered to be 'a big man'.

Filep Karma basically stepped forward to claim the legacy of the OPM in that July 1998 rally although he had no ties to the guerilla fighters, the remaining followers of Permenas Ferry Awom, who were lying low in nearby jungles in western Biak island, nor the rival camps operating from the border areas. Karma also had no connections with West Papuan leaders in exile.

On 2 July 1998, he helped organise a large pro-independence rally and raised the Morning Star flag on the water tower near the Biak seaport. A violent clash ensued in which approximately a dozen police were wounded.

Kris Padwa, an electrician who was detained shortly for his political protest in 1985, told me that most Papuans, if given a chance to speak freely, would likely talk about independence. 'We suffer a lot under Indonesia'. He joined the Filep Karma–led protest around the water tower, 'We cassowaries cannot fly, by God, we can run'.

On 6 July, the Indonesian military opened fire on the protesters and took control of Biak island. The full death toll remains unknown as many bodies reportedly were loaded onto trucks and allegedly dumped into the sea from two Indonesian navy ships. 'Once I travelled to villages around Biak. Villagers told me about graves where they buried dead bodies from the seashore', Karma said.

He estimated more than 150 protesters were killed. Kris Padwa saw naval war ships near the Biak seaport and many Indonesian soldiers on the streets. 'It reminded us of World War II'.

Human Rights Watch has reported that the Indonesian government has continuously failed to carry out a serious investigation of these allegations, or hold accountable the perpetrators of abuses against the people in Biak. Without an independent and impartial investigation to ensure accountability, the memories of those killings will continue to inflame tensions and varied death-toll estimates will continue to circulate.

Karma was wounded in his legs by rubber bullets. The police arrested him and held him in detention from 6 July to 3 October 1998. 'I had maggots from my wound. No medical treatment. It healed naturally', he said.

On 25 January 1999, the Biak district court found him guilty of treason and sentenced him to six-and-a-half years in jail. Karma appealed this sentence and was freed on 20 November 1999 with an amnesty from President Abdurrahman Wahid.

I left the Abepura prison, and started to research the OPM activism in West Papua.

Jim Elmslie's explanation about the OPM is a practical guide to understanding the independent movements in West Papua. Elmslie, in his book *Irian Jaya under the Gun*, divided the Indonesian control into four periods.

The first is from 1 October 1962 to 1 July 1971. It marks the time between the arrival of the United Nations and Seth Rumkorem's 'Declaration of the Independent Republic of West Papua'. Rumkorem was a former Indonesian Army intelligence officer who became frustrated to see the so-called Act of Free Choice in 1969. His protest caused him to end up in a military prison. But the resistance against Indonesia grew from disorganised and short-lived rebellion, including in Permenas Ferry Awom's efforts in Manokwari and Biak island, to a centralised ongoing guerilla war, waged by, essentially, full-time fighters that Rumkorem established in 1973 around Wutung. Rumkorem called his guerilla forces the National Liberation Army (Tentara Pembebasan Nasional, TPN) and the jungle head office 'Victoria'. It operates within a loose military hierarchy and is accepting of a broad set of common goals.

The second period is from 1971 to mid-1986, during which the OPM became a well known, if little understood, group within West Papua, Indonesia and Papua New Guinea. It was engaged in armed opposition against the Indonesian state, mostly with bows and arrows, prompting a vicious retaliation and causing the exodus of over 10,000 refugees into PNG in 1984. The exodus happened after Indonesian Special Forces arrested musician-cum-anthropologist Arnold Ap, whose Mambesak band had popularised various traditional songs from all over West Papua, in November 1983. Ap was allegedly tortured inside a Special Forces clearing house to reveal his knowledge about the OPM network. In April 1984, he reportedly escaped his detention but was 'found' on a Jayapura beach and shot to death. His band mate, Eddie Mofu, was also killed.

These refugees are seen as 'live documents' by the OPM because their existence cannot be denied. They provide concrete evidence that all is not well inside West Papua. But these years were also marked by bitter factional fighting within the OPM, especially between Seth Rumkorem and his colleague, Jacob Prai, who later set up the Pemka faction. In September 1982, Rumkorem ran away from a seaport near Jayapura and landed in Rabaul, PNG. The two rivals obviously had little real impact on the functioning of the Indonesian government.

The third period, between 1986 and 1995, was militarily quiet. Many of the OPM early leaders were dead or in exile. This was also during the height of President Suharto's military rule. Filep Karma was then just graduating from a university in Java, moving back to Jayapura and working as a civil servant. Theys Eluay was a Golkar politician.

The fourth period started from 1996 when Kelly Kwalik, an OPM commander in Papua's Central Highlands, ordered the kidnapping of more than a dozen European and Indonesian biologists from the World Wildlife Fund research station in Mapunduma, near Wamena. This thrust Papua into the headlines of global newspapers and televisions.

The Associated Press sent me to Wamena for six weeks to cover the kidnapping. I also wrote for other newspapers, including the Perth-based *West Australian* and the Bangkok-based *Nation* dailies, and I did a BBC radio interview. I befriended Octovianus Mote of *Kompas* newspaper, never imagining that Mote would one day become one of West Papua's most important leaders from his exile in New Haven, Connecticut.

Jim Elmslie also analysed the geopolitical consequences of these West Papuan problems. He argued that the Papuans are Melanesians, predominantly Christian, and the non-Papuan migrants are Indonesians, predominantly Muslim. Javanese and Bugis are the two largest racial newcomers in Papua. Racial and religious tensions are inevitable, heightened by competition over land and resources, the Papuans' exclusion from the formal economy and the paucity of government services that they receive.

The different racial breakdown of the Indonesian migrant-dominated cities and the bush, and the fact that many Papuans are openly expressing their dissatisfaction with the status quo and calling for independence, or at least a referendum on independence, is fuel to the fire of violent conflict.

The Indonesian government's response is primarily military and repressive: viewing Papuan 'separatists' as criminals, traitors and enemies of the Republic of Indonesia. This is a recipe for ongoing military operations to search for and destroy Papuan 'separatists', a term that could be applied to a large, if not overwhelming, portion of the Papuan population.

While most of Indonesia has enjoyed a huge growth in democratic freedoms since the fall of Suharto in 1998, this has not been the case in West Papua. The Indonesian military retains almost absolute control over Papua and West Papua provinces. Civilian political figures and groups in West Papua have little power to influence policy, and no say in how the military and police operate. It is like what Filep Karma had told me in our 2008 meeting in the Abepura prison.

After his November 1999 release, Filep Karma joined the TPN-OPM Forum of Former Political Detainees and Prisoners (Forum Mantan Tahanan dan Narapidana Politik TPN-OPM) whose objectives include helping Papuan prisoners and their families. Their chairman, John Mambor, joined the Papua Presidium Council and headed a faction within the council, representing former political prisoners.

In June 2000, when the Papua Presidium Council organised the huge congress, Filep Karma also joined and stood near Theys Eluay in the preliminary session. 'I saw Theys put aside a prepared speech to declare West Papua's independence', said Karma.

Karma thought it might take a new generation to revive what Theys Eluay, assassinated on 10 November 2001, and his peers had started. He concluded there is a culture of impunity for security personnel guilty of frequent and gross human rights abuses, including murder and torture, in Indonesia. Corruption is endemic, with some observers calling Papua and West Papua now the most corrupt provinces in Indonesia.

'The most important impact of the Theys assassination was that it created the atmosphere of fear in Papua. Activists, students, politicians, and many people raised their anger after the killing, prompting many migrants to leave Papua. But it did not stay long. What I felt was an atmosphere of fear. If they could kill Theys Eluay, it means they could eliminate anyone'.

The Indonesian military, having lost their previous power bases in East Timor and Aceh, ruthlessly maintain their control over West Papua, both as a power base and as a considerable source of revenue. The Indonesian military involvement in legal businesses, such as mining and logging, and, allegedly, illegal businesses, such as alcohol, prostitution, extortion and wildlife smuggling, provide significant funds for the military as an organisation and also for individual officers.

On 1 December 2004, Karma decided to break that atmosphere of fear. He brought along Yusak Pakage and organised a small celebration of the

West Papua declaration as a nation 43 years earlier – 1 December 1961. In a video of the event, Karma spoke passionately about West Papua's independence, criticising the 2001 special autonomy program but also talking about the West Papuan nationalism. He argued that West Papua should be an open society, accepting not only 'dark skin, curly hair people' but also Javanese, Minahasan or even Americans, who want to help West Papua. 'In Java, there're also native Javanese, straight hair, who also care about our independence. That's why they also cry for freedom in Papua. And these friends, when the Indonesian authority try to arrest and to kill them. We say to them, "Comrades, you come here!"'

When the protesters tried to raise the Morning Star flag, Indonesian police attempted to forcibly disband the rally. Clashes broke out and the crowd attacked the police with blocks of wood, rocks and bottles. The police responded by firing into the crowd. Karma was arrested immediately and charged with treason.

On 27 October 2005, the Abepura district court sentenced him to 15 years' imprisonment. Yusak Pakage was sentenced to 10 years. In August 2009, his friends and family told me that Karma had difficulties urinating. He requested medical assistance from the prison clinic but was only instructed to drink more water and to take a rest. Finally, through the intervention of media and NGOs, prison personnel were persuaded to send Karma to Dok Dua public hospital in Jayapura.

The doctors at Dok Dua hospital examined Karma several times between August and October 2009. They recommended Karma immediately be sent for urology surgery either in Makassar or Jakarta. Karma made an official request for surgery in Jakarta. But the prison argued that the Indonesian government lacked funds to send Karma for treatment.

Between December 2009 and February 2010, Karma's family members and supporters negotiated with Indonesian officials for the medical transfer, running a campaign to raise funds for Karma and Ferdinand Pakage. They raised enough money to send Karma to Jakarta and to buy a fake eye for Pakage. But the bureaucracy continued refuse to proceed with the permit.

'I used to be a bureaucrat myself. But I have never experienced such [use of] red tape on a sick man', Karma said. On 27 May 2010, the Ministry of Health sent two Jakarta-based doctors to the Abepura prison to check Karma's health situation and determined he could have urology surgery in Jakarta. This finally took place in July 2010 when Karma was sent to Jakarta and got his surgery in a Christian hospital. His daughters, Audryne and Andrefina, who were studying in Bandung, West Java, visited their father in the hospital. I also met him during his 11-day treatment in the hospital.

He spoke about racism against Papuans, not only in West Papua but also in Java. He talked about his experience, when studying in Solo in the 1980s, where he was often taunted as 'monkey' or 'ape'. He argued that the Javanese, who were mostly familiar with shadow puppet stories, consider black figures as the bad guys in the Ramayana and Mahabarata epics. 'The good guys are always light skinned. The giants are always dark', Karma said. 'Papuans are treated like half-human and half-animal'.

In Jakarta, he also agreed to appoint the Washington-based Freedom Now to represent him as his international legal counsel, to file a petition at the United Nations Working Group on Arbitrary Detention in New York. Eklefina Noriwari, Karma's mother, represented her son in the law suit.

Numerous organisations have cited Karma's wrongful detention, including Kontras and Imparsial in Jakarta as well as Human Rights Watch and Amnesty International. In addition, numerous members of the US Congress have called for his release, and the US State Department has cited Karma's status as a political prisoner.

In November 2011, the United Nations Working Group on Arbitrary Detention condemned the imprisonment of Filep Karma, specifically referring to his as 'arbitrary' under international law and asking the Indonesian government to release him 'immediately and unconditionally'.

But most Papuans seem to have lost faith in the Indonesian government and its ability to deal fairly with them. After decades of what is in effect an Indonesian armed occupation, they feel that the Indonesian state is unable and unwilling to give them even their most basic human rights as Indonesian citizens. Hence the pleas to the international community calling for recognition of their plight and for third party mediation – an outcome flatly rejected by Jakarta. Thus, the tensions fuelling the conflict in West Papua continue to intensify.

In May 2015, President Joko Widodo had just started his presidential term, and decided to enact three of his Papua policies: releasing political prisoners, ending the isolation of West Papua from international media and building infrastructures.

I decided to be in Jayapura, visiting Filep Karma in the Abepura prison hall when the presidential announcement was made. It was totally different from our 2008 meeting. Most prison guards understood that Karma had come to international attention. The United Nations had already asked for his release.

We chatted and joked. He reiterated the need to engage the Indonesian government with a non-violent movement. It was quite a challenge to debate with his fellow political prisoners, especially the younger ones, who got reckless seeing rights abuses and impunity from the Indonesian security.

He even walked me out of the prison gates. He simply walked back in, and closed the gate, after I entered my car.

On 9 May 2015, President Jokowi visited the prison – the first Indonesian president to visit this historical prison – and granted clemency to five Papuan prisoners; each of them had spent 12 years in prison, for their role in an arsenal raid in Wamena in 2003. Apotnalogolik Lokobal, Jefrai Murib, Kimanus Wenda, Linus Hiluka, and Numbungga Telenggen talked to President Jokowi in the prison hall, thanking Jokowi but also asking him to release other prisoners, Papuan and Moluccan detainees.

Jokowi promised to release all of them.

That evening, three of them came to a two-storey church guest house where I was staying and had a chat with some human rights defenders. Apotnalogolik Lokobal and Jefrai Murib had suffered strokes, having difficulty climbing stairs. They were staying in an NGO office, next door. All of them experienced torture and ill-treatment in detention.

The three slept in two rooms next to mine. At 3.00 am, Numbungga Telenggen got out of his room, walking to the dining area. I woke up and asked him what happened.'Where am I? What am I doing here?' asked Telenggen. I told him that he had been released from the prison.

It was saddening to see how they felt uncomfortable, uneasy, but also relieved, when taking a morning stroll outside the guest house. 'We have never walked outside the prison', said Kimanus Wenda. We organised a stone burning feast to welcome them.

Filep Karma's release came on 19 November 2015, four years before the end of his sentence. He called me after he was told that he had to leave the prison. He asked for one more night to sleep in his cell. The prison management agreed. 'Abepura prison is already like home to me. I always had in mind that I was going to be released in 2019, and suddenly I was kicked out – so I was shocked', he said.

I only read in the news when Filep Karma finally walked out of the Abepura prison with his lawyer Olga Hamadi. Hundreds of West Papua National Committee activists waited for them outside the prison. They made a convoy, with motorcycles, cars and a truck, to Waena neighbourhood in Jayapura and held a celebration. Karma made a speech. They grilled pork and brought a lot of sweet potatoes. He only returned home in Dok Lima area that night, meeting his daughter, his son-in-law and holding his first grandson.

Peace Proposal and Consolidation

In November 2014, I visited Wamena, teaching an NGO writing class, meeting bloggers, camerapersons and journalists. It brought back memories from my first Wamena visit in 1996 when I was covering the OPM kidnapping. Wamena is small. It's mild in the day and cool enough at night to sleep under a thick blanket.

Baliem Valley and the Central Highlands are the homeland of the Danis – the largest ethnic group in West Papua. They're often portrayed with their deep dark skin, penis gourd and colourful bird-feather headdress. Their warriors also wear boar tusks, in their noses or ears, in traditional ceremonies. Wamena in Dani language literary means 'my pig'. Don't be surprised if many Danis ask you to have *wam* or roast pork.

This time, I stayed in a Catholic guest house close to the office of the Indonesian Institute of Sciences (Lembaga Ilmu Pengetahuan, LIPI).

John Jonga, a Catholic priest and human rights defender, invited me to visit his church in Hebuba, outside Wamena. We had a barbecue and talked about our common friend, Muridan Widjojo, who had just died seven months earlier, in March 2014, at 47.

'He was a very good man. His heart is in Papua', said Djonga. Theo Hesegem, a human rights advocate who knew Widjojo since 1994, talked about the Widjojos in Jakarta, 'Pak Muridan will be remembered because of his Papua peace road map'.

Widjojo obviously had many friends in Wamena and the surrounding Baliem Valley. He was a historian at LIPI who mostly did research on West Papua. He graduated from Leiden University in 2009, writing his PhD thesis on local resistance on Tidore island in the Moluccas in the 19th century. Those islanders built an alliance with native Papuans and British traders in their fight against the Dutch East India Company.

In 2009, a LIPI team, with Widjojo as the editor, published a book, *Papua Road Map: Negotiating the Past, Improving the Present and Securing the Future*. It was intended to be a model for conflict resolution with a justice approach in West Papua.

They provided new insight to decision makers in Indonesia, especially President Susilo Bambang Yudhoyono, hoping to change the five-decade

-old approach to the West Papua conflict and to stimulate a willingness to take new steps to achieve justice.

The government's policy goal appeared to be to paralyse the Papuan independence movement, so it would not endanger Indonesia's territorial integrity. It was pursuing this goal through a security approach: using military and intelligence operations.

'Resources in Jakarta and Papua are wasted on political measures that are reactionary, symbolic and, ultimately, irreconcilable. The security approach does not address the heart of the conflict. Rather, it breeds further conflict and discontent', he wrote in a 2008 essay for *Inside Indonesia* magazine.

LIPI's approach has four key dimensions: *recognition*, *development*, *dialogue* and *reconciliation*.

- Recognition requires that Indonesia responds to a number of pressing problems that have caused the marginalisation of indigenous Papuans including the radical demographic change that has brought dislocation and displacement. Indonesian migrants are already dominant in most sectors including governance and businesses. Indigenous Papuans are a minority in West Papua.

- Recognition must focus on Papuans and their identity. It should include a social strategy of positive affirmation. It should support processes that will help Papuan individuals and local institutions compete more effectively in the market and be better able to protect their interests in the struggle for control of resources.

- Economic development has long been the Indonesian government aim. It has practically left many vulnerable Papuan groups. A new paradigm for development in Papua is that it is necessary to raise the quality of life of Papuans to the level of other Indonesian citizens. Development programs must be able to meet the basic needs and rights of Papuans in education, health and economic welfare. Papuans must have the capacity to participate effectively in, and feel themselves part of, the project of social change in West Papua. 'This will ensure that Indonesia and Indonesian-ness is considered integral to the provision of public services, which will gradually help Papuans to feel comfortable in and proud of being a part of Indonesia'.

- A dialogue should also be considered between Jakarta and Papua. It is the framework for reaching agreement and later a compromise. LIPI team argue that the dialogue can end the present political stalemate and cycle of violence.

'If it was possible to negotiate a resolution in Aceh, then it is possible to negotiate on Papua'.

The challenge is to persuade the parties in the conflict of the potential of dialogue at local and national levels, with or without international mediation. There will be many difficult questions, beginning with a decision on the team of acceptable negotiators. The involvement of a well-respected international third-party mediator would help the dialogue. According to Widjojo, paranoia about the involvement of foreigners based on so-called 'nationalism' should be discarded.

Reconciliation can be pursued through two potential transitional justice mechanisms: prosecutions before the Indonesian human rights court. But LIPI noted that past experiences with the court, including the 2006 Abepura killings, has demonstrated that victims are unlikely to obtain justice. The LIPI team prefers a truth telling mechanism. 'The Special Autonomy Law provides the legal basis for the creation of a truth commission. Truth commissions focus on the experiences and testimonies of the victims, which form the basis for exposing the pattern, motive and the extent of the crimes. Truth commissions aim to create an historical record of the events, providing restitution and reparations to victims and restoring their dignity. They do not punish perpetrators (though they may recommend prosecutions)'.

The Center for Nusantara Studies, a little-known organisation in Jakarta, published a response to the LIPI proposal, with a book entitled *Integration: A Done Deal – Critical Comments on Papua Road Map*. It's an anthology with 13 contributors including some former OPM members. Its editors are Agus Edy Santoso and Yosef Rizal.

Nicholas Messet, a former OPM member who used to work as a pilot in PNG, calls Widjojo's road map 'a strong provocation'. Messet argues, 'The Indonesian government would never want to conduct a dialogue if the agenda was the issue of rectifying Papua's history and status. I lived abroad for a long time and associated with world leaders. From the global geopolitical aspect, one sees there's no opportunity for Papua to be independent. Currently there're no countries that speak of the issue of independence. Should extraordinary human rights abuses be committed in Papua then perhaps there would be independence. If not, there is no reason to hope for an independent Papua'.

The editors questioned LIPI's methodology and accused the LIPI team of 'voic[ing] the interests of outside parties'. It did not specifically mention those parties. They accused LIPI of 'wrapping Indonesia with a geopolitically biased imperialism'.

Muridan Widjojo collaborated with Neles Tebay, a Papuan pastor, setting up the Papua Peace Network in Jayapura. They see themselves as facilitators of dialogue, and do not wish to determine its outcome. They organised 'public consultations' in nine regions in 2010–11: Jayapura, Timika, Wamena, Fakfak, Merauke, Nabire, Biak, Enarotali and Sorong.

Markus Haluk, a Wamena native who knew Muridan Widjojo since 1993, joined the Papua Peace Network, becoming a facilitator in those consultations. They held the consultations with both Papuan and Indonesian migrant communities. 'In mid-2011, Muridan told me that he had had chemotherapy treatment in his neck. I am not sure how widespread his cancer was. He drank a lot of water. His voice became hoarse. I resigned in September 2011, deciding to help the Papuan People Congress. I talked to Pater Neles and Muridan. I told them that the Papua Peace Network should remain neutral. I am not going to create the impression that it is not neutral'.

On 16–19 October 2011, the Papuan Customary Council organised the Papuan People Congress in a field in Abepura, reviving what other West Papuan leaders had done in December 1961 and June 2000. It was a peaceful gathering, involving 1,000 Papuans from the nine tribal areas. I heard that some of the organisers had talked about UN Secretary Ban Ki Moon and Pope Benedict XVI also attending the congress. It was incorrect but those fake news items were widely circulated.

In the closing ceremony on 19 October, Forkorus Yaboisembut, the chairman of the Papuan Customary Council, read out the 1961 Declaration of Independence, and said that he and Edison Waromi of the West Papua National Authority, an OPM group, had been elected by the Congress as president and prime minister respectively of the 'Federal Republic of West Papua'.

Indonesian police and the army assumed that it was treason. They fired warning shots to disperse the event, killing at least three men, injuring dozens and arresting about 600 people. Witnesses said several victims had gunshot wounds. The security officers even ransacked a Catholic college near the congress site, prompting Neles Tebay, the Catholic pastor, to protest. The police charged Yaboisembut, Waromi and three other congress leaders with treason. In March 2012, they were sentenced to a three-year jail term.

Those humiliations, as well as the almost daily abuse that Papuans suffered, dissuaded neither Neles Tebay nor Muridan Widjojo. They kept moving with their works. It culminated in a conference on 5–7 July 2011 in Jayapura, opened by Djoko Suyanto, then the coordinating minister for political, legal and security affairs, and attended by Bambang Darmono, then head of the Unit for the Acceleration of Development in Papua and West Papua, along with some 500 Papuans. They welcomed the idea of having a dialogue with the Indonesian government. They discussed 17 criteria to elect their negotiators with any party, including the Indonesian government. Those criteria included good English skills, aspiration to have freedom, gender proportionality and independence from the Indonesian bureaucracy.

They finally elected five West Papuan negotiators: Rex Rumakiek (Canberra); John Otto Ondawame (Vanuatu); Benny Wenda (Oxford); Octovianus Mote (New Haven); Leonie Tanggahma (The Hague). All of them were Papuan exiles.

Darmono considered that the conference set unacceptable conditions for dialogue. The selection of the five Papuan exiles soured those in Jakarta. The Jakarta elite kept on thinking that a good Papuan is not a pro-independence Papuan.

'The Papua Peace Network did not direct the conference. It just facilitated the process', said Markus Haluk. President Yudhoyono announced that his government was willing to pursue the strategy and held meetings with two groups of church leaders in December 2011 and February 2012. But Yudhoyono did not pursue any more before the end of his term in 2014.

John Djonga, the Catholic priest, said it's extremely difficult to change the mindset of the bureaucracy in Indonesia.

These are the banyan trees. They have deep roots. They have difficulty accepting a dialogue. They assume a dialogue means a demand of West Papua independence.

In Vanuatu, John Otto Ondawame's West Papua National Coalition for Liberation tried to be a member of the Melanesian Spearhead Group, an intergovernmental organisation of four Melanesian states – Fiji, Papua New Guinea, Solomon Islands and Vanuatu – as well as the Kanak and Socialist National Liberation Front which seeks the independence of New Caledonia from the French rule.

The WPNCL was a merger of Seth Rumkorem's Victoria faction and Jacob Prai's Pemka guerillas. It was based on a reconciliation when both armed groups had realised that they had gone nowhere with their rivalries.

Rumkorem died in Wageningen, the Netherlands, in 2010. Rex Rumakiek, a fellow ethnic Biak, replaced Rumkorem, living in Canberra. Jacob Prai retired in exile in Sweden. John Otto Ondowame, who joined Pemka guerillas in the 1980s, replaced Jacob Prai. Ondowame did his PhD at the Australian National University in Canberra, graduating in 2000. It apparently helped that both Rumakiek and Ondowame live in Canberra.

The WPNCL argued that West Papuans should get help from fellow Melanesians. It is about a black Melanesian solidarity. The word 'melanesia' comes from the Greek words *melano* (black) and *nesos* (islands). The move apparently worried the Indonesian government. This lobbied the bigger Melanesian countries, PNG and Fiji, to block the application. Jakarta also asked Canberra to use its influence in the South Pacific to block the application, using the 2008 Lombok Treaty between Indonesia and Australia, which compels both countries to support each other's territorial integrity.

In June 2014, the WPNCL application was discussed when the Melanesian countries were convening in Port Moresby, PNG. But Forkorus Yaboisembut's Federal Republic of West Papua claimed that it was also a legitimate representative of the West Papuan people. They insisted that they were a better representative. The MSG leaders unsurprisingly asked the West Papuans to solve their differences and to unite first.

Vanuatu helped facilitate these rival groups to meet in Port Villa in December 2014. On 7 December 2014, the three largest factions in West Papua – the Federal Republic of West Papua (NRFPB), the WPNCL and the National Parliament of West Papua under Buchtar Tabuni – agreed to set up a unified group called the United Liberation Movement for West Papua with its secretariat in Vanuatu. They also agreed to set up a secretariat with five elected members: Octovianus Mote as the general secretary; Benny Wenda as the spokesperson; and three members Rex Rumakiek, Leonie Tanggahma and Jacob Rumbiak (Melbourne).

The line-up is similar to that the peace conference elected in July 2011. Muridan Widjojo might argue it would probably be the same, if John Otto Ondamawe had not died in September 2014. The new merged group, the United Liberation Movement for West Papua, was finally given observer status with the MSG in June 2015 which guarantees equal rights and recognition with Indonesia, an associate membership. Leonie Tanggahma has a specific assignment. She is assigned to deal with the Indonesian government if Jakarta under President Jokowi is to hold a dialogue, according to Markus Haluk. The other four members are assigned to advocate independence.

I returned from John Djonga's church that night and went back to the guest house in downtown Wamena, with a full stomach, thinking how these West Papuan rhizomes had became resilient. Some of their leaders have died, even been killed, but they continue to resprout.

The American Goldmine in Mount Grasberg

Timika, the largest mining town in West Papua, has a street intersection named after a local businessman: *Titi Teguh*. It is located on a row of shops, intersecting another road with a big white house where Titi Teguh lives. His real name is Irwanto Tenggowijaya. But everyone in Timika calls him Titi Teguh. It literally means 'persistent little brother'.

Titi Teguh owns those shops as well as two hotels, trading companies, an alcohol distribution network, and the *Timika Express* daily.

In April 2010, a group of angry Papuan housewives raided a shop next to his house, smashing bottles and demanding that the Timika police take action against his alcohol sales. It became a news headline. Native Papuans still use the original name of the area: Koperapoka intersection. But it is now easier to use Titi Teguh.

I went there one evening in May 2015, seeing the small shop, with a lot of bottles...Johnnie Walker, Absolut Vodka, as well as Indonesian beers, Bintang and Anker, plus Minahasa's well known liquor *Cap Tikus*.

Juliana Daudo, Titi Teguh's wife and the publisher of the *Timika Express* newspaper, welcomed me and asked me to wait in their house. There were some family pictures in the living room, showing their vacation in Australia.

She returned with her husband, a stocky ethnic Chinese man, who shook my hand. 'Some of our children study in Australia', he said. Titi Teguh was born in Makassar to a poor ethnic Chinese family, only finishing primary school. In 1989, he moved to West Papua's Fakfak and in 1990 worked in Timika. 'I had no job. I was only a coolie in the Timika seaport. In 1991, I smuggled alcohol and got arrested. I was jailed for three months in Fakfak. I dated the prosecutor's daughter. The Daudos are Timorese. Her father obviously disagreed that his daughter should date a convict. But we were young. We decided to run away and marry in Timika. We're married happily and now my father-in-law has no problem with us'.

In Timika, Titi Teguh befriended some Special Forces officers, who were assigned to secure PT Freeport Indonesia's mining operation, from the giant Grasberg Mine in the mountains to Timika seaport. Grasberg is the largest goldmine in the world. It is mostly owned by the Phoenix-based Freeport-McMoRan which owns around 90 per cent of PT Freeport Indonesia, the principal operating subsidiary in Indonesia.

President Suharto approved the Freeport operation in 1967 based on Indonesia's newly passed foreign investment law. It was built at 4,100 metres above sea level in a remote area, involving a capital and technology input beyond Indonesia's resources in the 1970s. Freeport built a 79-mile (127-kilometre) road and pipeline, port, airstrip, power plant as well as two new towns called Tembagapura (at Mile 68) and Kuala Kencana (at Mile 32). It officially opened in 1973 and soon became Indonesia's largest taxpayer.

Titi Teguh said, 'Freeport then did not care if one or two or even five containers went missing in a single week. These officers stole them and asked me to sell the goods. They stole Nescafe, apples and frozen chicken from Australia, spare parts...everything. I sold them in Timika, Tual, Dobo. They brought the stuff on the weekend. I had already sold them by Wednesday. I still had cash to buy other goods and paid them on the weekend. I made my fortune. The soldiers stole and I sold. I thought it was a good business. Freeport also initially thought they were mining copper but found gold instead'.

His statement reminded me of Lexy Lintuuran, Freeport's corporate security chief, who told me in 2006 about the security situation in Timika. Freeport operated 14 security checkpoints to register every car and person travelling along the 79-mile road. Workers showed their employee cards at the checkpoints. Locals showed special permits issued by Freeport's Community Liaison Office. There were also special Freeport-issued visitor cards. 'Only the soldiers usually refuse to report at the checkpoints', said Lintuuran.

Security is a major problem since OPM guerillas routinely attack the pipeline. The checkpoints are manned by Freeport security plus various Indonesian security units such as the Special Forces, the Kostrad army reserves, the Marines, the Air Force's Paskhas elite unit, the Army Battalion 752, the Army's Cavalry, as well as the Mobil Brigade police troops.

Freeport has a division called the Emergency Planning Operation that provides logistical, transportation and communication support for the more than 3,000 Indonesian security personnel stationed in the area, according to Lintuuran.

It is obviously common to see soldiers in jungle camouflage in Timika. In December 2005, *The New York Times* published a report about such an arrangement. Freeport records obtained by the *Times* showed that from 1998 through 2004, Freeport gave military and police generals, colonels, majors and captains, and military units, nearly US$20 million. Individual commanders received tens of thousands of dollars, in one case up to $150,000. Freeport said it had 'taken appropriate steps' in accordance with American and Indonesian laws to provide a secure working environment for its more than 18,000 employees and contract workers.

In Timika, Titi Teguh was putting himself in the right node. He expanded his friendship, nurturing the Special Forces' younger officers and getting to know officers from other forces. The couple decided to set up *Timika Express* in April 2010 after the women's raid. Juliana Daudo said it was initially the idea of some journalists under Marthen Moru, an editor at *Radar Timika* newspaper. 'Marthen Moru is also a Timorese. It's a kind of Timorese solidarity. Sometimes people called our newspaper *Timor Express*', laughed Daudo.

Titi Teguh said, '*Timor Express* just celebrated its fifth anniversary. Now it prints around 1,000 copies every working day. It is the second largest newspaper after *Radar Timika*. It has a staff of around 30 people. My wife is the commissionaire. We own nearly 100 per cent of the newspaper's shares. My sister-in-law, Judith Daudo, is the financial director. I do not intervene in the editorial content of the newspaper. I only ask them in a few cases to tone down certain coverage'.

Recently the newspaper published a story about a high-ranking officer in the Timika police precinct who had reportedly taken money from an illegal gambling den. It's common for police officers in West Papua to take regular security money. But this officer, according to *Timika Express*, was acting as if he was 'an angel'.

Timika police chief Yustanto Mujiharso was not happy with that story. Titi Teguh said, 'He invited me to meet him in the precinct. He told me, "It tarnishes my good name". I said I cannot intervene in the newsroom. It's true that I am the owner but they have their independence. He said, "Who owns *TV One*? Aburizal Bakrie! Who owns *Metro TV*? Surya Paloh! It's a lie that a media owner cannot intervene…I know you sell alcohol. I never bother to disturb your business. I know you have connections up to the headquarters in Jakarta. We need to understand each other"'.[3]

---

3 Aburizal Bakrie is the chairman of the Bakrie Group which owns *TV One*. Surya Paloh is the chairman of the Media Indonesia group which controls *Metro TV*. Both Bakrie and Paloh are also politicians whose political views are reflected in their respective media.

Titi Teguh got the message. He went to the newsroom and told his reporters to tone down their reporting. 'Newspaper business does not make money but it's good for security'.

That night, he decided to walk me to the Titi Teguh intersection to get a taxi. 'It's a rather dangerous neighbourhood. You're a stranger. It's safe with me'.

* * *

The most prominent and long-running disputes between a mining company and local community in Indonesia arguably centred on the operations of Freeport McMoran's Grasberg copper and goldmine in Timika.

The Grasberg mining resulted in the displacement of two indigenous tribes, the Amungme and Komoro, from their traditional lands. Many Amungme sons and daughters became frustrated and angry about Freeport, including guerilla-turned-academic John Otto Ondamawe, environmentalist Tom Beanal, teacher-turned-OPM commander Kelly Kwalik and nurse-turned-rights defender Yosepha Alomang. Tom Beanal and Yosepha Alomang used to file law suits against Freeport. It took years and produced small changes.

The Grasberg mining also resulted in the regular dumping of unprocessed tailings, widespread deforestation and the destruction of the Grasberg landscapes through open cut mining. According to Freeport's website, in 2015 it produced respectively 349 million and 215 million tons of waste rock and tailings.

I did a small calculation. If a trailer truck could hold 20 tons of cargo, it means Freeport had produced 28.2 million trucks of waste in 2015. If I lined up those 28.2 million trucks in a single line, assuming a truck is 9 metres long, those trucks would be 3,100 kilometres long. It's roughly three times the length of Java. In April 2015, I used Google Maps to see the scale of the dumping grounds along the Otomona and Ajkwa rivers. The dumping grounds are six times bigger than Timika's total area.

When displacing those Amungme and Kamoro people in the 1970s, Freeport built a neighbourhood called Kwamki Lama to relocate those poor people without considering their social, economic and cultural backgrounds. Denise Leith wrote in her book, *The Politics of Power: Freeport in Suharto's Indonesia*, that no Indonesian was living in Kwamki Lama when she was visiting in September 1998. Her Indonesian taxi driver was also reluctant to bring her there. Once the driver dropped Leigh in Kwamki Lama, he did not even wait for his fare – something that she rarely witnessed in Indonesia. Now Kwamki Lama is the site of frequent crimes and gang fights. Human rights abuses, including torture and killings, were also alleged to have been committed by security and company personnel.

Saul Paulo Wanimbo, the head of the Catholic Office of Peace and Justice, told me that communal violence is chronic in Timika. 'Freeport obviously draws many people, not only from Papua, but also many other parts of Indonesia, to get jobs and to find a decent living. Many do decent jobs, from mining to trades, but thousands of people are involved in illicit activities. It often borders to deadly violence. They cannot rely on the police. They rely more on their kins, clans or families or gangs. It involves indigenous Papuans but also migrants. It involves people from the Central Highlands but also people from Kei Islands. I am afraid it is getting bigger'.

Wanimbo complained about the lack of a mechanism for correcting mistaken impressions. 'Many (Indonesian) journalists often came to my place, sitting here and interviewing me. But they used racist terms such as 'tribal war' when addressing human rights violations. I need to rely on the church network and NGOs, in Jakarta and overseas, to pay attention to rights abuses in our area. Not the media'.

I am trying to check about Freeport and these media problems with Octovianus Danunan, the chief editor of *Radar Timika*, the largest newspaper in Timika. Danunan is an ethnic Torajan, originally from South Sulawesi, who started his career with the *Cenderawasih Pos* daily in Jayapura in 1989.

We had dinner in a grilled fish restaurant in downtown Timika. He said, 'Freeport is a very difficult subject to cover. It's a limited area. It's highly secured. Journalists need to have permits to enter the many Freeport checkpoints. You also need to use a four-wheel drive to travel there. Anyone without a travel ID cannot pass the checkpoints. You will also have guards to travel with you. Journalists have to rely on police sources to write anything that happened along the 79-mile road to Freeport.[4] Since 2003, there has been a regular shooting along that route with a total of 45 or 46

---

4   I had asked PT Freeport Indonesia for access to the Grasberg mine, since Freeport had sponsored Pantau Foundation, where I worked, to do journalism training in Jayapura and Timika in 2005. Freeport never answered my request to visit their concession. Freeport also decided to stop working with Pantau Foundation after American anthropologist Eben Kirksey and I had published a report on the Freeport school teachers' killing published in November 2006.

victims. It's been 12 years now and the police could never find out who they are. Not a single shooter was known'.

I asked him about the Antonius Wamang shooting case in August 2002. Eben Kirksey and I wrote a 2007 report about the case in which one Indonesian and two American school teachers were shot dead while on a weekend picnic on Mile 63. We suspected 11 Indonesian soldiers were somewhat involved in the case but only Wamang and his peers were arrested, tried and jailed.

Danunan responded, 'It's only opinion that Wamang had shot the Freeport teachers. It is still not clear who shot the teachers. I wrote an op-ed in 2003 on that case. I basically argued there were three components that we must suspect for the shooting:

- A rivalry between the Indonesian police and the military in getting the security contracts with post-Suharto Freeport. Now we know that the military does not have the contract. Freeport is now using the police in the Grasberg mine. I also wrote that the Indonesian military cannot totally control their own soldiers plus…the hundreds, if not thousands, of deserters in Papua.

- A campaign to get, at least, part of Freeport mining area into two other regencies: Nabire and Puncak Jaya. Now the Freeport area is under the Mimika regency with Timika as its capital. But it's bordering the other two regencies. Those two also want to get a piece of Freeport. Mimika is probably Indonesia's richest regency. Tembagapura, the mining centre in Mount Grasberg, is located next to Puncak Jaya regency. They also want a share from the Freeport exploration.

- The political decision of the OPM to get the world's attention on their freedom struggle. In 1996, OPM commander Kelly Kwalik ordered the kidnapping of international biologists in Mapenduma to get international media attention. Kwalik was strategic in making that decision. It's also possible that OPM does the shooting to keep the world's attention on Papua. Armed groups in Timika are obviously not only the Indonesian military and police. OPM also has guns. OPM is fractured with many dissent groups'.

He continued: 'I have to be very careful working in Timika. Many groups have guns or have the ability to use armed men to attack. The problem with journalism in Papua is that it's not monitored. The Press Council is very far away in Jakarta. People do not understand the complaint mechanism with the Press Council. No media watchdog in Papua'.

Danunan said racial sentiments are very sensitive in Timika. Some migrant groups have sizeable populations: Javanese, Torajan, Timorese. 'Politicians use these racial sentiments to protect their power. Anyone can be a journalist in Papua. They do not get training in journalism. New recruits could immediately join a newsroom. Perhaps, a new recruit is given an internship for some days and then sent to the field immediately. During the President Suharto period, Timika had no newspaper. *Radar Timika* was only published in 2001. Now newspaper competition is very fierce. Timika is a small town but it has five daily newspapers'.

I cannot agree more as Timika only had a population of around 130,000 in 2015.

Danunan reminded me that his newspaper is the only one owned by a media group. *Radar Timika* is a subsidiary of the Surabaya-based Jawa Pos media group. The other four newspapers are owned by businessmen and politicians in Timika. 'Titi Teguh published *Timor Express* obviously not for the sake of journalism', said Danunan.

Danunan's statement is not a surprise. I interviewed more than 30 other journalists in West Papua – both Indonesian and Papuan reporters – for a 2015 Human Rights Watch report. They routinely self-censor to avoid reprisals for their reporting. That environment of fear and distrust is magnified by the Indonesian security forces' longstanding practice of paying journalists to be informers and even deploying agents to work undercover as journalists. Danunan named some Timika journalists who worked as police or military informers. He also mentioned police officers who work as undercover journalists. These practices are carried out both to minimise negative coverage and to encourage positive reporting about the political situation in West Papua.

In May 2015, President Joko Widodo announced that West Papua was opened to international journalists. His statement created a controversy within the banyan trees. Unfortunately, Jokowi did not follow it up with an official presidential instruction, allowing room for non-compliance by government agencies and security forces opposed to the change. Various senior officials have since publicly contradicted Jokowi's statement. Even the Ministry of Foreign Affairs, which said it had 'liquidated' the clearing house, also said that prior police permission is required for access to Papua and that foreign journalists should inform the ministry of likely sources and schedules. The deep state rejected Widodo's policy. West Papua remains a restricted area.

Staff members of international nongovernmental organisations, academics, and some foreign observers have also been denied access to Papua. The security forces closely monitor the activities of international groups that the government permits to operate in Papua – those that seek to address human rights concerns are especially scrutinised.

International NGOs that the government asserts are involved in 'political activities' have been forced to cease operations and their representatives banned from travel to the region, including the International Committee for the Red Cross and the Dutch development group Cordaid. Peace Brigades International (PBI), an international organisation that promotes nonviolence and human rights protection in conflict areas, ceased its operations in Papua in 2011 due to what it described as unremitting government surveillance, harassment, and intimidation of its staff and volunteers.

Government restrictions on foreigners have extended to United Nations officials and academics Indonesian authorities perceive as hostile. In 2013 the government rejected the proposed visit of Frank La Rue, then the UN special rapporteur on freedom of expression, because he insisted on including Jayapura on his itinerary. It seems that La Rue had learned what the Bolivian diplomat, Fernando Ortiz Sanz, had faced in the 1960s during the Act of Free Choice implementation.

According to Human Rights Watch, the Indonesian government has legitimate security concerns in West Papua stemming from periodic attacks, mainly targeting police and security forces, by OPM fighters. But the threat from the OPM insurgency does not provide a legal justification for the broad-brush and indefinite restrictions on freedoms of expression, association, and movement that the Indonesian government has imposed on West Papua since the 1960s. Any such restrictions, including those on non-nationals, must be based in law, narrowly construed in application and timed to address a government concern, and proportionate to achieving a specific aim.

In Timika, I learned that removing access restrictions alone, like what President Jokowi had proposed, would not resolve the Grasberg environmental degradation or the underlying political tensions in West Papua or dispel the suspicions of Indonesian officials. But this is an essential step toward broader respect for human rights: shining a light on West Papua, not keeping it hidden from view.

It is the best way to ensure West Papua has a rights-respecting future.

The Papuans lost not only their lands to migration but also jobs and rights. In many urban areas in Papua – Sorong, Biak, Jayapura, Manokwari, Merauke, Nabire, Timika, Wamena – I often hear Papuans complaining about difficulties in getting jobs. Most jobs, from drivers to construction, from office clerks to restaurant waiters, are occupied by migrants. Papuans usually want to be politicians or civil servants, but obviously very few succeed. Employers view workers from other parts of Indonesia as more reliable and efficient than the local population.

West Papua is always a place that fascinated me. I met a lot of people who for a long time had been waiting and hoping for things to get better. Many of them hope that West Papua will become a sovereign state, I guess; more than many other areas in Indonesia. Others do not have such hopes, concluding that Indonesia is just too strong, having the backing of many powerful countries, like the United States, Russia and China, and West Papua is just too tiny. Unfortunately, West Papua is rich in minerals and other natural resources. It is precious and to be divided among these big powers. These Papuans want to do things that Indonesia could tolerate such as environmental protections, education improvement, health services, sports activities and arts. But the killing of Yohame, the environmentalist, again reiterated the frustration among Papuans.

Jim Elmslie concluded that the Papuan issue is even more dire: they are faced with either independence or eventual extinction. 'Having prospered on the island of New Guinea for some 50,000 years their future is now in question. Without independence they will be rapidly swamped by the Indonesians and every valuable resource or piece of land will be expropriated. Those who resist will be shot, as in the past. As the new arrivals are almost entirely Muslim, the West Papuans will become a racial and religious minority, consequently subject to the treatment of minorities received in a poor, overcrowded and violent society like Indonesia: discrimination, then persecution, then murderous pogrom. This is what has occurred for the Christians in Ambon and East Timor, and the Chinese in Java. This is what West Papuans feel is in store for them'.

EPILOGUE

On a summer afternoon in August 2005, I stepped out of Thornton Heath train station, south London, to take a 10-minute walk to Northwood Road to interview Carmel Budiardjo, 80-year-old British human rights campaigner, who founded Tapol human rights group in 1973. Her two-storey townhouse had a hedge and a small front yard. She welcomed me in her living room with racks of books and a vase of burgundy chrysanthemum. Tapol's office is located on the second floor.

Budiardjo first came to know Indonesia in 1947 when she met an Indonesian official in Prague. They married and she moved to Jakarta in 1952. She worked as a translator and later wrote economic analyses for both President Sukarno's administration and the Indonesian Communist Party. When General Suharto toppled Sukarno in 1965, her husband was jailed for 'political offences' and spent 12 years in prison without trial. She spent three years in detention, also without trial, before being deported from Indonesia in 1971.

In Indonesia, *tapol* stands for *tahanan politik* (political prisoner). Tapol campaigned to release nearly 100,000 leftist political prisoners in Indonesia. Tapol also worked on Aceh, East Timor and West Papua. In 1995, she received the Right Livelihood Award in Sweden. In August 2009, East Timor President José Ramos-Horta presented her with the Order of Timor Leste.

I told her about my journey, from Sabang to Merauke, concluding that most people who live in Java, myself included, do not realise the disparity between Java as an 'inner' or 'core' island compared with the 'outer' or 'peripheral' ones – in Dutch colonial parlance, the *Buitengewesten*, or Outer Territories.

'It also applied to me when I lived in Jakarta in the 1960s. Only when I left Indonesia in 1971, I began to understand the problem. I was caught up by the concept of the liberation of West Papua', Budiardjo said. 'I have to be outside of Indonesia to begin to think about the reality of Indonesia. West Papua is not necessarily a legitimate part of Indonesia'.

Some of her colleagues were quite upset with her. She was seen to be anti-Indonesia, anti-nationalism. She said, 'I am not an advocate of break-ing apart of Indonesia. But in West Papua and Aceh, there are strong feeling of injustice and their own nationalisms. Of course, Aceh and West

Papua are different. West Papua was an international issue. The Act of Free Choice in 1969 was an absolute fraud'.

As noted earlier, according to Merle C. Ricklefs' standard *History of Modern Indonesia*, the Dutch didn't create Indonesia but merely defined its territorial border. By establishing that territorial extent, the colonial power also determined who was to be Indonesian and who was not. Millions of Indonesian citizens do not understand this fact. It was the Dutch who brought together hundreds of kingdoms and sultanates into a single administration headquartered in Batavia. It was not Majapahit. It was not Sriwijaya.

In Indonesia, the grand narrative has always referred to the Dutch as '*penjajah*' or 'exploiter'. This logic creates a problem. How could this blood-sucking coloniser also define Indonesia? Indonesian founding fathers, such as Muhammad Yamin and Sukarno, simply created the myth that Indonesia used to be a big country prior to the Dutch colonialism. Yamin talked about Indonesia Part I (Sriwidjaja), Indonesia Part II (Majapahit) and Indonesia Part III.

Budiardjo argued that Sukarno and his peers had also introduced the concept '*bhinneka tunggal ika*' or 'unity in diversity'. Sukarno knew that Indonesia is a country with thousands of islands, with hundreds of racial, religious and language groups. It is not a single entity although Sukarno genuinely wanted to build a unity. He called it a 'nation building process'.

In the 1950s, Yamin embarked on a very ambitious project: creating myths. He argued that Indonesia needed to have a 'national history' and an 'Indonesia-centric' one. Some Minahasan intellectuals said Yamin actually fabricated Java-centric history. Yamin mixed fiction and fact, intertwining Javanese myths and the Indonesian nationalist movement. His 'history' books almost never mention Minahasa's first election in 1919. Some historians, like Getrudes Johan Resink and Asvi Warman Adam, later wrote that Yamin's 'national history' borders on chauvinism and lies.

Yamin legalised the slogan that the Dutch had colonised Indonesia for '350 years' as if the Dutch took over power in a splash, from Sabang to Merauke, conquering more than 400 kingdoms and sultanates. The 'national history' also manipulated issues related to 'the rebellions' like those in Aceh, Sumatra, Minahasa, the Moluccas, East Timor and West Papua. Yamin also introduced what he called 'national heroes'. His first choice was Prince Diponegoro, a Javanese aristocrat who wrote in his own memoirs that he wanted to subjugate Java – not the Netherlands Indies. In the 1820s, when Diponegoro was fighting the Dutch, the concept of Indonesia was totally unknown in Java. Berlin academic Adolf Bastian only popularised the terminology 'Indonesia' in 1884, three decades after Diponegoro's death in 1855.

By 2015 Indonesia had 163 official 'national heroes', probably the most numerous in a single country in the world. Asvi Warman Adam wrote that every regency, every ethnic group in Indonesia, are trying to recommend a national hero to the Ministry of Social Affairs, which administers the nomination process. Ironically, two Indonesian communist leaders, Tan Malaka and Alimin, who were decreed national heroes by President Sukarno, went missing from public memory.

When General Suharto took power in 1965, Suharto boosted Yamin-approach myths through tightly censored school textbooks, media propaganda, museums, monuments, movies and public speeches. His military regime knew very well that Indonesia's diversity could also create political problems. They created the acronym 'SARA' – *suku* (tribes), *agama* (religion), *ras* (race) and *antar-golongan* (inter-group relations), legitimising much repression in the name of SARA. Suharto also banned many newspapers and restricted international journalists, human rights researchers and scholars, including Budiardjo.

Millions of children who grew up in the Suharto period were taught that the Indonesian Communist Party was a 'latent' danger to Indonesian unity. Their teachers made sure that the students all knew that communism was lurking everywhere and may strike us unawares.

All of Indonesia's media conglomerates were set up during the Suharto era. These news organisations' top editors always talked about the need to preserve the Unitary State of the Republic of Indonesia, censoring stories of rights abuses, environmental degradation and injustice in places like East Timor or West Papua.

Suryopratomo, the chief editor of *Kompas*, the largest national newspaper, admitted the many extreme human rights abuses by Indonesian soldiers in Aceh, West Papua and others. 'Still it is better to be united in this age of global competition', he said.

Carmel Budiardjo admitted that such views were common even in her Indonesia in the 1950s. Frequently, managers and editors put forward their nationalism – or in some other cases also their Islamic interpretation – when confronted with racial or religious problems in their coverage.

Muslim executives, like Widjojo Hartono of the Jawa Pos Group, when assigned from his headquarters in Surabaya to work at their subsidiary, *Suara Maluku* daily in Ambon, advocated the opening of a new newspaper exclusively for the Muslims in a bid to balance what he considered to be the dominance of the Ambonese Christians in *Suara Maluku*. He had the group backing, setting up the *Ambon Ekspres* newspaper. This helped fan sectarian violence in the Moluccas.

Even in the post-Suharto period, many bannings were still in place. President Susilo Bambang Yudhoyono tolerated the burning of around 30,000 history books not considered to be placing enough blame on the communists in 1965.

When I left Carmel Budiardjo's townhouse, I remembered what she stressed: 'The way Indonesia is governed is so Java centric. The Javanese in general do not really understand what happened in the country'.

* * *

Subro, the Madurese activist in Pontianak, told me that ethnic Madurese currently suffer an inferiority complex, 'Many of my friends are ashamed to say that they are Madurese. We are ashamed to be Madurese'. It's an impact of the discrimination and the killing of around 6,500 Madurese from 1997 and 2001.

The visitors on Jalan Roda in Manado share a general feeling: a discriminated Muslim minority inside a Christian enclave. Ethnic Minahasan control the bureaucracy, the academic circles, the police and the military. The Muslims, mostly ethnic Gorontaloan, are middlemen or street vendors.

Ethnic Chinese are also a discriminated against minority in Indonesia, going back to the 1740 massacres in Batavia under the Dutch Indies government. The Suharto regime banned Chinese characters, Chinese-language school and restricted ethnic Chinese from working in the civil services. The regime also officially used the term *pribumi* (sons of the land) as well as *non-pribumi* for the Chinese.

Ironically, in post-Suharto Indonesia, that racist term has also given birth to similar phrases such as *putra daerah* (sons of the region) or *penduduk asli* (native). Indonesian migrants are now called *pendatang* (newcomers) when they should be treated and looked upon as fellow Indonesian citizens. Another term is *masyarakat adat* (tribal group). The Malay and the Chinese in West Kalimantan claimed themselves as *putra daerah* whereas the Madurese have been treated as *pendatang*. The Dayak claimed to be *penduduk asli*.

Should migrants have to assimilate or should their cultures be recognised? According to *Human Development Report 2004: Cultural Liberty in*

Today's Diverse World, three principles are critical: (1) respect diversity; (2) recognise multiple identities; (3) build common bonds of belonging to the local community. The United Nations' report stresses the need for respecting diversity and building more inclusive societies by adopting policies that explicitly recognise cultural differences – multicultural policies. It stressed that identities are not a zero-sum game.

Many Javanese born in Aceh, for example, are frequently told by their Aceh colleagues, 'You speak Acehnese *fluently*. You don't look like most Javanese'. The assumption here is that a Javanese person has become less Javanese, because it is common to think about identity as a zero-sum game; if you have more of one identity, you have less of another. Identity is somehow imagined like a square box with a fixed size.

Indonesia should recognise these multiple identities and multicultural policies.

One reason for optimism is electoral democracy and a change in Indonesian laws. Indonesia organised democratic, presidential and parliamentarian elections, in 2004, 2009 and 2014, plus thousands of local elections. Indonesia has 34 provinces and more than 500 regencies and cities. These were relatively peaceful although the campaign financing needed a lot of money, unfortunately, also prompting corrupt campaign finances.

Indonesia has also redefined what it means to be a citizen. A citizenship law passed in 2006 proclaims that an Indonesian is someone who was born in Indonesia to Indonesian citizens, a radical departure for a society that separated the Chinese and the Eurasian, in one way or another, through colonial times and post-independence Indonesia. Indonesian parliament has also ratified two major international human rights covenants: the International Covenant on Civil and Political Rights as well as the International Covenant on Economic, Social and Cultural Rights.

But old habits die hard. Hundreds of decrees and regulations are made to discriminate against racial, religious and gender minorities in Indonesia. When Basuki Purnama, the ethnic Chinese politician 'Ahok', became Jakarta governor in 2014, his presence also triggered anti-Chinese sentiment in Indonesia. He became an effective governor, reforming public services but also being notorious for his blunt speeches. In December 2016, he was charged with blasphemy and brought to trial. As recounted above, in May 2017 he was found guilty of blasphemy against Islam and sentenced to a two year jail term.

Rumours, fake news and propaganda undermine quality journalism. Law enforcement is a huge challenge in Indonesia.

I am afraid nationalism guru Benedict Anderson's suggestion is definitively needed in Indonesia: a radical change in the mindset of the political leaders. His remark resonated for me again when I was meeting Jacob Matheis Soselisa, a Tobelo politician, who viewed the problems in the Moluccas islands as related to the fact that Eastern Indonesia suffered 'structural marginalisation' in the fields of education and health care, and was neglected 'in the hands of the central government'. Soselisa concluded that Indonesia's narrow nationalism doesn't serve its people from Sabang to Merauke.

* * *

Violence in post-Suharto Indonesia, from Aceh to West Papua, from Kalimantan to the Moluccas, is evidence that Java-centric nationalism is unable to distribute power fairly in an imagined Indonesia. It has created unnecessary paranoia and racism among Indonesian migrants in West Papua. The Papuans simply reacted by saying that they're Melanesians – not Indonesians. They keep questioning the manipulation of the United Nations–sponsored Act of Free Choice in 1969.

In East Timor, President Suharto's successor B. J. Habibie agreed to have a referendum. Indonesia lost and it generated a bloodbath. Habibie's predecessors, Megawati Sukarnoputri and Susilo Bambang Yudhoyono, refused to admit the Indonesian military's occupation despite a United Nations' finding that the Indonesian occupation there had killed 183,000 people between 1975 and 1999.

In Minahasa, Bert Adriaan Supit examined the composition of the so-called founding fathers of Indonesia. Supit told me that 63 per cent of the 75 members of the Japan-made independence committees were Javanese; 13 per cent were Sundanese; Sumatra had 11 per cent; Kalimantan had 4 per cent; Ambon and Sulawesi four men (5 per cent). The Javanese disproportionately dominated the committees.

In 1945, Indonesia's non-Javanese founders Mohammad Hatta, Sam Ratu Langie and Johannes Latuharhary wanted an Indonesia that was democratic and decentralised. They advocated a federation. 'Sukarno, Supomo and Yamin advocated a centralised unitarian state', Supit said.

Understanding the urgency to fight incoming Dutch troops, Johannes Latuharhary accepted Supomo's proposal but suggested the new republic hold a referendum as soon as it became independent. Sukarno agreed but this decision has never been executed. Adriaan Supit, however, learned from the failures and the social cost of the Permesta rebellion in the 1950s, moving carefully not to provoke violence in Minahasa.

A unitarian state naturally creates the Centre. Jakarta becomes the Centre. Jakarta has been accumulating and controlling political, cultural, educational, economic, informational and ideological power. The closer a region to Jakarta, the better it will benefit from the Centre. Java is the closest to the Centre. The further a region is from the Centre, the more neglected it will be. West Papua, Aceh, East Timor and the Moluccas are among those furthest away from Jakarta.

A centralised power demanded a long and complex bureaucracy. Red tape naturally created corruption. Indonesia is frequently ranked as the most corrupt country in Asia. Political and Economic Risk Consultancy Ltd., listed Indonesia as the most corrupt country in Asia in 2005.

The centralised power also created an imagination that Indonesia has a majority – religious and ethnic. It helps create a climate in which that majority has more power, and thus is justified to have privileges and to rule over the minorities.

Sumatran poet Leon Agusta summarised, 'They're the two most dangerous words in Indonesia: Islam and Java'. Muslim majority and Javanese dominance!

In 1997, the Asian economic crisis rocked the Centre, forcing Suharto to step down in May 1998. The peripheries used the crisis to each find new equilibrium in their respective domains. Ethnic Dayak leveraged their power in Kalimantan, showing their muscles against their ethnic rival Malay and killing the much smaller ethnic Madurese. The Malay also massacred the Madurese, sadly, to counter the Dayak.

In Ambon, the crisis created an opening among the Christian Moluccans to leverage against the demographic changes which they considered to favour Muslims during the Suharto era. This created sectarian violence, killing around 10,000 people from 1999 to 2004. The violence also spread to Ternate, Tidore and Halmahera, witnessing the older sultanate powers fighting against one another and killing around 15,000 people.

Joseph Saunders of Human Rights Watch told me in 1997, 'Indonesia has sadly taken a step back under Suharto and New Order. The government has not just promoted the national language, a positive, they've effectively banned a lot of local publications…for a long time you couldn't publish in local languages. It's a step backward as it's all dictated by the centre'.

Nearly 100,000 people died in violence in the decade after Suharto stepped down from power. But Indonesian opinion leaders keep the idea of a centralised Indonesia. In 1999, a new law was passed in which political parties must have their head offices in Jakarta. They should have at least provincial chapters in two-thirds of Indonesia. The Centre still holds huge power in Indonesia.

* * *

The idea to switch Indonesia into an Islamic state also gained support in post-Suharto Indonesia. It started at the People's Consultative Assembly in 1999 when some Islamist parties suggested an equilibrium, replacing state ideology Pancasila with the Jakarta Charter.

The 1945 Jakarta Charter didn't make Islam the state religion but could be interpreted to mean the state had a special responsibility to uphold Islamic sharia. It contained a phrase in the preface of the Constitution which read: *'With the obligation for adherents of Islam to practice Islamic sharia'*. The Pancasila, as a political compromise, simply deleted that phrase.

But the 1999 assembly decided not to have a vote. The Islamist parties also agreed, as a loss might have created serious damage to the idea.

The appeal, however, did not decrease. It grew quickly because the Suharto government had failed to protect human rights, to fight corruption, and to the protect the environment. Suharto maintained political stability and economic development but he himself was widely seen to be a corrupt despot.

Many Islamist parties and organisations, ranging from the moderates to the extremes, began to campaign for the sharia provisions, especially in conservative Muslim areas such as Aceh, West Sumatra, West Java and West Nusa Tenggara. Political Islam was seen as an alternative to the idea of secular nationalism.

Presidents Abdurrahman Wahid and Megawati Sukarnoputri did not favour political Islam. Wahid, himself a prominent Muslim scholar, defended religious freedom and promoted multiculturalism. Megawati, who replaced Wahid, faced the Islamists' criticism as they argued that a woman should not be a leader. Still they agreed with Aceh having a special autonomy to implement the Islamic sharia. This was to overcome Aceh's growing nationalism and widespread secessionist guerilla war. They helped open the Islamists' Pandora's box.

In Aceh, women are required to dress modestly, alcohol is prohibited, and numerous offenses – from adultery to homosexuality to selling alcohol – are punishable by public whipping. They even made the Sunni school of

Shafi'i as the province's official religion, while permitting three other major Sunni traditions – Hanafi, Maliki and Hambal – only on the condition that their followers promote 'religious harmony, Islamic brotherhood and security among Muslims'. The law excludes Aceh's sizable Shia and Sufi minorities.

In 2004, Megawati lost the presidential election to Susilo Bambang Yudhoyono, a retired general, who received support from Ma'ruf Amin, the chairman of the Indonesian Ulama Council. In return, President Yudhoyono made Ma'ruf Amin his religious affairs advisor. In July 2005, when opening their *ulama* congress, Yudhoyono stated his intention to 'take strict measures against deviant beliefs'. Ma'ruf Amin's council immediately issued fatwas against Ahmadiyah Muslims as well as against 'secularism, pluralism and liberalism'.

Yudhoyono assigned Amin to draft a decree on *religious harmony*. It's based on an Islamic practice on how to treat the *dhimmies* (Arabic means 'protected'). Arab-Muslim conquerors applied that practice to non-Muslim populations who surrendered to Muslim domination. In Indonesia, Hindus in Bali or Christians in the Moluccas never had such a deal. Ma'ruf Amin didn't use the term *dhimmies*. He used the term 'religious harmony'.

In March 2006, Yudhoyono approved Amin's draft, making it into a regulation. It requires Indonesia's 34 provinces and some 500 cities and regencies to establish a so-called Religious Harmony Forum (Forum Kerukunan Umat Beragama, FKUB) as advisory bodies to governors, mayors and regents. It is stipulated that the composition of FKUBs should 'mirror the composition of religions' in each area. Consequently, the dominant religion in any given area has the majority of members in a 17-strong FKUB (in a regency or mayoralty) or a 21-member provincial FKUB.

Yudhoyono basically replaced the constitutional principle of 'religious freedom' in Indonesia. The result of the decree has been a legally sanctioned block on construction of new houses of worship for religious minorities in areas where Muslims are in the majority, including the islands of Java and Sumatra. In some cases, the decree has even blocked Christian congregations from renovating existing church buildings. Militant Islamists effectively hijacked the decree and imposed vigilante-style enforcement of alleged violations. The Communion of Churches in Indonesia, a grouping of Protestant churches, criticised the 2006 decree and listed more than 1,000 churches closed down while Yudhoyono was in power for a decade.

The Yudhoyono government also aggressively enforced the 1965 blasphemy law, an overbroad and vague legal holdover from Sukarno's authoritarian rule. More than 100 individuals were prosecuted for blasphemy under Yudhoyono.

In 2008, Yudhoyono and Amin also introduced an anti-Ahmadiyah decree. Yudhoyono also made it compulsory for all schools, including international schools in Indonesia, to teach 'religion', and the government provides a disproportionally high number of Sunni Muslim teachers.

Aceh under Yudhoyono became a model for other areas in Indonesia to introduce sharia provisions. An official survey in 2015 found that more than 442 sharia ordinances have been passed throughout Indonesia, modelled on Aceh, mostly making it mandatory for women – Muslims and in some areas also Christian women – to wear the hijab.

Daoed Joesoef, a Sorbonne-educated scholar, told me that President Sukarno had consistently forbidden government schools from having such classes, 'When Suharto rose to power, he allowed the schools to have these religion classes'. Joesoef himself became the education minister under President Suharto in the late 1970s. He tried to eliminate these classes but there was no way to undo that Islamist policy. Yudhoyono expanded the ruling to all schools. Ma'ruf Amin became the chairman of the Nahdlatul Ulama, the largest Muslim group in Indonesia, in August 2015.

Political Islam is not the answer to corruption, rights abuses, and the environmental degradation in Indonesia. It is also not the answer to communal and sectarian violence in post-Suharto Indonesia. It decrease the protection of rights in Indonesia.

President Joko Widodo also embraced Ma'ruf Amin, appointing him to be his religious affairs advisor. In August 2018, he even picked up Amin to be his running mate in the 2019 presidential election.

Novelist Pramoedya Ananta Toer reminded me that the answer is to protect secular nationalism, to deal with past human rights abuses, to enhance the checks-and-balances in a democratic system, and to keep on promoting humanity. If Indonesia is to fail, according to Pramoedya, wars will take place everywhere. 'It's been more than 100 years that Java sent murderers to Aceh and other places. If Indonesia is to break up, it will also happen again. Java has too many people and they are mostly poor'.

If Indonesia is not to change, as Benedict Anderson suggested, it will find colossal difficulties in removing fascism – whether in the name of Pancasila or Islam. Like what J. R. R. Tolkien's shaman character Gandalf says in the series *The Lord of the Rings*, 'Do not be too eager to deal out death and judgement, for even the very wise cannot see all ends…All we have to decide is what to do with the time that is given to us'.

NOTES ON PLACES

I visited more than 90 locations between July 2003 and December 2006. Many of my stops were in Indonesian cities such as Pontianak, Surabaya, Kupang, Jayapura or Manado. My journeying also took me to the most remote corners of this vast archipelago – to 41 small towns, 15 villages, 11 islands and two peculiar coasts. Many names of my stops – Karatung, Karakelang, Binongko, Tomea and Mansinam – would barely ring a bell of recognition among many Indonesians.

I climbed Mount Kelimutu on Flores island, witnessing the breathtaking red, green and dark brown hues of the volcano at sunrise. Unfortunately, a car hit the motorcycle that was bringing me down from the mountain. The motorcycle driver, a teenager from Ende, suffered a broken leg. A passing car took him to Ende while I walked his wrecked motorcycle for an hour.

I sampled every mode of transportation available. In Aceh, I hopped on a chopper to visit the tsunami-ravaged coastal town of Lamno. In Kalimantan, I took small boats and smoke-filled public buses. I didn't get seasick but the small cockroaches that shared my cabin on the Manado–Miangas ship posed problems, tormenting me during the entire two-night trip. I took a small wooden boat to visit unpopulated Ndana Island. The waves were pretty rough.

In Pontianak in western Kalimantan, I met Sapariah Saturi, a Madurese journalist, who helped me to understand the suffering of ethnic Madurese. She later moved to Jakarta, coincidently staying near my apartment and later becoming an environmental specialist. We got to know each other better and married in 2007 in Jakarta. My son, Norman, was only six years old when I began the reporting. Now he is a young journalist. His sister, Diana, was born in 2011, and accompanied me in the final phase of writing this book. They grew along with my reporting, Norman daring to jump into the sea from our ship near Tomea Island and Diana taking pictures of sea turtles.

Papua is Norman's favourite destination. 'It's good for my health', he said, referring to his asthma. Diana basically loves beaches.

I read relevant documents and books prior to each trip. In Aceh, I stayed mostly in Banda Aceh's Hotel Sulthan, reading Aceh rebel leader Hasan di Tiro's analysis of *Indonesia*, but also travelled to the Aceh guerilla-controlled areas of Sakti, Sigli and Lhok Nga. I crossed the Banda Aceh strait to do some interviews in Sabang and visited Iboih Beach, Balohan seaport and the Ujung Batu tip on Weh Island. Between 2005 and 2011, I travelled to most parts of Aceh to cover the post-tsunami reconstruction and the rise of conservative Islamism.

In Kalimantan, I didn't cross any sea – it is already the third-largest island on Earth – but used *dongdong* motorboats to travel through swampy areas. It was one of the most gruelling trips I have ever taken. I went to Pontianak, Tebang Kacang, Singkawang, Roban, Selakau, Pemangkat, Tebas, Jawai, Sentebang, Sambas, Semalantan, Bengkayang, Sanggau-Ledo, Menjalin and Mempawah.

In Sulawesi, I began my trip in Makassar to conduct interviews on the Bugis rebel fighter Kahar Muzakkar. I then flew to Manado to interview Minahasan activists. I took a car from Manado to visit Minahasa's intellectual capital – Tomohon. Later I used speedboats and ferries to travel around Sangihe and Talaud islands. From southeast Sulawesi, I boarded a ferry to go to Baubau on Buton island and drove across the island to reach Pasarwajo, the site of the Butonese sultanate. From there, Norman and I boarded a Bugis ship, or *phinisi*, to roam around Wangiwangi, Kaledupa, Tomea, Binongko and Hoga islands. This archipelago has been turned into a protected environmental preserve and is a diving paradise.

In Java, I travelled to Semarang and Salatiga, where I used to live. Later I visited Blitar, where the tomb of Sukarno is located and the Panataran village, the site of the Palah Temple of the Majapahit era. I lost my laptop and my camera inside the Jakarta-Blitar train. Thieves probably opened my bag and took them while I was sleeping.

On East Timor, I began my travel from western Timor with some reporting in Kupang, including the Tuapukan refugee camp, and later Soe, Nikiniki, Kefamenanu, Atambua as well as crossing the border into newly independent East Timor to visit Matoain, Liquisa and Dili. When returning to Kupang, I took a ferry to visit Baa, Oelaba and Oeseli on Rote Island. From Oeseli, I took the small wooden boat to see Ndana Island.

In the Moluccas, my trip started in Ternate. I then took a speedboat to go to the neighbouring Halmahera island, visiting Galela, Tobelo, Kao, Malifut, Sosol, Tahane and Sidangoli. I spent the nights in Tobelo and Tahane. I also went to Soasiu on Tidore island, where I discovered that Christians were not allowed to settle on that Muslim-controlled island. I also stayed in Ambon, doing extensive reporting and interviews, which included a visit to the Waiheru prison to meet Ambonese nationalist Semuel Waileruny.

Between 2003 and 2007, I was involved in a newspaper improvement project with the Jakarta-based Pantau Foundation, helping the *Flores Pos* daily in Ende on Flores island, and the *Serambi* daily in Aceh. Helena Rea introduced me to her relatives, including the teenager who brought me to see Mount Kelimutu. I also visited Ambon, Makassar, Manado, Medan, Pontianak, Pekanbaru, Semarang, Surabaya and Yogyakarta, helping me to better understand the challenges of many journalists in Indonesia.

Human Rights Watch, which employed me in 2008, allowed me to visit Papua every year between 2008 and 2016. This enriched my contacts in almost every major urban area in Papua: Biak, Jayapura, Manokwari, Merauke, Sorong, Timika and Wamena. In Manokwari, I twice made a short boat ride to Mansinam Island, the site of the first Christian missionaries in Papua. In Merauke, I rented a mini-van to visit several transmigration villages, a vast area around Merauke where Javanese transmigrants live.

I also conducted interviews in Kuala Lumpur, London, New York, Singapore, Stockholm, Tokyo, and Washington DC. I did much of my writing in my Jakarta apartment where Norman and Diana waited for me, with Sapariah enriching my understanding of Indonesia from her environmentalist point of view.

NOTES ON SOURCES

I met many remarkable people when reporting for this book. We had our interviews mostly in their offices or living rooms, but several interviews were conducted inside prisons or in tsunami-ravaged villages.

Some of these sources died tragically. A policeman fatally beat Jonli Awalla, a Miangas islander, in May 2005. His death prompted the whole of Miangas to fly a Filipino flag, protesting not only against the policeman but also showing their distaste toward Indonesia.

The tsunami also killed my Acehnese sources who included Aceh police spokesman Sayed Hoesayni and reporter Taufan Nugraha. Acehnese poet Z. Afif, who taught Acehnese language in Stockholm, died in October 2004. Afif went into self-exile in 1965, moving from Beijing to Hanoi and later to Stockholm. Afif was the first person to brief me about Aceh's nationalism.

On 30 April 2006, Indonesian novelist Pramoedya Ananta Toer died in his Jakarta home. It was less than a month after our interview. Nationalism guru Benedict Anderson died in December 2015 in Batu, East Java. Another source, George J. Aditjondro, also my mentor, died in December 2016 in Palu, Central Sulawesi. Oktovianus Pogau, a talented West Papuan journalist who set up the *Suara Papua* news portal, died in January 2016.

Many other sources have also died during the 15-year reporting and writing of this book. I just didn't keep in touch with all of them. I interviewed more than 700 people. Many sources are not quoted in the book. I also learned a lot from them too.

Sumatra

Field Research and Interviews

This chapter is an expansion from an essay that I wrote for *The Star* weekly in Kuala Lumpur, 'Starting From Kilometre Zero' published on 14 September 2003. *The Star* sent me to Aceh in June 2003, two weeks after the martial law was declared in Jakarta. I visited post-tsunami Aceh to work for Pantau Foundation (2005–08). On 17 April 2013, I testified at the Aceh provincial parliament in Banda Aceh on behalf of Human Rights Watch.

My sources in Banda Aceh included Abdi A. Wahab, Abdullah Puteh, Hakim Nyak Pha, Imam Syuja, Muslim Ibrahim and Yuli Suriani. Indonesian army captain Solih and Colonel Ditya Sudarsono gave me to access military zones. Politician Afdhal Yasin invited me to stay in his house.

In Tiro area, I interviewed Second Lieutenant Eka Andang, Second Sergeant Asep Setiaman, farmers Muhammad Husin, Sapari and Muhammad Abubakar. Reporter Mansur Amin quit *Tempo* immediately after the allegation from Hasan Tiro in 1977. I met Amin in January 2005 in Banda Aceh.

In Stockholm, I interviewed GAM leaders Zaini Abdullah and Bachtiar Abdullah as well as their rivals Husaini Hasan and M. Yusuf Daud. Bertil Lindner, a Swedish journalist based in Chiang Mai, Thailand, briefed me about GAM's Stavanger meeting in July 2002 during which most Acehnese leaders agreed to advocate referendum – not merely guerilla war. Bertil also reminded me of Hasan di Tiro's connection to CIA operative Edward Lansdale in Vietnam.

In Sabang, I interviewed politician Husaini, prison warden Sianto and his wife Nyik Siti Absyah, mayor Sofyan Haroen, privates Sutrisno and Wahyu Hanes as well as the family of Liyan Ramli. Jupri, a Sabang police officer, drove me around town.

In Lamno, I interviewed survivors that included Hendi, Muhammad Ali, and Mustafa Ibrahim. World Vision let me take a ride in their chopper.

I attended a Jakarta discussion on Aceh and the tsunami on 24 February 2005 organised by the Reform Institute, during which I interviewed Surjadi Sudirdja, former Indonesian Home Affairs Minister, Aceh acting governor Azwar Abu Bakar and Jakarta's former chief negotiator in Geneva Wiryono Sastrohandoyo. I also learned a lot from Aceh legislator Farhan Hamid and many of Indonesia's hardline views from Golkar legislator Yuddy Chrisnandy and army general Lieutenant General Kiki Syanakri.

Hasan di Tiro confused many scholars about his age. He claimed in his diary that he was turning 46 on 4 September 1976, meaning that he was born in 1930. In another book, *Demokrasi Untuk Indonesia*, which was written by Tiro in 1958, he describes in the writer's box that he was born in 1923. Media reports quoted the Swedish authorities as stating that he was born in 1925.

In November 2004, Ed Aspinall and Anthony Reid, two Australian scholars who have written books on Aceh, became involved in an internet discussion about his age. Both were sceptical about 1930. Reid decided to use 1925. Reporter Murizal Hamzah, who wrote a biography about Hasan Tiro, told me that Tiro had gone to the Dutch 'Normal' school in Bireuen in 1939. I don't think one goes to high school at nine. Yusuf Daud, another Aceh leader in Stockholm, told me in September 2005 that Amir Mahmud, an older brother of Malik Mahmud, the so-called prime minister of the Aceh exile government, went to the same Bireuen school. Amir Mahmud was born in 1925. Yusuf said Amir always said that he is younger than Hasan di Tiro. It means Hasan Tiro was born in 1923, according to Murizal Hamzah's conclusion.

Material Sources

Adinegoro, *Melawat ke Barat*, Batavia: Balai Poestaka, 1926.

Alfian, Ibrahim, *Perang di Jalan Allah: Perang Aceh 1873–1912*, Jakarta: Pustaka Sinar Harapan, 1987.

Amnesty International, 'Shock Therapy Restoring Order in Aceh, 1989–1993', 2 August 1993.

Anderson, Benedict R. O'G, *Imagined Communities: Reflections on the Origin and Spread of Nationalism*, Verso (Revised edition), July 1991.

Armstrong, Karen, *A History of God*, London: Vintage, 1999.

Di Tiro, Hasan, 'Declaration of Independence of Acheh–Sumatra', National Liberation Front of Acheh, Sumatra, Acheh, Sumatra, 4 December 1976.

Di Tiro, Hasan, *The Price of Freedoms: The Unfinished Diary of Tengku Hasan di Tiro*, Ontario: Open Press, 1984. It recorded his activities from 4 September 1976 to 29 March 1979.

Di Tiro, Hasan. '*The Legal Status of Acheh–Sumatra Under International Law*', Acheh Sumatra National Liberation Front, 1980.

Di Tiro, Hasan, 'The Case and the Cause of the National Liberation Front of Acheh-Sumatra', Acheh Sumatra National Liberation Front, 1985.

Harsono, Andreas. 'A nation that refuses to succumb', *The Nation*, Bangkok, 31 January 31, 2001.

Harsono, Andreas, 'Starting from Kilometre Zero', *The Star*, Kuala Lumpur, 1 September 2003.

Human Rights Watch, *Aceh Under Martial Law: Inside the Secret War*, New York, December 2003.

Human Rights Watch, *Policing Morality: Abuses in the Application of Sharia in Aceh, Indonesia*, New York, November 2010 (https://www.hrw.org/ report/2010/11/30/policing-morality/abuses-application-sharia-aceh-indonesia downloaded on 5 December 2011).

Human Rights Watch, 'Aceh's New Islamic Laws Violate Rights', New York, 2 October 2014 (https://www.hrw.org/news/2014/10/02/indonesia-acehs-new-islamic-laws-violate-rights downloaded on 2 October 2014).

Human Rights Watch, 'Human Rights Watch Complaint on the Rights of LGBT people in Indonesia's Aceh Province', several letters sent to some United Nations human rights officials, February 2016 (https://www.hrw. org/news/2016/03/29/human-rights-watch-complaint-rights-lgbt-people-indonesias-aceh-province downloaded on 1 November 2016).

Human Rights Watch, 'Indonesia: Megawati Should Investigate Aceh Killing', New York, 7 September 2001 (http://hrw.org/english/docs/2001/09/07/indone2033.htm downloaded on 25 January 2017).

Hurgronje, Snouck C., *Aceh: Rakyat dan Adat Istiadatnya,* Leiden-Jakarta: INIS, 1987 (translated from Dutch entitled *De Atjehers*).

Jaringan Pemantau Aceh 231, *Catatan Dwi Tahunan: Kekerasan terhadap Perempuan di Aceh 2013–2014,* Banda Aceh, July 2015.

Jones, Sidney, 'Finding Solutions, Winning People's Hearts', *Tempo,* 22–28 July 2003.

Kell, Tim, *The Roots of Acehnese Rebellion 1989–1992,* Ithaca: Cornell Modern Indonesia Project, 1995.

Komnas Perempuan, *Menjelujur Pengalaman Kekerasan Perempuan di Aceh,* Jakarta, June 2013 (http://www.komnasperempuan.go.id/menjelujur-pengalaman-kekerasan-perempuan-di-aceh/ downloaded on 15 January 2017).

Lansdale, Edward Geary, *In the Midst of Wars: An American's mission to Southeast Asia,* Harper & Row, 1972.

Lansdale, Edward Geary, 'Register of the Edward Geary Lansdale Papers, 1910–1987', Online Archive of California (http://content.cdlib.org/view?docId=tf6v19n8cp&chunk.id=dsc-1.7.6&brand=oac downloaded in August 2007).

Lombard, Denys, *Kerajaan Aceh: Jaman Sultan Iskandar Muda (1607–1636),* Jakarta: Balai Pustaka, 1986 (translated from *Le Sultanat d'Atjeh au Temps d'Iskandar Muda 1607–1636*).

Majelis Permusyawaratan Ulama, *Kumpulan Undang-undang, Perda, Qanun dan Instruksi Gubernur tentang Keistimewaan Nanggroe Aceh Darussalam* (2002), *Vikalah, Sulhu, Ikrar dan Qadha* (2002), *Perampasan, Hajru, Syuf'ah dan Syarikat* (2002), *Jual Beli, Sewa Menyewa, Kafalah* (2002), *Hiwalah, Gadai, Amanah dan Hibbah* (2002).

Munir, Lili Zakiyah, 'Simbolisasi, Politisasi dan Kontrol terhadap Perempuan di Aceh', in *Syariat Islam: Pandangan Muslim Liberal,* Jakarta: Jaringan Islam Liberal, 2003.

Noerdin, Edriana, *Politik Identitas Perempuan Aceh,* Jakarta: Women Research Institute, 2005.

Pour, Julius, 'Teuku Ibrahim Alfian, Keterikatan Samudera Pasai-Mataram', *Kompas,* 6 May 2003.

Reid, Anthony, *The Contest for North Sumatra: Atjeh, the Netherlands and Britain, 1858–1898,* Kuala Lumpur: Oxford University Press, 1969.

Rini, Chik, 'Sebuah Kegilaan di Simpang Kraft', *Pantau,* Jakarta, May 2002 (https://www.pantau.or.id/?/=d/161 downloaded on 25 January 2017).

Sulaiman, Muhammad Isa, *Mosaik Konflik di Aceh,* Banda Aceh: Acehkita, 2006.

Winchester, Simon, *Krakatoa: The Day the World Exploded: August 27, 1883,* Harper Perennial, 2005.

Zentgraaf, H. C., *Atjeh* (a translation from the Dutch), Jakarta: Beuna, 1986.

Kalimantan

Field Research and Interviews

I visited West Kalimantan for three weeks in December 2004 and January 2005, staying in Pontianak, Singkawang and Bengkayang. Apo Apriady, a Dayak youth, drove me around Pontianak, telling me that he had once eaten a 'Madurese heart'. Sapariah Saturi, a Pontianak native, makes visiting Pontianak almost annually.

In Pontianak, I researched the Dayak-oriented *Kalimantan Review* magazines. My interviewees included Dayak activist Stepanus Djuweng, who helped set up the Dayakology Institute. A. R. Mecer, the founding member of Pancur Kasih group, gave me his 2006 biography, *Berjuang untuk yang Terbuang*. Other Dayak sources included Alexander Mering, Tanto Yakobus and Yusriadi.

Malay sources included militia Abbas Fadillah and Chairil Effendi of the Tanjungpura University. In the Malay areas of Jawai, Pemangkat and Tebas, I interviewed Arman Ayub (born 1976), whose father, Ayub Tahir, was killed by the Madurese gang on 19 January 1999, in the Parit Setia village. Koranic teacher Idham Chalid helped me to interview Hamidi Hadran, the ironsmith in Parit Setia. Idham also introduced me to Erman Tungkat, a Malay militia, who was involved in the killing and lives in Sentebang.

Muhammad Lase, the head of hamlet Serang in Sari Makmur village, and Zainal Sidik, the village head of Sari Makmur, explored the history of the Rambayan village, whose name, was changed into Sari Makmur after the massacre.

Rambayan was a Madurese village. My Madurese sources lived in Rambayan prior to the Parit Setia attack. Now it is a Malay village. I learned a lot about how the Madurese properties were occupied or sold in Sari Makmur from Lase and Zainal. They told me the Madurese owners could only do the land transaction in Singkawang as they are not allowed to enter Sambas villages.

I also talked to the family of Mawardi bin Haji Sude, who was killed in the Senangi massacre. His wife Romina, their son Dedi Kustian, Dedi's wife Susi Kurnia, and Dedi's sister Anita, provided information about Mawardi. Masya Hasan alias Mat Kedang granted me a long interview in the Pusaka village. He also gave me stories on the death of Mawardi.

Madurese sources included husband-and-wife Abunawas-Karimah, Mariyama and her aunt Sarunah, Haji Marhayat, Samsuri, Sari, Chodijah and

Jasudin. I interviewed Madurese leaders Nagian Imawan as well as Subro and Mustain Said. Nagian told me about his 'missing niece' Novi Alfonita. I also interviewed Subro's parents, Sanali and Sariti, in the Tebang Kacang relocation area, about three hours off-road driving from Pontianak. I talked to some other Sambas displaced villagers: Mat Sukri, Ismail, Pak Tosin, Sabirin and Marhatap.

In Singkawang, my Malay sources included Ikhdar Salim of the Communication Forum of Malay Youth (Forum Komunikasi Pemuda Melayu, FKPM), Sukarmi, and Zulkarnain Bujang, the head of the FKPM.

I also interviewed Kenny Kumala, a German-educated ethnic Chinese politician in Singkawang, who is also a provincial parliament member. Andi Suhardi, another politician, gave me more stories. Ng Djan Ho alias Nugroho Setiadi, the eldest son of Ng Miau Khui, who was detained for several months in 1967, also granted me an interview.

I interviewed husband Siau Fut Jiu and wife Tjong Tjhiu Djin in the Roban area, outside Singkawang. Roban was the relocation destination of the Chinese refugees in the 1967. Now it is still a poor village with many houses that have not changed from their original condition in 1967. I also interviewed Chin Sjin Luk in Roban. Husband Lie Syak Liung and wife Tju Nyan Tjau also live in Roban.

The case of Novi Alfonita took my special interest. I heard her case initially from her Madurese uncle Nagian Imawan in Pontianak. Idham Chalid helped me to trace Novi by looking for her Malay mother Hajiah. It took us two days to find Hajiah. I interviewed Hajiah binti Saleh and her new husband Hamidi bin Usman in the Bekut village in Tebas.

Hajiah's first husband, Thalib, himself a Madurese, was murdered during the Madurese massacres. Hajiah is a Malay. Her second husband is also a Malay. Hajiah gave birth to her second daughter, with Hamidi, in September 2002. I also interviewed Hajiah's father, Saleh bin H. Achmad, his wife Farida, her sister Sanimah, in their Mausere village. This family lives next door to Mawardi. I found this a bitter tragedy.

In the town of Sambas, I interviewed Delyuzar and Ronald Dachlan, two close friends to Raden Wimpi or Pangeran Wira Dinata. I managed to talk over the phone with Raden Wimpi himself who was about to go for the hajj pilgrimage to Mecca. I also talked to Endang Sri Muningsih, Wimpi's wife, inside the Alwadzikoebillah palace. Endang is a mixed blood. Her father is a Banjar while mother is a Javanese.

Urai Hasanuddin, an uncle to Raden Wimpi, briefed me about the royal family. Urai Riza Fahmi, the head of the Keraton Secretariat, briefed me about how the Sambas palace tried to avoid the Madurese killing in Sambas.

In Bengkayang, I interviewed Iskandar Oton, the Dayak owner of a billiard house, Khoen Sin Fah alias Halijah and her husband Agus Lazim. Sodikin, an employee of bank BNI, took me on a tour of the small town and we saw swallows. Petrus Alyosius Simuk, the head of the Coop Pelita Bengkayang (since 1975), a retired school teacher and an actor in the 1967 Chinese massacre, also granted me an interview.

In Jakarta, I interviewed Piet Herman Abik and Maria Goreti, members of the Indonesian Senate, representing West Kalimantan. I interviewed Jamie Davidson, the expert on the Sambas violence, while he was visiting Jakarta in July 2005. I brought Davidson's 400-page thesis, *Not Since Time Immemorial: Ethnicity, Indigeneity and Collective Violence on an Indonesian Periphery*, in my Kalimantan trip and practically used it as a travel guide.

The population figures in this chapter come from a census summarised in the 2003 *Indonesia's Population: Ethnicity and Religion in a Changing Political Landscape*. Many Dayak groups challenged the census result which did not categorise 'Dayak' as a single group. Instead, it categorised Kendayan, Pesaguan and other 'Dayak sub-ethnic' groups. It puts Sambas ethnic group as the largest category in West Kalimantan (about 444,000 or 12 per cent of the total population). The Chinese became the second largest ethnic group at 9.46 per cent. The Pontianak office of the Central Board of Statistics finally withdrew the result.

Later, many Dayak groups cited a 'statistic' produced by West Kalimantan military commander Major General Namoeri Anum. He described that the Dayak compose 41.5 per cent of the total population in West Kalimantan, the Malay 39.5 per cent, the Chinese 11.3 per cent and the Madurese 0.4 per cent (Kalimantan Review, December 2004). The new number of the Madurese is much lower than the result of the 2000 census at 5.46 per cent.

I doubted such a drastic reduction despite the widespread massacres and the eviction of the Madurese. Many Madurese fled to Madura Island or eastern Java. Others said the number of the Madurese, prior to the ethnic cleansing, was as high as 8 per cent of the total population. It is also difficult to verify as the latest census that included ethnicity in this archipelago was organised in 1930 by the Netherlands Indies government. I decided to use the 2000 census although I know it does not satisfy everyone, myself included.

Pontianak has three dailies dominated by Malay journalists. The *Pontianak Post* (formerly *Ackaya*) and *Equator* dailies have their main market in Pontianak while *Kapuas Pos* is aimed at the hinterland of Kapuas Hulu. The Surabaya-based Jawa Pos Group controls their shares.

Material Sources

Adhi Ksp, 'Ketika Supremasi Hukum Ambruk di Sambas Kamis', *Kompas,* 1 April 1999.

Aditjondro, George J., 'From "Ganyang Malaysia" to "Ganyang Fretili": Lessons Learned from the Konfrontasi Period that Maybe Relevant in Ending the Indonesian Occupation of East Timor'. A paper presented at the International Conference on Peacemaking Initiatives for East Timor, organised by the Department of Political Science of the Australian National University in Canberra, 10–12 July 1995. Revised edition on apakabar@clark.net mailing list on 26 July 1995.

Bamba, John, 'The Role of Adat In The Dayak and Madurese War', Paper presented on International NGO Forum on Indonesian Development conference in Bonn, Germany, 4–6 May 1998. The Institute Dayakology's website also provided me with information about their programs as well as the Credit Union's activities.

Davidson, Jamie and Kammen, Douglas, 'Indonesia's Unknown War and the Lineages of Violence in West Kalimantan', *Indonesia,* No. 73, April 2002.

Davidson, Jamie, *Violence and Politics in West Kalimantan, Indonesia,* PhD thesis, Washington University, Seattle, October 2002.

Davidson, Jamie, 'The Politics of Violence on an Indonesian Periphery', *Southeast Asia Research,* Vol. 11, No. 1, March 2003.

Djuweng, Stefanus (ed.), *Manusia Dayak: Orang Kecil yang Terperangkap Modernisasi,* Pontianak: Institute of Dayakology Research and Development/ IDRD, 1997.

Effendy, Machrus, *Penghancuran PGRS-PARAKU dan PKI di Kalimantan Barat,* Jakarta: PT Dian Kemilau, 1995.

Equator, 'Dominasi Etnis di Kalbar Picu Konflik Baru', 7 April 2003. This report quoted Chairil Effendi.

Eriyanto and Rusman, 'Panglima Burung', Pantau, May 2001.

Harsono, Andreas, 'Panasnya Pontianak, Panasnya Politik', Gatra, 5 July 2008.

Heidhues, Mary Somers, 'A history of diversity', *Inside Indonesia,* April–June 2004.

Human Rights Watch, *Communal Violence in West Kalimantan,* New York, 1 December 1997 (http://www.hrw.org/reports/1997/wkali/ downloaded on 1 November 2003).

Human Rights Watch, Persecution of Gafatar Religious Group, New York, 29 March 2016 (https://www.hrw.org/news/2016/03/29/indonesia-persecution-gafatar-religious-group downloaded on 13 February 2019).

Jenkins, David, 'The Last Headhunt', *Far Eastern Economic Review,* 30 June 1978.

Kalimantan Review, 'Menghilangkan Etnis dengan Statistik', *Kalimantan Review* Edisi Khusus, 2003. The whole issue addresses the ethnic and statistical problem in West Kalimantan.

Mackie, J. A. C., *Konfrontasi: The Indonesia-Malaysia dispute 1963–1966,* Published
   for the Australian Institute of International Affairs by Oxford University Press,
   Kuala Lumpur, 1974.
Mackie, J. A. C., *The Chinese in Indonesia,* Melbourne: Nelson, 1976.
Parry, Richard Lloyd, *In the Time Madness,* London: Jonathan Cape, 2005.
Petebang, Edi and Sutrisno, Eri, *Konflik Etnik di Sambas,* Jakarta: Institut Studi
   Arus Informasi, 2000.
Putra, Nico Andas and Djuweng, Stepanus (ed.), *Sisi Gelap Kalimantan Barat:
   Perseteruan Etnis Dayak-Madura.* Jakarta: Institut Studi Arus Informasi. 1999.
Soemadi, *Peranan Kalimantan Barat dalam menghadapi Subversi Komunis Asia
   Tenggara,* Pontianak: Yayasan Tanjungpura, 1974.
Suryadinata, Leo; Arifin, Evi Nurvidya; Ananta, Aris, *Indonesia's Population:
   Ethnicity and Religion in a Changing Political Landscape,* Singapore: ISEAS,
   2003. It used and analysed the 2000 census taken by Indonesia's Central Board
   of Statistics.
Van Klinken, Gerry, 'Ethnic fascism in Borneo', *Inside Indonesia,* June–July 2000.
Wawa, Jannes Eudes, 'Warga Kalbar Impikan Kedamaian', *Kompas,* 3 July 2000.

Sulawesi

Field Research and Interviews

I visited more than a dozen small towns and their harbours in the Sangihe
and Talaud islands in September 2004. I interviewed about 30 people
during the trip, which included Adelito Papea Pagtun, school teacher
Agus Tege, Alfredo Papea Pagtun, Arnold Abbas, Benita Bagus Pvillaflor,
Carlito Niebres, husband and wife Djonyor Namare and Lukring Binulang,
Eldon Matoneng, Ennos Nangori, Firdaus Majusip, Hengky Vantriardo,
Joppy Luppa, Nanlis Pade, Miangas fisherman Petrus Essing (plus wife
Kalarita Tientang, daughter Nova Tine, daughter-in-law Meyiske Palense),
wife Rita Matama and husband Jonli Awalla, wife Rosana Sari and
husband Lukas Bawala as well as three North Sulawesi's civil servants in
charge on public works who were travelling to islands during my trip: Chris
Laotongan, Alfons Limboh and Jefri Sundana. Djonyor Namare welcomed
me to stay in his house as there is no hotel in Miangas.

I interviewed Markarius Velmus Janis, an election official in Tahuna,
Sangihe Besar Island. I also got some information about transport matters
on those rather isolated islands from two Indonesian Navy captains,
Muhammad Syarif Alamsyah and Totok Prasetijo, at the Kairagi naval base
in Manado.

I visited Manado and Tomohon twice, in July and September 2004, interviewing Abdurahman Lakasan, Adil Polontalo, Yuni Husain, Arudji Radjab,

Rosyifa Amiri, Aif Darea, Alex John Ulaen, Arnold F. Parengkuan, journalist Benny Allo, Sangihe politician Edison Humiang, editor Friko S. Poli, Jackried Maluenseng, realtor Janto Widjaja, activist Jemmy Lumintang, street vendor Lukman Tune, radio broadcaster Noverius Bulango, linguist Paul Nebath, lecturer Reiner Ointoe, Royke Rarumangkay, Suardi Hamzah and editor Suhendro Boroma of the *Manado Post*. I also interviewed Willy Roeroe in his retirement home in Tomohon who briefed me about the *manguni* bird (owl) and the history of Christianities in Minahasa. I interviewed Bert Adriaan Supit in July and September 2004 in Tomohon.

Tidorean Muin Sumaila and Boolang Mongondowan Coen Husain Pontoh gave me insight into Manado's political situation. Both are former activists of the Manado branch of the Himpunan Mahasiswa Islam or the Islamic Students' Association. Muin is a school teacher. Pontoh is now the editor of the New York–based Indo Progress website.

Alex John Ulaen of the Ratulangi University in Manado helped me with documents on Miangas. Ulaen himself is a Karatung native on the Talaud Islands.

In Jakarta, I interviewed Herman Nicolas Sumual and some of his colleagues in the office of PT Konsultasi Pembangunan as well as Syenni Inneke Smith Watulango of Brigade Manguni.

In Makassar, I interviewed Boet Philip Manuel Rompas, a retired photographer, who took the photograph of Muslim militia leader Kahar Muzakkar in 1965. Boet is married to Lily Rompas, a linguist at the Hasanuddin University, who briefed me about Bugis-Minahasa relations in Makassar. I visited Palu, near Poso, only in December 2016, doing some interviews about Poso violence.

Material Sources

Conboy, Kenneth and Morrison, James, *Feet to the Fire: CIA Covert Operations in Indonesia, 1957–1958,* Annapolis: Naval Institute Press, 1999.

Dhakidae, Daniel, *Gerungan Saul Samuel Jacob Ratulangi: Pijar-pijar Bintang Kejora dari Timur.*

Harvey, Barbara, *Permesta Half a Rebellion,* Ithaca: Modern Indonesia Project, Cornell University, 1976.

Henley, David, *Nationalism and Regionalism in a Colonial Context: Minahasa in the Dutch East Indie,* Leiden: Koninklijk Instituut voor Taal-, Land- en Volkenkunde, 1996.

Henley, David, 'The Fate of Federalism: North Sulawesi from Persatuan Minahasa to Permesta', Paper prepared for the KNAW symposium 'Indonesia in transition: crises, conflicts, continuities'. Amsterdam, 25–27 August 2004.

Kahin, George McTurnan, *Nationalism and Revolution in Indonesia,* Ithaca: Cornell University Press, 1952.

Kerukunan Keluarga Kawanua, *Manifesto Manusia Kawanua*, Jakarta: Dewan Pembina Kerukunan Keluarga Kawanua, 2004.

Lam, H. J., *Miangas (Palmas): Scattered Annotations*, Batavia: G. Kolff & Co, 1932.

Manado Pos, 'Jadi Lini Terdepan Jaga Minahasa, Turun Gunung BM Setia terhadap NKRI', 9 March 2003.

Matindas, B. E. and Supit, Bert, *Ventje Sumual: Menatap Hanya ke Depan: Biografi Seorang Patriot, Filsuf, Gembong Pemberontak*, Jakarta: Penerbit Bina Insani, 1998.

McRae, Dave, *A Few Poorly Organized Men: Interreligious Violence in Poso, Indonesia*, Leiden: Brill, 2013.

Nairn, Allan, 'General Lumintang Trained by the U.S', 28 March 2000 (https://www.etan.org/news/2000a/suit/nairn.htm downloaded on 7 August 2017).

Pangkerego, Aneke Sumarauw, 'Gunung Lokon dan Gunung Kelabat' from the book *Cerita Rakyat dari Minahasa* (http://members.tripod.com/~MandaRatulangi/Lokon01.html downloaded 1 November 2004).

Parengkuan, Arnold, *The Presence, Place, and Role of the Christian Evangelical Church in Minahasa in the Midst of the Struggle of Minahasa Society and Indonesian Nation in the Period of 1934-1979*, PhD thesis at the South East Asia Graduate School of Theology, Jakarta, 1994.

Persatuan Minahasa, 'Menuju Minahasa Baru: Pergerakan Persatuan Minahasa', Tomohon, 2003. It is a 38-page leaflet.

Saruan, Josef M., 'Gereja dan Masyarakat 1930–1945: Masa Awal Pertumbuhan GMIM'. This is a 76-page undated leaflet used by Saruan to teach his students at the Program Pasca Sarjana Teologi seluruh Indonesia in Tomohon.

Sarundajang, S. H., *Arus Balik Kekuasaan Pusat ke Daerah*, Jakarta: Sinar Harapan, 2002 (fourth edition).

Sulu, Phill M., *Permesta: Jejak-jejak Pengembaraan*, Jakarta: Sinar Harapan, 1997.

Supit, Bert, *Minahasa: Dari Amanat Watu Pinawetengan Sampai Gelora Minawanua*, Jakarta: Sinar Harapan, 1986.

Supit, Bert Adriaan, 'Provinsi Minahasa: Suatu Wacana Pemberdayaan Daerah dan Rakyat Melalui Reformasi Struktur Pemerintahan Daerah Menuju Indonesia Baru', Manado, 10 July 2001. It is a 24-page leaflet prepared to disseminate Supit's idea to establish Minahasa province.

Supit, Bert Adriaan, *Menuju Minahasa Baru: Pergerakan Persatuan Minahasa*, Tomohon: Suara Nurani, Tomohon, 2003.

Supit, Bert Adriaan, *Melawan Arus: Wacana Federalisme Untuk Indonesia*, Manado: Yayasan Suara Nurani, 2004.

Supit, Bert Adriaan, *Otobiografi Bert Adriaan Supit: Pengalaman, Kesaksian, Pikiran & Harapan*, Tomohon: Yayasan Suara Hati, 2004.

Supit, Bert, Nainggolan, Jun N. H. and Matindas, B. E., *Apa Beda Permesta dan PRRI*, Jakarta: LSPMM Minaesa, 2004.

Suryadinata, Leo; Arifin, Evi Nurvidya; Ananta, Aris, *Indonesia's Population: Ethnicity and Religion in a Changing Political Landscape*, Singapore: ISEAS, 2003. It used and analysed the 2000 census taken by Indonesia's Central Board of Statistics.

Ulaen, Alex J., *Nusa Utara: Dari Lintasan Niaga ke Daerah Perbatasan*, Jakarta: Sinar Harapan, 2003.

Van Klinken, Gerry, *Minorities, Modernity and the Emerging Nation: Christians in Indonesia, a biographical approach*, Leiden: KITLV Press, 2003.

Yunarti, D. Rini, *BPUPKI, PPKI, Proklamasi Kemerdekaan RI*, Jakarta: Kompas, 2003.

Java

Field Research and Interviews

I learned about the excision of the Islamic sharia from the Indonesian constitution in a 1997 book written by seven student activists, which included O. E. Engelen, as well as other analyses by Australian scholar Gerry van Klinken and Indonesian political scientist George J. Aditjondro. I also checked with Ventje Sumual, then a young Minahasan militia, guarding the Eastern Indonesia delegates at Hotel des Indes in August 1945. Engelen's wife told me that Engelen died soon after finishing the 1997 book.

I interviewed Ventje Sumual initially on 20 November 2004 in Jakarta. I later read a book written by Gerry van Klinken, *Minorities, Modernity and the Emerging Nation*, in which an interview with O. E. Engelen was extensively used. Van Klinken also gave me the transcript of his 24 July 1994 interview. I interviewed Sumual again on 15 March 2007.

I used many obituaries written by Cornell University's George McTurnan Kahin when describing Indonesia's foundaing fathers.

In Jakarta, I interviewed Pramoedya Ananta Toer, Rahman Tolleng, Daoed Joesoef, Ibarruri Aidit, and Suryopratomo. In Blitar, I interviewed tourists Daud Mesriadi, Choirul Anam, Wajiman and his wife Sutinem, Hermawan Wibisono, Riza Hafizatullah and Rama Wardhana. Masya Spek, who manages Hanacaraka.com, helped me to check ancient Javanese manuscripts in the Panataran temple in Blitar.

Material Sources

Adam, Asvi Warman et al., *Soeharto Sehat*, Yogyakarta: Galang Press, 2006.

Adam, Asvi Warman, 'Kasus Biografi Soekarno', *Kompas*, 6 June 2007. Adam wrote of a stark difference between Cindy Adams' English and Indonesian versions. Sukarno was quoted as saying, in the Indonesian version, that Hatta did not appear on 17 August 1945 until Sukarno asked Hatta to accompany Sukarno declaring independence. Sukarno said he could declare independence himself. The English version didn't have these controversial paragraphs.

Adams, Cindy, *Sukarno: An Autobiography*, Indianapolis: Bobbs-Merrill, 1965.

Aidit, Murad, *Aidit, Sang Legenda*, Jakarta: Panta Rei, 2005.

Anderson, Benedict R. O'G., *A Preliminary Analysis of the October 1, 1965 Coup in Indonesia*, Ithaca: Cornell Modern Indonesia Project, With Ruth T. McVey and Frederick P. Bunnell, 1971.

Anderson, Benedict R. O'G., *Java in a Time of Revolution*, Ithaca: Cornell University Press, 1972.

Anderson, Benedict R. O'G., *Language and Power: Exploring Political Culture in Indonesia*, Ithaca, NY: Cornell University Press, 1990.

Anderson, Benedict R. O'G., *Mythology and the Tolerance of the Javanese*, Ithaca: Cornell University, Cornell Modern Indonesia Project, 1997 (revised edition).

Anderson, Benedict R. O'G., 'Indonesian Nationalism Today and in the Future', *Indonesia*, No. 67, April 1999.

Anderson, Benedict R. O'G., 'Petrus Dadi Ratu', *New Left Review*, May–June 2000.

Anderson, Benedict R. O'G., *Violence and the State in Suharto's Indonesia*, Ithaca, NY: SEAP Cornell University, 2001.

Anderson, Benedict R. O'G., Introduction in *Indonesia Dalem Api dan Bara* by Tjamboek Berdoeri, Jakarta: Elkasa, 2004.

Anderson, Jon Lee, *Che Guevara: A Revolutionary Life*, Grove Press, March 1998.

Bayuni, Endy M., 'Symposiums aim to invoke Pancasila to bind nation', *The Jakarta Post*, 18 May 2006. It quoted Rahman Tolleng, a politician and former journalist, in describing the phenomenon as 'the creeping Talibanization' of Indonesia.

Borsuk, Richard and Chng, Nancy, *Liem Sioe Liong's Salim Group: The Business Pillar of Suharto's Indonesia*, Singapore: ISEAS, 2014.

Candraningrum, Dewi, Negotiating Women's Veiling: Politics and Sexuality in Contemporary Indonesia, IRASEC, 2013.

Coppel, Charles A., *Indonesian Chinese in Crisis*, Oxford University Press, 1983.

Emmerson, Donald K., 'What Is Indonesia?' in *Indonesia: The Great Transition*, John Bresnan (ed.), Boulder, Colorado: Rowman & Littlefield, 2005.

Engelen, O. E. and Lubis, Aboe Bakar, *Lahirnya Satu Bangsa dan Negara*, Jakarta: Universitas Indonesia Press, 1997.

Fellowship of Indonesian Christians in America, 'Penutupan, Perusakan, Dan Atau Pembakaran 374 Gereja Di Indonesia Pada Tahun 1945–1997'. On the number of churches burned in Indonesia, I referred to a database built by the Fellowship of Indonesian Christians in America (http://www.fica.org/persecution/374.html downloaded on 17 June 2016).

Harsono, Andreas, 'Indonesia's courts have opened the door to fear and religious extremism', *The Guardian*, 10 May 2017.

Human Rights Watch, *In Religion's Name: Abuses against Religious Minorities in Indonesia*, New York, February 2013 (https://www.hrw.org/report/2013/02/28/religions-name/abuses-against-religious-minorities-indonesia#abedd5 downloaded on 7 August 2015).

Hidayatullah.com, 'Pelajaran dari Brunei Merdeka' had Abubakar Basyir's quotation, 1 March 2007. In possession of the author.

Ien Ang, 'Remembering Today', *Inside Indonesia*, April–June 2004.

Ingleson, John, *Road to Exile: The Indonesian Nationalist Movement, 1927–1934*, Singapore: Published for the Asian Studies Association of Australia by Heinemann Educational Books (Asia), 1979.

Joesoef, Daoed, *Dia dan Aku: Memoar Pencari Kebenaran*, Jakarta: Penerbit Buku Kompas, November 2006. I used the chapters that described Joesoef's relations to Sukarno, Mohammad Hatta, Suharto and Ali Moertopo. Joesoef also described his attempt to block another session of "religion class" in the national school curriculum in Indonesia.

Joshua Oppenheimer directed two films on the 1965 massacres in Indonesia, *The Act of Killing* (August 2012) and *The Look of Silence* (August 2014), produced by Signe Byrge Sørensen.

Kahin, George McT., *Nationalism and Revolution in Indonesia,* Ithaca: Cornell University Press, 1952.

Kahin, George McT., 'In Memoriam: Mohammad Hatta (1902–1980)', *Indonesia,* 30, October 1980.

Komisi untuk Orang Hilang dan Korban Tindak Kekerasan, *Bunuh Munir! Sebuah Buku Putih,* Jakarta: Kontras, 2006.

Latief, Abdul, *Pledoi Kol. A. Latief: Soeharto Terlibat G30S,* Jakarta: Institut Studi Arus Informasi, July 2000.

Lesmana, Surya, *Saksi dan Pelaku Gestapu: Pengakuan Para Saksi dan Pelaku Sejarah Gerakan 30 September 1965,* Yogyakarta: Media Pressindo, 2005.

Lindsey, Tim and Pausacker, Helen, *Chinese Indonesian: Remembering, Distorting, Forgetting,* Singapore: ISEAS, 2005.

Maier, H. M. J., "A hidden language: Dutch in Indonesia," UC Berkeley: Institute of European Studies, 2005.

Malaka, Tan, *Dari Penjara Ke Penjara,* Jakarta: Teplok Press (three volumes), July 2000.

Mangkusasmito, Prawoto, *Pertumbuhan Historis Rumus Dasar Negara dan Sebuah Refleksi,* Jakarta: Hudaya, 1970.

Melvin, Jess, *The Army and the Indonesian Genocide: Mechanics of Mass Murder*, New York: Routledge, 2018.

Mortimer, Rex, *Indonesian Communism Under Sukarno: Ideology and Politics, 1959–1965,* Ithaca: Cornell University Press, 1974.

Mrázek, Rudolf, *Sjahrir: Politics and Exile in Indonesia,* Ithaca: Cornell Modern Indonesia Project, Southeast Asia Program, Cornell University, 1994.

Muljana, Slamet, *Runtuhnya Kerajaan Hindu-Jawa dan Timbulnya Negara-negara Islam di Nusantara,* LKIS Yogjakarta, 2005 (first printing in 1968 by Penerbit Bhratara in Jakarta).

Munir, *Membangun Bangsa Menolak Militerisme: Jejak Pemikiran Munir 1965–2004,* Jakarta: Komite Aksi Solidaritas untuk Munir, 2006.

Perlez, Jane, 'Obituary: Pramoedya Ananta Toer, Indonesian novelist', *International Herald Tribune,* 1 May 2006.

Pigeaud, Th. G. Th., 'Java in the 14th Century. A Study in Cultural History', the Nagara-Kertagama by Rakawi Prapanca of Majapahit, 1365 AD, 3rd. ed., rev. & enlarged, The Hague: Martinus Nijhoff, 1960–1963.

Prapanca, *Desawarnana (Nagarakrtagama),* translated by Stuart Robson, Leiden: KITLV Press, 1995.

Purwanto, Bambang and Adam, Asvi Warman, *Menggugat Historiografi Indonesia,* Yogyakarta: Ombak, 2005.

Ricklefs, M. C., *A History of Modern Indonesia Since C. 1200,* Stanford University Press, 2002.

Rose, Mavis, *Indonesia Free: A Political Biography of Mohammad Hatta,* Ithaca: Cornell Modern Indonesia Project, Southeast Asia Program, Cornell University, 1987.

Saafroedin Bahar, Ananda B. Kusuma, Nannie Hudawati, *Risalah Sidang Badan Penyelidik Usaha-usaha Persiapan Kemerdekaan Indonesia (BPUPKI) dan Panitia Persiapan Kemerdekaan Indonesia (PPKI) 28 Mei 1945-22 Agustus 1945,* Jakarta: Sekretariat Negara Republik Indonesia, 1995.

Salmon, Claudine, *Literature in Malay by the Chinese of Indonesia: A Provisional*

Annotated Bibliography, Paris: Association Archipel, 1981.

Schwarz, Adam, *A Nation in Waiting: Indonesia's Search for Stability,* Allen & Unwin, 2nd edition, July 2000.

Schwarz, Adam, and Paris, Jonathan (eds), *The Politics of Post-Suharto Indonesia,* Council on Foreign Relations, New York, 1999.

Scott, Margaret, 'The Indonesian Massacre: What Did the US Know?' *New York Review of Books,* November 2016.

Setiono, Benny G, *Tionghoa dalam Pusaran Politik: Mengungkap Fakta Sejarah Tersembunyi Orang Tionghoa di Indonesia,* Jakarta: Transmedia, 2008.

Sjahrir, Sutan, *Our Struggle,* Ithaca: Cornell Modern Indonesia Project, 1968. Translation with introductory essay by Benedict R. O'G. Anderson (translator) of Sjahrir's *Perdjoeangan Kita.*

Sluimers, Laszlo, 'The Japanese Military and Indonesian Independence', *Journal of Southeast Asian Studies,* Vol. 27, 1996.

Soedjatmoko and Mohammad Ali, G. J. Resink and G. McT. Kahin, *An Introduction to Indonesian Historiography,* Ithaca: Cornell University Press, 1962. This book features contributions from John Bastin, C. C. Berg, Buchari, J. C. Bottoms, C. R. Boxer, L. Ch. Damais, Hoesein Djajadiningrat, H. J. de Graf, Graham Irwan, Koichi Kishi, Koentjaraningrat, Ruth T. McVey, J. Noorduyn, J. M. Romein, R. Soekmono, Tjan Tjoe Som, F. J. E. Tan, W. F. Wertheim and P. J. Zoetmulder. I used this extensively in understanding the historiography of Indonesia.

Steele, Janet, '"Reformasi total": Lessons from Indonesia on media reform', *Jakarta Post,* 23 July 2018 (http://www.thejakartapost.com/academia/2018/07/23/reformasi-total-lessons-from-indonesia-on-media-reform.html downloaded on 21 January 2019).

Steele, Janet, *Wars Within: The Story of Tempo an Independent Magazine in Soeharto's Indonesia,* Singapore: ISEAS, 2005.

Sudisman, *Kritik Oto Kritik: Seorang Politbiro CC PKI,* Teplok Press, November 2000.

Sukarno, *An Autobiography as told to Cindy Adams,* Indianapolis: Bobbs Merrill, 1965.

Suryadinata, Leo, *Ethnic Relations and Nation-Building in Southeast Asia: The Case of the Ethnic Chinese,* Singapore: ISEAS, 2004.

Suryadinata, Leo, *Political Thinking of the Indonesian Chinese 1900–1995,* Singapore University Press, 1997 (new edition).

Suryadinata, Leo, *The Ethnic Chinese Issue and National Integration in Indonesia,* Singapore: ISEAS, 1999.

Taylor, Jean Gelman, *Indonesia: Peoples and Histories,* New Haven & London: Yale University Press, 2003. I used Taylor's box 'Majapahit: Symbol of National Unity or of Javanese Imperialism?' in tracing the subchapter on Majapahit.

Thukul, Wiji, *Kebenaran Akan Terus Hidup,* Jakarta: Ikohi Yappika, 2007.

Toer, Pramoedya Ananta, 'The book that killed colonialism', *The New York Times Magazine,* 18 April 1999.

Toer, Pramoedya Ananta, *The Mute's Soliloquy: A Memoir,* Penguin, April 2000.

Toer, Pramoedya Ananta, *Sang Pemula,* Jakarta: Lentera Dipantara, 2003 (first printing in 1985).

Touwen-Bouwsma, Elly, 'The Indonesian Nationalists and the Japanese 'Liberation' of Indonesia: Visions and Reactions', *Journal of Southeast Asian Studies,* Vol. 27, 1996.

Van Klinken, Gerry, *Minorities, Modernity and the Emerging Nation: Christians in Indonesia, a biographical approach*, KITLV Press, Leiden 2003.

Vlitchek, Andre and Indira, Rossie, *Saya Terbakar Amarah Sendirian! Pramoedya Ananta Toer dalam Perbincangan dengan Andre Vltchek & Rossie Indira*, Jakarta: Kepustakaan Populer Gramedia. January 2006. Pramoedya aired an argument about Javaism in this interview.

Wardaya, F. X. Baskara (ed.), *Mencari Demokrasi*, Jakarta: ISAI, 1999. It has several interviews, including with Benedict R. O'G. Anderson on the 1944–46 revolution in Java.

Widjaja, I. Wangsa and Swasono, Meutia F. (eds.), *Mohammad Hatta: Kumpulan Pidato II*, Jakarta, Idayu, 1983. This collection included a speech that Hatta made in Makassar on 22 May 1967, in which he described the situation when he decided to drop the 'seven words' from the Jakarta Charter. The 1960 speech in New York is also included here.

Wisnoewhardono, Soeyono, *Memperkenalkan Komplek Percandian Panataran di Blitar*, KPN Purbakala, Mojokerto, 1995.

Yamin, Muhammad (ed.), *Naskah Persiapan Undang-Undang Dasar 1945*, vol. 1, Jakarta: Yayasan Prapanca, 1959.

Yamin, Muhammad, *6000 Tahun Sang Merah Putih*, Penerbit Siguntang, 1954.

Yamin, Muhammad, *Gadjah Mada: Pahlawan Persatoean Noesantara*, Djakarta: Balai Poestaka, 1945.

Zed, Mestika, 'Menggugat Tirani Sejarah Nasional', Paper presented at the 7th National History Conference, Jakarta, 28–31 October 2001.

The Moluccas

Field Research and Interviews

Many names and terms are used in a different way in the Moluccas' or Maluku. In Ambon, the Bugis youth 'Nursalim' is an example. Muslim newspapers said he had asked for his 'van rental money'. Christian news-papers said he had asked for 'cigarette money'. The Muslim version called him 'Usman' while the Christians said that his name was 'Nursalim'. I went to see people involved and checked names, version, fighting etc. It turned out that his official name was 'Nursalim' (only one word) but friends called him 'Usman'. I am using the term 'the Moluccas' for consistency.

In Ambon, I interviewed *Ambon Ekpres* editor Ahmad Ibrahim and *Suara Maluku* editor Novi Pinontoan, lawyers Antoni Hartane, John Pattihawea and Chris Latupeirissa, filmmaker Des Alwi Abubakar, refugees Dongratina Ratuanik, Lusiana Latuny, Maria Latuny and Herman Latuny.

Journalists always provided me with much information. I thank Febi Kaihatu, Flourida Attamimi, Indah Heluth, Insany Syahbarwaty, Dien

Kelilauw, Joanny Maryorie Pesulima, Lucky Sopacua, Ricky Rumaruson, Rudi Fofid, Semmy Sahureka and Yany Kubangun.

Semuel Waileruny's wife Elsina Titaley and his lawyers Fileo Pistos Noija and Z. Aponno provided me with background on Waileruny's political works. I also interviewed Waileruny's inmate Idi Amin Thabrani Pattimura, who allegedly organised some 'terrorist activism'. It was a surprise to know that Pattimura considered Waileruny his 'leader' and Titaley his 'mother'. When I saw them talking to one another, I didn't get the impression that they belonged to two deadly clashing Christian-versus-Muslim sectarian parties.

Government attorneys M. A. Pattikawa and Zainul Arifin Wijaya helped me with information on Waileruny. Judge Maenong was involved in a productive conversation. He gave me speedy permission to interview Waileruny. In 2011, Human Rights Watch gave Waileruny the Hellman/Hammett grant, helping him to finish his book on the sectarian violence. Wa Malia and her mother Wa Djalia invited me to visit their makeshift house.

I visited Ternate twice. I interviewed Sultan Mudaffar Syah, Sjahrini Sad, Syaiful Bahri Ruray, Agus Salim Bujang, Janib Achmad and M. Adnan Amal. I also visited Tidore and talked to Rustam Fabanyo, Daud Muhammad and Muhammad Amin Faaroek.

In Malifut, I had Fahmi Hasan, a Makian student in Tahane, helping me to travel around the area. Makian students were highly involved in lobbying the Indonesian government to create the Makian Mainland in Malifut subdistrict. Fahmi helped me interview Muhlis Idrus and Husin Syawal, who were involved in the jihad troops. I also interviewed Sosol villagers Erwin Makahiking, Barbalina Rajangolo and Yuningsih Sabaika. Sosol and Tahane are separated by only a 3-metre wide road! I thank Mohammad Irvan, Rosdiana Din, Badawi Saleh and Naya Sam of the Malifut Indah eatery.

In Tobelo, I interviewed Heri Manonata (owner of Hotel Villahermoza), reporter Febbyola Lilipory, Javanese transmigrants Poniyem and Suyanto, electrician Victor Magany, politician Jacob M. Soselisa, red troops commander Benhard Bitjara (nicknamed 'Benny Doro' as he originates from Doro village) and food vendor Ani Sawal. I visited Duma village with Hernata Lasamahu, meeting her remaining family members as well as her remaining two children. Artist Grace Siregar and her husband Alexander Davey, who worked for World Vision, gave me some backgrounds on the North Molucca war.

Material Sources

Aditjondro, George J., 'Guns, Pamphlets and Handie-Talkies: How the military exploited local ethno-religious tensions in Maluku to preserve their political and economic privileges' in *Violence in Indonesia* edited by Ingrid Wessel and Georgia Wimhofer, Hamburg: Abera Verlag Markus Voss, 2001.

Amal, M. Adnan and Djafaar, Irza Arnyta, *Maluku Utara: Perjalanan Sejarah 1800–1950* Volume 1, Ternate: Universitas Khairun, 2003.

Amal, M. Adnan and Djafaar, Irza Arnyta, *Maluku Utara: Perjalanan Sejarah 1800-1950* Volume 2, Ternate: Universitas Khairun, 2003.

BBC News, 'Ferry survivors' dreadful ordeal', 4 July 2000 (http://news.bbc.co.uk/2/hi/asia-pacific/818126.stm downloaded on 21 January 2019).

BBC News, 'Profile: Jafar Umar Thalib', 30 January 2003 (http://news.bbc.co.uk/2/hi/asia-pacific/1975345.stm downloaded on 21 January 2019).

Bubandt, Nils, 'Towards a New Politics of Tradition? Decentralisation, Conflict and Adat in Eastern Indonesia', *Anthropologi Indonesia*, No. 74, May–August 2004.

Bubandt, Nils, 'Mobilising for Conflict: Rumours, Pamphlets and the Politics of Paranoia' in J. Goss and K. Lange (eds.), *What Went Wrong? Explaining Communal Violence in Eastern Indonesia*, Cornell University Press, 2013.

Chauvel, Richard, *Nationalists, Soldiers and Separatists: The Ambonese Islands from Colonialism to Revolt 1880–1950*, Leiden: KITLV Press, 1990.

Duncan, Christopher R., 'The Other Maluku: Chronologies of Conflict in North Maluku', *Indonesia*, 80, October 2005, pp. 53–80.

Duncan, Christopher R., *Violence and Vengeance: Religious Conflict and Its Aftermath in Eastern Indonesia*, Ithaca: Cornell University Press, 2013.

Eriyanto, 'Koran, Bisnis dan Perang', *Pantau,* September 2002.

Eriyanto, *Media dan Konflik Ambon,* Jakarta: Radio 68H, 2003.

Freestone, Ian, 'Duma, Indonesia, Emerges from Tragedy: Refugees Rebuild Their Lives in the Maluku Islands', *Compass Direct,* 12 September 2003. With acknowledgments to Reverend James Haire, Uniting Church, Australia, for his research on the early Halmaheran church.

Harvard Divinity School published a profile of "Abul A'la Maududi" on "The Religious Literacy Project" (https://rlp.hds.harvard.edu/faq/abul-a%E2%80%99la-maududi downloaded on 21 January 2019).

Heynneman, Ron, *Ibu Maluku: The Story of Jeanne van Diejen,* Hartwell, Victoria: Sid Harta Publishers, 2002.

International Crisis Group, 'Indonesia: Overcoming Murder and Chaos in Maluku', Asia Report No. 10, 19 December 2000.

Kastor, Rustam, *Konspirasi RMS & Kristen Menghancurkan Umat Islam Ambon & Maluku,* Yogjakarta: Wihdah Press, Maret 2000 (second edition).

Kastor, Rustam, *Suara Maluku Membantah Rustam Kastor Menjawab,* Yogjakarta: Wihdah Press, Maret 2000.

Leirissa, Richard Z., *Maluku Dalam Perjuangan Nasional Indonesia*, Lembaga Sejarah, Fakultas Sastra Universitas Indonesia, 1975.

Lim, Meryyna, *Archipelago Online: The Internet and Political Activism in Indonesia*, PhD dissertation at Technology and Sustainable Development Group, School of Business, Public Administration and Technology, University of Twente, Enschede, 2005.

McCawley, Tom., 'The Enduring Allure of the Bandas', *Destinasian,* August/September 2005.

Nanere, Jan (ed.), *Halmahera Berdarah,* Ambon: Yayasan Bina Masyarakat Sejahtera dan Pelestarian Alam, 2000.

Newcrest, 'Newcrest operation in Halmahera', published in 2004 on the mining company website (http://www.newcrest.com.au/upload/reports/2004AnnualHTML/02_operations/toguraci.html downloaded on 16 June 2010).

Newsweek, 'Vice President Hamzah Haz defends his choice of friends', 1 July 2002.

Pieris, John, *Tragedi Maluku: Sebuah Krisis Perdamaian,* Jakarta: Yayasan Obor Indonesia, 2004.

Poerwowidagdo, Judo (ed.), *Menuju Rekonsiliasi di Halmahera,* Jakarta: Pusat Pemberdayaan untuk Rekonsiliasi dan Perdamaian, 2003.

Richard Z. Leirissa, *Maluku Dalam Perjuangan Nasional Indonesia,* Lembaga Sejarah Fakultas Sastra Universitas Indonesia, 1975.

Ron Heynneman, *Ibu Maluku: The Story of Jeanne van Diejen,* Victoria: Sid Harta Publishers, 2002.

Smith, Alhadar, 'The forgotten war in North Maluku', *Inside Indonesia,* July–September 2000.

Spyer, Patricia, 'Fire Without Smoke and other phantoms of Ambon's violence', *Indonesia,* No. 74, pp. 21–36.

Sukidi Mulyadi, *Kekerasan Di Bawah Panji Agama: Kasus Laskar Jihad dan Laskar Kristus,* Conference on Islam and Children, Ohio University, Athens, 10–12 April 2003. This paper has a lot of information on Laskar Jihad.

Syahril Muhammad, *Kesultanan Ternate: Sejarah Sosial, Ekonomi dan Politik,* Yogyakarta: Penerbit Ombak, 2004.

Van Dijken family tree, 'Parenteel van Jacob Bruin De', undated publication (http://members.chello.nl/j.vandijken2/frame3.htm downloaded in August 2007).

Van Klinken, Gerry, *Communal Violence and Democratization in Indonesia: Small town wars,* London and New York: Routledge, 2007.

Van Klinken, Gerry, 'The Maluku Wars: Bringing Society Back In', *Indonesia,* No. 71, April 2001.

Waileruny, Semuel, *Membongkar Konspirasi di Balik Konflik Maluku,* Jakarta: Obor, 2011.

Wangkar, Max, 'Jawa Pos adalah Dahlan Iskan', *Pantau,* May 2001.

Wilson, Chris, 'The Ethnic Origins of Religious Conflict in North Maluku Province, Indonesia, 1999–2000', *Indonesia,* No. 79, 2005.

Lesser Sunda

Field Research and Interviews

In Kupang, I interviewed human rights workers Sarah Lerry Mboeik, Apolos Dewa Praingu and Darius Beda Daton as well as teacher Sukedah Prayitno. Helio and Dian Soares met me and talked about their East Timor experience. Winston Rondo, Meri Djami and Volkes Dadi Lado of CIS

Timor provided me with a lot of information on the East Timor refugees. I also got assistance from journalists Yemris Fointuna, Matheos Messakh and Dion DB Putra. Governor Piet Tallo also talked to me about the refugees as well as Pasir Island's legal status.

When visiting the Tuapukan camp, I talked to scores of refugees as well as locals. They included Yakob and Selvince Dethan, Alfonso Soares and Olandina da Silva. Meri Djami accompanied me in Tuapukan.

In Rote, I interviewed Jerzy and Ruth Messakh as well as their colleagues Uce Adoe Pingak and Lasarus Yonas Pah. Mes Mulle, the publisher of the *Media Rote Ndao* newspaper, briefed me about Baa's only newspaper. His newspaper was published irregularly. Jerzy Messakh brought me to Ndana Island where I interviewed fishermen Stefanus Benggu and Rie Tayang. Also in Rote, I went to Oelaba village and talked to Anwar Idris and Hasan Saidah.

In Dili, I interviewed Nugraha Katjasungkana and Titi Irawati as well as journalists Russell Anderson and Nelyo Isaac of TVTL. In the Maukiak canteen, I met many activists, including Tomas Freitas and Jaime Agostinho Hanjam. Katjasungkana showed me the Comarca prison. I interviewed Jacinto Alves also in Dili. I also interviewed José Ramos-Horta in Vancouver in 1997.

In Jakarta, Irawan Saptono refreshed my memory about the 1995 experience in Dili. Yeni Rosa Damayanti told me her connection with the East Timor clandestine operation in Java. I regularly talked to Clementino dos Reis Amaral between 1993–95 when I was a reporter covering Indonesia's National Commission on Human Rights.

Material Sources

Commission for Reception, Truth and Reconciliation in East Timor, *Chega!* Dili, October 2005. This report is available on some websites, including East Timor Action Network's www.etan.org and International Center for Transitional Justice www.ictj.org.

Deborah Cassrels, 'The businessman who aims to turn Bali into the new Palm Islands', *Australian Financial Review*, 9 September 2016 (https://www.afr.com/lifestyle/anguish-bali-tourist-development--and-the-enigmatic-tomy-winata-20160829-gr3v4r downloaded on 7 August 2018).

Fernandes, Clinton, *The Independence of East Timor: Multi-Dimensional Perspectives – Occupation, Resistance, and International Political Activism*, Sussex Academic Press, 2011.

Fointuna, Yemris, 'NTT can only accept 6,000 Timorese families', *The Jakarta Post*, 12 June 2001.

Fointuna, Yemris, 'Refugees start use violence, terror to survive', *The Jakarta Post*, 28 February 2002.

Goodman, Amy and Nairn, Allan, *Massacre: The Story Of East Timor*. A documentary about the Santa Cruz massacre. Pacifica Film, 2002.

Habibie, Bacharuddin Jusuf, *Decisive Moments: Indonesia's Long Road Towards Democracy*, Jakarta: Ilthabi Rekatama, 2006.

Harsono, Andreas, 'Indonesia Deports Rights Activists From East Timor', *American Reporter*, 13 November 1995.

Makarim, Zacky Anwar, 'Kambing Hitam Sejarah Kolonial' in *Gado-gado Kalibata: Kumpulan Kolom Gatra*, Hery Pamudi (ed.), Jakarta: Gatra Pustaka, January 2007.

Matsuno, Akihisa, 'The Balibo Declaration', A paper prepared for the 2nd Course on Indonesia and East Timor, Lisbon, March 1995 (http://www.hamline.edu/apakabar/basisdata/1995/04/16/0003.html).

Nairn, Allan, 'A Narrow Escape From East Timor', *USA Today*, 21 November 1991.

Pour, Julius, *Benny Moerdani: Profile of a Soldier Statesman*, Jakarta: Yayasan Kejuangan Panglima Besar Sudirman, 1993. It is an official translation of the original Bahasa Indonesia version. The translator is Tim Scott.

Ramos-Horta, José, *Funu: The Unfinished Saga of East Timor*, New Jersey: Red Sea Press, January 1987.

Romesh Silva and Patrick Ball, *The Profile of Human Rights Violations in Timor-Leste 1974–1999*, Benetech, February 2006 (https://hrdag.org/content/timorleste/Benetech-Report-to-CAVR.pdf downloaded on 7 December 2018).

Santoso, Aboeprijadi, *Jejak Jejak Darah: Tragedi dan Pengkhianatan di Timor Timur*, Published jointly by Stichting Inham (Amsterdam) dan Pijar-Yogyakarta (Yogyakarta), December 1996.

Santoso, Aboeprijadi, 'Trio Habibie & Timor Timur', *Indo Progress*, 6 September 2016.

Tallo, Piet A., *Pelayanan Kemanusiaan Dalam dan Dengan Pelbagai Keterbatasan: Pertangungjawaban Publik – Penanganan dan Pemanfaatan Dana serta Bantuan Barang dalam Rangka Penanganan Pengungsi Timor Timur Tahun Anggaran 1999/2000-2001*. This report was published by the office of Nusa Tenggara Timur Governor Piet Tallo, Kupang, 2001.

Taylor, John G., *Indonesia's Forgotten War: The Hidden History of East Timor*, London: Zed Books, 1991.

West Papua

Field Research and Interviews

Jayapura, along with Abepura and Sentani, was the metropolis that I visited the most in both Papua and West Papua provinces. I interviewed Frans Maniagasi, Karel Phil Erari, Benny Giay, Terry Aronggear, Arnolda Menufandu, Srihartati Harto, Herman Awom, Martina Damimetou, Frans Alexander Wospakrik, Willy Resubun, Charmain Mohamed, Markus Haluk, Socrates Yoman, Filep Karma, Dominikus Surabut, Mathias Reffra, Oktovianus Pogau.

I also visited Wutung, a village divided by the Indonesia-Papua New Guinea border, in May 2005, talking to Angela Flassy, Husni Ali, and Irvan Tarigan. It was about four hours' drive from Jayapura. I drove there with my Pantau Foundation colleagues: Budi Setiyono and Indarwati Aminuddin.

I Interviewed Sergeant Ukas in his house in Merauke. Anita Ayu Sulandri came to my Merauke hotel for a one-on-one interview. I also talked to Leo Mahuze, Perwita Sari, and Wensislaus Fatubun.

In Timika, Ans Gregory da Iry of PT Freeport Indonesia, Octovianus Danunan, Vinsentius Hendra, Yulius O. Lopo, Irwanto 'Titi Teguh' Tenggowijaya, Juliana Daudo, Saul Wanimbo gave me their time about Freeport and Timika.

In Wamena, I interviewed Theo Hesegem, John Djonga, Akhy Logo, Fransiska Asso, Meki Elosak, Naftali Pawika, Roni Hisage, and Asrida Elisabeth.

In Jakarta, I interviewed Antonius Wamang, Deminikus Bebari, Ed McWilliams, Eltinus Omaleng, Esau Onawame, Hardi Tsugumol, Ishak Onamawe, Jairus Kibak, Janes Natkime, Johni Kacamol, Lexy Lintuuran, Mahmud Trikasno, Patsy Spier, Saul Tahapary, Yulianus Deikme. I also interviewed Joseph Saunders of Human Rights Watch and Freeport commissionaire Simon Patrice Morin.

Material Sources

Aditjondro, George Junus, *Cahaya Bintang Kejora: Papua Barat dalam Kajian Sejarah, Budaya, Ekonomi, dan Hak Asasi Manusia*, Jakarta: Elsam, 2000.

Agus A Alua, *Dialog Nasional Papua dan Indonesia 26 Februari 1999: Kembalikan Kedaulatan Papua Barat, Pulang dan Renungkan Dulu*, Jayapura: Biro Penelitian STFT Fajar Timur, 2002.

Allard, Tom, 'Coral sea paradise faces ruin from mining', *Sydney Morning Herald*, 2 July 2011 (http://www.smh.com.au/environment/coral-sea-paradise-faces-ruin-from-mining-20110701-1gv6w.html downloaded on 7 August 2011).

Antara News, *President Yudhoyono proceeds to Manokwari from Raja Ampat*, 24 August 2014 (http://www.antaranews.com/en/news/95399/president-yudhoyono-proceeds-to-manokwari-from-raja-ampat downloaded on 7 August 2015).

Aspinall, Edward, 'The Helsinki Agreement: More Promising Basis for Peace in Aceh?' Policy Studies, No. 20, Washington: East-West Center, 2005 (http://www.eastwestcenter.org/publications/helsinki-agreement-more-promising-basis-peace-aceh downloaded on 7 August 2015).

Blade, Johnny, *West Papua leader Ondawame dies*, Radio New Zealand, 5 September 2014 (http://www.radionz.co.nz/international/pacific-news/253864/west-papua-leader-ondawame-dies downloaded on 5 December 2015).

Budiardjo, Carmel and Liem Soei Liong, *West Papua: The Obliteration of a People*, London: Tapol (third edition, revised), 1988.

Chauvel, Richard, *Papua: dialogue as the road to peace,* 6 July 2015, Blog (http://indonesiaatmelbourne.unimelb.edu.au/papua-dialogue-as-the-road-to-peace/ downloaded on 7 August 2016)

Drooglever, Pieter, *An Act of Free Choice: Decolonisation and the Right to Self-Determination in West Papua,* Oneworld, 2009.

East Timor and Indonesia Action Network, *Kopassus Organizes Propaganda Offensive Targeting U.S,* February 2012 (https://www.etan.org/issues/wpapua/2012/1202wpap.htm downloaded on 7 August 2012).

Eben Kirksey, *Freedom in Entangled Worlds,* Duke University Press, 2012.

Elmslie, Jim, 'West Papuan Demographic Transition and the 2010 Indonesian Census: 'Slow Motion Genocide' or not?' a paper for *Comprehending West Papua Conference* at Sydney University, 23–24 February 2011.

Elmslie, Jim, *Irian Jaya under the Gun: Indonesian Economic Development versus West Papuan Nationalism,* University of Hawai'i Press, 2002.

Farhadian, Charles E., *The Testimony Project: Papua Jayapura,* Deiyai Press, 2007.

Freeport Indonesia, *Controlled Riverine Tailings Management at Freeport Indonesia,* January 2009 (http://www.fcx.com/sd/pdf/riverine2009.pdf downloaded on 7 August 2018).

Freeport McMoran, *Tailings and Waste Rock* (http://www.fcx.com/sd/env/tailings.htm).

Gartley, Elizabeth, *Filep Karma Speech West Papua 2004,* video published on 13 January 2013 (https://www.youtube.com/watch?v=3RY-iEjbtkY downloaded on 7 August 2018).

Giay, Benny, *Pembunuhan Theys: Kematian HAM Di Tanah Papua,* Yogyakarta: Galang Press, May 2006 (second printing).

Harsono, Andreas, *Murder At Mile 63 – Part One: A Trip to the Big City,* 7 November 2006, (http://www.pantau.or.id/?/=d/428 downloaded on 7 August 2018).

Human Rights Watch, *'What Did I Do Wrong?': Papuans in Merauke Face Abuses by Indonesian Special Forces,* New York, June 2009.

Human Rights Watch, *Free All Political Prisoners: Clemency for 5 Papuans Leaves Dozens Behind Bars,* 9 May 2015 (https://www.hrw.org/news/2015/05/09/indonesia-free-all-political-prisoners downloaded on 7 August 2018).

Human Rights Watch, *Indonesia: End Access Restrictions to Papua,* 10 November 2015 (https://www.hrw.org/news/2015/11/10/indonesia-end-access-restrictions-papua downloaded on 7 August 2018).

Human Rights Watch, *Indonesia: Military Documents Reveal Unlawful Spying in Papua,* 14 August 2011 (https://www.hrw.org/news/2011/08/14/indonesia-military-documents-reveal-unlawful-spying-papua downloaded on 7 August 2018).

Human Rights Watch, *Something to Hide? Indonesia's Restrictions on Media Freedom and Rights Monitoring in Papua,* New York, November 2015.

Human Rights Watch, *Too High a Price: The Human Rights Cost of the Indonesian Military's Economic Activities,* London-New York, June 2006.

International Crisis Group, 'Indonesian Papua: A Local Perspective on the Conflict', Asia Briefing No. 66, 19 July 2007 (http://www.crisisgroup.org/home/index.cfm?l=1&id=4945 downloaded on 7 August 2018).

International Crisis Group, 'Papua: The Dangers of Shutting Down Dialogue', Asia Briefing No. 47, 23 March 2006 (http://www.crisisgroup.org/home/index.cfm?id=4042&l=1 downloaded on 7 August 2018).

Ipenburg, At, 'The life and death of Theys Eluay', *Inside Indonesia*, April–June 2002.

Kabar24, Hery Lazuardi (ed.), *Kapolri: Kerusuhan Sorong Ulah Simpatisan Papua Merdeka*, 22 April 2014 (http://kabar24.bisnis.com/read/20140422/78/221406/kapolri-kerusuhan-sorong-ulah-simpatisan-papua-merdeka downloaded on 7 August 2018).

Kompas, 'Buku Kisah Kematian Theys Diluncurkan di Jayapura', 27 October 2003.

Leith, Denise, *The Politics of Power: Freeport in Suharto's Indonesia*, University of Hawai'i Press, 2003.

Liputan 6, *Ibu Rumah Tangga Gerebek Gudang Miras*, 8 April 2010 (http://m. liputan6.com/news/read/271432/ibu-rumah-tangga-gerebek-gudang-miras downloaded on 7 August 2018).

MetroTVnews, *Perda Minuman Keras di Sorong Berlaku Maret 2016*, 13 March 2016 (http://ekonomi.metrotvnews.com/read/2016/03/13/497793/perda-minuman-keras-di-sorong-berlaku-maret-2016 downloaded on 7 August 2018).

Mitchell, Scott, 'After Decades, Indonesia to Allow Foreign Journalists Into West Papua', *Vice News*, 11 May 2015 (https://news.vice.com/article/after-decades-indonesia-to-allow-foreign-journalists-into-west-papua downloaded on 7 August 2018).

New Matilda, *West Papuan Independence Leader Found Floating In Sack At Sea*, 1 September 2004 (https://newmatilda.com/2014/09/01/west-papuan-independence-leader-found-floating-sack-sea/ downloaded on 7 August 2018).

Osborne, Robin, *Indonesia's Secret War: The Guerilla Struggle in Irian Jaya*, Allen&Unwin, 1985.

Papua Post, *Sejarah Perjuangan Papua Merdeka*, 20 December 2012 (http://papuapost.com/negara-west-papua/sejarah-papua-merdeka/ downloaded on 7 August 2018).

Perlez, Jane and Bonner, Raymond, 'Below a Mountain of Wealth, a River of Waste', *The New York Times*, 27 December 2005 (http://www.nytimes.com/2005/12/27/world/asia/below-a-mountain-of-wealth-a-river-of-waste.html?_r=0 downloaded on 7 August 2018).

Peyon, Steven, *Kronologi Lengkap: Aparat Keamanan Negara, Menculik Ketua KNPB Sorong Papua Barat*, Blog, 3 September 2014 (https://bysteveneyon.wordpress.com/2014/09/03/kronologi-lengkapaparat-keamanan-negara-menculik-ketua-knpb-sorong-papua-barat/ downloaded on 7 August 2018).

Pour, Julius, *Benny Moerdani: Profile of a Soldier Statesman*, Jakarta: Yayasan Kejuangan Panglima Besar Sudirman, 1993. It is an official translation of its original Bahasa Indonesia version. The translator is Tim Scott.

Priatmojo, Dedy and Ambarita, Banjir, *Bentrok di Sorong Tiga Orang Luka-luka*, Viva.co.id, 21 April 2014 (http://nasional.news.viva.co.id/news/read/498409-bentrok-di-sorong-tiga-orang-luka-luka downloaded on 7 August 2018).

Radio New Zealand, *Vanuatu PM appeals to Melanesian solidarity on West Papua*, 26 July 2016 (http://www.radionz.co.nz/international/pacific-news/309416/vanuatu-pm-appeals-to-melanesian-solidarity-on-west-papua downloaded on 7 August 2018)

Reporters Without Borders, *RSF tells Indonesia to stop flouting journalists' rights in West Papua*, 9 May 2016 (https://rsf.org/en/news/rsf-tells-indonesia-to-stop-flouting-journalists-rights-west-papua downloaded on 7 August 2018).

Saralana Declaration on West Papuan Unity, 6 December 2014 (https://www.etan.
   org/issues/wpapua/2015/Saralana%20Declaration.pdf downloaded on 7
   August 2018)
Supriatma, Made, *Melacak Tim Mawar*, Harian Indoprogress, 27 May 2014
   (http://indoprogress.com/2014/05/melacak-tim-mawar/ downloaded on 7
   August 2018).
Supriatma, Made, *Pembunuh Theys Hiyo Eluay Dipromosi Jadi Ka Bais*, Suara Papua,
   20 September 2016 (http://suarapapua.com/2016/09/20/pembunuh-theys-
   hiyo-eluay-dipromosi-jadi-ka-bais/ downloaded on 7 August 2018).
Tapol, 'The Neglected Genocide', Asian Human Rights Commission and Human
   Rights and Peace for Papua, 2013 (http://www.tapol.org/sites/default/files/
   sites/default/files/pdfs/NeglectedGenocideAHRC.pdf downloaded on 7
   August 2018)
Tapsell, Ross, 'Q&A: Australia's reaction to arrest of French journalists in West
   Papua', *The Conversation*, 6 October 2014 (http://theconversation.com/qanda-
   australias-reaction-to-arrest-of-french-journalists-in-west-papua-32503
   downloaded on 7 August 2018).
The Free West Papua Movement (http://www.converge.org.nz/wpapua/opm.
   html) OPM Revolutionary Council based in Madang, Papua New Guinea.
   Headed by its Chairman Moses Werror downloaded 3 September 2007. Latest
   Interview with Moses Werror, Chairman of the Free West Papua (OPM)
   Revolutionary Council. Interviewed by phone from Madang, Papua New
   Guinea, by Ben Saul for *Honi Soit*, the Sydney University student newspaper,
   Sydney, Australia. Interviewed on 22 August 1996.
Widjojo, Muridan S., *Papua road map*, Inside Indonesia, 4 October 2008
   (http://www.insideindonesia.org/papua-road-map downloaded on 7 August
   2018).

Epilogue

Field Research and Interviews

I interviewed Carmel Budiardjo in her Thornton Heath home office on 1
August 2005. Budiardjo's colleague, Liem Sioe Liong, also gave me a lot of
his time during interviews spanning three years in Jakarta.

I interviewed Aceh figures such as Irwandi Yusuf, Mohammad Nazar.
M. Jafar and Nasruddin Abubakarin in October 2006 in Banda Aceh. Two
months later, Irwandi, Nazar and Nasruddin won their respective elections,
sending me text messages about their jubilation.

Material Sources

Adam, Asvi Warman, *Seabad Kontroversi Sejarah*, Ombak Yogyakarta Maret, 2007.
Anderson, Benedict R. O'G., 'Indonesian Nationalism Today and in the Future',
   Indonesia, No. 67, April 1999.

Budiardjo, Carmel, Surviving Indonesia's Gulag: A Western Woman Tells Her Story, Cassell, May 1996.

Crisis Management Initiative. It has a webpage dedicated to all documents and press speeches related to the Aceh peace agreement (http://www.cmi.fi/?content=aceh_project downloaded on 7 August 2018).

Human Rights Watch, 'Indonesia: Vice Presidential Candidate Has Anti-Rights Record,' Jakarta, 8 August 2018.

Husain, Farid, To See The Unseen: Kisah di Balik Damai di Aceh, Jakarta: Health & Hospital Indonesia, April 2007.

Pusaka Indonesia, Ini Dia Daftar 163 Pahlawan Nasional, 15 May 2015 (http://www.pusakaindonesia.org/ini-dia-daftar-163-pahlawan-nasional/ downloaded on 21 January 2019).

United Nations Development Programme, Human Development Report 2004: Cultural Liberty in Today's Diverse World, New York, 2004. The director and lead author of this report is Sakiko Fukuda-Parr.

Zurbuchen, Mary S. (ed.), Beginning to Remember: The Past in the Indonesian Present, University Press, 2005.

ACKNOWLEDGEMENTS

In Jakarta, where the bulk of my time was spent, and research done, I owe a special debt of gratitude to Pantau Foundation, a small non-profit group whose members encouraged and supported me in travelling for and writing this book: Agus Sopian, Anugerah Perkasa, Artine Utomo, Budi Setiyono, Esti Wahyuni, Fahri Salam, Imam Shofwan, RTS Masli, Ruth Ogetay, Siti Nurrofiqoh and Syahar Banu. Two female staff, Erni Mei Ruly and Sri Maryani, provided tremendous assistance to me.

I joined Human Rights Watch in July 2008, covering Papua and religious minorities in Indonesia. Ali Dayan Hasan, Aruna Kashyap, Brad Adams, Elaine Pearson, James Ross, John Sifton, Joseph Saunders, Kyle Knight, Kriti Sharma, Margaret Wurth, Meenakshi Ganguly, Phelim Kine, Phil Robertson and Sophie Richardson, nurtured my intellectual journey to understand international laws.

I also received input from some international researchers who regularly visit Jakarta: investigative journalist Allan Nairn of New York; Donald K. Emmerson of Stanford University; Gerry van Klinken of KITLV Leiden; Janet Steele of George Washington University; Margaret Scott of New York University. Sidney Jones of the Institute for Policy Analysis of Conflict always opens her door to answer my questions. Jim Simon in Seattle and Oei Eng Goan in Jakarta helped edit my manuscript. Clinton Fernandes, a fellow activist in Canberra, read this manuscript for Monash University Publishing.

The Ford Foundation funded the 1.5-year seed money in writing this book. I thank Hans Antlov, Philip Yampolsky and Suzanne Siskel, who trusted me to take the trips. Nabil Foundation in Jakarta helped finance my trip to Jayapura, Merauke and Biak. Mary Kaplan of New York helped finance my research on Freeport McMoran, the largest gold mine in the world, in Papua.

In Kuala Lumpur, I thank my editors at *The Star* newspaper: Chua Yew Kay and Ng Poh Tip. They sent me to cover the Aceh war in June 2003 along with P. K. Katharason, Philip Golingai and Shahanaaz Habib.

In Banda Aceh, journalist Taufik Al Mubarak and Hotli Simandjuntak taught me to realise the bias among Jakarta mainstream media. Politician Afdhal Yasin drove me to tour the tsunami-devastated coastal areas.

In Pontianak, I stayed at the house of editors Sarmini and Yasmin Umar. Fellow reporters in Pontianak, including Alexander A. Mering, Hairul

Mikrad, Nur Iskandar, Tanto Jacobus and Yusriadi, helped me in my reporting. Subro, a Madurese activist, gave his time and his books to help me understand the widespread Madurese discrimination in Kalimantan.

In Manado, I received maps, books, and travel tips from Alex John Ulaen of Sam Ratulangie University. In Miangas, I thank island head Djonyor Namare and his wife Lukring Binulang, who welcomed me in the middle of the night and let me sleep in their house. When leaving Miangas, I used the *Daraki Nusa* ship. I thank its crew who were very friendly during the Miangas–Tahuna trip.

In Kupang, I thank CIS Timor, which helped many former East Timorese militias and their families return to East Timor. Winston Rondo, Olkes Dadi Lado and Roby Lay provided many insights. Merry Djami accompanied me to visit the Tuapukan camp. Ita Bouna welcomed to stay in her house. I thank human rights campaigner Sarah Lerry Mboeik who opened many doors in Kupang to me.

In Ambon, journalists Rudi Fofid, Ricky Rumaruson, Yany Kubangun and Febby Kaihatu helped me to get background material. In Tobelo, Febbyola Lilipory, a radio broadcaster, helped me with names and backgrounds. Lilipory herself was a victim in the violence. I especially thank Hernata Lasamahu, another victim of the conflict, who opened her past to me. In Ternate, I thank artist Fadriah Syuaib for walking me around the tiny island.

In Jayapura, I thank my college friend Hendrikus A. Ondi who currently works at the Evangelical Christian Church of Papua. In Merauke, journalist Agapitus Batbual accompanied me to the Benny Moerdani monument. In Biak, I learned a lot from Filep Karma and his family. In Wamena, I thank Theo Hesegem and pastor Yohanes Jonga.

I stand on the shoulders of giants. These giants included my college professors Arief Budiman and George J. Aditjondro (well known for hunting the wealth of the Suhartos) and Goenawan Mohamad of the Institute for the Studies on Free Flow of Information. Bill Kovach, a journalism guru at Harvard University, opened my world on long form writing.

I also got tremendous support from my wife Sapariah Saturi, herself an ethnic Madurese from Pontianak, as well as our two children, Norman and Diana, who grew up seeing their father shaping this book. I dedicate this book to these loving people in my life.